No. 1844
$25.95

58
HOME
SHELVING &
STORAGE PROJECTS

PERCY W. BLANDFORD

TAB BOOKS Inc.
Blue Ridge Summit, PA 17214

Other TAB Books by the Author

FIRST EDITION

FIRST PRINTING

Library of Congress Cataloging in Publication Data

Blandford, Percy W.
58 home shelving and storage projects.

Includes index.
1. Cabinet-work.   2. Shelving (Furniture)
3. Storage in the home.   I. Title.   II. Title:
Fifty-eight home shelving and storage projects.
III. Title: Home shelving and storage projects.
TT197.B585   1985   684.1′6   85-2566
ISBN 0-8306-0844-3
ISBN 0-8306-1844-9 (pbk.)

Contents

Introduction

Do you accumulate things? I do. In this modern society, many household and personal goods seem necessary to life, and our possessions surround us. Maybe it has always been so, but not to the extent it is today. We must have a place to put these things, or our homes, offices, shops, schools, work places, and anywhere we live or meet will be untidy places where we cannot find things.

So we must have storage arrangements. There was a time when personal possessions were few, and almost everything a family had would go in a large chest. Those days are long past, and we need much more storage accommodation than that. Fortunately, most of our storage needs can be met by furniture we make ourselves, and that is what this book is all about.

Wood is the obvious material to work with. Like most other furniture in the home, most things you make will be basically wood. While solid wood is attractive, it has its limitations in some ways. Some better woods are now difficult to get, and many are expensive. There is also a limitation of widths available; you cannot get a board wider than the tree from which it came. Widths can be made up by gluing pieces together, but for wide pieces, we now have the advantages of some man-made developments in wood. In particular, plywood and particleboard can be used today where wide, stiff, and flat panels are needed. These materials have altered the woodworking scene and made the building of storage furniture that much easier. The projects in this book take advantage of these new materials, where applicable, without forsaking traditional craftsmanship in natural wood.

If you are a skilled craftsman with a well-equipped shop, you can use your resources to the fullest in making some of the storage projects described. If, however, you are a beginner with only a few hand tools, you can also make many attractive items.

Every home needs shelves. They are basically simple to make, and you can develop them into hanging cabinets. If you have doubts about your ability, start with shelves. If you do not feel capable of making dovetails or mortise-and-tenon joints, there are usually dowel or nail alternatives, but if you never try more advanced construction, you will never progress in your woodworking craft.

This is not a book on woodworking skills. I assume that you have some knowledge of tool handling and woodworking techniques, but there are some instructions provided where particular processes are involved. Most of the book consists of projects, which are complete as they are, or you can use them as ideas for developments to suit your needs. A big advantage of making your own storage furniture, instead of buying it, is that the sizes can be made to suit your exact needs; they do not need to be a compromise.

Where a project is described to be a certain size, it is accompanied by a materials list in which widths and thicknesses are mostly exact, but lengths are a little full to allow for cutting and fitting joints. All dimensions on drawings and in lists are in inches, unless indicated otherwise.

May you and your home benefit from the shelves and storage projects that you make from this book.

Chapter 1

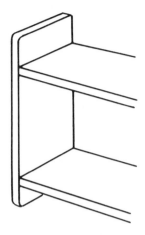

Shelf Design

A *shelf* is a flat panel projecting from a wall, usually horizontally. It must be supported, and there are many ways of doing so. The mechanics of shelving depend on many factors, which must be considered if the result is to be satisfactory, and the shelf is to do its job correctly without any risk of it collapsing.

The load on a shelf applies leverage to the means of attaching it to the wall. The wider the shelf, and the farther the load from the wall, the greater is the leverage (Fig. 1-1A); so it is usually advisable to make a shelf no wider than its intended purpose requires. There may be other factors, such as reducing interference with people moving about the room, that also influence the choice of width. The load on a shelf tries to pull it away from the wall and make it slide down its surface. All of the fastenings tend to resist sliding, but only the upper ones have to resist the tendency to pull away. If there is a bracket under a shelf, the top screws have to resist pulling out under a load (Fig. 1-1B), but the lower ones are not pulled, at least not until the whole thing is about to fall. If the bracket is above, the main pulling away is from the top (Fig. 1-1C).

BRACKETS

A shelf nearly always must be supported by the ver-

tical surface against which it fits. Sometimes there can be one or more supports to the floor, but otherwise the rigidity and security of the shelf depends on the brackets or other attachments to the wall. Practical considerations are dealt with in Chapter 2, but when designing, you must make sure the shelf gets all the support it needs. In design the main concern is with triangulation. A triangle with rigid members cannot be pushed out of shape (Fig. 1-2A); that is how a load is taken by the shelf support. Some brackets are made triangular (Fig. 1-2B), but even with a closed end between two shelves, the upper shelf transfers its load to the wall via a triangle (Fig. 1-2C) with its base upwards, while the lower shelf has its supporting triangle with its base downwards (Fig. 1-2D).

If a shelf is to get maximum support, the triangle should reach quite close to the front edge (Fig. 1-2E). A smaller triangular support would obviously not be as successful (Fig. 1-2F); it would have more of a bending and sagging effect on the shelf itself, and the load would be increased on the support.

A support with the same distance on the wall as on the shelf would be theoretically satisfactory (Fig. 1-2G), but if the part on the wall is increased (Fig. 1-2H), loads thrust nearer vertically, and a bracket looks better with a longer leg on the wall. If a support reaching to the floor seems advisable, yet something as far from the wall as

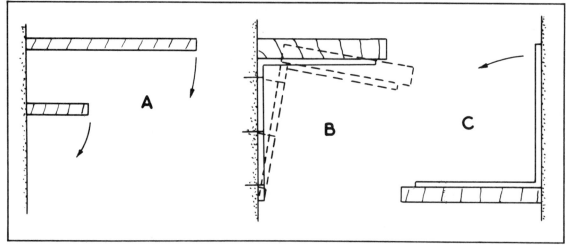

Fig. 1-1. Loads on a shelf are greater if it is wide (A), and most strength is needed at the highest points (B,C).

a vertical post would cause an obstruction, it may be possible to use a sloping support (Fig. 1-2J), which would represent triangulation taken as far down as it could be in the circumstances.

Some manufactured pressed-steel shelf brackets cause minimum obstruction because they do not project much. Although there is no diagonal strut, the load is still taken by triangulation. Within the body of the bracket (Fig. 1-2K). There are limits to what such an arrangement will support without a diagonal piece, but for many household applications, these shelf brackets are adequate.

In some manufactured shelving systems, brackets are made with the shortest side of the triangle towards the wall. This method of support would be a weakness if the only attachment to the wall was within that side, but these systems usually provide adjustment of shelf spacing by moving up and down on vertical parts, which are attached to the wall or otherwise supported throughout their length (Fig. 1-2L). It would be unwise to use individual shallow triangular brackets without the help of vertical pieces.

If a shelf comes in a corner or recess, its end can be supported on a strip screwed to the wall (Fig. 1-3A). This choice is obviously superior to a bracket on a surface in resisting any tendency for the shelf to tilt under the load; so arranging at least one end of a shelf in this way is worthwhile whenever possible. The end support also helps any brackets farther along to resist tilting.

Something similar can be arranged by using an end support on a shelf (Fig. 1-3B). It may be cut with a dado groove as well as having screws into the shelf. To attach

it to the wall, there can be metal plates (Fig. 1-3C) or a strip of wood outside or let into the back of the shelf (Fig. 1-3D). The end support may go above and below the shelf, when it will offer the best support, or it could be just arranged above or below, when strength will be at least as good as brackets.

LEVELS AND STIFFNESS

Lengthwise stiffness of a shelf, as well as security in attachment to the wall, can be increased if there is a strip along the back of the shelf, above or below it, with screws through into the wall (Fig. 1-4A). Even when there seems to be enough initial stiffness in a shelf, it may develop a sag after protracted use under a heavy load, such as a row of books. A strip at the back, added during the first fixing, is a precaution against such a happening. A strip under the front (Fig. 1-4B) will also prevent sagging, but care is needed to see that this extra thickness in an assembly does not interfere with the removal of a book or other object from the shelf below.

The number of needed supports cannot be decided by any rules. It is largely a matter of common sense and experience. A stiff shelf with good fastening for supports can have fewer supports than a lighter shelf, both to take the load and to prevent sagging. If the surface to which the shelf is to be attached is not very stiff or substantial, it is better to spread the load by having more supports. This situation could occur where the attachment is to light paneling rather than substantial wood; however, quite often it is possible to arrange brackets to come over studding instead of unsupported panel surfaces.

A shelf should be horizontal. If it is out of level in its length, even by a small amount, it will be very obvious to anyone viewing it from the other side of the room. Normally, you may expect that if the shelf is parallel with the floor or ceiling, it will be horizontal, but that is not always so. In some rooms, the floor may be out of horizontal, or the part below where the shelf is to come may have warped or sagged. When marking for a shelf it is advisable to measure from the floor or ceiling to the end positions of the shelf, then put a straight piece of wood across these points, and test it with a spirit level (Fig. 1-4C). If necessary, make new level marks on the wall and align the shelf with them.

It is important that a shelf is not lower at the front than the back. During its life, loads on it may tend to push down the less-supported front; so make sure it does not start low in that direction. Check that the wall is upright. It is unlikely to be far out. If it is inaccurate, you can make

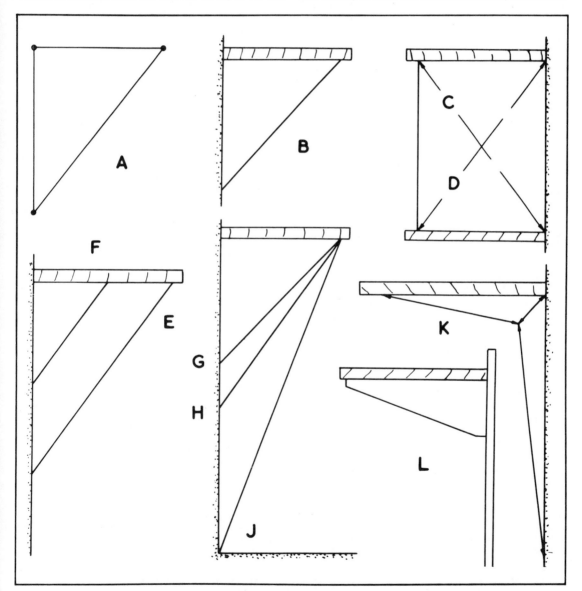

Fig. 1-2. Loads on shelves are triangulated, with the greatest strength coming when the triangle of forces is large.

3

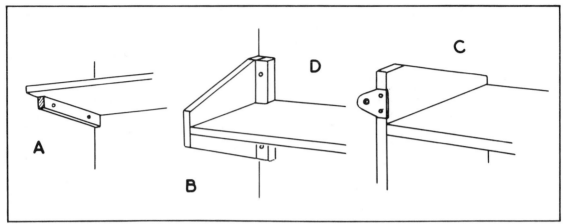

Fig. 1-3. A shelf may rest on strips (A) or have a bracket (B) with screws through wood or metal (C,D) to the wall.

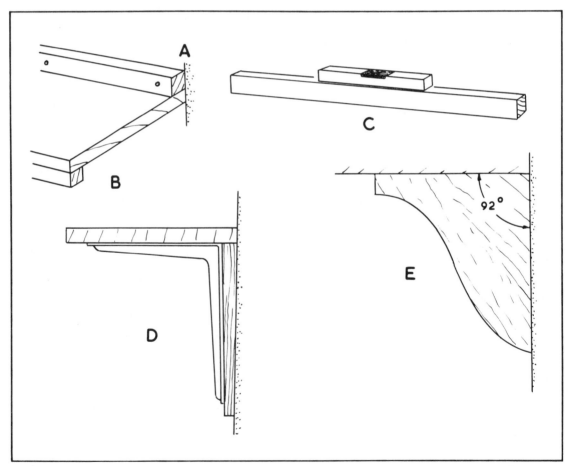

Fig. 1-4. The stiffness of a shelf can be increased with strips (A,B). Check levels (C) and allow for possible sag from square (D) by increasing the angle of brackets (E).

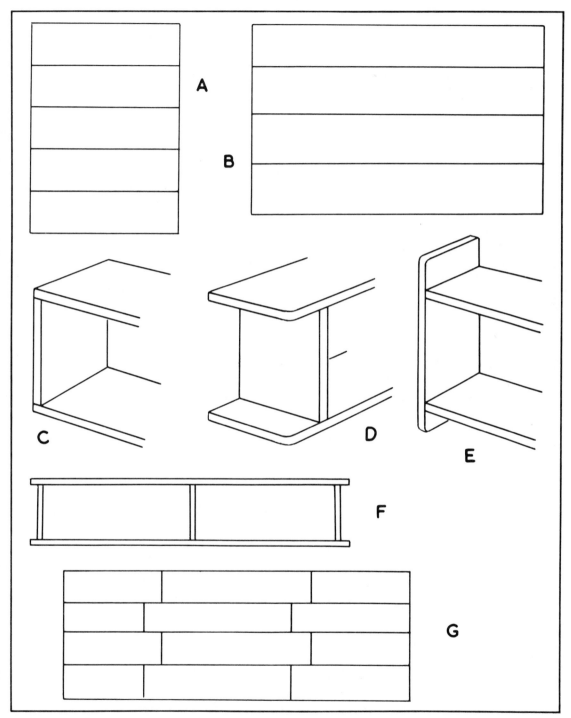

Fig. 1-5. With equal spacing, gaps appear to narrow towards the bottom (A); so it is better to taper spaces (B). Vertical supports may come at the ends or be set in, and intermediate supports will be needed for long shelves (C-G).

allowances when making supports. If you intend buying shelf brackets, however, you should put wood behind the brackets (Fig. 1-4D) and taper or shape each back so its front surface presents an upright surface to the bracket. There is some advantage to starting with the front of a shelf slightly higher than the back, particularly if it is to be heavily loaded. Then, if it sags a little, it should not go below horizontal. If you are making the supports, arrange them to be a degree or so above horizontal (Fig. 1-4E).

SHELF SPACING

There is an optical illusion you may need to consider if you are making a block of shelves. The illusion applies whether there are to be a few shelves hanging near eye level, or they are to fill a wall from floor to ceiling. If you space the shelves evenly, the lower gaps will seem to be closer than the upper ones (Fig. 1-5A). It may not matter, but the arrangement is visually more pleasing in most situations if the block of shelves appears to have wider gaps at the bottom and the spaces get less toward the top. Usually, for books and many other objects, you want to put the larger and heavier items lower down in any case; so shelf gaps to suit are arranged to get progressively narrower from top to bottom (Fig. 1-5B).

A square and a circle are not as attractive to look at as a rectangle or an ellipse. Except for details, curves do not occur in shelf design, but if you are planning a block of shelves, try to avoid a square outline. It is better if the size is greater one way. Somewhere between 1 1/4 and 1 1/2 times the other size is considered to give the best-looking shape. There may be other considerations governing proportions, but otherwise use this overall outline for the block.

If there are two or more shelves, they can be arranged to give mutual support. Loads on the shelves are shared, and attachments to the wall take even shares of the combined load, instead of one set of screws or other fastenings having a greater load than another set. Joining the shelves may also have practical advantages in preventing things from falling off the ends or books from falling over within the body of the shelving. At the end, the shelves can be joined with a piece between them (Fig. 1-5C). For the sake of appearance, the piece could be set back (Fig. 1-5D), or it could extend above, below, or both ways (Fig. 1-5E). Besides uniting the shelves, the end may have its own attachment to the wall and so share the support of the whole assembly.

Long shelves can be united with pieces between at intervals. This method will prevent warping or other movement, even if they are not strictly necessary for putting things on the shelves. They can separate different items or prevent books from falling over. They also break up the plain appearance of an otherwise unbroken length; so they may be considered worthwhile for that reason (Fig. 1-5F). With a long block of more than two shelves, there is some advantage in staggering the divisions; besides appearance, this arrangement simplifies construction and increases strength (Fig. 1-5G).

Chapter 2

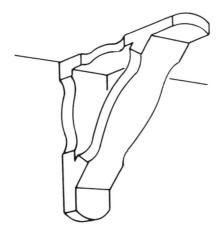

Shelf Details

A shelf has to be rigid and stiff in relation to the load it is to carry. If it will have to support only a few light display items, it will obviously not need the stiffness of a shelf made to hold a row of heavy books. Paper in bulk is heavy, and stacked paper or large, bound books can put a considerable load on a shelf and its supports. A shelf that is not stiff enough may develop sags between supports, but it may be a year or more before it becomes obvious.

Stiffness may be inherent in the material, but it is also related to the closeness of brackets or other supports. A thick, stiff board may have its brackets at wider intervals than a lighter board with more supports. For instance, a shelf made with a hardwood board 1 inch thick may be satisfactory with brackets 36 inches apart, but a piece of softwood 3/4 inch thick may be better with brackets only 20 inches apart, if it is to withstand the same load without sagging. There is no rule that can be quoted; it is a case of experience. Even if your own experience is slight, you can judge what would be satisfactory for your purpose by looking at shelves elsewhere and noting the sizes and spacings.

Stiffness is needed in the length. That is what you get in any natural wood board cut with its grain lines in the length. The lesser strength across the grain is more than enough in the width of a shelf supported by brackets. Boards cut from any part of the tree should usually be satisfactory, but if you want the minimum risk of twisting or warping, choose wood cut radially. If a log has been cut across into boards, the radially cut ones are those through or near the center slice (Fig. 2-1A). You can identify them by looking at the grain marks on the end of a board and noting if they go across the thickness (Fig. 2-1B).

SHELF MATERIALS

Many shelves are made of natural wood, which is generally superior to the alternatives. If you need to match furniture, that may govern the choice of wood. Otherwise, for a shelf where appearance is not important, you can use softwood for cheapness and lightness. Hardwood, such as oak, has considerably more strength than any softwood, however, and should be more durable and capable of being finished more attractively. Whatever the wood, look for reasonably straight grain and freedom from large knots. Grain lines that wander much may cause the shelf to warp, and large knots are weak spots and possible places where the wood may go out of shape.

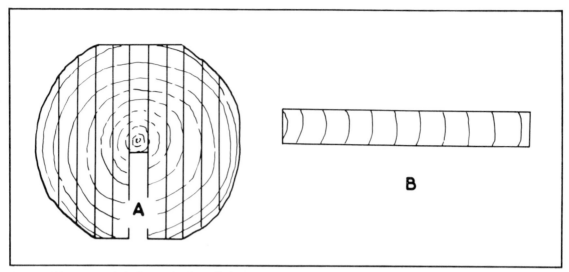

Fig. 2-1. Wood cut radially from a log is unlikely to warp.

Plywood can be used. It may be thick enough to use in the same way as solid wood. The grain of the outer plies looks better lengthwise, and stiffness should be slightly better that way. For a shelf in an unimportant position, the untreated edge may be acceptable, but for a better front edge, there can be a lip of solid wood attached. Screws or nails through (Fig. 2-2A) might be unsightly, although stopping over the sunk heads would hide them, particularly if covered by a painted finish. It would be better to cut a joint. A tongue on the lip piece can fit into a groove in the plywood (Fig. 2-2B). This joint can be cut with hand or power tools. If additional stiffness is wanted, the lip could be thicker and carried under the plywood (Fig. 2-2C). The front edge of the lip does not have to be left square; it could be rounded or molded. For convenience and safety in handling and gripping the lip while cutting the shape, it is best to make the piece on the edge of a wide board and not cut it off until it is ready to fit to the plywood. If you first make the lip so it stands a little high on the plywood, it can be planed level after the glue has set. If you try to make it the same width as the plywood, and the surface finishes low, leveling the plywood to it by more than a very slight amount could spoil the appearance.

A shelf could be made of thinner plywood suitably stiffened. A lip piece on the front may take the plywood glued into a rabbet (Fig. 2-2D). There could be a similar piece at the back, but as that part will be hidden, a strip underneath (Fig. 2-2E) is all you need. At the ends, other strips make up the thickness and can be rabbeted,

mitered, and rounded if the corner is exposed (Fig. 2-2F); otherwise you only need a thickening piece underneath (Fig. 2-2G). Similar thickening pieces are placed where the brackets will come (Fig. 2-2H). In a simple shelf, all bottom surfaces can be the same level, but you can make the front strip deeper, providing it comes forward of bracket ends. It can be molded or made quite deep to provide stiffness and to take a curtain track, or to serve some other purpose (Fig. 2-2J).

Particleboard makes good shelves because it is a uniform thickness and comes in flat pieces and many sizes, some larger than will be needed for shelves. If it is bought with the surfaces and edges veneered with plastic or wood, it needs little preparation. Cut ends that will be exposed can be covered with strips of the same material as the surface. These strips are usually supplied in a self-adhesive form that can be pressed on with heat.

Particleboard has the same stiffness in all directions, but it is not as great as the stiffness in the length of solid wood of the same thickness. It is liable to develop sags between supports that are too far apart, usually not until it has been subjected to a load for a long time, however. This means that brackets should be closer than they would be for solid wood.

Particleboard can be stiffened in the same way as suggested for plywood, however, except that grooving it may not be satisfactory, because much depends on the resin and wood chip composition of the particular board. A simpler way of stiffening, that avoids this problem, is to put the wood underneath set back a little from the front

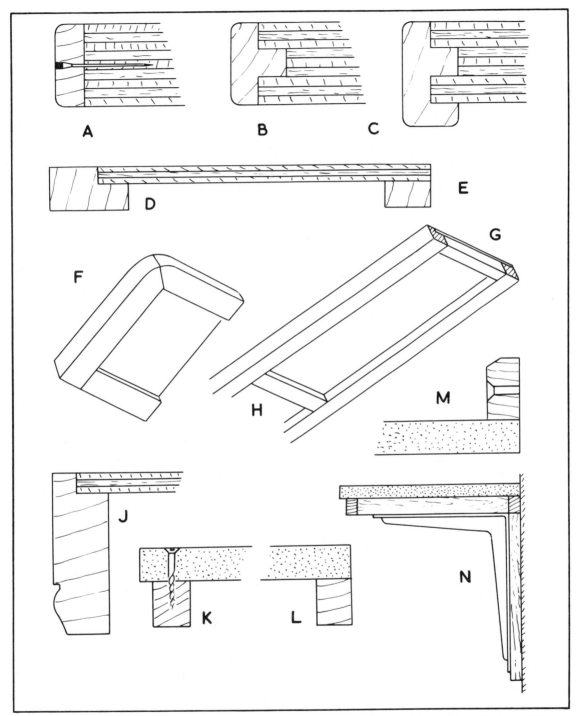

Fig. 2-2. Plywood may be edged (A-E). Edges give the effect of greater bulk (F-J). Particleboard benefits from solid wood stiffening (K-N).

(Fig. 2-2K) and screwed through at intervals from the top. Another strip can go along the back edge, but there it may be level and used for screwing to the wall (Fig. 2-2L). It could be above the shelf if the brackets below are to go close to the wall (Fig. 2-2M). If having the strip below is preferable, brackets can be packed out from the wall (Fig. 2-2N).

Metal shelving requires stiffening lips turned in at front and back. As this process requires special shop equipment, metal is unsuitable for making individual shelves in a normal shop, but there are satisfactory metal shelves you can buy that may include supports with adjustable brackets. Such equipment is intended for storage in industrial applications, rather than for domestic use, but it could be usefully employed in a garage or small shop. Elsewhere, if a metal surface is required, sheet metal can be screwed on a wood shelf. For a shelf subject to frequent movement of heavy goods over its front, there are metal edge moldings that can be put on wood or other boards to reduce wear and maintain a better appearance.

METAL BRACKETS

A shelf unconnected with any others is usually supported by a number of individual brackets. If another shelf is united to it in any way, the connecting parts can serve the purpose of brackets in keeping the shelves level and in attaching to the wall.

Brackets can be metal (usually mild steel) or wood and bought ready-made or made as needed by the craftsman. Metal brackets have less bulk than wood ones, and bought metal brackets are usually less bulky than individually made metal brackets. Bulk may not matter, but it does if there has to be the minimum obstruction under a shelf. In another place bulk may be attractive, as when shaped and carved brackets hold a shelf above a fireplace.

The simplest metal bracket is a plain L shape (Fig. 2-3A). Stiffness then depends on the cross section of the metal. Iron or mild steel of, say, 1- × -3/8-inch section, forged to shape, can be surprisingly stiff and support a considerable weight without bending. A bracket can be made by heating to redness the part to be bent in a fire or with a blow torch and pulling it round while one part is held in a vise. It need not be bent to a sharp angle. A curve in the corner does not matter (Fig. 2-3B).

A variation achieves a lighter result by using a section that is thick at the edges (Fig. 2-3C). Screw holes come in the thinner web, while the outer flanges provide stiffness.

Additional stiffness for a bracket comes from providing a diagonal support, which could be a plain strut (Fig. 2-3D), with its ends welded or riveted, or a steel plate welded on (Fig. 2-3E). A scroll may be both decorative and serve as a strut (Fig. 2-3F).

Some mass produced metal brackets get their strength from pressing thin sheet-metal into sections that give stiffness. These manufactured brackets are lighter and generally preferable unless you want a traditional appearance. There are many variations, but one form has the sheet metal forced into a section (Fig. 2-3G) that is deeper towards the root of the bracket (Fig. 2-3H). Screw holes come in the flat flange outside of the shaped part.

A further development of this uses a pressed steel main part, but another stiff piece of steel makes a shaped decorative strut (Fig. 2-3J). Most of these manufactured brackets are made in many sizes, but usually one leg is longer than the other and intended to be the upright one.

Holes in manufactured brackets dictate the size and position of screws, unless you redrill them. Thick brackets may have countersunk holes, but the sheet metal brackets are too thin for countersinking without weakening; so roundhead screws are normally used. If screw holes have to be drilled in brackets, keep in mind the loads that will come on the bracket in use. A weight on a shelf tries to pull the top of a bracket away from the wall. To prevent this, put two screw holes as high as you conveniently can in the vertical leg (Fig. 2-4A). Usually, they are arranged at slightly different levels; then if they go into wood with its grain near horizontal they will not engage with the same grain lines, and so cause splitting. Another hole near the tip of the leg shares some support and serves to vertically locate the bracket (Fig. 2-4B). The number of other holes that should be drilled depends on the size of the bracket, but screws at 3-inch intervals should be adequate.

Screws upwards into the shelf only have to keep the shelf in place. They are not normally subject to much load. You may only need two upwards (Fig. 2-4C), but an arrangement similar to the vertical leg is usually found in manufactured brackets.

If you want the shelf to be easily removable, metal brackets can be given a lip at the front (Fig. 2-4D). They prevent the shelf from moving forward; yet it can be lifted off. To prevent the shelf from moving out of position in its length, use light battens across it against the inner edges of the end, or other brackets to locate it (Fig. 2-4E).

WOOD BRACKETS

Where wood brackets are to be made, their design

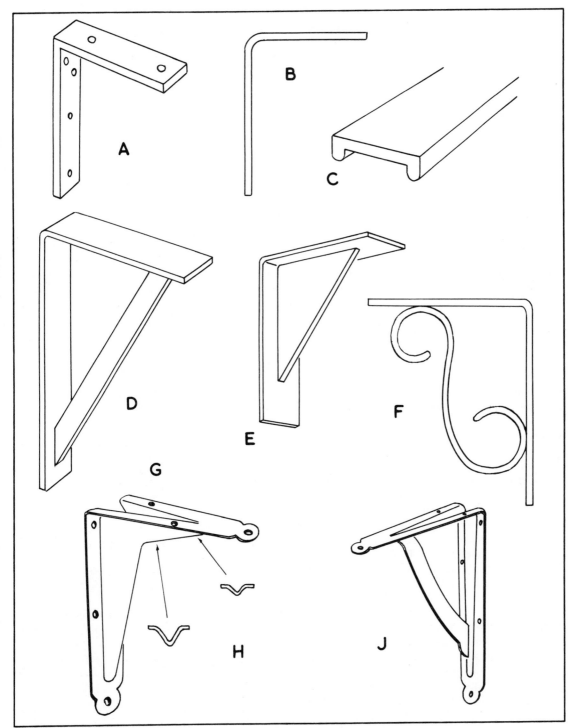

Fig. 2-3. Flat or formed strip brackets (A-C) may be stiffened by various forms of struts (D-J).

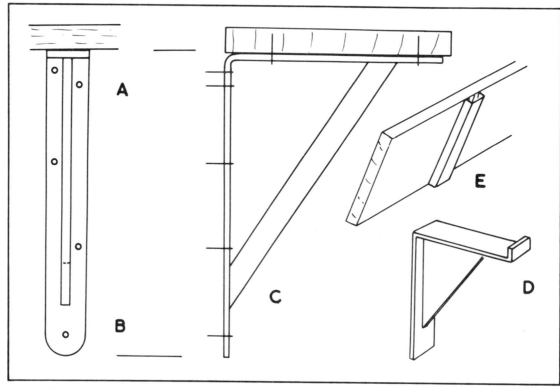

Fig. 2-4. Bracket screw holes are located for greatest strength (A-C). A shelf to lift off may be retained by the bracket and located with a batten (D,E).

depends on purposes and appearance. if the bracket is to provide strength without too much regard for appearance, a basic triangular form is best (Fig. 2-5A). The top leg should almost reach the front of the shelf, and the vertical leg is best about 1 1/2 times this length, if there are no space restrictions below the shelf. It could be made shorter if that is the only way of fitting it into a space. The diagonal strut is set back a short way from the ends of the bracket legs. The section of wood that should be used depends on the overall size, but a 3/4- x -2-inch section would do to support a shelf 12 inches wide.

The greatest load comes on the joint between the vertical and horizontal parts, with the top piece trying to pull forward away from the other. A dovetail, with its tapered direction horizontal, is best able to resist this pulling. It could be single or double, depending on the wood section (Fig. 2-5B). A comb or finger joint could also be used (Fig. 2-5C); it would depend on glue to prevent pulling, but with modern glues the joint would be very strong. Any joint can be reinforced with screws or nails.

The strut might go flat against the legs and be screwed through (Fig. 2-5D), but a better resistance to movement under load would be provided by notching the ends into the legs (Fig. 2-5E). To mark out the strut and notches, draw a full-size side view of a complete bracket. The notches are cut square to the legs at the outer ends and tapered back to the thickness of the strut (Fig. 2-5F). They need not be very deep—1/4 inch in 3/4-inch wood should not be exceeded.

Cut the notches in the legs to match the drawing. Make the corner joint and let the glue set. Put the bracket on the drawing and lay the strut across it so its ends can be marked from the notches. Cut the ends slightly too long and try the strut in position. Pare the ends to a close fit so the corner angle is a little more than 90 degrees. The notched joints may close under load; so be careful not to have the strut so short that the shelf may eventually tilt forward slightly. Joints may be strong enough just glued, or the strut ends can also have nails or screws from outside (Fig. 2-5G).

Make all the brackets you need at the same time, do-

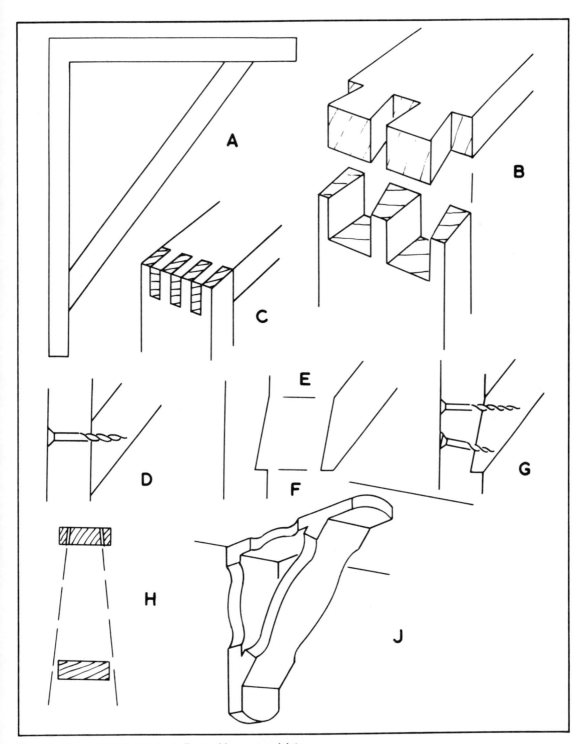

Fig. 2-5. Wood brackets may be built up with common joints.

ing similar work together, so all the parts match. Arrange at least two screw holes near the top of each vertical leg. Have another one at the end below the strut and one or two elsewhere. If the holes behind the strut are drilled diagonally, the screws are easy to drive (Fig. 2-5H).

This type of bracket can be decorated. The ends of both legs can be rounded and the sides shaped, then the strut given similar decoration (Fig. 2-5J). You could also fret or carve the surfaces. The strut might be rounded in section as well as carved. It could be made as a turned spindle with square ends that are fitted to the bracket legs.

Another way of providing the diagonal support, particularly in smaller brackets, uses a solid piece between the legs (Fig. 2-6A). It should be narrow enough to allow screws into the wall or shelf on each side of it (Fig. 2-6B) and itself may be glued and screwed through the legs, where the screw heads will be hidden after the shelf is located (Fig. 2-6C). Cut the triangular pieces so the grain is parallel to the diagonal edge.

The filler piece does not have to be a simple triangle. Its exposed edge may be decorated in any way you wish. It could have simple curving (Fig. 2-6D); the outline could follow a classical molding shape (Fig. 2-6E). There might be edge shaping that develops into carving (Fig. 2-6F), or even goes as far as including carved figures if the bracket is to be used in a church or other appropriate situation.

Making a bracket as a single thick block allows for carving or other decoration in some depth, but it brings a problem in screwing, as you cannot easily screw from the front into the wall. Attachment to the shelf is simple, because you can screw downwards through it. If the shelf is to be attached to a panel which has not yet been put in position, screws can be driven from the back (Fig. 2-6G), but if you have to screw from the front there could be a back piece (Fig. 2-6H) or strips put on each side of the block (Fig. 2-6J). The block might be designed so a small piece at the top projects enough to take two screws close under the shelf, and another screw can be driven and plugged at the bottom (Fig. 2-6K).

END SUPPORTS

Some shelves need uprights at the ends to hold up whatever they are to carry. This situation is particularly common with a row of books, which must be prevented from falling over. End supports can then also double as attachments to the wall, with no need for brackets. They can be used for single shelves or blocks of two or more.

An example is a shelf with each upright end projec-

ting above and below the shelf (Fig. 2-7A). The upper part is high enough to support books, while the lower part is tapered. The upright could be nailed or screwed to the shelf in the simplest construction, or it could be doweled. It would be better, however, to use a dado joint (Fig. 2-7B). This joint is simplest going right through, but if the joint is to be hidden at the front, you can use a stopped dado (Fig. 2-7C).

Make the notch to within about 1/4 inch of the front. If you use a router, square the forward end of the stopped dado with a chisel to take the shelf end (Fig. 2-7D) or round the shelf end to match. If the groove is cut by hand, you will need to chop out a notch at the forward closed end so the saw has enough movement to cut the grooved sides (Fig. 2-7E).

To avoid screws or nails through the outer surface, you can use them to supplement glue in the joint by driving them diagonally upwards from below the shelf (Fig. 2-7F). For extra strength in the joint, the lower edge of the groove and shelf may be given a dovetail angle (Fig. 2-7G). The ultimate in strength for this type of joint is to taper it from the back, as well as give it a dovetail form (Fig. 2-7H). When it is assembled with glue by driving the shelf in from the back, the result should be so secure that nothing short of breaking the wood will separate it. The same construction can be used for two or more shelves, with the ends suitably extended (Fig. 2-7J).

You can choose from several ways of attaching the shelves to the wall. A strip of wood might go outside each end (Fig. 2-8A), so screws through it go into the wall. A strip could go inside (Fig. 2-8B); it is usually stronger if it is made in two parts—above and below the shelf—rather than if the shelf is cut away to let one piece through. Either arrangement could be supplemented with a strip under the rear edge of the shelf (Fig. 2-8C), with more screws through it into the wall.

Another attachment uses metal plates, sometimes called *mirror plates*, from their use in hanging looking glasses flat on a wall. They can be bought, but suitable plates are easily made (Fig. 2-8D). Their size and thickness depend on the load, but a possible size, suitable for most purposes, is shown in Fig. 2-8E and can be made out of brass plate less than 1/16 inch thick.

Let each plate in flush with the back edge of the wood. Countersink the screws that go into the wood level with the plate and either use roundhead screws through the plate into the wall or countersink for it on the other side.

It is possible to arrange to take down the shelves without disturbing screws into the wall, if the hanging plates are given keyhole slots. Each plate is the same as

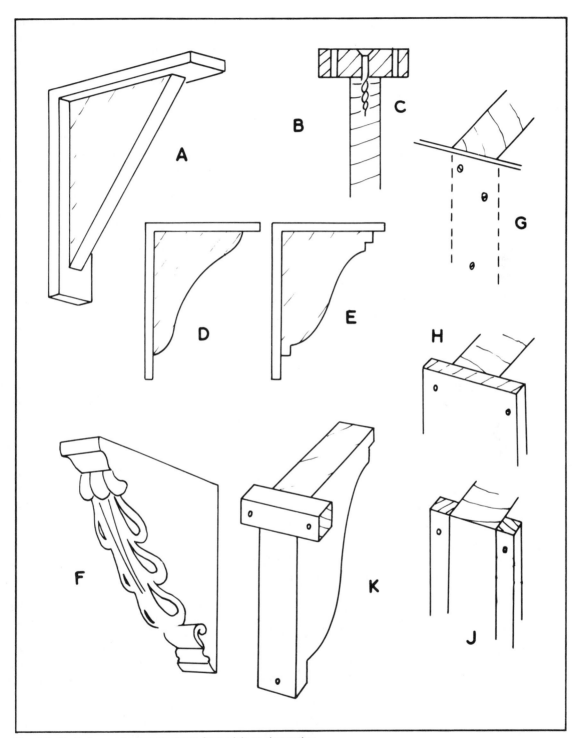

Fig. 2-6. Struts in wood brackets range from plain to decorative.

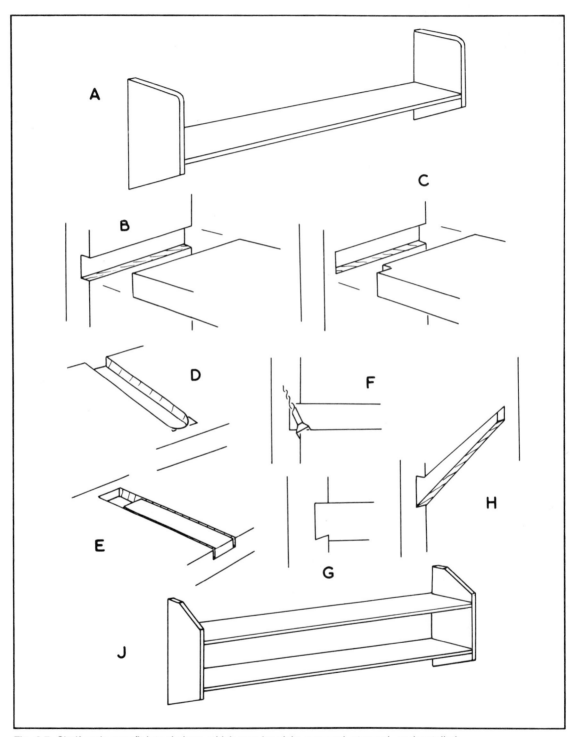

Fig. 2-7. Shelf ends may fit into dadoes, which may be plain, screwed, stopped, or dovetailed.

before, except for the different hole. The large hole must pass over the hanging roundhead screw, and the upward slot makes a sliding fit over the neck of the screw (Fig. 2-8F), which is driven into the wall to within a little more than the thickness of the plate. Make the slotted part at least as long as two screw neck diameters (Fig. 2-8G).

In some situations, an end is required above a shelf, but nothing has to project below. If there can be a very small projection downward, a dado joint is possible. If the end must finish level with the bottom of the shelf, however, a different joint is needed if the shelf and the weight of its load are to be taken by the ends. In this type of assembly it is helpful to arrange for some of the weight to be taken along the shelf, with plates or wood strips, if possible.

The best joint for an end that does not project below is a multiple dovetail (Fig. 2-9A), with the tails arranged in the direction to take the load. This joint could be cut by hand, with the tails wider than the pins, or by machine,

with them the same width. A tongue or finger joint is an alternative. Dowels could be used (Fig. 2-9B), but drilling must be carefully done to avoid breaking out the short end grain below the holes in the ends.

A strip along the top of the rear edge of the shelf could be matched by another of the same thickness joining the tops of the end uprights (Fig. 2-9C). Screws through these strips into the wall would probably provide all the support needed, without any wall attachment to the uprights.

A further step is the closing of all or part of the space behind a block of shelves. Plywood is the most simple solution. Nailing it on directly might be sufficient where appearance is unimportant, but in most situations, it is better to let it into a rabbet in the ends (Fig. 2-9D). Any rail across may be let in more deeply (Fig. 2-9E). One effect of a plywood back is to stiffen the whole assembly and keep it square. You may find it adequate to screw through the plywood into the wall, without any other attachment points.

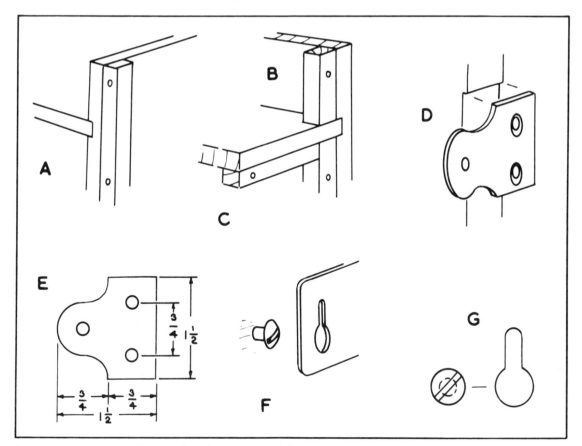

Fig. 2-8. Attachment to a wall may be through wood blocks (A-C) or through metal plates (D,E), which could be keyholed (F,G).

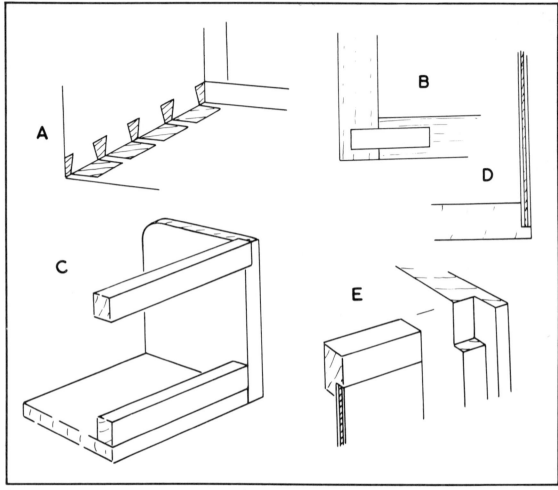

Fig. 2-9. Shelf ends could be dovetailed or doweled (A,B). At the back there may be strips, rabbeted plywood, and a wider top rail (C-E).

As with wood brackets, the ends can be decorated in various ways. It is also possible to arrange for shelves in a block to have variable positions. These developments are described later in projects.

FASTENINGS

To attach shelves and their brackets to walls, the usual fasteners are wood screws. These screws are described by their length from the surface of the wood and by a gauge number. Screws become thicker as the gauge number gets larger. Screws are made in many lengths for each gauge number, but only a limited range is normally available. Most stores will only have the even

numbers, except for very small screws. As a guide to approximate sizes, gauge 6 is slightly more than 1/8 inch diameter, and gauge 14 is near 1/4 inch. To hang most shelves, you need screws between these sizes; gauges 8 and 10 are mostly commonly required. For length, you must choose what will go through the part you are hanging and extend far enough into the wall. Choice is a matter of experience, but as a guide, a screw should go through the shelf part and any wall panel, so that about 1 inch, at least, goes into a stud or other solid wood part.

Screws commonly available are made of steel. They are strong and suitable for most purposes, but they will rust in damp conditions. Then and in good-quality indoor work, you may prefer to use brass or stainless-steel screws, which are more costly. Other metal alloys are used for special-purpose screws, but are unlikely to be needed for hanging shelves.

General-purpose screws have flat countersunk heads (Fig. 2-10A). A countersink drill bit will let in a head, but in some woods the head will pull in, at least partly. Experiment in scrap wood before countersinking the shelf part, otherwise you may find the head going far below where you expected as you tighten it. If it is a hole in metal, obviously you must countersink fully because the head should finish level, and it cannot be expected to pull in. Roundhead screws (Fig. 2-10B) are attractive and must be used on sheet-metal parts that are too thin for countersinking. An oval, or raised, head (Fig. 2-10C) fits a countersunk hole, but it stands slightly domed above the surface. It looks better than a flat head on an exposed metal part. There are other screw heads, but those I have mentioned are the only ones needed for shelving. Most screw heads are slotted for a normal traditional screwdriver, but some have the crossed Phillips head, primarily intended for mass production methods. If you have them, they require special screwdrivers.

A screw holds by pulling whatever is immediately under its head against the part the screw thread is in; so there is nothing to be gained by forcing the screw thread into a top piece of wood. In that part, there should be a hole which is a sliding fit on the neck of the screw (Fig. 2-10D). In the lower part, you need a smaller hole so the

screw thread can cut its way in. This hole should basically be the root diameter of the screw thread, but in softwood it should be less. In very hard wood, this hole should go as far as the screw is expected to reach (Fig. 2-10E), but in soft wood it can stop short (Fig. 2-10F), because the screw point will cut its own way to the full depth. If you are screwing a thin metal part in place, drill far enough for the unscrewed neck to slide in (Fig. 2-10G) before making the smaller tapping hole, unless the part the neck has to pull into is soft, and there is no fear of it breaking out.

If you are attaching to wood, you can get the locations of two bracket holes fairly far apart, and drill for them, then screw the brackets at these positions. For the other screws, you can drill through the bracket holes, since no hole must be bigger than them. If you are attaching to brick, stone, or other masonry, or to a hollow wall, you cannot do so, because the holes behind the bracket must be larger than the screw diameter.

For masonry you have to plug the wall for each screw. There are several plastic and fiber plugs available, although you can make your own from wood. The way you make the holes depends on the material and the equipment available. There are wall drills for hand use that must be hammered to make a hole, but for most brick and stone walls, the cleanest and most accurate way to make the hole is to use a tipped drill bit in an electric drill. It is easier if the drill is of the hammer type. A tip-

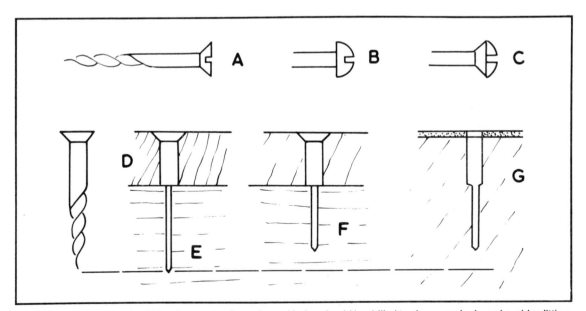

Fig. 2-10. Screw heads should be chosen to suit needs, and holes should be drilled to give a good grip and avoid splitting.

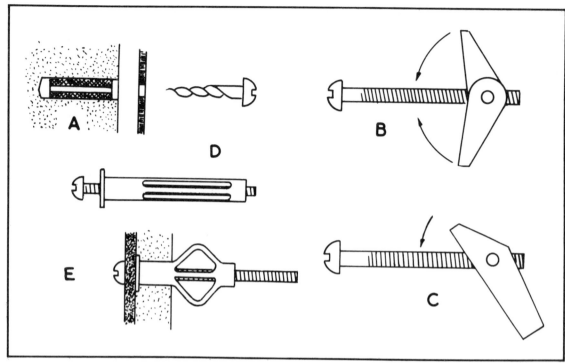

Fig. 2-11. Plugs are needed in masonry (A). For hollow walls there are special fasteners (B-E).

ped bit looks like an ordinary twist bit for metal, but it has a special hard tip.

The size hole to make depends on the plug, which will usually be about twice the diameter of the screw it is to take. If you make your own wood plugs, use that proportion. The plug should be a push fit in the hole, and it will expand as the screw bites into it. If the wall is plastered, go far enough through to get the plug at least 1 inch into solid masonry. In any case, push the plug a little way below the surface (Fig. 2-11A). It can be pushed in with a piece of wood or a flat punch. If you leave it level with the surface, its end will rise and expand outwards as the screw enters and may prevent the part being attached from pulling level with the surface.

Bought plugs are hollow. Mark the center of a wood plug with a spike and drill a small hole for the screw thread, after the plug has been driven into its hole. For strength, you should attach to solid masonry and not to the mortar line between laid bricks or slabs, but if the wall is plastered, you will have to chance what you penetrate. With several fastenings, many of them should obtain a strong hold.

Because all of the holes are large and must be drilled before you start mounting the parts on the wall,

you have to mark the locations of the holes first. You cannot drill through the brackets or other parts. Put the shelf with its brackets attached in place, preferably with help, then mark through all the holes with a spike or center punch, so you get a positive dent and not just a surface mark, as you would with a pencil.

When you have plugged the wall, enter each screw partly and check that the assembly is as you want it before tightening all around. Check that no dust, wood chips, or other things are between the surfaces to prevent close joints.

It is unwise to attach a shelf by fastenings only to wallboard and other soft materials, unless it is a very light assembly to carry small display items. In some situations, most of the screws can go into studs and carry most of the load, but there may have to be others into parts of a hollow wall, to provide secondary support. There is no strength to be obtained by driving screws into soft wallboard, and it cannot be plugged, so another method must be used.

There are several hollow wall anchors that provide something large enough on the other side of a wall panel for the screw to pull against. To get that piece to the other side, a fairly large hole must be drilled; so the wood or metal part that is to be screwed on should not have its screw hole too near its edge, or the large hole underneath will not be hidden.

A toggle bolt has a pair of spring-loaded wings that fold flat along the bolt as it is pushed through the wallboard, then they spring open at the other side (Fig. 2-11B); or it may have a single wing with one heavier side, that falls by gravity after being pushed through (Fig. 2-11C). The screws are of the metal-thread type and may have heads, or they could be without heads so a nut can be put on the projecting end. Some makes differ in detail, but the action is usually in one of the ways just described.

Another way of getting something to grip inside a hollow wall uses an expansion bolt (Fig. 2-11D). The whole thing pushes through a hole as wide as the tubular body, then when the screw is tightened, the further end is pulled back and the cut flexible central part expands against the back of the panel (Fig. 2-11E) until it is flattened. This type can have the screw fully withdrawn without losing the other part inside, as may happen with some toggle bolts, so it may be more convenient to use when driving the fairly large number of bolts needed in a shelf with several brackets.

If a wall is made of hollow concrete blocks, it will probably be possible to plug in to it the same way as into solid masonry. If the concrete is very thin, however, there are toggle bolts with long screws that can be pushed through to the hollow inside of a block.

There are some light plastic plugs that will expand slightly on the far side of a wallboard panel when the screw is driven. They are only for light loads, however, and should not be used for shelf brackets.

Chapter 3

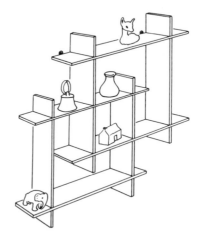

Shelf Projects

Shelves must be made to suit circumstances and needs, and the possible variations are almost infinite. There are, however, some types which can be defined and which may form bases for development into particular projects. The shelf designs in this chapter are offered as examples which can be modified to suit your needs.

Shelves can be single and mounted on a wall away from any other furniture; they may have to fit against something already there or have one or both ends in corners. You may need several shelves, either mounted independently or built into blocks. The shelves may be quite small, or they may form part of an assembly covering a whole wall. Shelves are obviously being made to be used, and how they are made will be governed to a certain extent by the size and weight of the intended load.

You can probably make a solitary shelf without much advance planning, but even then it may be advisable to lightly pencil on the wall where it is to come. You may then decide that it would be better a different length or at a higher or lower location. If the assembly is to be bigger or more complicated, it may be advisable to make a scale drawing of the wall and what you want to add. The drawing need not be very detailed, providing you show the overall sizes and parts in the correct proportions.

Another point to consider is the relation of what you

are adding to existing furniture and parts of the house structure. Will the shelves you want to add interfere with the opening of a door? You may need to move them or cut back a shelf to solve this problem. What about the use and layout of furniture that is already there? Will the shelf interfere with someone sitting at a table? Maybe a few inches higher will give enough clearance. Consider accessability to things on the shelf. A shelf between eye and waist level is more accessible than one higher or lower. You may want to put things out of reach of children, or there may be an advantage in using space near the floor. You may want to use all available space, whatever its height. Consider all these things before you make holes in the wall, which would be unsightly if you changed your mind and moved the shelves.

SIMPLE SHELF

Many shelf requirements are met with a simple board on two or more brackets (Fig. 3-1A). Although this project is simple, there are a few points to consider. Decide on width and length. Remember the undesirable extra leverage and possible obstruction of an excessively wide shelf; so select a width no more than is reasonably adequate. This width will have to be related to bracket

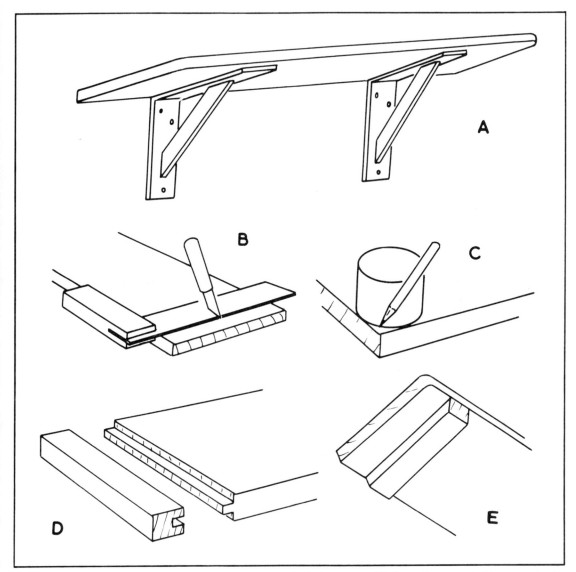

Fig. 3-1. A plain shelf should be cut square and may have rounded corners, while it may be prevented from warping by battens.

sizes, if you are using ready-made metal brackets. The end of the horizontal leg of each bracket should come fairly near the front edge.

If you buy the wood already machine-planed, or you put the board through your own planer or jointer, there will be a slight cross-grained ripple effect on the surface. For the best finish this effect should be removed by light hand planing or sanding. Even if the machine finish is unimportant for the broad surfaces, it is usually advisable to smooth the front edge, which is the part most in view. Ripples there may become very obvious under a gloss paint or varnish.

The end of a piece of wood, as bought, may be rough from a coarse saw; it may be dirty from standing on end, and it may have opened slightly as a result of cracks or shakes drying out. It is always advisable to allow some excess length so you can cut off a short piece. To ensure a clean cut, mark with a knife all around (Fig. 3-1B). Exposed front corners should be rounded; the amount depends on the situation. Instead of using a compass to get a good shape, you can draw around a large washer or the end of a can for a bigger curve (Fig. 3-1C).

For most shelves, the end grain of a board is acceptable if it is left exposed, but if you wish to hide it and prevent warping of a wide shelf, you can glue on a clamp piece that is tongued and grooved (Fig. 3-1D). The alternative to restrict warping is to arrange a batten across where each bracket comes (Fig. 3-1E). If the brackets are fairly close to the ends, this method should provide adequate stiffening. All that has been said about solid wood shelves is mainly applicable to the use of plywood or particleboard with edging and framing as described in Chapter 2.

You may choose to paint or varnish the shelf in position, but it is easier to get a good finish, without the risk of getting paint on the wall or elsewhere that it should not be, if you apply the paint or varnish while the board is free, and you can turn it about while using the brush. It will usually be best to fit the brackets to the shelf temporarily, then put the assembly against the wall and level it, so you can mark the screw holes in the wall. Then take it down and remove the brackets so you can paint the shelf, unless you intend to paint the brackets as well.

To get a good finish on wood, do not be too hasty. You must fill the grain, put some paint thickness on the surface, and finally apply the gloss or other paint finish to the surface that will be seen. The effectiveness of that final appearance depends very largely on what goes under the last coat. You can get primer paint, which is particularly intended for filling the grain of softwoods. For the undercoat which follows it, there are colors that are compatible with the top coat. With some woods you can go straight into undercoat, but if the grain still shows through, and there is unevenness, put on two or even more undercoats. If necessary, lightly sand the matt undercoat. Make sure the undercoat is absolutely dry, then apply the top coat of finishing paint. Read the directions on the can; with some modern paints, the minimum of brushing is advised.

Varnish is simpler to use, since it provides its own primer and undercoat. Modern synthetic varnish can be applied successfully in most atmospheric conditions. Older, natural varnishes would not set properly, or they became cloudy, if applied in cold or humid conditions. It is still advisable to avoid such conditions, but if you cannot, modern varnish should not be affected. You can apply the first coat directly, although some makers advise you to thin it to get better penetration of the wood. The first coat will soak into many woods. Add another when it is dry and follow with a third. That may be enough for a shelf. Lightly sand between coats. For an exceptionally fine finish, use more coats, sanded every time, except the last. Some older varnish took a long time drying and would collect dust from the atmosphere. Modern varnishes are mostly dust-free in about an hour, although they may not be fully dry for about a day, so avoid stirring up dust for an hour or so in a room where you have been varnishing.

TWO-SHELF BOOK RACK

An arrangement of two shelves between ends is often wanted, and the most common need is for books on the lower shelf and display items on the upper one. This arrangement can be made in almost any size, from something to hold a dozen paperbacks to a longer rack for larger hardcover books. The example in Fig. 3-2A has some suggested sizes, but they can be modified to suit your needs. A hardwood with a clear finish will look good. Softwood finished with paint, possibly with decals on the ends, would be appropriate for a child's room.

Mark out the pair of ends together (Fig. 3-2B). Prepare and mark out the two shelves and the back, all to the same length (Fig. 3-2C). The shelves will fit into stopped dadoes, but they are shown narrower than the ends, so they do not have to be notched.

Cut the dadoes in the ends before you shape the outlines. Try to make the shelves a good push fit. If necessary, you can slightly chamfer a shelf on the underside to make it fit, without affecting appearance. Cut the notches in the back of the ends for the top (Fig. 3-2D).

Shape the tops and bottoms of the ends. The hollows in the front edges are optional, but they break up the straightness and improve appearance. Be careful to remove saw marks and maintain even curves, or badly shaped curves will be very obvious.

Drill the shelf ends to take screws from below (Fig. 3-2E). One near the back and another about 2 inches from the front should be enough in each end. Drill the ends of the back for screws into their notches. A rack of the size shown may hang from two screws through the back, with holes arranged fairly near each end (Fig. 3-2F). It is always advisable to arrange hangings as widely spaced as the construction allows. Widely-spaced screws make the rack stronger and resist any tendency to tilt sideways better than closer screws. For a larger rack, there can be additional screws into the wall; a strip of wood across below the lower shelf can be drilled through,

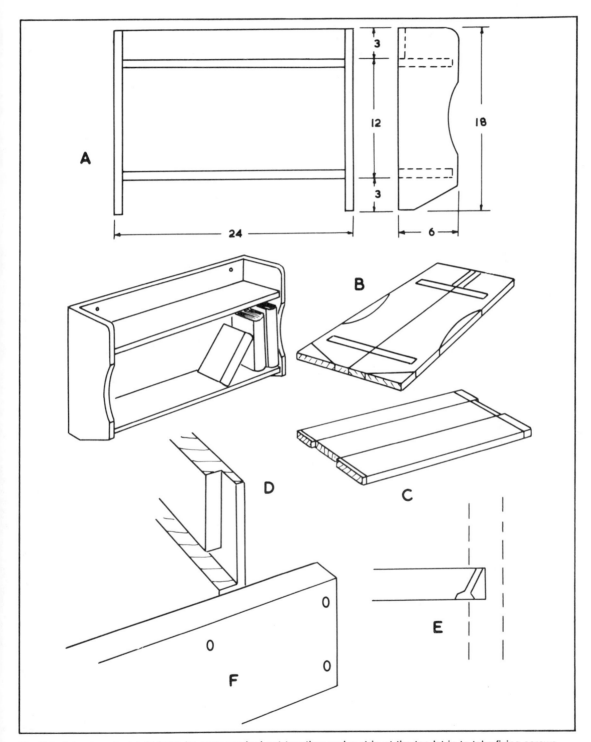

Fig. 3-2. A book rack should have its parts marked out together and a strip at the top let in to take fixing screws.

or there could be metal plates inside the ends or below the lower shelf.

Assemble the book rack with glue as well as screws. Although you can do some sanding and final cleaning of the surfaces after assembly, it is easier to get at internal surfaces before you put the shelf together; so finish the parts as far as possible before assembling them. Even if you then get glue where it is not wanted or otherwise affect the surfaces, the cleaning off that must be done is reduced.

As with any furniture assembly, it is best to pull the joints together with clamps; otherwise you have to hammer the parts together, with scrap wood to spread the blows. You need at least two bar or pipe clamps that will open enough to span the rack with a little to spare for scrap wood under the jaws.

Put glue in all the joints and have a drill ready to make the tapping holes for the screws. Draw the parts together with the clamps. Try to estimate the amount of glue to be sufficient, yet not enough to ooze out of the joints excessively. Cleaning off surplus glue is always a nuisance and difficult to do completely and smoothly.

Drill for and drive the screws, but at the same time check squareness. The back should not allow the assembly to go far out of square, but measure diagonals between the extreme corners at the rear. Push the parts into shape so the diagonals measure the same before the glue starts to set.

Materials List for Two-Shelf Book Rack

2 ends	6 × 19 × 3/4
2 shelves	5 1/2 × 24 × 3/4
1 back	3 × 24 × 3/4

SHELF WITH CORNER SUPPORT

If a shelf along a wall can have one end in a corner, there can be a support on the adjoining wall instead of a bracket near that end (Fig. 3-3A). Further along there may be one or more brackets, according to the length of the shelf. The end attachment is more positive than a bracket because the shelf end is supported solidly instead of in the cantilever manner of a bracket; so there should never by any risk of the end of the shelf tilting.

It is unwise to assume that the corner of a room is square. It may be, but you should check the angle of the corner at the height the shelf will be. Test it with a carpenter's square or set an adjustable bevel to the corner angle and test that. Another way is to have the shelf

too long and first cut and put its end square in place. You can see if the end needs adjustment, then alter it to fit before cutting the other end of the shelf to length.

There are at least two ways of supporting the end of the shelf in the corner. Simplest is a batten held to the wall with screws. It looks neatest if it is slightly shorter than the width of the shelf, with an angled front end and sharpness taken off exposed edges (Fig. 3-3B). The shelf can be held by screws downwards into it. Check the level of the batten when you screw it into place (Fig. 3-3C). As with brackets, it is better for the batten to hold the shelf a degree or so higher at the front than to risk having it tilt forward.

The batten under a shelf end works quite well, but may not be considered attractive, particularly if the shelf is above eye level, and the batten is in full view. It may be better then to use a piece against the wall, into which the shelf fits with a dado joint. This piece could have its grain go the same way as the width of the shelf (Fig. 3-3D), or it could be a deeper piece with the grain vertical (Fig. 3-3E), similar to a closed end of a bookcase. A plain dado is satisfactory in most situations because the attachment to a bracket further along the shelf should prevent the shelf from pulling out. A dovetail form could be used, however.

Attach the wood or metal bracket to the other part of the shelf. Support the shelf at the corner and check its level as you position the bracket for marking holes into the wall (Fig. 3-3F).

SHELF IN A RECESS

If a shelf is to fit into a recess, it can be supported at both ends in the way just described for one end in a corner (Fig. 3-4A), but there is a problem in fitting. You cannot make a shelf too long and trim it to length by trial, as it will not go into the recess. The first time the shelf is put into the recess it must be right. If the corners of the recess are exactly square. this is a straightforward process, but usually they are out of square. If the two corners are more obtuse than 90 degrees, you can cut the shelf to length at the front and plane off the ends toward the back until the shelf will go in fully. Usually it is not as simple as that, however.

Mark on the walls where the shelf is to come, including where its front edge will meet the walls (Fig. 3-4B). Measure exactly where the front edge will be between the marks. Use that measurement as a base from which to work along the edge of the board that will make the shelf (Fig. 3-4C).

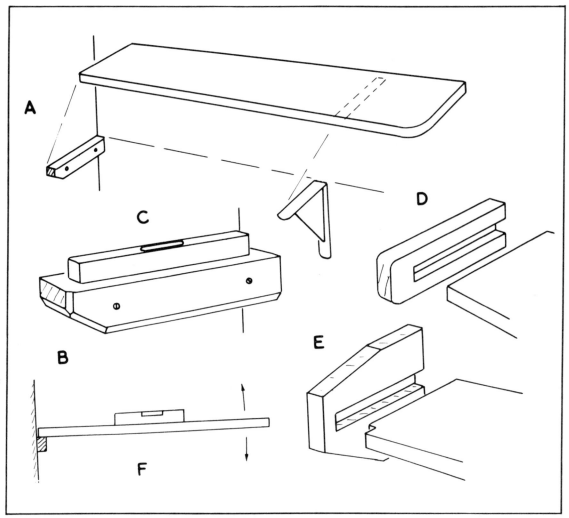

Fig. 3-3. A shelf in a corner may rest on a batten and bracket. It should be level both ways. End pieces can be used instead of battens.

Measure diagonally from one point on the wall at the intended position for the front of the shelf to the opposite corner (Fig. 3-4D). This is difficult to do with a tape rule or other measure. It is more accurate to have two strips of wood tapered to thin ends and with enough length to overlap. Place them between the points to be measured, with the tapered ends making contact, and pencil where the inner end of one comes on the other (Fig. 3-4E). Put the strips back together with one tapered end in place on the shelf and mark where the other end comes on the back edge (Fig. 3-4F). Join that mark to the mark on the front edge to indicate the place to cut for that end. Do

the same the other way to get the cut line for the other end (Fig. 3-4G).

A simple shelf may just be supported on battens at the ends. There could be another batten under all or part of the back edge, also. You can also have the ends in dado pieces, but they would need to be fitted to the ends of the shelf and the whole assembly slid into place before screwing to the wall. If the shelf is in a very wide recess, there may have to be a bracket under its center for additional support.

With a shelf in a recess, it is easy to hide the battens with a strip along the front, which would fit against square

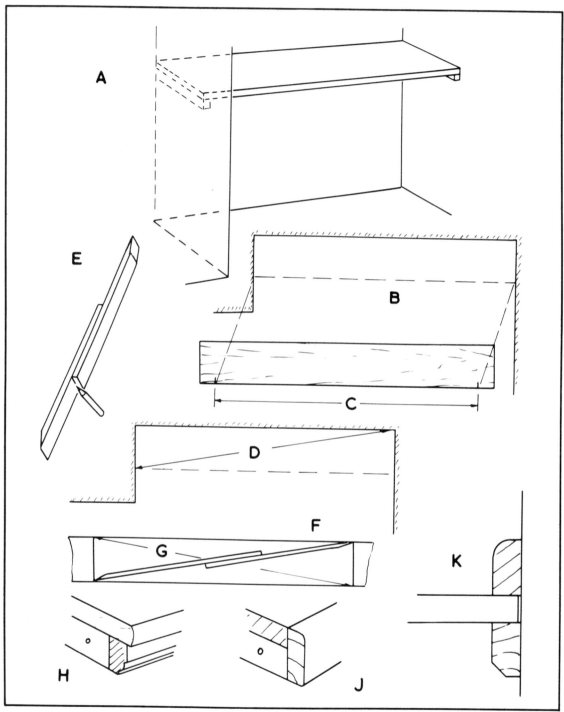

Fig. 3-4. Fitting a shelf in a recess involves careful measuring to get a good fit (A-G). The edges may the thickened and protected (H-K).

ends of the battens. It may go under the shelf and could have its lower edge molded (Fig. 3-4H). It could be arranged in front of the shelf (Fig. 3-4J), but it would then have to be nailed or screwed into it. The heads would be apparent, even if plugged, unless you trusted to glue only.

It may be worthwhile to cover the edges of the top of the shelf (Fig. 3-4K). This method has several advantages if it is carried across the ends and along the back with mitered corners. The cover strips protect the wall from knocks as a result of objects being moved on the shelf. They also disguise a possibly poor fit of the shelf against the wall. You could make the shelf a more open fit and rely on the cover strips to hide spaces. In some houses, the walls are not flat. Without the cover strips, you would have to be careful to shape the edges of the shelf that would be in contact, but with cover strips pulled tightly to the wall, any slight discrepancies will be hidden.

CORNER SHELVES

In most rooms the least-used parts are the corners. A shelf across a corner may provide storage or be a good place to display a vase of flowers or other decoration to improve the decor of the room. There could be a block of shelves or a cabinet with a door, as described later, but a triangle does not offer anywhere near as much storage space as a square; so capacity is limited, although it may still be enough for some things.

The simplest corner shelf is a plain triangle supported on two battens screwed to the wall (Fig. 3-5A). It could be a simple board cut with its grain lines parallel with the front edge. It should be made a close fit into the corner, even if that is not 90 degrees. You can get the angle with an adjustable bevel or make the fit by trial. The battens underneath may meet at the corner, although there is no need for a precision fit there. The forward ends can be bevelled or rounded (Fig. 3-5B).

Like the shelf in a recess, the appearance of a triangular shelf can be improved with a strip across the underside to hide the battens (Fig. 3-5C), and there could be cover strips on top (Fig. 3-5D).

Although it is usual to make the shelf with sides of the same length, it is not essential, and in some places it may be better to have uneven sides (Fig. 3-5E), but making one side very much more that the other reduces the available shelf area. An uneven triangle would be appropriate to the corner of a long room, when a picture or a loudspeaker on it is to face along the room.

The front edge of the shelf does not need to be straight. Curving it outwards increases the shelf area. Too much curve leaves a large unsupported area forward of a line between the batten ends (Fig. 3-5F). A moderate curve there as part of an ellipse looks better and has less overhang than a part of a circle. If you want to make the shelf as 1/4 a circle, the curved edge should be stiffened; one way of doing so is to build up laminations underneath, glued together (Fig. 3-5G). If you wish, the curved edge of the laminated part could be covered with veneer.

Another way of obtaining more shelf area is to cut the ends of the front edge square to each wall before making the line across (Fig. 3-6A). There is a limit to how much is practicable, but a few inches cut squarely does not leave too much forward of the line of a supporting strip (Fig. 3-6B). There could be strips under the front, set back a little and mitered to each other (Fig. 3-6C). They provide decoration, but not much stiffness, so a diagonal piece behind them is still advisable.

There could be wood brackets under the squared parts (Fig. 3-6D), and the shelf made stiff enough not to need a supporting strip under the long side. The brackets forward of the battens would be decorative, and the edge of the shelf might be shaped similarly (Fig. 3-6E). As with the plain triangular shelf, the sides along the walls need not be the same length.

BOXED SHELVES

Strong shelves can be arranged without brackets or external projections if a pair of shelves are made in the form of a box, with its opening forward. If a single row of heavy books must be accommodated, or you wish to provide a place for heavy tools or a stock of metal in a shop, or even a place to put pans in a kitchen, this form a shelving makes a good choice.

For a moderate length, there need only be ends between the shelves (Fig. 3-7A), but for a greater length, or even if you only want to separate things on shorter shelves, there could be one or more divisions (Fig. 3-7B) to keep the shelves straight. The back could be left open to the wall, or it might be closed with plywood or hardboard. Some typical sizes are given in Fig. 3-7C and D to provide an indication of sections and proportions, but they will need to be modified to suit circumstances.

For solid wood construction with the best appearance and greatest strength, the best joints for the corners are dovetails, with the tails vertical (Fig. 3-8A) in the direction of the load. Alternately, use dowels, rather less in diameter than half the thickness of the wood and at about 2-inch intervals across the joint. Care is needed when drilling the ends to get as much depth as possible, while not letting the point of the drill break through (Fig. 3-8B). For a less important situation, you could nail or screw the sides into the shelves, not the other way around.

If the shelves are plywood of at least 1/2-inch thickness, you can screw the sides to the end. The heads should be counterbored and plugged (Fig. 3-8C), or you could leave roundhead screws on the surface and treat them as decoration (Fig. 3-8D). Screws with flat or oval heads and in cup washers could also be regarded as decorative (Fig. 3-8E). Dowels can be used in plywood, but much depends on the quality and thickness of the plywood. If the grain is very coarse, it is difficult to make

clean holes in the shelf ends. Try drilling a scrap piece before deciding on this method.

If the shelves are particleboard covered with plastic or wood veneer, the joints can be screwed, with the heads sunk enough to allow for plastic plugs (Fig. 3-8F). Dowels could be used, but there is even more of a risk of the drill breaking through than there is with solid wood. To avoid this situation, you could drill right through and regard the dowel ends as decoration (Fig. 3-8G). The contrasting colored circles, carefully spaced, can be quite attractive. As a further step, the dowel ends might be rounded before they are driven, so each projects a little from the surface (Fig. 3-8H).

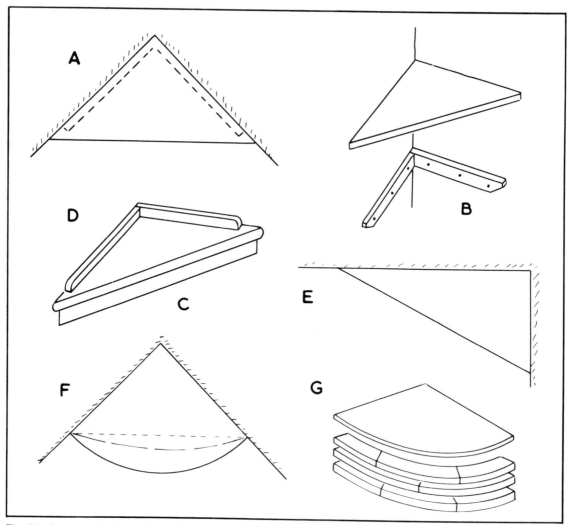

Fig. 3-5. A corner shelf may be a triangle, but need not be symmetrical or straight.

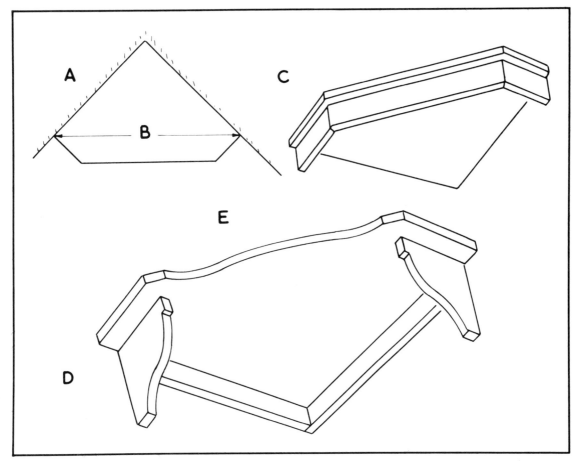

Fig. 3-6. A corner shelf can be given increased area by squaring its ends; then brackets and edging provide support.

A simple division is a plain piece of the same section as the shelves, with dowels into them (Fig. 3-8J). In some situations, it might be better set back a little from the front edge. Access to books or other items stacked against it would be easier, and the appearance improved, if the front edge was hollowed (Fig. 3-8K).

If there is to be a back, the plywood or hardboard could be merely glued and nailed to the rear of the assembly, but that would leave its edges showing, which may not matter. For better appearance the parts should be prepared with rabbets for the back before the joints are cut. If there is a back, screws into the wall can go through it. The number depends on the size of the assembly and its intended load, but screws fairly close to the top shelf are more effective than any lower down. If the back is open, mirror plates can be used, projecting inwards from the ends and top, or strips can be added inside or outside the ends and top for screws to the wall.

Materials List for Boxed Shelves

Short

2 pieces	7 × 25 × 3/4
2 pieces	7 × 11 × 3/4
1 back	10 × 25 × 1/4 plywood

Long

2 pieces	7 × 43 × 3/4
4 pieces	7 × 11 × 3/4
1 back	10 × 43 × 1/4 plywood

EXTENDED BOXED SHELVES

The simplest way to extend boxed shelving is to dou-

31

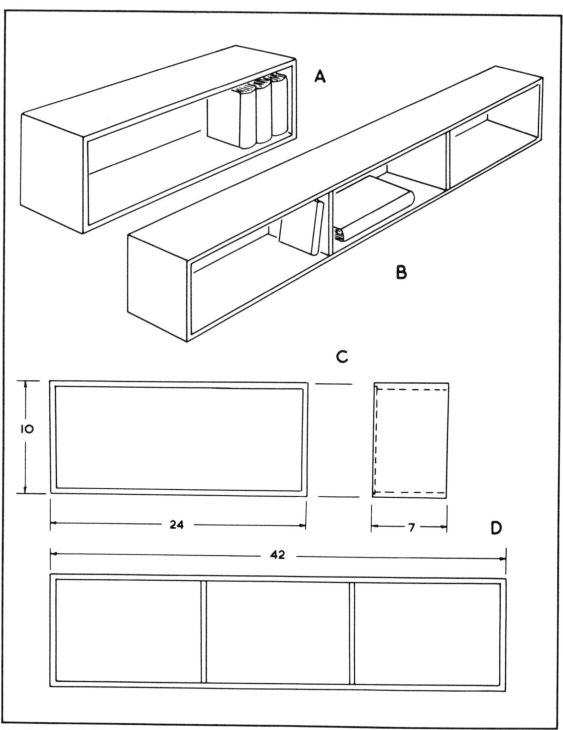

A

B

C

10

24

7

D

42

Fig. 3-7. A pair of shelves can be made like a box on edge.

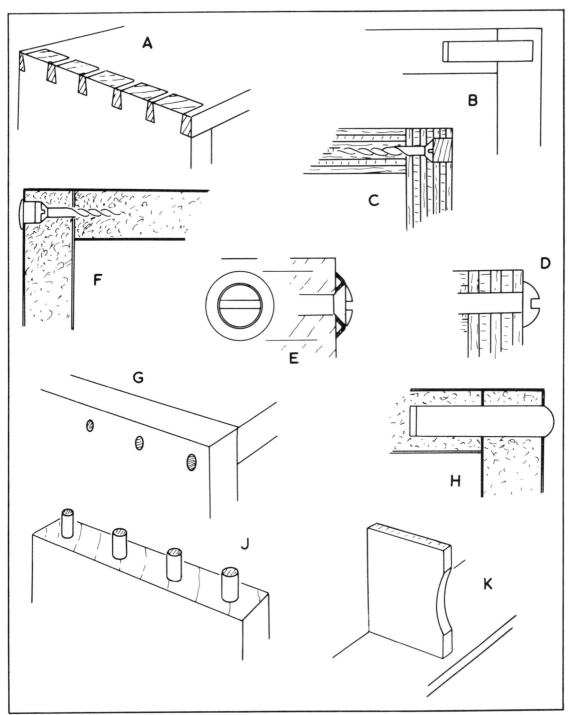

Fig. 3-8. Solid wood corners may be dovetailed or doweled (A,B). Plywood and particleboard can be screwed (C-F). Dowels can go through (G,H). Divisions can be doweled and shaped (J,K).

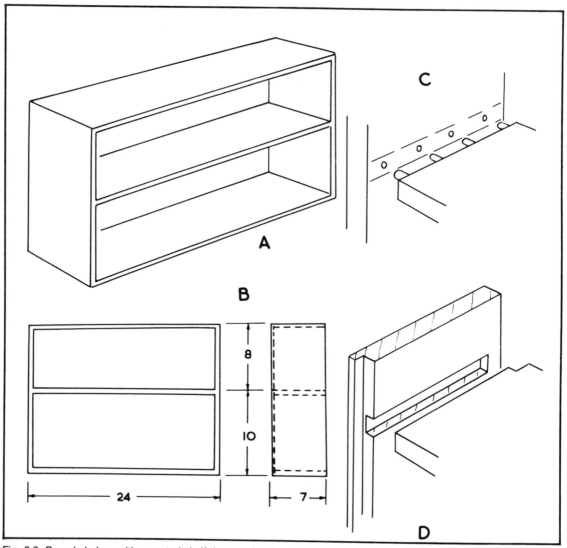

Fig. 3-9. Boxed shelves with a central shelf that can be doweled or let into a dado, with a recess for a plywood back.

ble the depth. The box shown in Fig. 3-9A is made high enough to have a shelf across it. Possible sizes are suggested. For the sake of appearance, if not for the books or other items to be accommodated, the shelf is better located above the halfway mark (Fig. 3-9B).

Construction methods are the same as in the previous examples, except for the extra shelf. If veneered particleboard is used, dowels make the most convenient joints (Fig. 3-9C). If you are using solid wood, dowels are also possible, but the traditional joints would be dadoes (Fig. 3-9D).

If you make the assembly without a back, be very careful to see that it is square by comparing diagonal measurements before the glue has set. If there is a back, it should keep the other parts true. Any block of shelves on a wall is in a very obvious position, and viewers will be quick to notice anything out of square.

Materials List for Double-Depth Boxed Shelves

| 2 sides | $7 \times 19 \times 3/4$ |
| 3 shelves | $7 \times 25 \times 3/4$ |

Deep-Boxed Shelves

The boxed shelves can be extended further, so there are séveral intermediate shelves (Fig. 3-10A). By firmly jointing the corners, you can ensure strength and rigidity, but if the assembly is tall, there is a risk of the sides bowing outwards if they are not restrained. Dovetailed dadoes for at least some of the intermediate shelves will hold them in. An open-backed block of shelves can be held in shape with a rear rail under a central shelf, with its ends let into the sides, screwed, and preferably dovetailed (Fig. 3-10B). This and another similar rail under the top (Fig. 3-10C) will take screws into the wall.

Materials List for Deep-Boxed Shelves

2 sides	7 × 31 × 3/4
5 shelves	7 × 16 × 3/4

Outward Extension

Boxed shelves can be extended outside the normal outline. If they will be fairly close to the ceiling, you can take the sides up to the ceiling for extra accommodation (Fig. 3-11A). If the assembly is to come close to the floor, you may find it worthwhile extending downwards so some of the weight is taken on the floor (Fig. 3-11B), relieving wall fastenings.

If the space below is sufficient, it may form extra storage. If it is to remain open, make sure there is enough depth for a brush or other cleaner to go under the bottom shelf. If the gap is not more than a few inches, it may be better to close it with a plinth. Strips of wood may go across the front and sides level with the bottom shelf (Fig. 3-11C). The top edges of these plinth strips may be left square, rounded, beveled, or molded, and the corners mitered. This method can be done around particleboard,

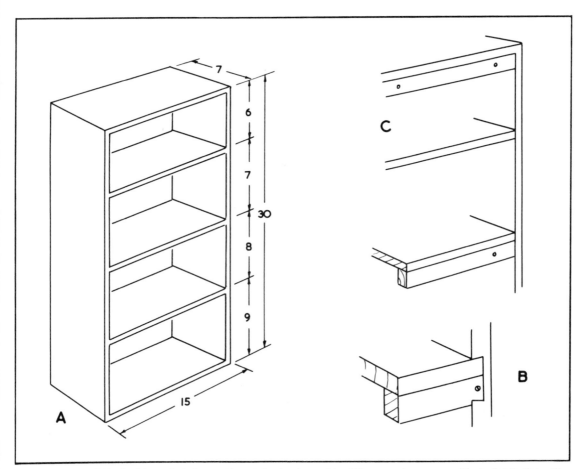

Fig. 3-10. In a tall block of boxed shelves, strips at the back provide stiffness and a means of fastening to the wall.

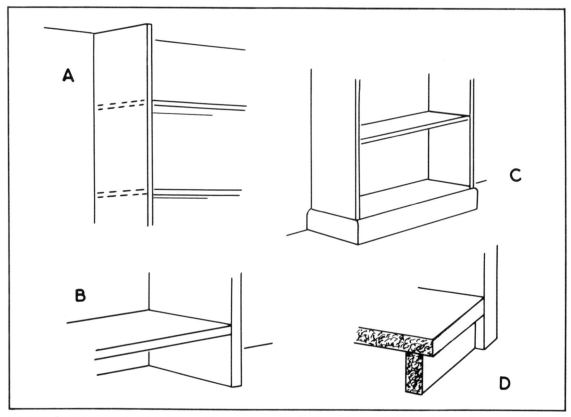

Fig. 3-11. Shelf ends may be taken to the ceiling or extended to the floor, where a plinth may fit around or be let in the front.

but a simpler way is to set back a strip at the front as a plinth (Fig. 3-11D).

There may be a good reason to extend a shelf outwards. Suppose, in a kitchen, a food mixer has several accessories. The mixer itself might have a compartment on a shelf with a divider to enclose it; then the bottom shelf can be extended outside, and holes can be drilled in the extension to take accessories (Fig. 3-12A). There cannot be a dovetail or other strong corner joint at this point, but dowels should provide ample strength (Fig. 3-12B). If you prefer to screw from below, make sure the screws are long enough into the side. End grain does not provide as much grip on a screw thread as cross grain; so screws that way should be longer to compensate. A good way of increasing the grip of a screw is to let a piece of dowel rod into a hole, so the screw cuts its way across the grain (Fig. 3-12C).

A further problem in a kitchen is the storage of food processor blades so they are accessible, but placed so you won't cut yourself on them, and the vital edges won't get damaged. For most sorts of processor blades, you can provide a strip with notches, held forward with spacers at the ends (Fig. 3-13A). If the blade axle parts extend on both sides of the rotary blade, there will have to be a similar piece behind the strip. Sizes depend on the particular blades, but the best place for the rack is fairly high on the back of a boxed shelf, and deep enough to take other things below, yet keeping the cutters out of the way, but not so close to the top that they cannot be lifted out (Fig. 3-13B).

The undersides of shelves can be used for storage. There is usually space to spare above the contents of the shelf below. Things that will push into holes, such as pens, some kitchen mixer parts, and many tools, can fit into a drilled block below a shelf (Fig. 3-13C). For parts that are not round in section, a strip of plywood with spacers will make suitable compartments (Fig. 3-13D). For other items, it may be more convenient to use loops of leather or webbing strap (Fig. 3-13E). Use screws between loops, but put washers under the heads so they do not pull

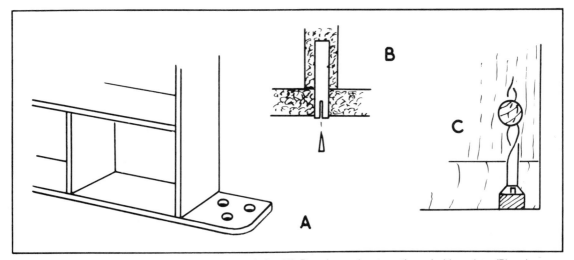

Fig. 3-12. A shelf extension provides extra accommodation (A). Dowels may be strengthened with wedges (B) and screws give a better grip in end grain with dowels (C).

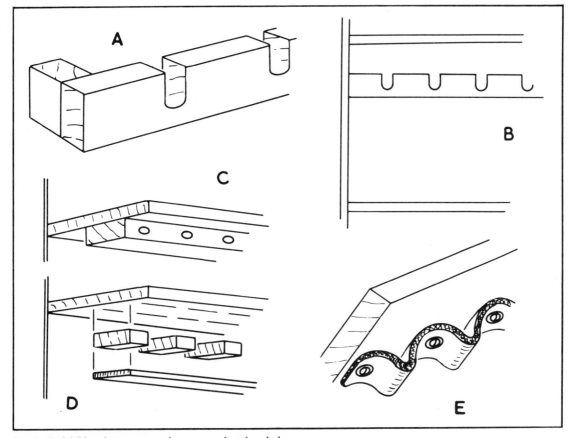

Fig. 3-13. Additional storage can be arranged under shelves.

through. For tapered tools, the flexibility of the loops allows pushing in until the tool is gripped, which cannot be done as readily with rigid wooden sockets.

HANGING BOOK RACK

Books in bulk are fairly heavy. There are two main considerations when you are planning to make a multi-shelf rack supported solely by screws into a wall. If it is to reach the floor, much of the weight will be taken there; so wall fastenings will have reduced loads.

The shelves themselves must be stiff enough to resist bending. A row of books appear to have little effect on the shelf at first, but after a few months, a weak shelf may develop a sag. There might be no fear of it breaking, but the curve downwards in the middle will spoil its appearance. Solid wood with its grain lengthwise is less likely to bend after long use than plywood or particleboard. Length affects the tendency to bend under load; so a rack consisting of a larger number of shorter shelves will be stiffer than a rack with a fewer number of longer shelves for the same capacity.

You must also consider attachment to the wall. If it is masonry, plugs for the screws can be located almost anywhere. If the wall is light board over vertical studding, you have to get the screws into the studding; so may have to plan the size of the rack to suit this need.

The suggested design in Fig. 3-14A suits solid wood. Plywood could be the same thickness or a little thicker. Alternatively, you could use thinner plywood strengthened with strips of solid wood at the edges, but to get enough stiffness, the edges, and therefore the appearance of the front of the shelf, would be thicker than solid wood or plywood. Veneered particleboard may have to be in a stock thickness, but ideally it should be a little thicker than the specified solid wood.

The sizes given in Fig. 3-14B will give a good capacity with a width that overlaps two studs at normal spacing; so two screws of adequate length can be driven at top and bottom, and they should be enough. If you have doubts, additional screws can go through a strip under an intermediate shelf, or mirror plates could be put behind any shelf. Distances between shelves should be made to suit your books, with the larger ones at the bottom and an inch or so clearance above the books.

The book rack is shown with an open back. If you wish to close it with thin plywood or hardboard, cut rabbets in the wood for the sides before marking them out for other parts. Deep books are usually wider than shallow books; so to avoid the smaller books being almost lost at the back of full-width shelves, the rack tapers toward the top.

Mark out the pair of sides together (Fig. 3-15A). Do not plane the taper or do any end shaping until after you cut the joints. It is easier to handle the wood while it is parallel and there is spare length at the ends.

From the marked-out sides, you can discover the exact width of each shelf (Fig. 3-15B). Cut the shelves to width and length and make the dado joints into which they fit. It would be sufficient to make each shelf the same width as the dado length (Fig. 3-15C), but it is easier to get a close, good-looking joint if you cut back for stopped dadoes (Fig. 3-15D).

The top and bottom strips must take the weight of the whole assembly; so notch them into the sides enough to take stout screws (Fig. 3-15E) and allow for a few screws through the shelf as well (Fig. 3-15F).

It may be sufficient to merely taper the top and bottom of each side (Fig. 3-15G). If that is done cleanly and accurately, it will look better than shaped ends which are poorly finished. Shaped ends are shown in Fig. 3-15H. You could bevel at the bottom and shape at the top, or the other way around, if you wish. You could also leave the tops standing higher to act as supports for another row of books.

The pieces across the back could be left straight, but if you shape the tops and bottoms of the sides, they could be made to match (Fig. 3-15J). A simple and effective decoration is a variation on wagon beveling along the front edge (Fig. 3-15K), done by careful work with a spokeshave, a chisel used with the bevel downward, or with a Surform tool. Mark on the front only and keep the tool always at about 45 degrees.

Sand all the inner surfaces before assembly. Drill all screw holes, including those for screws to the wall, then assemble with glue as well as screws. Screws driven upward under the top and bottom shelves into the dado joints should be enough to prevent all joints from opening. Even better would be to make these joints with a dovetail section. The screws into the wall could have round heads or be driven through decorative washers. If you want to hide them, they could be counterbored and plugged, but that would make removal difficult if you wanted to move the rack.

Materials List for Hanging Book Rack

2 sides	8 × 41 × 7/8
1 shelf	8 × 30 × 7/8
1 shelf	7 1/2 × 30 × 7/8

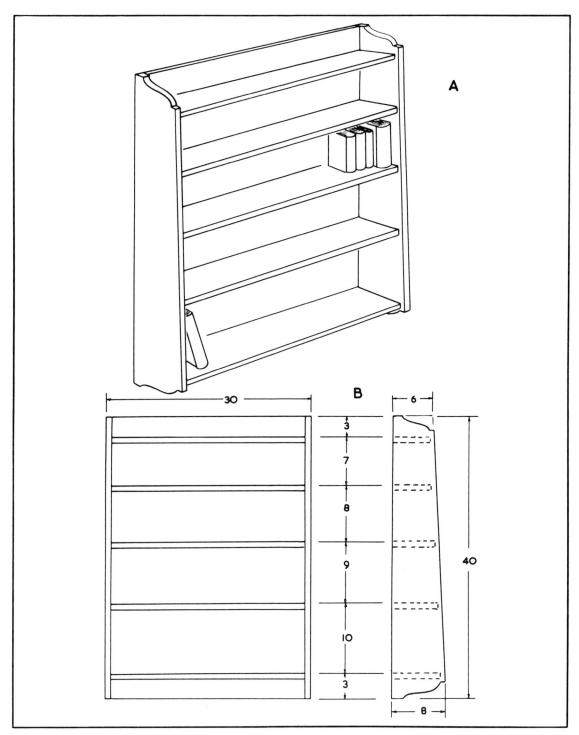

Fig. 3-14. Suggested sizes for the hanging book rack.

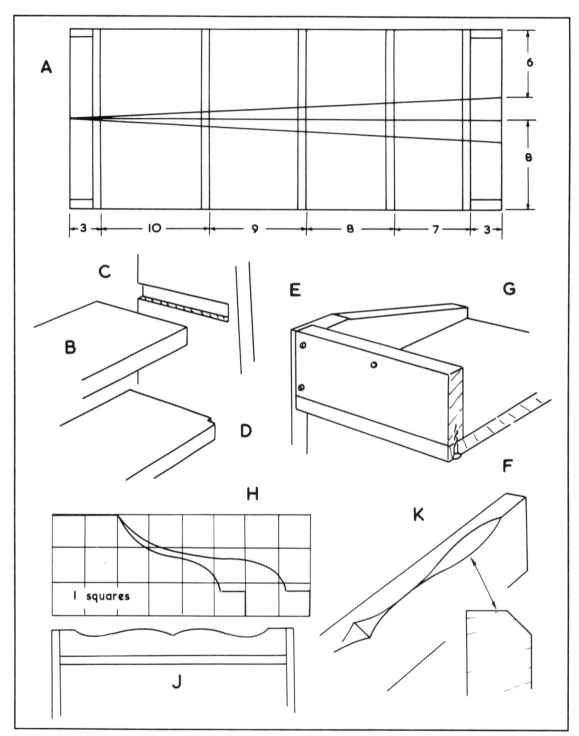

Fig. 3-15. Marking out, shaping, and joining parts of the hanging book rack.

1 shelf	$7 \times 30 \times 7/8$
1 shelf	$6\ 1/2 \times 30 \times 7/8$
1 shelf	$6 \times 30 \times 7/8$
1 top	$3 \times 30 \times 7/8$
1 bottom	$3 \times 30 \times 7/8$

LARGE STORAGE SHELVES

In a storeroom, warehouse, or other place where it is convenient to stack things like magazines and boxes on shelves, the important consideration is safe capacity for the maximum amount in the space available, without much regard to appearance. Quite often the shelves need to be wider than the usual household shelving, which brings problems of support. If you are thinking of 12-inch shelves almost to the ceiling, you will be asking the shelves to take a considerable weight.

Supports should go to the floor, if that is possible; otherwise the loads on screws into the wall could be more than they can take, particularly if you must depend on comparatively few screws into studding. If the wall is only a partition, it might not be able to withstand the strain if the floor does not share it; so make some supports to the floor. There are ways of doing so without much obstruction.

The example in Fig. 3-16 is a composite arrangement to show various methods of construction. It is intended to be made of plastic-veneered particleboard about 3/4 inch thick, with the edges as well as the broad surfaces veneered and strips of veneer glued over the cut ends.

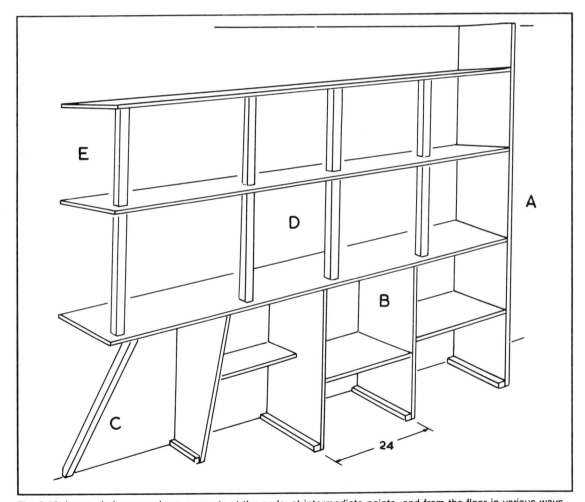

Fig. 3-16. Large shelves may have supports at the ends, at intermediate points, and from the floor in various ways.

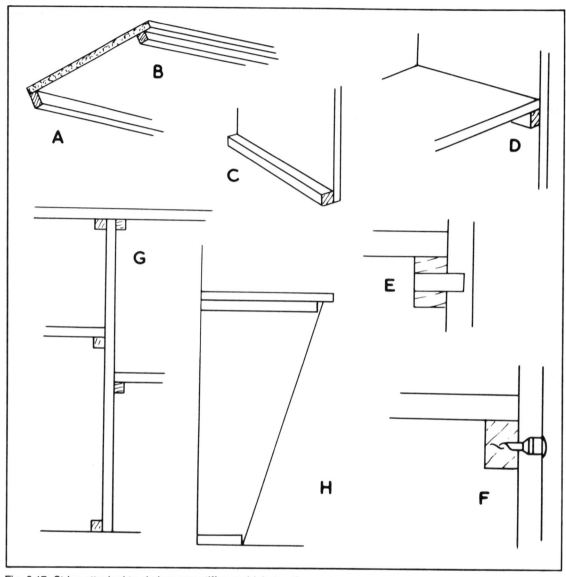

Fig. 3-17. Strips attached to shelves can stiffen and join to other parts.

The backs of all shelves rest on strips of 1-×-2-inch wood (Fig. 3-17A), screwed through to the shelves and drilled at intervals for screwing to the wall. It may be advisable to put stiffening strips under the front edge (Fig. 3-17B). Supports are shown at 24-inch intervals. Unless what is to be stored is exceptionally heavy, that spacing should be enough to keep unstiffened particleboard from sagging; however, much depends on where main loads are concentrated and the quality of the board.

The end upright goes from floor to ceiling (Fig. 3-16A). Prepare it and mark it out. It may then be used as a gauge for other upright parts, to get all the heights correct and matching. At the foot of this piece, add a strip of 1 1/2-inch-square wood for one or two screws into the floor (Fig. 3-17C). All any downward screws must do is keep the end in place, so they need not be many or long.

At the shelf levels, there can be 1-×-2-inch strips (Fig. 3-17D). If you want the outer surface to remain unmarked, there can be glued dowels (Fig. 3-17E); otherwise, use screws with their heads covered with plastic plugs (Fig. 3-17F).

The main supports for the lowest long shelf are full-width pieces (Fig. 3-16B). Use feet similar to the end, but you can add strips each side of the tops of the supports (Fig. 3-17G) and batten supports for any other lower shelves. Besides their use for storage, such shelves help with stiffness.

If you do not want the supports to come as far forward at floor level, you can taper them to reduce obstruction (Fig. 3-17H). If you are using particleboard already veneered on the edges, cut the taper at the back and square the ends to match. If you do it the other way, you will have to plane the taper and put a strip of veneer on it. If the cut edge is toward the wall, you will not have to do much to it.

If you want a support to the floor with negligible obstruction, there can be a post sloping back to the angle between the wall and floor (Fig. 3-16C). A piece of hardwood 1 1/2 inches square would suit the shelf sizes I am considering. There are problems with making joints at its ends (Fig. 3-18A). The bottom must be prevented from moving. You can use a dowel for this purpose, but another way is to drive in a screw with a long neck and cut off the head (Fig. 3-18B). Press the screw on the floor where it is to go to mark the position, then drill for it. At the top, pull the post into position, and drill downward through the shelf for a dowel into it (Fig. 3-18C).

The supports for the upper shelves are pieces of 1 1/2-inch-square hardwood near the front edges. As far as possible, arrange them away from other supports (Fig. 3-16D) as that makes fitting easier. It should be sufficient to use glued dowel joints (Fig. 3-18D). If you think additional support across the width of a shelf would be advisable, there can be strips notched into the rear supports and screwed or doweled in place (Fig. 3-18E).

Towards the ends of the shelves, it would be better if the posts came in line (Fig. 3-16E), even if the joints are staggered further along. There could be one dowel going into both parts (Fig. 3-18F), but that could bring assembly problems. It might be better to get all the joints made at one level before moving on to the next one. There is not enough thickness in a shelf for dowels to meet halfway, but strength could be improved on that by cutting the dowel ends diagonally (Fig. 3-18G). Another way would be to use a large dowel for the lower post and drill it for a smaller one after fixing (Fig. 3-18H).

You could use tenons. Two offset tenons may fit into one mortise (Fig. 3-18J), or the lower tenon could be divided for a single tenon from the post above to fit into it (Fig. 3-18K). Tenoning involves cutting mortises with square corners, which is difficult to do in some particleboard without the edges crumbling; so dowel arrangements are preferable.

OPEN-ENDED SHELVES

A block of shelves does not have to be made with wide, closed uprights at the sides. It may suit the decor of a room to have a much lighter appearance at the sides. If the shelves are to support plants in pots or flowers in vases, it would be better if these items were visible from the sides, and foliage could spread that way as well as forward.

The shelves in Fig. 3-19 are intended to be attached to a wall, but the supports are narrow and slope back, although the shelves remain all the same width. Suggested sizes are given in Fig. 3-20A. If you modify them, arrange for the foot of the sides to extend to the same width from the wall as the shelves and for the top extension to come above the top shelf, so it gets the benefit of a full-width joint. The shelves do not have to be all the same width; you could make one or more of the higher ones narrower.

Lay out the main lines (Fig. 3-20B) full-size on the edge of a sheet of plywood or other convenient board. They are all contained in a rectangle 8 × 45 inches, and that should be drawn first. Set an adjustable bevel to the angle that the shelves all cross the diagonal line and use that when marking shelf positions on the side strips so you get all shelves the same. As with any shelving, avoid letting the shelves finish lower at the front than the rear. It is better to mark out with a very slight upward angle toward the front, than to risk getting a downward slope when cutting.

Cut the two side pieces to shape and check that they match as a pair. There are two possible ways of attaching the shelves to the sides: you can depend on glue and screws only, or you can let the shelves into dadoes. Dadoes help to positively locate shelf ends and reduce any risk of a shelf dropping when in use.

Make all the shelves to identical lengths, and make enough supporting end strips. The front edges of the shelves may be chamfered or rounded (Fig. 3-20C). Cut back the supporting strips from the front (Fig. 3-20D) and round all exposed edges.

Attach the supports to the ends of the shelves. For most purposes glue can be supplemented with nails or screws, with their heads sunk and covered with stopping. The crossings with the sides are different at each level. Mark where they come from your full-size drawing and drill for two screws at each place, arranged diagonally (Fig. 3-20E), so they cannot go through the same grain lines either way. Screw from the inside outwards so there are no screw heads showing outside the sides. During assembly, use a straightedge against the backs of the shelves to check that they and the cut tops of the sides will come flat against the wall.

It should be sufficient to screw to the wall through mirror plates on the rear of the top shelf or through a strip of wood under it, since most downward thrust will be taken by the legs on the floor. There will probably be no

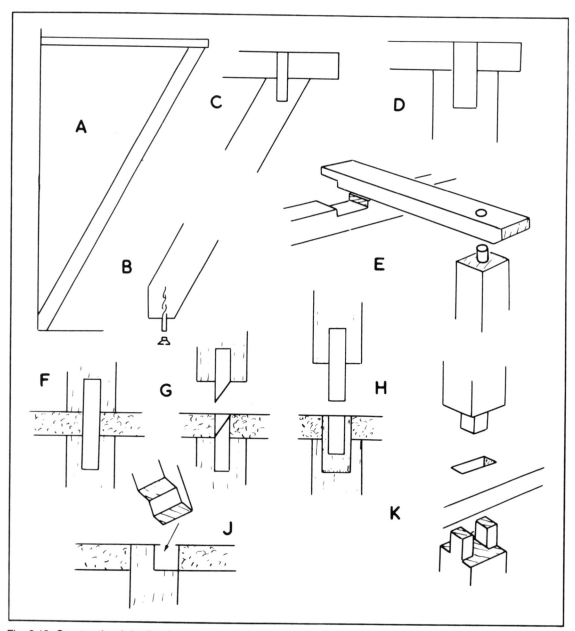

Fig. 3-18. Constructional details of struts and supports for large shelves.

Fig. 3-19. A set of open-ended shelves with sloping supports.

need to attach the legs to the floor. If attachment is considered necessary, there could be cutoff screws, as described for a strut under shelves (Fig. 3-18B). There could be a mirror plate screwed under each leg so a screw could go through its projecting part into the floor. If something more would be preferred, a foot can be dow-

eled or tenoned on each leg (Fig. 3-20F).

Materials List for Open-Ended Shelves

2 sides	2 1/2 × 48 × 1
4 shelves	8 × 36 × 3/4
8 supports	2 × 8 × 3/4

45

NOVELTY SHELVES

Most of us accumulate souvenirs from trips and vacations and wish to display them. This little block of shelves is intended to hang on the wall and provide somewhere to put the smaller souvenirs so they look attractive. The whole display serves the same purpose as a picture in breaking up the plainness of a wall, while reminding us of where the many items came from.

The shelves are arranged as interlocking squares (Fig. 3-21). The sizes suggested in Fig. 3-22A should suit most objects, but obviously variations are possible. For use on the wall of a room, it would be inadvisable to make the arrangement much bigger. Its size should not be such that the items displayed look small, while drawing too much attention to the shelves themselves. Relate the wood sizes to the things to be displayed. If you have just one large item, and the others are all of a comparable smaller size, it would be better to put the large object elsewhere and relate the shelf sizes to the smaller things for a more even display.

The parts are simple, but they must be made accurately to match each other. Because you must cut halfway across each piece, the wood should be fairly close-grained hardwood. Softwood might break along the short grain. Plywood could be used, if you are willing to accept the edge view of the plies at the front. There are eight pieces to finish 3 inches wide by 14 inches long and 1/4 or 5/16 inch thick. Make sure the pieces are of uniform width and thickness; otherwise you will have trouble making secure, close-fitting joints. You should aim at joints that will hold together dry.

There are four pieces with three notches (Fig. 3-22B)

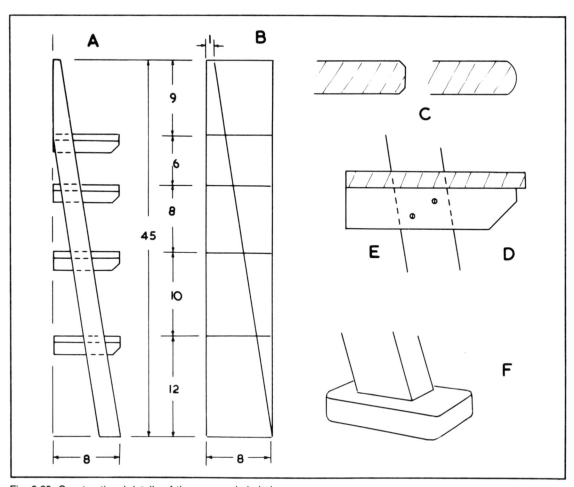

Fig. 3-20. Constructional details of the open-ended shelves.

46

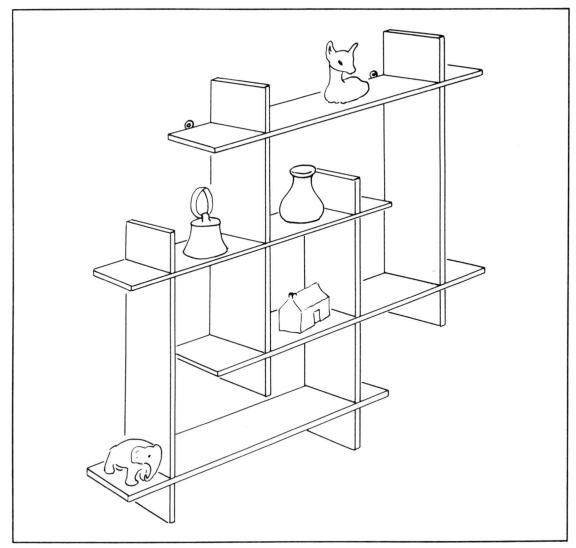

Fig. 3-21. Novelty shelves for displaying small items.

and four with two notches (Fig. 3-22C). The end notches in all eight pieces must match, and the center notches in four should be exactly central, so any piece can be reversed during assembly. Use the actual wood to mark the widths of the slots. After cutting, a slot should be a push fit on any other piece of wood.

Take the sharpness off all edges and ends. You could round the front corners of each shelf, but you will have to make a trial assembly to determine which will be the front corners. The front edges might be rounded as well.

When you assemble, the joints can be left dry if they are a good fit. This method would allow you to disassemble later, if you wished. Otherwise use a minimum of glue in each joint. In any case, check that the parts are square to each other.

The whole assembly, even when loaded, is quite light, and there is no need for very substantial hanging arrangements. There could be two small screw eyes driven downward into the top shelf to hang on nails in the wall or on picture hooks. Ordinary mirror plates are too large for this assembly, but you could cut small ones from thin sheet aluminum (from a drink can) so there can be one or two small nails through each into the back of the top shelf and nails the other way into the wall. If the shelves hang only slightly out of true, it will be rather obvious, so check with a spirit level.

HANGING SHELVES

In many rooms, shops, stores, and garages, the space that is least used is overhead. There must be some clearance above you to make the room feel airy and spacious, and you would not be happy with a ceiling only a few inches above your head, but there are some situations where storage space could be arranged under the ceiling without impeding movement or affecting the normal use of the area. In a crowded storeroom or a shop with tool and other racks all around the walls, the only direction you can look for possible further storage place is upward. In a garage with all the usual accumulation of things around the walls, it would be possible to arrange storage above the car without interfering with other uses of the place. Hanging shelves make good places to store things that are only occasionally needed. In a woodworking shop, they can hold stocks of wood, with long pieces lengthwise and short pieces across.

Of course, a major problem is getting a strong enough attachment to whatever is above, because only upward fastenings will hold the shelves, unless the shelf is within reach of a wall, where some additional support there might be provided. If it is a garage with roof rafters exposed, or a shop where the joists for the floor above are exposed, making secure attachments is easy. The hangers for the shelf may be taken up the side of the rafter or joist for screws driven horizontally (Fig. 3-23A). A screw will take a much greater load across its diameter than in its length, when only the threads take the strain. Arrange the screws diagonally, so they go into different grain lines of both parts (Fig. 3-23B). If not much of the wood above is exposed, you can include a plywood gusset to allow more screws both ways (Fig. 3-23C).

If there is a ceiling, you must find where the joists or rafters are above it, because screws must be driven upward into them. Driving them elsewhere would soon bring the ceiling down. You will have to look for evidence to show you where the stronger parts above the ceiling are. From a room overhead you may be able to trace lines of nails in floorboards. From outside, you may be able to see the ends of rafters or indications of where they are supported. Even if you can only find evidence of one piece of wood and the spacing of others, you may be able to establish one sure point to drive a screw and get the other

positions by measurement.

Usually the plaster or other board used for a ceiling is not very thick. If you look across a ceiling, particularly toward a light, you can often see the lines of joists where the board has curved upward very slightly between them. This process shows you the direction, and you may get a positive location of at least one joist to provide a start in measuring. If all else fails, you may have to probe through the ceiling. If you use a very fine awl, the holes will not be very obvious later and will disappear when the ceiling is painted. Use a piece of hard steel in a handle—a fine knitting pin would be very suitable.

A hanging shelf will have to be supported by a series of hanging frames, which may have a strip at the top for attachment (Fig. 3-23D), particularly if the joist above is in the same direction as the length of the shelf. It may be better to give each vertical piece its own pad to take screws in a line going the width of the shelf (Fig. 3-23E).

So that the vertical hangers are as secure as possible in their pads, it is best to use joints that resist pulling. One or more dovetails into the side of the pad (Fig. 3-23F) or its end (Fig. 3-23G) could be used. The hanger could have a tenon into the pad and be spread above into a tapered mortise with wedges (Fig. 3-23H). For screws upwards, it is best to use roundheads with large washers (Fig. 3-23J) to resist any tendency of heads to pull into the wood in use.

At the shelf level, the crossbars can be dovetailed to the hangers (Fig. 3-23K). For a simpler construction, it may be satisfactory to merely overlap the surfaces and screw through them (Fig. 3-23L).

The spacing of hangers may be governed by the attachment points above. If these points are wide apart, the shelves must be thicker than if they are closer. Ideally, the shelves should be kept as light as possible. Much depends on the loading, but hangers made from 1- x -2-inch strips spaced at about 24-inch intervals might have boards on them about 5/8 inch thick, but if the spacing was doubled, the boards should be 1 inch thick.

The shelves could be screwed to the hanging frames, but it may be better to arrange them to lift off, to aid cleaning and allow you to rearrange storage more easily. A surprising amount of dust settles on overhead things, and you may want to get them all down occasionally. If the shelving is made up of several boards, fit each of them with cleats across to keep them in place (Fig. 3-23M). If the frames hang some distance from the ceiling, the cleats will also reduce any tendency of the frames to wobble.

The shelf need not be made of closed boards. If it is to be mainly used for smaller items arranged across

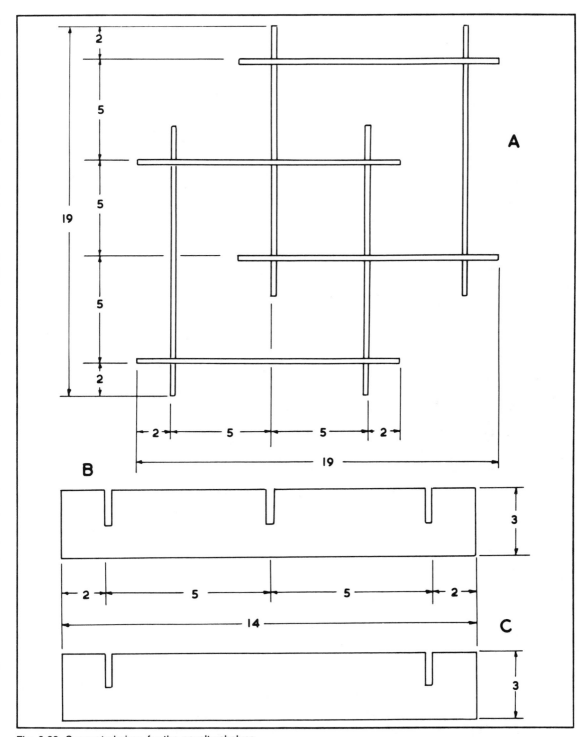

Fig. 3-22. Suggested sizes for the novelty shelves.

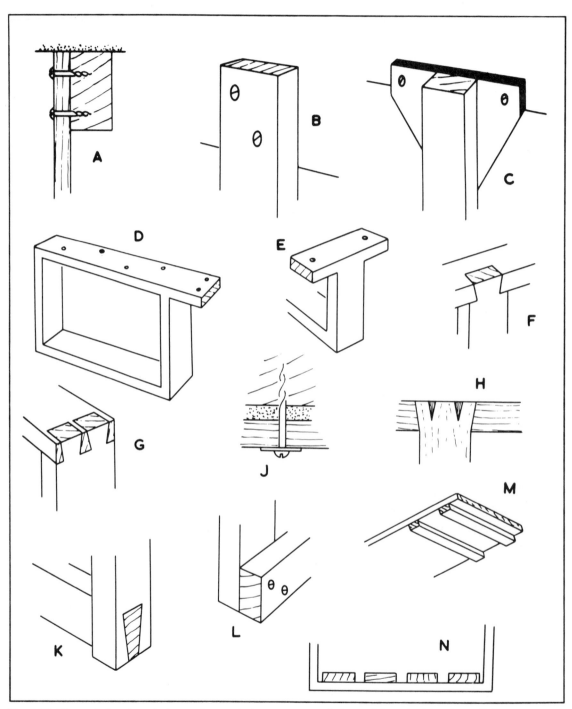

Fig. 3-23. Where shelves have to hang, strong attachments are needed, possibly to the joist above (A-C) or by screws (D,E). Dovetails will resist downward pulls (F,G). Wedges provide strength (H). Washers prevent screw heads pulling in (J). Frames may be dovetailed (K) or screwed (L) and shelves fitted over them (M,N).

or for short pieces of wood, an assembly of strips on battens might be better (Fig. 3-23N) so you can see between them.

SPOON RACK

Anyone who collects spoons with badges, costs of arms, or other indication of where they were obtained on their ends, will want to display them. In a suitable rack

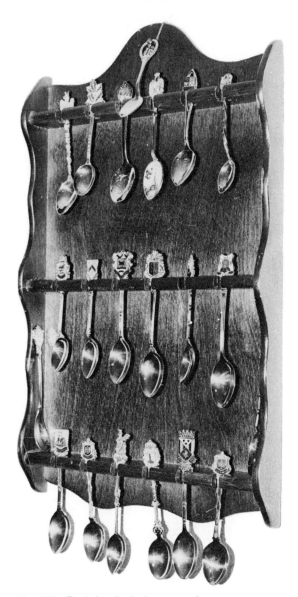

Fig. 3-24. Rack for displaying souvenir spoons.

they make a decorative display and a reminder of where you have been. Any rack should not hold the spoons in a way that does not allow them to be removed. It is better to arrange it so the spoons can be taken down and examined or used. Because of the shape of a spoon, it hangs and looks best with its bowl downward; so a display rack needs to be in the form of a block of shelves with suitable slots.

This spoon rack (Fig. 3-24) will display eight spoons on each shelf. It could be made with any number of shelves. It is shown with three, to take 24 spoons (Fig. 3-25A). The sizes should suit the usual type of souvenir spoons, but you should check your collection. You may find a narrower or wider spacing between shelves and spoons would suit some of them.

Although the assembly is very similar to a hanging bookcase or other block of shelves, it does not have to carry much weight; so it can be made with wood of quite light sections. It is shown with wood 1/4 inch thick for the main parts, and that should be hardwood with reasonably straight grain so the thin wood does not warp. The back may have to be 1/4-inch plywood, but if you can get it thinner, that would be better. Ideally, its front surfaces will be veneered to match the other parts, but you may have to settle for plain plywood and stain it to match. A fairly dark finish will show up the silvery color of the spoons and any enamelwork on their ends.

The sides set the sizes for the other parts. Mark out the pair of them (Fig. 3-25B) and rabbet the rear edges to suit the back plywood. There is not much thickness for this joint, and you will have to drive a few thin nails diagonally when you glue in the back (Fig. 3-25C).

The shelves go into stopped dadoes (Fig. 3-25D). There is not much thickness to cut away and provide glue surfaces; so drive two thin pins into each joint (Fig. 3-25E). Punched below the surface, they can be stopped and will not show.

The slots for the spoons should be marked out carefully. Regular, even spacings are important. Check the sizes of the parts of your spoons where they will hang, but most will go through a slot 1/4 inch wide and hang on a widened part 1/2 inch wide. If you have any spoons of unusual size, you will have to cut special slots to suit them. Spoons of different sizes might go into the bottom row and be arranged symmetrically.

Mark the position of each slot and the centers of the holes on a line 1/2 inch back from the front (Fig. 3-26A). Drill 1/4-inch holes cleanly (Fig. 3-26B), then cut in to make the entry slot 1/4 inch wide (Fig. 3-26C). Trim the edges cleanly and sand off the edges above and below.

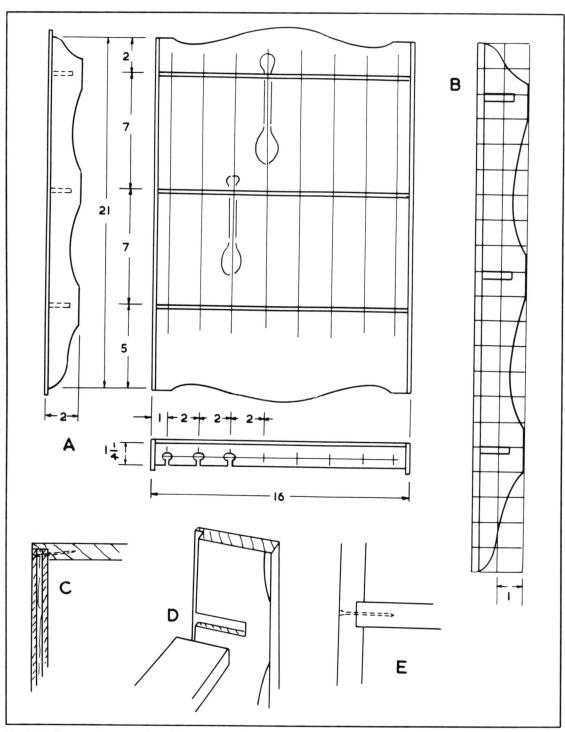

Fig. 3-25. Sizes and construction of the spoon rack.

Perform each step on all the slots at the same time; this may be a little tedious, but it will ensure uniformity.

Shape the top and bottom edges of the back plywood to curves that match the sides. A half template will help you mark the curves symmetrically (Fig. 3-26D). The top could be curved higher at the center around a central hanging screw hole, or you could fix the rack with a pair of screws through the back underneath the top shelf.

Materials List for Spoon Rack

2 sides	$2 \times 22 \times 1/4$
3 shelves	$1\ 1/4 \times 16 \times 1/4$
1 back	$16 \times 23 \times 1/8$ or 1/4 plywood

PLATE RACK

A plate with a decorative center is meant to be displayed, rather than used, particularly if it commemorates some event or place. If it is a single plate, it may be hung with a wire clip that grips the edge and has an eye at the back to go on a hook or nail. If there are several plates in a set, it may be better to make a wooden rack which could be arranged vertically, horizontally, or combined with a spoon rack. Suggestions for all three types are given here. Much depends on the number and size of the plates.

The example of a vertical rack (Fig. 3-27A) is designed around three 7-inch plates. You will have to lay out your rack to suit the actual plates. If you prepare a piece of wood for the back longer than you need, you can experiment with the plates to get the best positions for the supports. In most situations it will be best to arrange the plates as close together as possible. The amount they are dished will affect the projection of supports. If the set of plates is graduated in size, spacings will be affected, usually with the biggest at the bottom. So the plates cannot roll out sideways, they rest on two pegs, notched a little at the front (Fig. 3-27B) and spaced fairly wide apart behind retaining front strips (Fig. 3-27C), which look best shaped and rounded at the edges. Keep the strips light, so they are as inconspicuous as possible and do not take attention from the plate designs.

The back is mainly parallel, but you can shape the ends in any way you wish. With plain-rimmed plates, plain curved wood will do, but if the plates have shaped outlines, an outline on the wood that reflects the shape may be better. If you wish, you may fret or carve the ends. Attachment to the wall will usually be with screws through the centers of the end circles.

If the rack is firmly fixed to the wall and is in a position where it is unlikely to be knocked, the plates may be safe enough just resting in place. If you want to secure

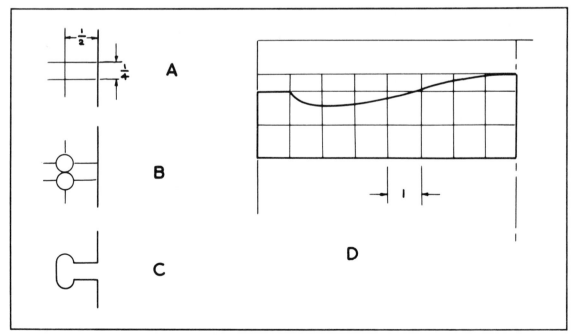

Fig. 3-26. Cutting slots for the spoons and shaping the top and bottom.

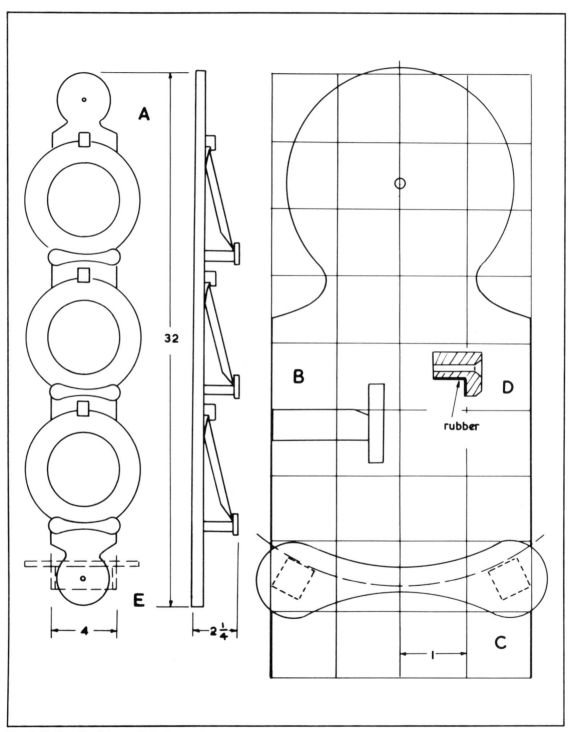

Fig. 3-27. Details of the vertical plate rack.

the plates, there can be little turnbuttons above each one (Fig. 3-27D). Size will depend on how much the plate extends, due to its dishing. Arrange the turnbutton to turn on a screw. Gluing in a rubber lining would be advisable.

If you have a few souvenir spoons to display with the plates, the bottom of the rack could be extended downward to allow space for a slotted shelf. The shelf might be extended beyond the width of the backboard and would look right if made about the same length as the diameter of the bottom plate (Fig. 3-27E).

If you prefer to arrange your plates in a horizontal row, the rack becomes a fairly simple shelf (Fig. 3-28A). The main problem then is keeping the plates evenly spaced. There could be pegs holding out the front strip, in a similar manner to those on a vertical rack, but a solid shelf is simpler, and you can locate the plates by hollowing the front edge of the shelf (Fig. 3-28B) before putting on the front strip. If you want to secure them against

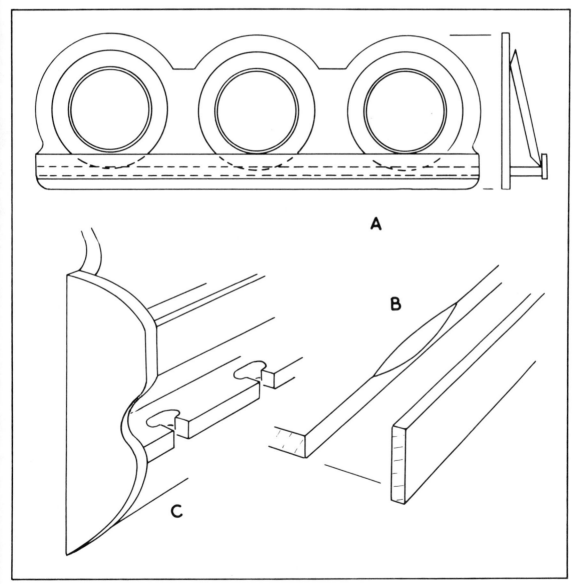

Fig. 3-28. Suggestions for the horizontal plate rack, which could have spoons hanging below.

knocks, put individual turnbuttons above the top edges.

The back of the horizontal rack can be decorated in any way you wish. There could be straight edges at the top and bottom, or you may prefer a shaped outline unrelated to the shapes of the plates. The drawing shows curves which have the effect of framing the plates. Care is needed to get the hollows on the shelf accurately positioned so the plates settle centrally against the back curves.

If the rack is for plates only, its lower edge can finish just below the shelf or be taken further down and given a matching shape to the top edge. Alternatively there can be a shelf for spoons, or you could extend even further for two or more spoon shelves, where the effect would be something like the spoon rack already described, with plates on top. A single shelf under three 7-inch plates should hold about 12 spoons.

The spoon shelf need not project as much as the plate rack. Its main sizes can be taken from those of the rack for spoons only and slots cut in the same way. The two shelves can be linked with shaped end pieces (Fig. 3-28C) which come outside the edges of the back, and the curves can follow around. The main shelf need not be more than 1/2 inch thick, but most of the other parts could be 1/4 inch. Assembly would be with glue and thin nails or pins punched below the surface and covered with stopping.

Chapter 4

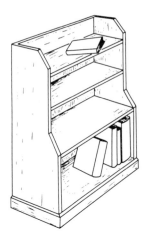

Free-Standing Shelves

Any mention of shelves produces a picture in the mind of boards attached to a wall, but shelves do not always have to be attached to a vertical surface. There are situations where a block of shelves is more useful if it is possible to move all around them. They are still better described as shelves than as tables or cabinets. Such free-standing table- or floor-mounted shelves have to be made stable. It would be disastrous if their design made them liable to topple. A broad base and a height no more than is justified are needed; heavier loads must be located lower down.

A block of free-standing shelves may still be used against a wall, but because it is not attached to the wall, it becomes another piece of portable furniture. It can be moved for cleaning or reorganization of the room layout. A bookcase is a typical example. If it is designed so the larger volumes are lowest, it can achieve stability without the need to make the base much larger than would be needed to hold the books in any case. Similar stability might be obtained with shelves for other purposes away from the wall, by having larger lower shelves and legs which extend outside the area of the load.

Slotted steel angle strips with matching brackets and pressed steel shelves can be cut and bolted together to make blocks of shelves of any required size. They have many uses for industrial and office storage, but they could not be considered attractive for use in a home. Wooden structures of a generally similar design can be finished to give a better appearance and are preferable where something more than just utility is required.

Examples in this chapter show projects intended to stand without help from attachments to a wall, but some of them could be used against a wall and be attached to it for the sake of greater stability, if they will not need to be moved.

FOUR-LEGGED BLOCK OF SHELVES

This project is a block of three wide shelves supported on legs that extend the full height and are brought closer together toward the top (Fig. 4-1). The shelves could be used to store many things, such as industrial parts, but in the home they would take magazines, boxes of toys, records, books, and many other things that would otherwise be scattered elsewhere. The extensions of the legs above the top shelf will prevent things from falling off it. If there are books on edge or papers in piles, the ends keep them in place and tidy. If you do not require as much projection, the tops of the legs can be cut down.

Fig. 4-1. A four-legged block of shelves.

The arrangement would look best with veneered particleboard for the shelves. The other parts could then be made of hardwood and finished in a contrasting shade to the shelves. Alternately, the whole thing could be finished so it matches other surrounding furniture. With the sizes shown (Fig. 4-2A), the proportions give a stable assembly when empty and increasing stability as the shelves are loaded.

Because of the taper, the end view should be set out full-size, although half of it would be sufficient (Fig. 4-3A), with just the main lines. The shelf widths follow a slightly broader taper than the legs (Fig. 4-2B). There are lengthwise supports under the shelves (Fig. 4-2C). They serve two purposes: besides stiffening the shelves and preventing heavy loads from causing them to sag, they give some lengthwise ridigity to the assembly. There is plenty of rigidity across, but this further stiffening is important in the length. If you think you need more stiffening, there could be small brackets between the shelf ends and the legs.

From the full-size setting out, you can see the lengths of the end shelf supports and how much taper to put on their ends. You can also mark where the lengthwise supports will come. They could be doweled (Fig. 4-3B), or you could use mortise-and-tenon joints (Fig. 4-3C). Make the shelves and veneer any cut edges or ends. Assemble the underframes and attach them to their shelves (Fig. 4-3D) so nothing spoils the appearance of the top surfaces, screw through the wood from below. Screws can be

counterbored (Fig. 4-3E), but because the holes are not normally visible, there will be no need to plug them.

Mark out and cut the legs, but leave a little extra at the top until after the joints are made. The short piece across the top could be doweled to the legs (Fig. 4-3F), and the outer corners rounded. A more interesting joint as an open bridle (Fig. 4-3G), made with a little extra projecting each way for trimming level after the glue has set. When the corners have been rounded, the pattern of end and side grain in a bridle joint looks attractive.

When the whole block of shelves is assembled, the shelf ends keep the legs correctly splayed, but until then it is advisable to lightly tack a piece of scrap wood across

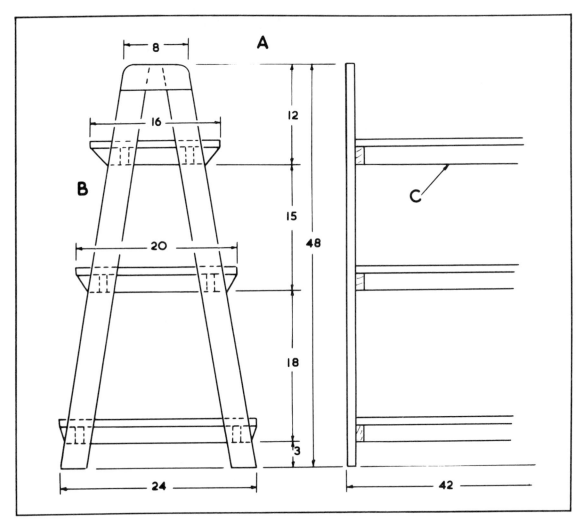

Fig. 4-2. Sizes for the four-legged block of shelves.

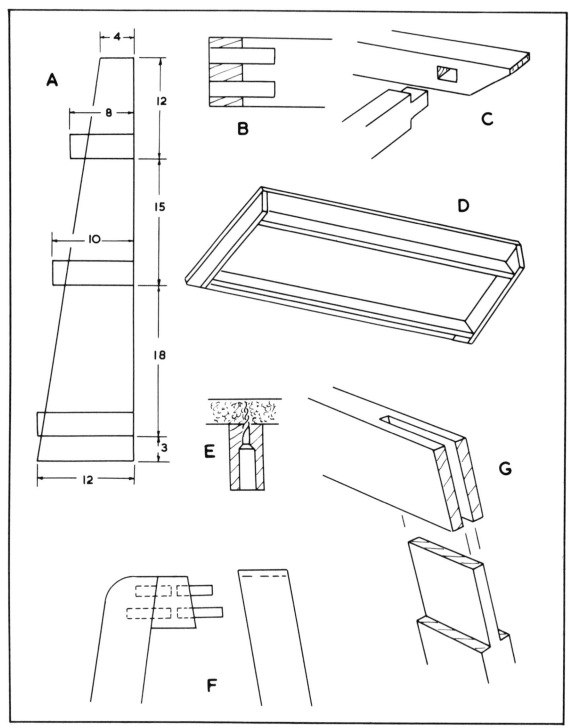

Fig. 4-3. Setting out and making the four-legged block of shelves.

near the bottoms to hold each pair of legs at the correct angles.

Mark across the leg assemblies where the shelves are to come and screw through the end shelf supports into the legs. If the woodwork is to be stained and varnished or painted a different color from the shelves, it will be best to make a trial assembly without glue, then disassemble and finish all the parts before final assembly. Where the surfaces are to meet and be glued, leave the wood untreated so the glue can enter the pores and get a good grip.

Assemble while the work is standing on a surface known to be flat. If you work on an uneven surface, you may finish with legs that suit that surface, but would wobble on any other. If you do finish with an assembly that is apparently out of true, measure downward from the bottom shelf to check leg lengths. If you are still doubtful, stand the whole thing upside-down and put straight pieces of wood across the bottoms of the upturned legs so you can sight one across the other. Sighting will show

if there is a twist as a result of one long or short leg; that will have to be adjusted.

Materials List for Four-Legged Block of Shelves

4 ends	$3 \times 51 \times 1$
2 ends	$3 \times 9 \times 1$
1 shelf	$16 \times 42 \times 3/4$
1 shelf	$20 \times 42 \times 3/4$
1 shelf	$24 \times 42 \times 3/4$
6 shelf supports	$2 \times 42 \times 1$
2 shelf supports	$2 \times 25 \times 1$
2 shelf supports	$2 \times 21 \times 1$
2 shelf supports	$2 \times 17 \times 1$

TABLETOP TIDY

A small block of shelves or trays on a desk, bench, or table allows papers, tools, bolts, nails, and other small things to be sorted and kept tidily. This tidy has three trays large enough to take papers or magazines and

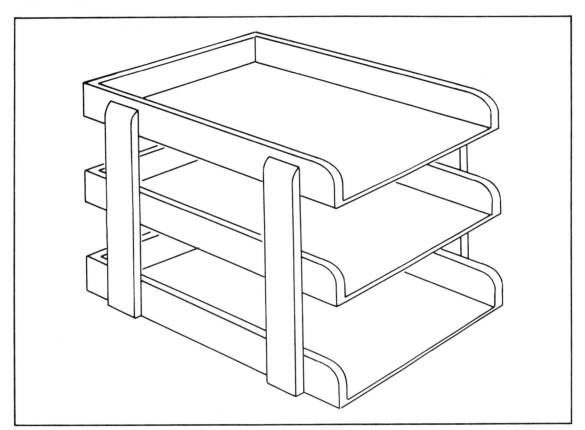

Fig. 4-4. A tabletop tidy.

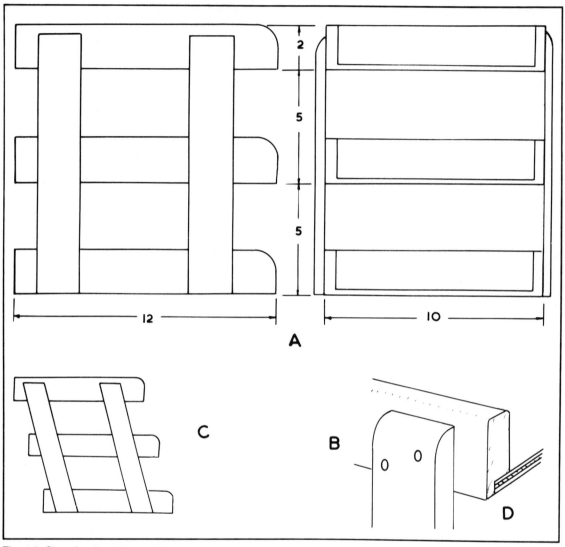

Fig. 4-5. Sizes for the tabletop tidy.

anything smaller (Fig. 4-4). The sizes allow for three trays with enough space between them for a hand to reach the back (Fig. 4-5A). The same method of construction could be used for trays of other shapes or for other numbers in a block.

The method of construction will depend on the purpose of the tidy. If appearance is unimportant, the parts could be nailed together, and the wood could be anything available. If it must match other furniture in a room or office, it would be better to cut joints and let the plywood bottoms into the tray sides, then finish the assembly with

stain and varnish or polish.

The trays are all the same. The plywood bottoms are best cut with the grain of the outer plies across the trays so the front unsupported part is stiff, and the grain is less likely to break out when planing in construction or pulling hard things over it in use.

For the simplest construction, glue and nail the rear corners of a tray and nail on the plywood bottom (Fig. 4-6A). Dovetail nailing (Fig. 4-6B) is slightly stronger than straight nailing. Screws will make stronger corners because they grip better in end grain.

For better construction, let the plywood bottoms into rabbets (Fig. 4-5D). It could go into plowed grooves, but that would reduce usable depth in each tray (Fig. 4-6C). There are several possible joints for the rear corners. Dovetails have a professional look (Fig. 4-6D). A comb joint is almost as attractive (Fig. 4-6E). If you have the facilities to machine it, a dado-tongue-and-rabbet joint (Fig. 4-6F) could be used. There is little strain on the corners; so almost any joint will do.

Round the front corners and take off the sharp edges before assembly. Take care that all trays finish exactly the same width, or you will have difficulty in fitting the uprights.

The supports are shown vertical with their tops lower than the top tray edges and rounded there. Make them all the same and screw them to the trays. Two screws arranged diagonally at each crossing should be sufficient (Fig. 4-5B). If you think you may want to separate the trays and rearrange them at any time, do not use glue in these joints.

For an interesting variation, and to make access to the trays easier, the supports can slope (Fig. 4-5C). Do not make the slope excessive, particularly if there are more than three trays, or weight in the back of the top tray may make the assembly topple backward. The problem would be reduced if the trays were made shorter toward the top, while combining sloping supports with a tapered arrangement of tray lengths.

It will be best to make a trial assembly, then take the sides off so the trays can be finished in whatever way you wish. If the tidy is to stand on a polished tabletop, cloth could be glued all over the bottom tray, or just at its corners. You could use rubber feet or discs of rubber in a similar way. Even if the surface does not have to be protected, cloth or rubber underneath will keep the tidy from slipping.

Materials List for Tabletop Tidy

6 tray sides	2 × 13 × 1/2
3 tray backs	2 × 11 × 1/2
3 tray bottoms	11 × 13 × 1/4 plywood
4 supports	2 × 12 × 1/2

SORTER

When papers must be sorted, it is convenient to have

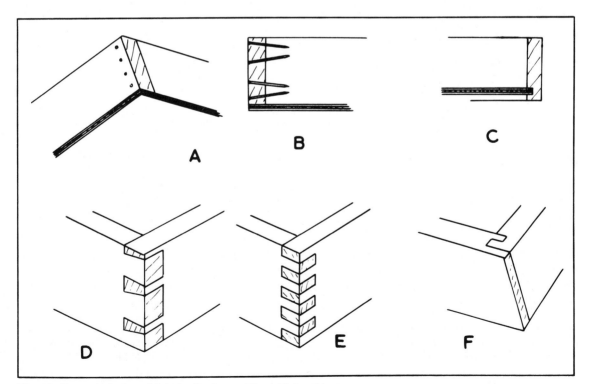

Fig. 4-6. Suggested corner joints for the trays of the tabletop tidy.

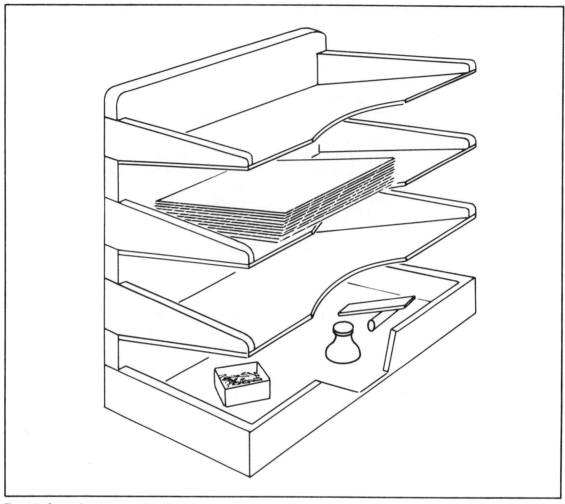

Fig. 4-7. Sorter for papers and mail.

a stack of shelves one for each of the separate papers that have to be arranged in sequence or stuffed into envelopes. The same thing can be used for sorting mail, leaves of loose-leaf books, and many other things. This sorter (Fig. 4-7) has three sorting shelves and a tray at the bottom that could be used for all the things that often clutter up a desk. Obviously, it could be made higher, but a tall sorter might be unstable and would then have to be attached to the wall, or it might be held to the back of a desk with a clamp. The shelves should not be brought much closer together, or it would be difficult to reach between them when a stack of papers is in position.

The sorter is shown as framed plywood with screwed or nailed joints (Fig. 4-8A). With a stained and varnished finish, this construction should be acceptable in an office, although solid wood and cut joints would make a more professional type of sorter.

Cut the piece of plywood for the back and mark on it where the other parts will come. Frame its rear surface. The top of the framing looks best if the corners are mitered, but at the bottom, the sides should go to the edge of the plywood, and the bottom framing strip fits between. Make sure the bottom edge is square; it affects whether the sorter stands upright or not.

Cut the eight pieces to size for the sides. Six of them are tapered (Fig. 4-9A), and they all notch into the back (Figs. 4-8B and 4-9B). The front of the bottom tray could be one piece of wood, but it is shown cut (Fig. 4-8C). So

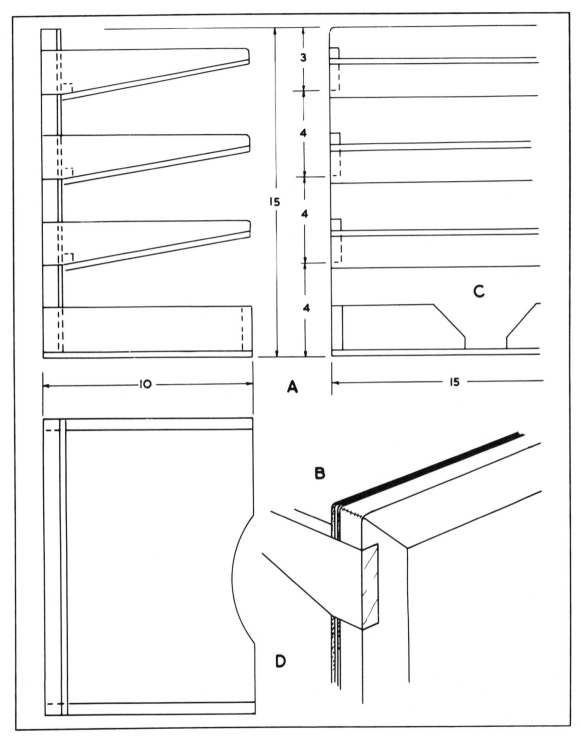

Fig. 4-8. Sizes of a sorter.

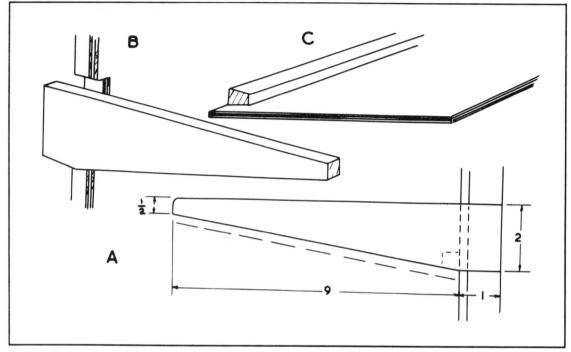

Fig. 4-9. Construction details of a sorter.

it is easier to remove small items or to clear out the tray after accidentally spilling a box of paper clips.

Make the shelves from plywood with the grain of its outer veneers the long way, for stiffness. Shelves go underneath the tapered sides, and the rear edge is stiffened with a fillet between the sides (Fig. 4-9C). Mark where the fillet comes against the back and drill through for small screws, which will be driven from the rear during assembly. The front edges of the shelves could be left straight, or a hollow could be cut for ease in pulling out papers (Fig. 4-8D). In any case, well-round the plywood edges.

Round the top corners of the back, but leave the other parts square. Attach the fillets to the rear edges of the plywood and check that they and the plywood are at the correct angles. Have the work inverted and start assembly from what will be the top shelf. Nail or screw the sides into their slots in the back, then nail and glue the shelf to them and through the back. Do the same with the other shelves and finally the bottom. Check squareness as you go. The sides will not look right if they slope downward. Make sure the top edges are square to the back before the glue sets.

Like the previous project, this sorter will benefit from having rubber or cloth glued under the bottom, to prevent it from scratching a desk surface or moving about in use.

Materials List for Sorter

8 sides	$2 \times 11 \times 1/2$
3 shelves	$10 \times 16 \times 1/4$ plywood
1 base	$11 \times 16 \times 1/4$ plywood
3 fillets	$1/2 \times 15 \times 1/2$
2 fronts	$2 \times 7 \times 1/2$
1 back	$15 \times 16 \times 1/4$ plywood
4 backs	$2 \times 16 \times 1$

BOOKCASE

Bookcases can come in many possible sizes and shapes to carry a stock of books of various sizes, some extending to cabinets that are much more advanced than a block of shelves. The example in Fig. 4-10 is a basic design that will serve its purpose well. It has an austere simplicity and an air of fitness for purpose that may be regarded as beautiful in appropriate surroundings. The lines can be softened by substituting curves for bevels and shaping the front edges of the uprights (Fig. 4-11).

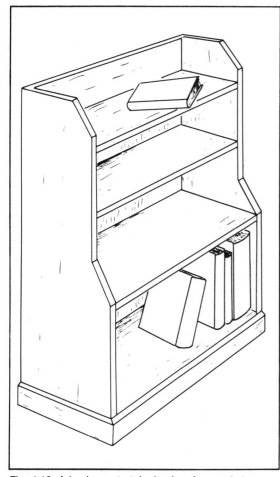

Fig. 4-10. A bookcase to take books of several sizes.

The top shelf has sides high enough to support a row of books there, so the back piece will be hidden by them. If the top is not to be used for books, the back may have a shaped edge, but otherwise decorating it is unnecessary.

If made of a good hardwood, the bookcase could grace any room. If it is intended for a child's room, it could be made of softwood and painted, possibly with decals on the sides. It would be possible to make all parts with veneered particleboard. A light-colored plastic veneer would suit a room furnished in a modern style.

The back is shown as plywood. If the bookcase is to stand against a wall, as it usually will, it does not matter what plywood is used, but if it is to go into a position where the back can be seen, plywood veneered to match the other wood would be more appropriate. Not much of the forward side of the plywood will show when the case

if full of books, so it should be sufficient to stain the normal surface something like the color of the finish on the other wood.

So the bookcase can accommodate large volumes at the bottom without narrow books higher up going to the back of excessively-wide shelves, there is a step in the width of the sides. A side could be made from a wide board and reduced, but it is easier and more economical to glue on a strip to make up the width. If a wide board is cut down, it is difficult to finish the front edge of the narrow part and get it smooth, but a narrow board can be planed quickly and accurately. It should be sufficient to prepare the meeting edges and glue the parts together. Modern glues will make a good joint if the parts are true and fit closely. You could use dowels as well (Fig. 4-12A). Cut and finish the bevel first, but the bottom edge may be leveled later.

Mark out the pair of sides first (Fig. 4-12B). Rabbet the rear edges for the full length to take the plywood back. The top of the rabbet will be opened out later above the top shelf to take the solid wood back.

Fit the shelves with stopped dado joints (Fig. 4-12C). The plywood back will prevent any movement of the joints at the rear, and the plinth should keep the bottom shelf's joint tight. It would be advisable to strengthen the joints of the top shelf, either by making them dovetail or driving a screw diagonally from below into each joint near its front.

Make all the shelves identical. Make the solid back and cut its rabbets in the sides. The plywood goes to the top edge of the shelf, and the solid piece fits above it (Fig. 4-12D). You can drive a few thin screws upward through the shelf into the solid wood before fitting the plywood. At the bottom, the plywood need not go to the floor if the bookcase is to stand against a wall, but if the back will be visible, it may be better if made full-length. When you assemble, glue and screw the back to all shelves so it provides maximum rigidity and makes it impossible for the bookcase to go out of shape.

After the other parts have been assembled, make and fit the plinth. At the front, it may come level with the shelf, although it looks well if stepped down slightly (Fig. 4-12E). Miter the front corners. In addition to glue, there can be a few screws driven from the inside outward into the side pieces of the plinth, while blocks in the corners allow some screws forward into the front piece (Fig. 4-12F).

The bookcase should stand level on most floors, but if you have doubts, keep the plywood back about 1/4 inch high and slightly hollow the undersides of the other three downward edges so the case stands on about 2 inches at each corner. About 1/4 inch of hollowing will not show on a carpet, but it will prevent the wood from rocking on any slightly high spot on the floor.

Materials List for Bookcase

2 sides	7 × 39 × 3/4
2 sides	2 × 20 × 3/4
2 shelves	6 3/4 × 18 × 3/4
2 shelves	8 3/4 × 18 × 3/4
1 back	5 × 18 × 3/4
1 back	18 × 34 × 1/4 plywood
1 plinth	3 × 21 × 5/8
2 plinths	3 × 11 × 5/8

MOBILE TROLLEY

There are situations where it is convenient to have a stack of shelves on wheels so they can be moved about with little effort. In an office or shop where large quantities of papers or parts for assembly must be moved, it

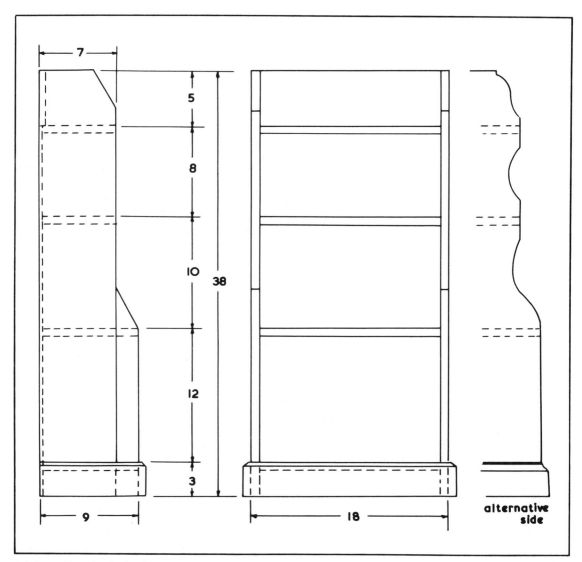

Fig. 4-11. Sizes for the bookcase.

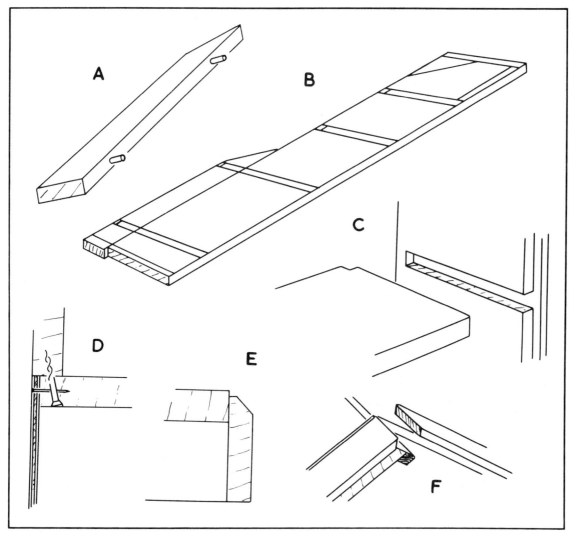

Fig. 4-12. Constructional details of the bookcase.

would be useful. In a restaurant, it would make a desert trolley. In the home, it would move food from the kitchen to the dining room or move books or magazines about the house.

The example in Fig. 4-13 has four shelves, arranged so two project on each side, supported on end posts that have broad feet equipped with casters. It may be best to have the shelves made of veneered particleboard, and the other parts solid wood. The sort of caster to use depends on circumstances, but if much movement is anticipated, they should be rubber-tired and over 2 inches in diameter. Smaller casters are intended just for moving a bed for

cleaning or other short-distance moves.

Sizes are suggested in Fig. 4-14A. If you alter them, make sure the feet spread enough for stability, and the ends are stiff enough to allow you to move the assembly without it wobbling, even when heavily loaded. The joint that gets most strain is where a post goes into its foot. Tenons are preferable there, even if other joints are doweled.

Mark out the posts (Fig. 4-15A). At each base cut double tenons with a haunch between (Fig. 4-15B) and make each foot with a mortise to match (Fig. 4-15C). The end supports for the shelves might be merely screwed to the

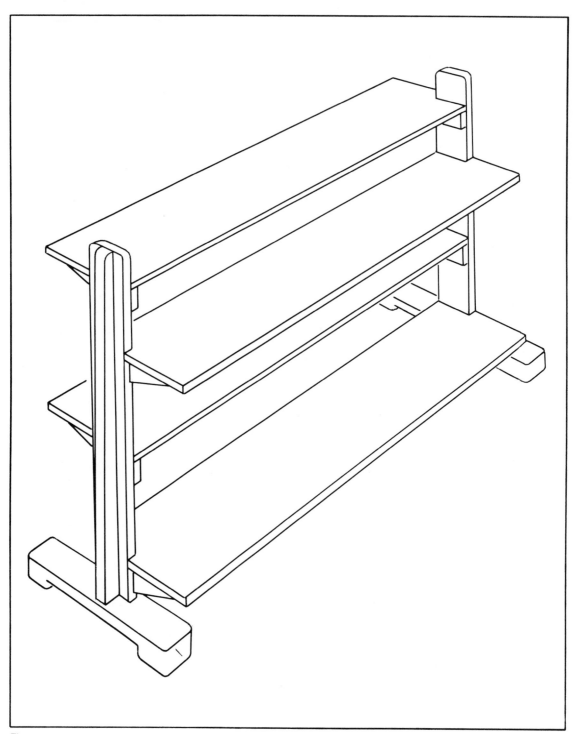

Fig. 4-13. A mobile trolley.

70

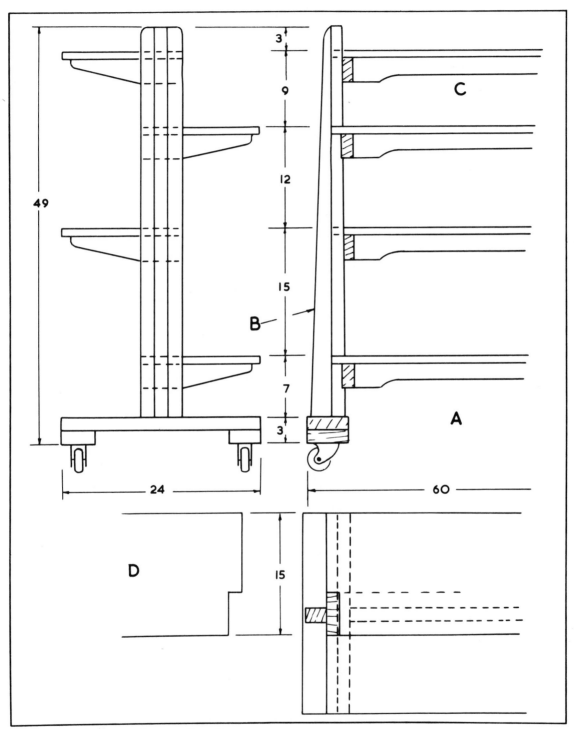

Fig. 4-14. Suggested sizes for a mobile trolley.

71

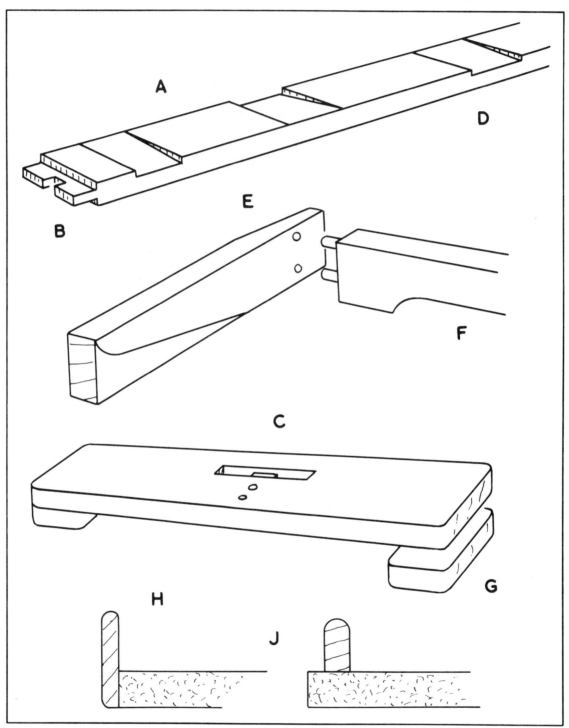

Fig. 4-15. Details for the parts of a mobile trolley.

posts, but that puts considerable strain on the screws. It is better to also notch them into the posts. To avoid cutting too much from the posts, the notches are tapered (Fig. 4-15D), and the ends of the supports are tapered to match (Fig. 4-15E). When the supports are glued in the notches and reinforced with screws, there should be no fear of movement.

Stiffness at the ends is increased with tapered pieces outside (Fig. 4-14B). Attach each to its post with glue and several dowels in the length and arrange two more to go downward into the foot. Attach the shelf supports to their posts and check that each is square.

Make the lengthwise shelf stiffeners (Figs. 4-14C and 4-15F). They are shown cut away below for the sake of appearance, but if this is not important, or where an industrial use calls for maximum strength, they can be left at the full depth. Drill the ends for dowels and make matching holes that go into the posts through the end shelf supports.

Add the thickening end pieces under the feet (Fig. 4-15G). Round the exposed corners and edges. Drill under the end pieces for screws or other attachment arrangements for the casters. Join the feet to their posts. See that these parts are square both ways, and the opposite ends make a pair. Join the ends together with the lengthwise shelf stiffeners. Check the accuracy of the assembly by measuring diagonals and adjusting if necessary before the glue sets.

Make the shelves so they are notched around the posts to project to their outside edges (Fig. 4-14D). Join the shelves to their supports with counterbored screws downward, but if you want to keep the top surfaces clear, drill upward through the woodwork for counterbored screws.

The shelves are shown with plain tops, which may be all that is needed for many purposes. If you want to prevent things from sliding off, as when transporting cups and plates, it would be better to put lips around some or all of the shelves. You could frame around the outside with closed mitered corners (Fig. 4-15H). There may be strips on top which could meet at the corners, but it is easier to wipe out dust or spilled liquids if small gaps are left there (Fig. 4-15J).

If the trolley is used for the regular transport of certain things, you may be able to add compartments or pierce shelves to take them. Cups might fit into holes; tools could go into slots. There might be guide pieces to hold trays or boxes.

Materials List for Mobile Trolley

2 posts	5 × 50 × 1 1/2
2 feet	5 × 25 × 1 1/2
4 feet	4 × 5 × 1 1/2
2 end stiffeners	2 1/2 × 50 × 1 1/2
8 shelf supports	3 × 13 × 1 1/2
4 shelf supports	3 × 58 × 1 1/2
4 shelves	15 × 58 × 3/4

Chapter 5

Considerations Storage

To get the maximum number of things into a given space, they may be merely piled on each other, fitted around each other, or stacked systematically, without any container being involved. To keep such a collection within bounds, particularly as the stack gets larger and higher, there may be boards or other rigid restrainers put around it, and the result is a box. Through much of history, most people's personal property was kept in a box with a lid. This chest was often also used as a seat, but it was the center of a family's existence, and its size, construction, and appearance was evidence of the status of the family.

We still use chests, and a box with a lid may be the best thing for storing blankets, linen, towels, and some clothing. An advantage of loading from the top is that you get the help of gravity. If you put something down, it does not try to fall out. Gravity is a help when you have to get as much as possible into a chest. A disadvantage is the difficulty of access. You have to lift a lid and reach down. Because the contents are arranged in a pile, articles on top must be moved to get at lower ones. You may have to almost completely unload and reload to get out one item, which also has to be searched for. There are better ways of storing so you can get at items without disturbing others.

When storage is mentioned, what is usually visualized is a cupboard or closet, having one or more front-opening doors. This storage is really a box with a hinged lid and resting on its side. You still must load it with the consideration of gravity, but as you pile up contents, you are looking edgewise at the items; so you can see where most things are and get them out without removing everything above them. Internal shelves may then act as dividers to separate different types of things or to take the weight of some of the contents when you are removing or replacing something from a low position. Most storage projects people tackle are of the box-on-edge, front-door type, usually with shelves.

If you walk around a supermarket or any store, the items which attract your attention most are near eye level. There may be more stock lower and other things higher, but what the owner most wants you to see and buy are above waist height and not much higher than the top of your head. We take most notice of things within that range, and this gives us a clue to how storage should be arranged. Things that you need frequently or want to be able to get at easily should be where you can see and handle them while standing, without needing to reach far up or down.

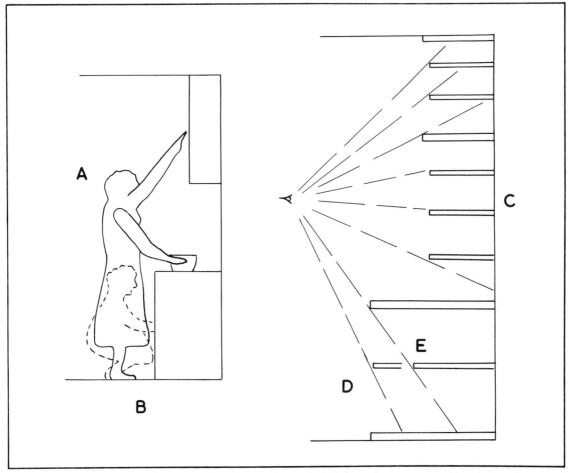

Fig. 5-1. Storage units have to be arranged so they can be reached (A,B), and you must consider what can be seen at various levels (C-E).

SIZES

There are certain recognized sizes and heights to take into account. Tabletops are usually within an inch or so of 30 inches high. Seats, other than those for relaxing, are between 15 inches and 17 inches high, which suits the leg length of most people and gives a suitable sitting position when using a table. The height of a seat is the height when any upholstery has been compressed; so an upholstered chair may appear to be higher. If a working surface is intended to be used more by a person standing, the height goes up to about 36 inches. If you then want to sit to work or eat, you need a high stool.

Table height is a guide to the lowest height for convenient storage. The greatest convenient height is about 72 inches. Between those two levels, an average person can reach without bending or excessive stretching (Fig. 5-1A). Less convenient heights are higher or lower. We want to make the most use of storage space, so less-frequently-used things go higher or lower, preferably light things high and heavy things low, but that selection is not always possible. Bending to get at low things is not very difficult (Fig. 5-1B), but a stool is needed to reach higher.

If what you are making must double as a working top, 12 inches is about the narrowest that will be much use against a wall, while 18 inches is better and 24 inches even more when used for office work, food preparation, playing with toys, and other usual tabletop activities in a home. Against that you must weigh problems of access. A back-to-front depth of around 24 inches is as far as you will be able to reach inside conveniently. If you will want to get at things near the back, remember this size.

Consider the placing of shelves. At around eye level, you can see the contents even if the shelves come almost to door level (Fig. 5-1C), no matter how many shelves you fit. This concept may also apply to storage arranged near the ceiling, particularly as you will be getting up there on a stool, and the effect will then be eye level.

From table level down, shelves will be better set back. If a full-width shelf comes near the center of a cabinet, your sight line is obstructed by its front edge (Fig. 5-1D), and you cannot see what is below the shelf without bending. If the lower storage space must be packed to capacity, shelves may have to come to the front, but if you want to see in more conveniently, set the shelf back a little (Fig. 5-1E).

What you plan to make for storage, whether it is built-in or movable, will occupy space; so the room is effectively made that much smaller. It may also obscure light, either from a window or an artificial source. Before you start work, measure or even make a mock-up from cardboard boxes or anything else available to see the effect. What about the opening of room doors? You should still be able to swing a door sufficiently. If you are thinking of making something that will occupy an entire wall, it will take perhaps 12 inches off the floor dimension. Is that acceptable in return for what the new unit provides?

DOORS

Door arrangements must be considered. If there is to be adequate access when the door is open, it must swing out more than 90 degrees and preferably nearer 180 degrees (Fig. 5-2A). If a door opens against a corner wall, that may be better than hinging it to the other side, depending on light and what would be obstructed if it swung that way. What about convenient access from the usual working position? You need to swing the door away from you and not have to go around the door to get at the space behind.

Sometimes the width is such that a single door would have to swing a long way forward, which would be a nuisance. In that case, double doors are better because they need only half the space for swinging (Fig. 5-2B). They also allow access at one side, if that is all you want. For a high cabinet, you may want to arrange a door to swing up (Fig. 5-2C), but you then must arrange a strut or other device to hold open the door. You may also arrange a lower door with its hinges at the bottom (Fig.

5-2D), but access at that level is not such a problem with normal doors.

Sliding doors are alternatives to swinging doors. They have the advantage of not projecting at any stage of their opening (Fig. 5-2E). This may be such an important consideration in some circumstances that they need to be adopted, but there are a few drawbacks to them. A pair of sliding doors are always there. Even when one is slid behind the other, you only have access and a clear view through half the front; so you can never see the whole of the interior, and things wider than half the width of the doorway cannot be moved in and out (Fig. 5-2F). Some sliding doors can be lifted out without much trouble; so occasional access to the full width is possible. If the sliding doors are glass, you get a better view of the interior, but access is still restricted.

It is possible to arrange doors that lift off, but you then have the problem of what to do with them. The arrangement may be worthwhile in a shop where tools are stored in the inside of the doors; then the doors are removed and used as wall panels so the tools are available above a bench.

Folding doors have been devised for cupboards, similar to those used for room doorways, but the tend to take up valuable space when they are moved backward and forward. Solid doors are not always necessary. A curtain that can be slid back on a rail may be all that is required, particularly with anything below table height. Doors give a tidy appearance, particularly when what is covered is a miscellaneous collection of items, not necessarily stowed untidily. There are places, however, where open-fronted storage is quite acceptable.

PROPORTIONS

You want what you are making to look good, even if the main reason for making it is utilitarian. When all you want is something to store equipment, books, or other gear, you may be inclined to go ahead and make a locker, cabinet, chest, or cupboard that has the right capacity, but if you get the proportions correct—using a few rules—it will look better.

Squares and circles are not good design features. It is better to use rectangles and ellipses (Fig. 5-3A). A box or other piece of cabinetry looks best if the measurement one way is between 1 1/4 and 1 1/2 what it is the other way, no matter at what angle you view it (Fig. 5-3B). You are unlikely to make anything completely elliptical, but the rule applies for only part of a curve. For instance, cutting away under a rail looks better with part of an ellipse

(Fig. 5-3C) than with part of a circle (Fig. 5-3D).

The optical illusion when divisions between horizontal lines are actually the same, but appear closer towards the bottom, was mentioned when laying out shelves (Fig. 5-3E). This illusion applies to drawer widths and other arrangements of horizontal lines in an assembly; so they should be made obviously narrower towards the top (Fig. 5-3F). A similar rule applies to the positioning of handles on a drawer front. If they are put at exactly half the height, they will appear to be below the middle; so it is usual to put them above halfway (Fig. 5-3G).

This illusion also applies to the appearance of a framed door. If you make the bottom rail the same width as the other three, it will appear narrower (Fig. 5-3H); so usually the bottom rail is made wider than the others (Fig. 5-3J).

The direction of principal lines will affect the apparent proportions. If you want something to look tall, provide plenty of upright lines. If you want it to look wide, provide plenty of horizontal lines. This rule can be seen where two squares of the same size actually look in different proportions according to the lines across them (Fig. 5-3K).

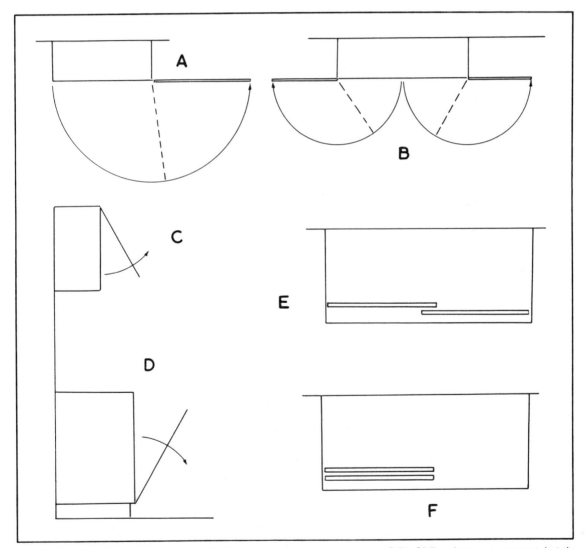

Fig. 5-2. Doors need space to swing (A,B). High or low doors may swing out (C,D). Sliding doors are compact, but do not show as much of the inside (E,F).

Diagonal lines should be used with great restraint. They can have a disconcerting effect on overall appearance if they are too prominent. There should be enough lines parallel with the general outline; then a few diagonals may be regarded as a panel or lesser design feature. One example is diamond-leaded glass panes in a door (Fig. 5-3L).

SELECTION

With a knowledge of the many ways storage furniture can be made, and how it can be arranged, you have to decide what will suit a particular purpose. If it is for your own use, selection may not be very difficult. If, however, you are to make something for someone else, it is important that you make them understand the various considerations and alternatives. Otherwise, you may find your time wasted if what you make is not what they want, after further consideration.

Function

You can divide the requirements into three sections: function, structure, and style. The function is storage of certain items, but is there any particular way they need to be stored? Will other things be added later? What sort of access is needed? Is storage the only function? Will some or all of the contents also need to form a display? Things may be stored behind doors; they could be open, or it may be better to use drawers. If it does not matter if things are stacked on each other, they will require much less space than if you must make compartments to keep them separate.

The storage function is the main requirement. It does not matter how you style an item, or how you use a new method of structure if at the end you cannot store what you started out to store. Your design is then unacceptable. If there are other possible ways of storing the same things, spend some time in weighing the advantages and disadvantages of each.

Think of how you want to pack things away, and how accessible they need to be. For instance, blankets and similar items may go in a pile in a chest and only have to be removed occasionally. If it is a record player or some other electronic equipment that is frequently used, you want to be able to uncover it and use it often with the minimum of trouble; so it may go behind a door in some sort of wall fitment, and be ready for use as soon as the door is opened. If you have scientific instruments or tools that need protection from each other, the best storage may be a set of shallow drawers with divisions for the

contents. If it is clothing to be stored, you have to decide if a full-length hanging closet is needed or if the clothing could be folded and put in drawers.

The function could be the desire to use up certain space, without being too specific about what the contents will be. A window recess may be a good place for a built-in seat; so you arrange that as a lifting top over an enclosed space. You can be certain that you will soon find things to fill it. There may be a recess that is little used, and you could build in an arrangement from the floor to ceiling that includes a working top, plenty of shelves, and a lower enclosed space. You will have improved the furnishing of the room, but much of what will be stored there will be found later. It could be that a part of one side of the room needs another piece of furniture to give a balanced effect to the layout; so you make a combination chest of drawers and storage cabinet that is free-standing so it can be moved if the layout is changed, or you wish to move home.

Structure

For the structure you make, the main divisions to consider are built-in or free-standing. Built-in furniture usually gives you the maximum storage with the minimum of space. You can also dispense with parts that would have to be made if the item was free-standing, because the walls and maybe floor and ceiling can become the sides and other parts of the furniture. Built-in furniture is rigid and cannot fall. You can move heavy things in and out without rocking it. A disadvantage is that it is always there and cannot be moved without taking it to pieces and probably leaving marks on the wall. You must be certain that what you propose to build in will be what is wanted, will be in the right place, and will perform the function you expect. It is difficult to alter your mind once it is there.

If you decide on free-standing furniture, it has to be made in its entirety, with back and sides that might not be needed if built-in. These parts must also be given a good finish because the object may be viewed from any direction.

You are not so limited for size; so you can make the furniture to suit the contents more easily than you can with a wall-mounted arrangement that must fill a certain space. Obviously, you still must think of the space the item will occupy, but there is more tolerance in size. Separate storage units can be moved around without affecting walls. You can rearrange a room layout. If what you have made is no longer required, or you make

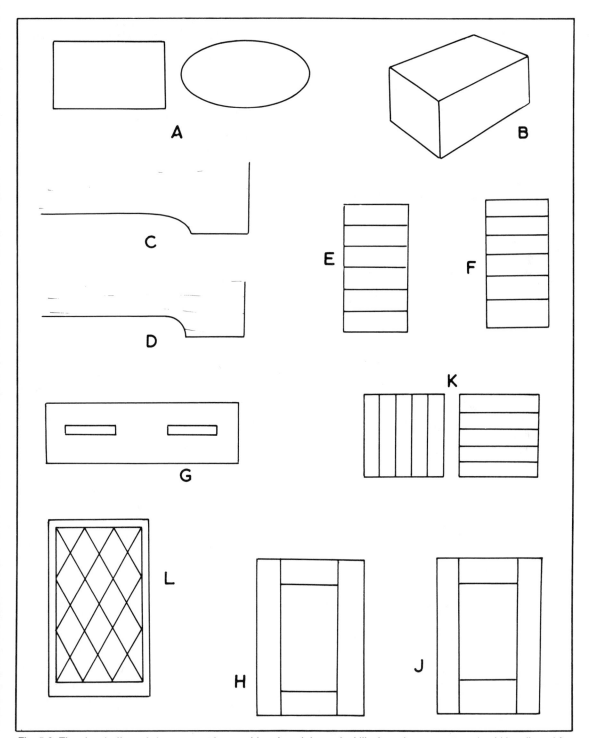

Fig. 5-3. The visual effect of shapes must be considered, and the optical illusions that may occur should be allowed for.

something in its place, it can be moved without regard to anything else.

It is possible to make free-standing storage furniture in modular form. You can have a chest or cupboard which takes matching shelves or other different storage arrangements, each made as independent units, but when they are stood on or beside each other, they match and appear to be single pieces of furniture. If you have enough modular units, you can rearrange the furniture to get a different effect and appearance, with different storage possibilities, or parts can be taken to another room to be put together in another way.

The structure consideration embraces the method and material of construction. You may favor solid wood throughout; you may make considerable use of plywood, or most of the work can be in veneered particleboard. The choice of material affects the method of construction. Solid wood will need methods based on traditional ways, but these methods must be modified and often completely altered for the other materials. What other furniture in the room is made of may affect what you use, if the new storage unit is to match. There are also practical and economic considerations. An enthusiastic woodworking craftsman may want to work in solid wood, but good wood in wide boards is not readily obtainable, and costs may be prohibitive. Plywood and particleboard give you wide pieces that remain flat and do not shrink or expand. For most furniture today, you must consider combinations of materials, using the good quality of some with the attractions of others. Carefully used, these mixtures take advantage of modern products to produce good-looking,

functional furniture. The only exception may be if you want to reproduce an antique; then you will need to find and use traditional woods.

Style

Style is linked with structure. Even if appearance is a secondary consideration, as it may be in a store room or garage, you want to be able to see what you have made and feel satisfied with the look of fitness for purpose. Elsewhere, the new piece of furniture must blend into its surroundings. It may not always match other furniture, but it should not look out of place. You may want to make the new piece of furniture a point of visual interest, with both a decorative and a storage function, or you may want it to be unobtrusive as possible, blending into the background or hidden in some way.

The three qualities must be looked at in relation to each other because they are interdependent. You will be making a storage unit; so its function is of prime importance. It must hold what is intended and do so in a way that is convenient to the user. Structure and style must be worked around these needs, bearing in mind the site the furniture will occupy. You must consider your own ability, and the equipment you will use, because it is no use being too ambitious. Most of us, however, can extend ourselves and produce work superior to what we thought was possible. There is a tremendous satisfaction in looking at something that does all it is intended to do, while looking good and being structurally sound, and saying "I made that."

Chapter 6

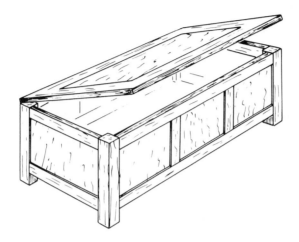

Boxes and Chests

You may not have so much use for massive chests; you do not keep all your possessions in the family chest; you may not even use a multitude of large boxes for storage, but boxes of many sorts are still the most used storage items in homes, offices, factories, and any place where things must be kept together. If you consider packaging, almost everything comes in cardboard boxes, which are often bulked in larger boxes that may be transported in containers which are really even larger boxes. Cardboard boxes are mostly disposable. They can be recycled, but many are destroyed.

Not so many things now come in wooden boxes, but machinery and other heavy goods need more than cardboard for protection, so they are crated. Wooden crates can often be adapted to make other containers. It may be possible to convert without fully disassembling. More often it is possible to carefully take a crate apart so the wood can be used again. You may not have to reduce it to single pieces, but may find you can use assembled sides as they are. Crates that have come from abroad can be a good source of useful wood. In a tropical country, where the predominant tree is mahogany, an exported machine may be put in a mahogany crate. It may not look like it and it may not be the best furniture-quality wood, but it

has possibilities. Usually the surface is as left from the saw. If you plane a part, you will get a better idea of what the wood is and if it might convert to something you want to make, without having to go to a lumberyard to buy the wood.

The simplest wooden box has its corners overlapped and a bottom overlapping the sides and ends, then the whole thing nailed. For many purposes this is all that is needed, but simple nailing does not have much resistance to force in the direction the nails were driven. Dovetail nailing, with closer nails near the open top, will be stronger (Fig. 6-1A).

Screws are stronger than nails, and the threads hold better than smooth nails in end grain. Barbed-ring nails (Fig. 6-1B) bring some of the advantages of screws to nailing. Most of them are made of bronze and other expensive metals to provide water resistance in boatbuilding; so they would not be chosen for a simple and cheap box. They have a good resistance to withdrawal. If you start to drive one, then try to withdraw it, it will break away surface fibers.

Because of the lesser holding power in end grain, screws at the corners of boxes with horizontal grain should be slightly longer than those that hold the bottom on, where the threads are gripping in side grain. If the screws are all the same length, you can get a similar compensation for lesser grip by using a closer hole spacing. When screwing box parts, you will be driving screws quite close to edges, with a risk of breaking the grain out if you do not do it right. Drill and at least partly countersink for each screw, with a hole that is an easy fit on the neck of the screw in the top piece (Fig. 6-1C). The small hole for the thread in end grain need not go very deep, because the screw will cut its own in once it has started, and there is not much risk of breaking out there.

You can give a greater grip to the screws at the top of a box, where strains in the direction of pulling apart may be greater, by putting a dowel through for the thread to get a greater grip in its cross grain (Fig. 6-1D).

The grip of nails can be increased in a box corner if they can be driven both ways. A miter would allow this (Fig. 6-1E), but you will encounter problems in cutting accurately and in holding wide boards in position while nailing. A simpler way is to cut a rabbet across one part to fit over the other (Fig. 6-1F). Do not make the overlapping piece too thin. Another way is to cut rabbets in both pieces (Fig. 6-1G) so nails can be driven through both lips.

If you want a corner without end grain visible, either of these joints can be cut with the corner mitered (Fig. 6-1H). Nail heads can be punched below the surface and covered with stopping. The mitered part can then be rounded—the amount of curve only being limited by the thickness of the overlapping piece.

Traditional large oak chests were iron-bound, often extremely heavily. This procedure certainly held the chest together, whether the corner joints were good or not. With plenty of retainers to move the chest, weight may not have mattered much. You do not want iron binding of that sort today, but some boxes can be reinforced with metal. It does not have to be massive. Sheet metal around corners may be worthwhile for heavy-duty boxes (Fig. 6-1J); in most cases, it can be iron or aluminum thin enough to cut with snips. Nails can go through holes made with a pointed punch, or, for a better appearance, round-head screws can go through drilled holes.

CORNER JOINTS

The best corner joints are dovetails. *Through dovetails* show details of the joint outside (Fig. 6-2A). That may not matter and, in the present-day attitude to design, may be regarded as a feature. If the joint is cut by hand, tails should be between 1 1/2 and 2 times the thickness of the wood, and there should be pins between them rather less

than the thickness, but opinions on dovetail proportions vary. There are jigs and devices for cutting dovetails by machine. With them you are limited in the choice of size, and most arrangements give you tails and pins the same width (Fig. 6-2B). One method of machine-dovetailing only allows you to make stopped dovetails, which may be acceptable for a box corner, providing the wood is thick enough to still have enough strength in the stopped direction (Fig. 6-2C). There is no need for stopped dovetails in a box unless it is to be one of many arranged in a row like drawers, and the dovetail construction is to be hidden at the front.

If the dovetail construction is to be hidden, there can be laps extending outside the tails and pins (Fig. 6-2D), leaving a narrow piece of end grain showing. If you want to avoid that situation, the lapped parts can be mitered (Fig. 6-2E). If you also arrange a miter at the top of a corner, only you will know that the joint is dovetailed, so this is called a *secret dovetail*. Both of these dovetail joints are more difficult to cut than through dovetails. They cannot be cut by machine. Not much can be sawn, and you must get the shapes by careful work with chisels. You will have to decide if such joints are worthwhile.

Comb, or finger, joints can be used (Fig. 6-2F). They are rather tedious to cut by hand accurately, and dovetails would be preferable then. If a suitable jig or machine is available, however, they can be used. This joint provides plenty of glued surface and is very strong without the aid of screws or nails.

The bottom of the box gets at least as much load as the sides and ends, but it is often just nailed or screwed on (Fig. 6-3A) even when more complicated joints are used at the corners. There is a better grip for the fasteners in side grain, and such a joint is usually satisfactory. It is stronger to enclose the bottom within the sides (Fig. 6-3B). When a bottom is put outside, its edges can be trimmed after attachment, but the inside arrangement calls for more careful cutting to size.

The bottom could go into a rabbet, then nails may be driven both ways (Fig. 6-3C). If metal fastenings are to be avoided, the bottom can be rabbeted and the tongue fitted into a plowed groove (Fig. 6-3D). This needs careful work for an accurate fit, but it makes a very strong joint. A simpler bottom gets part of the benefit of a rabbet and groove joint if only the sides are treated, then the ends are screwed (Fig. 6-3E). This construction is simpler because you can assemble the sides and ends, then fit the bottom and cut off surplus at the ends after you are satisfied with the joints. Another version of the joint has the bottom beveled to go into a sloping rabbet (Fig. 6-3F),

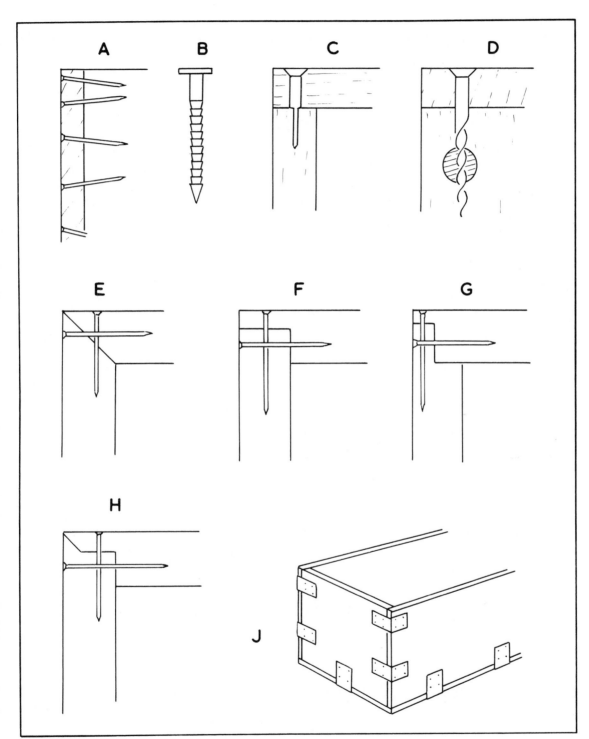

Fig. 6-1. Box corners may be joined in many ways.

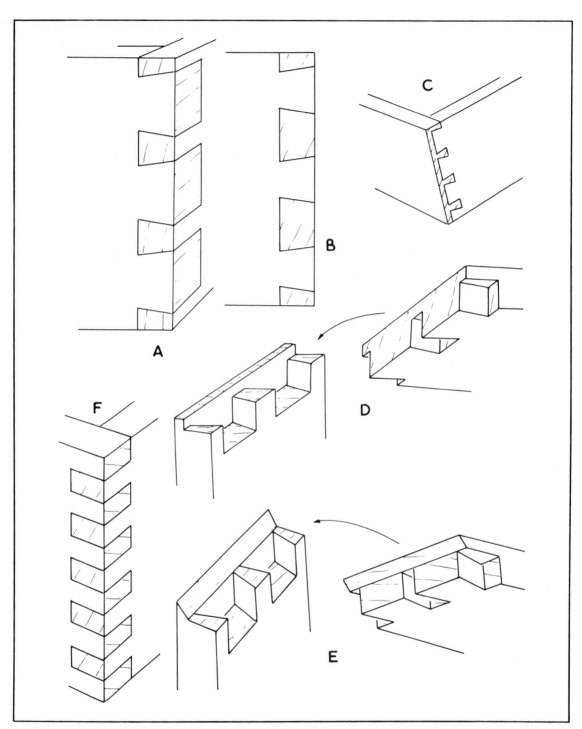

Fig. 6-2. Dovetails, as cut by hand or machine, make strong joints which may be concealed in one or both directions. The comb joint (F) is a simplified form.

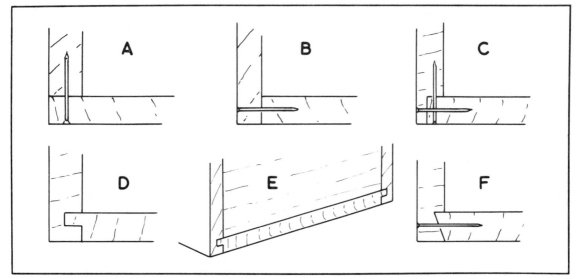

Fig. 6-3. A nail does not have much resistance to slipping in its length (A) and is better with the load across (B). Nails both ways in a rabbet are strong (C). A box bottom is best let in (D-F).

but that is not as good and may still need a few nails from outside.

There are ways of strengthening bottom and corner joints with strips of various sorts glued and screwed on, and details of them are shown in projects described later in this chapter.

INTERNAL-FRAMED PLYWOOD BOX

Wide boards of solid wood may be costly and often unobtainable in suitable thicknesses for making boxes. There is enough strength in comparatively thin wood for most boxes. Thicker wood may be unnecessary, and it could add unwanted weight. The alternative is plywood, which can be quite thin to provide adequate strength. Plywood does not take edge fasteners very well, however, and it is unsuitable for the usual solid wood joints; so it is better framed. You have to decide if you want the box to be smooth inside or outside. It may have a better appearance with a smooth exterior, but that means there are projecting edges inside, which may not matter for soft things, like cloth, but could be a nuisance if you are storing hard things that cannot be bent or compressed.

A simple box with inside framing (Fig. 6-4) has a lift-off lid. Typical sizes (Fig. 6-5A) show the proportions of parts. When anything is framed, it is normally best to frame the long sides first. In this case frame the two sides (Fig. 6-5B), with the top and bottom strips overlapping

the end ones. If appearance is not very important, you may just nail the plywood to the strips. For better work, use glue and fine nails that will be punched and stopped outside.

When you fit the ends, it may be sufficient to let the remaining framing pieces there go between the sides (Fig. 6-5C), but if you want a better appearance at the top, there can be miters (Fig. 6-5D). In that case, the ends of the top framing pieces should be prepared to take the end frames before they are attached to the sides. There will be no need for miters at the bottom corners.

Attach the end plywood panels to the sides with glue and nails into the framing. Fit the end framing pieces afterwards (Fig. 6-5E). This method gives you a better chance of making close fits than if you put the strips on the ends before nailing them on.

Level the bottom surfaces and screw or nail and glue on the bottom plywood (Fig. 6-5F). It is easiest if you make it slightly oversized and trim to the edges later, but have two edges of the sheet planed square and use them to get the sides and ends true as you put on the plywood. The box may stand directly on its bottom, but in many places it is better if it is raised on small corner feet. These feet are better if made of solid wood than plywood, which may disintegrate if the box is pulled about on a rough surface. Triangles with diagonal grain will do (Fig. 6-5G).

Make the lid with a piece of plywood cut to the size of the box, then put framing inside to fit inside the box framing (Fig. 6-5H). That could make a full frame, but if the plywood is stiff enough to remain flat without full stiffening, you could just put strips across the ends or along the sides. The size of the framing has to be judged to go in and out of the box top easily, yet not so loose that it moves about unnecessarily. If the box has not finished as perfectly symmetrical as you wish, the lid may fit better one way than the other. If so, mark on both lid and box the better way—not necessarily conspicuously, if you do not want to advertise the error.

Materials List for Internal-Framed Plywood Box

2 sides	12 × 25 × 1/4 plywood
2 ends	12 × 15 × 1/4 plywood
1 bottom	15 × 25 × 1/4 plywood
1 top	15 × 25 × 1/4 plywood
6 frames	3/4 × 25 × 3/4
4 frames	3/4 × 12 × 3/4
6 frames	3/4 × 16 × 3/4
4 feet	3 × 5 × 1/2

EXTERNAL-FRAMED PLYWOOD BOX

To give a box a smooth interior, all of the framing must come outside. If it is roughly made outside framing may be unattractive, but still adequate for industrial or amateur shop use. With a better construction and a good finish, the appearance is quite pleasing. If the surface veneer of the plywood and the solid wood match, a clear finish will produce a chest suitable for use in the home. With a painted finish, the box would be suitable for toy storage. If made with exterior or marine plywood and

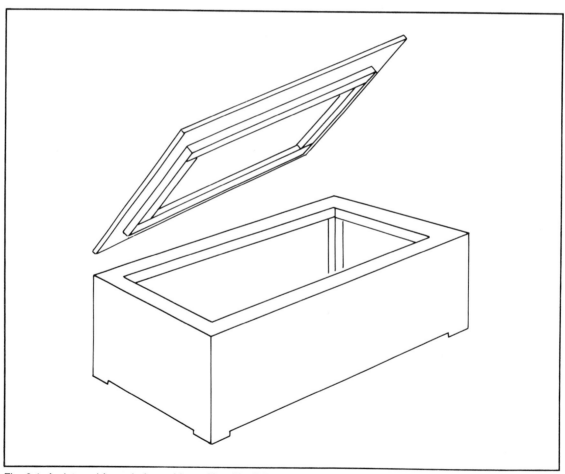

Fig. 6-4. An internal-framed plywood box with a lift-off lid.

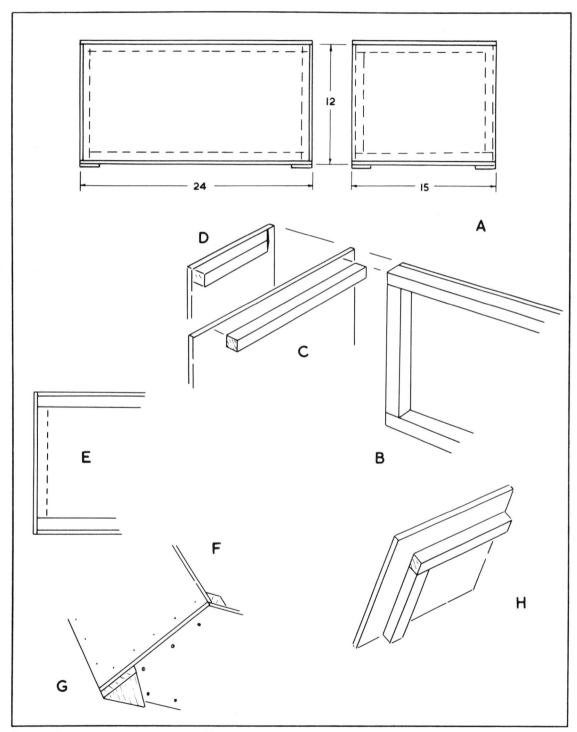

Fig. 6-5. Sizes and details of the internal-framed plywood box.

joined with waterproof glue, a chest would be suitable for sports gear or other outside equipment and could be taken outdoors and even left there in wet weather.

The typical box (Fig. 6-6) is shown with handles at the ends, a sliding tray, and a hinged lid. The sizes (Fig. 6-7A) will take a variety of things, but if you have particular equipment to store, check sizes before you start to work.

In this type of construction, it is better to start with the ends. Frame them with top and bottom overlapping the corner strips (Fig. 6-7B). Since fastenings will be driven from the inside outward, and there will be no need to punch the nail heads below the surface, you can use ordinary nails to supplement glue.

Bring in the side panels and attach them to the end frames (Fig. 6-7C). Add the top and bottom framing strips, with glue and nails from inside. Let the strips have a little extra overhang at the ends at first. The outer corners will be rounded when you finish the box. There should not be any nail or screw heads exposed that would interfere with rounding. It would be better to counterbore and plug a screw at each corner (Fig. 6-7D) or equally strong and simpler to put dowels there (Fig. 6-7E).

Screw and glue on the bottom (Fig. 6-8A). The box can be made completely waterproof. You may not want to fill it with water, but neither do you want water from outside to get in and damage the contents. If the box is to be used on grass or soil, you may want to put strips all around the bottom to raise the plywood, either underneath (Fig. 6-8B) or around the sides, with feet included at the corners (Fig. 6-8C).

Handles are strips across the ends (Fig. 6-8D). Round the parts that will be gripped. You may depend on screws and glue only, or you can make shallow notches in the end framing (Fig. 6-8E). Do not make the notches too deep because they reduce finger space between the handles and the plywood ends. If notches are to be used, they are easier to cut before the sides are added to the ends.

The lid is shown as an unframed piece of plywood. If it is 1/2 inch or more thick it should hold its shape unaided. Use two hinges positioned so their knuckles come outside the edges of the wood, so the lid will swing clear. Let the lower part of each hinge into the framing, but do not let them into the lid (Fig. 6-8F). The lower part can be screwed satisfactorily, but there is not much thickness in the lid to give screws a secure grip. It is bet-

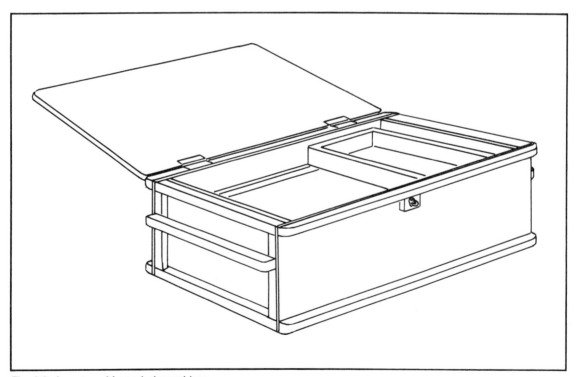

Fig. 6-6. An external-framed plywood box.

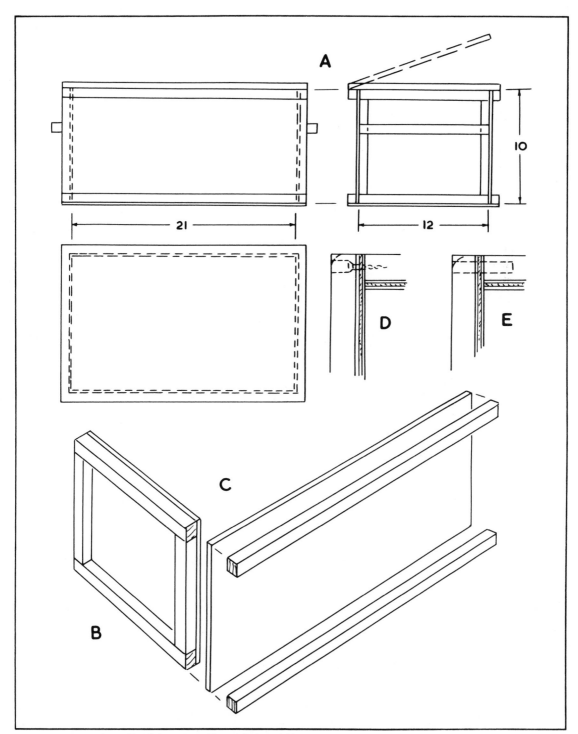

Fig. 6-7. Sizes and details of the external-framed plywood box.

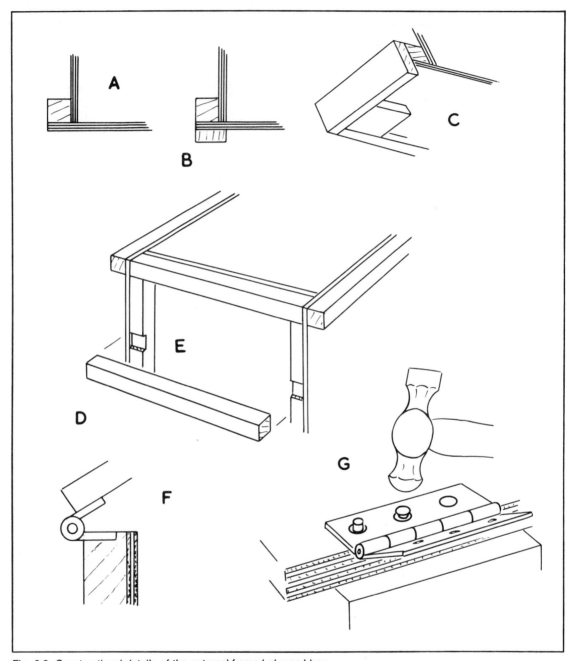

Fig. 6-8. Constructional details of the external-framed plywood box.

ter to use rivets for that part of the hinge. Choose aluminum, copper, or other soft rivets with countersunk heads. Cut off each rivet with what you judge to be enough metal to fill the countersunk holes of the hinge. Support the rivet heads on an iron block while you hammer over the ends (Fig. 6-8G), preferably with a small ball-peen hammer, although you can do it with the cross-peen of a normal hammer. To get the hinges correctly placed, temporarily fit them with single screws into the box edge while marking through where the holes are to come in the lid, then remove the hinges from the box and rivet them to the lid before finally screwing down.

The sliding tray can be whatever you like to make, depending on what you want to put in it. Remember that if it is to move along its runners, there must be space above at least part of the other contents to allow it to pass. It is a box resting on strips attached to the large box sides (Fig. 6-9A). If it is to slide easily, it should not be too narrow (Fig. 6-9B) because it would then tend to twist and stick as you tried to pull it along.

The box may be made in any way you choose, from simple nailing to secret dovetails. Make sure the runners are the same distance down from the top edge and parallel in height, otherwise the tray will wobble at the end of its run. There could be more than one tray, and even enough lift-out trays, or one big one, to fill the whole length. That may be worthwhile if there are many small items, such as tools, to be stored there, with larger items below.

If the box is to be locked, it is most easily done externally with a padlock and a hasp and staple (Fig. 6-9C). Rivet the metal to the lid and put a packing below the top framing strip at the side.

Materials List for External-Framed Plywood Box

2 sides	10 × 24 × 1/4 plywood
2 ends	10 × 13 × 1/4 plywood
1 bottom	15 × 24 × 1/4 plywood
1 lid	15 × 24 × 1/2 plywood
4 end frames	3/4 × 13 × 3/4
4 end frames	3/4 × 10 × 3/4
4 side frames	3/4 × 24 × 3/4
2 handles	3/4 × 13 × 3/4
2 tray sides	2 1/2 × 13 × 1/2
2 tray ends	2 1/2 × 7 × 1/2
1 tray bottom	7 × 14 × 1/4 plywood
2 tray runners	1/2 × 22 × 1/2

BOX WITH MATCHED LID

Making a lid to match a box can be troublesome. A simple way of making a lid that matches exactly is to form the lid and box sides and ends as one, then cut them apart after assembly. If the lid is carefully hinged, it will close exactly on the box.

This procedure can be done with a box of any size, but it is shown as a box to stand on a table and store small

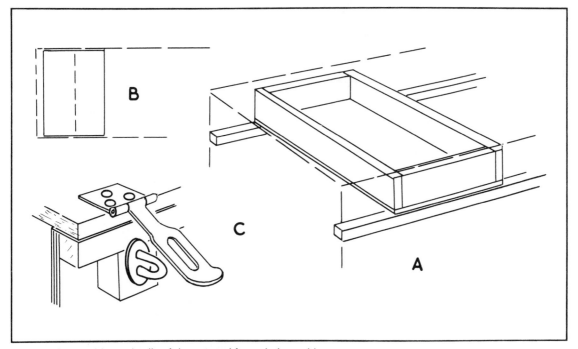

Fig. 6-9. Tray and hasp details of the external-framed plywood box.

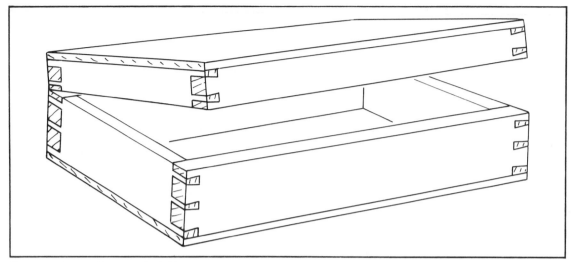

Fig. 6-10. A box with a matched lid.

items, such as handkerchiefs or jewelry. If fitted with a lock, it could become a cash box or a place to keep documents. Construction is shown as dovetailed (Fig. 6-10). The top and bottom may be glued flat on, or they could be let into rabbets.

Decide on the depth of the lid and mark on a side where the cut is to come. Dovetails must be arranged so the cut comes through a pin or tail and does not break into the line between them. This means that you cannot normally divide the width to be joined into tails of equal size. You must consider the lid and the body of the box as pieces that will be independent eventually. The sizes suggested (Fig. 6-11A) would permit a cut through a tail, giving two pins in the lid joints (Fig. 6-11B), or you could

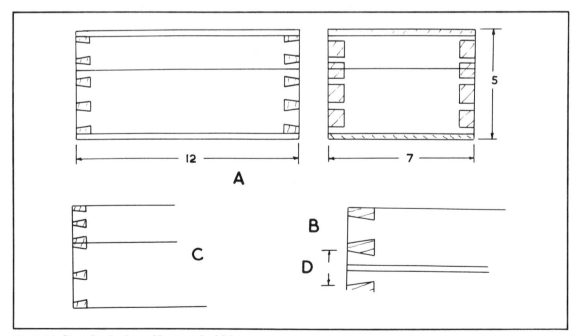

Fig. 6-11. Sizes for the box with a matched lid.

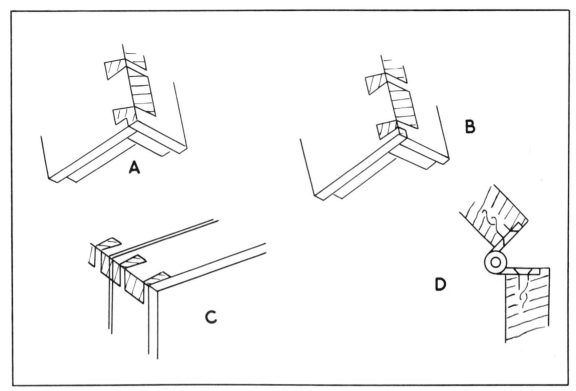

Fig. 6-12. Corner and hinge details of the box with a matched lid.

cut through a pin and have two tails in the lid (Fig. 6-11C). Below the cut you have more width to use and can space pins and tails suitably. Cutting the lid from the box and planing the edges will remove about 1/8 inch altogether, which could be allowed for in the pin or tail that comes across the cut (Fig. 6-11D).

If the bottom or top are to be let in, you must cut rabbets, then allow for them where they meet in the joints at the corners. There are two possible ways. You can notch the bottom pin (Fig. 6-12A) to cover the end over the rabbet the other way, or let that piece go through (Fig. 6-12B). Whichever way is chosen, glue the dovetail corners, then remove any excess glue inside. It is easier to do so before the top and bottom are fitted. Add the top and bottom and clamp the box until the glue has set, then plane and sand the outside. Do any rounding of edges and smooth the surfaces to the state you want the finished box to be.

The way you mark the cut between the lid and box depends on the method of cutting you choose. For most methods it will be advisable to use a marking gauge to scratch parallel lines all around (Fig. 6-12C), then the cut comes between them, and you have the gauge lines as a guide when planing. You can use a table saw with the lid against the fence. A hand-held circular saw with a fence or guide may also be used, or you may feel there is less risk of making a mistake if you cut with a hand saw. In any case, move around the four faces in turn and be careful to not let the parts or the saw slip on the fourth side.

Plane the surfaces level, being careful to avoid getting a twist anywhere. Try the parts together. Almost certainly they will not reverse perfectly, so keep them the right way when fitting hinges. A pair of hinges can be let partly into each meeting edge (Fig. 6-12D). Have the knuckles far enough out for the lid to open right back, otherwise the hinges or their screws will be strained.

Materials List for Box with Matched Lid

2 sides	4 1/4 × 13 × 5/8
2 ends	4 1/4 × 8 × 5/8
1 top	7 × 13 × 3/8
1 bottom	7 × 13 × 3/8

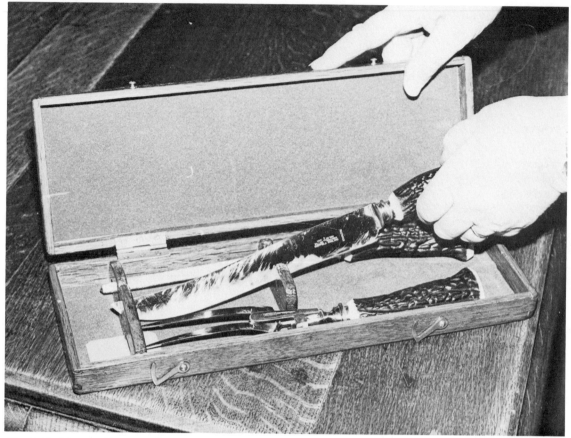

Fig. 6-13. A box for carving knife, fork, and steel.

CARVER BOX

This Carver Box is a variation on the last project and is made in the same way, with all the parts assembled before the lid is separated from the body of the box (Fig. 6-13). It is intended to hold a carving knife and fork, and a sharpening steel. Sizes obviously depend on these articles, but those shown are typical (Fig. 6-14A). For neatness the box should be made of an attractive hardwood, no bigger than necessary and with wood of quite light section. This involves constructional work finer and more delicate than the majority of storage projects.

Make the box in the same manner as the previous one, with a narrow tail in the lid and a slightly wider one in the box, and the cut through the pin between at each corner (Fig. 6-14B). Round the exterior edges. Cut the notches for small hinges, preferably brass. Fit the hinges temporarily to test their action, then remove them until after the box has been stained and polished.

Inside there are divisions for the knife, fork, and steel. The knife drops in at an angle (Fig. 6-14C); the fork drops into a slot, and its prongs go into a notch (Fig. 6-14D), while the sharpening steel drops into a slot and a hole (Fig. 6-14E). Do not be tempted to arrange the things in alternate ways or your hand may come against the sharp knife blade when reaching for one of the other things.

The box looks best if the top and bottom are lined with cloth, preferably green, which seems the accepted color for this purpose. It could be baize or other cloth glued in, or there are some suitable clothlike self-adhesive plastics that are easy to fit. Put the cloth in after the wood has been finished, but before you add the divisions. To protect the cloth from the fork prongs, you could put a little piece of sheet rubber or plastic under that notch.

There should be one, preferably two, catches to hold the box shut. The type where a hook swings over a screw is appropriate (Fig. 6-14F).

Materials List for Carver Box

2 sides	1 1/2 × 14 1/2 × 5/16
2 ends	1 1/2 × 5 × 5/16
1 top	5 × 14 1/2 × 1/4
1 bottom	5 × 14 1/2 × 1/4
2 divisions	1 × 5 × 5/16

PORTABLE TOOL BOX

When you need to take tools away from the shop, it is convenient to have a box or case that is easy to carry and will hold all of the hand tools you are likely to need, together with screws, nails, and other items. You must compromise between large size and portability. This tool box (Fig. 6-15) is a reasonable size, and it could be arranged on a shelf over the bench so it becomes a tool rack there, as well as being available when you want to work elsewhere. It is a suitable height to use as a trestle if you have nothing else on which to work.

It is another example of a box and lid that can be made as one and then separated, so the lid or flap will make a good fit when closed. The box shown (Fig. 6-16A) will hold some tools inside the flap; there is a removable tray, and the rest of the box will take the tools needed for the particular job in hand. There are two catches and a handle; so the box may be carried like a suitcase. A lock would be easy to fit.

There are several possible means of construction: The whole box could be made of wide boards of solid wood 1/2 inch thick or a little more. Top, bottom, and sides could be solid wood, with thinner plywood at the back and front. The whole box could be made of 1/2 inch plywood. The use of thin plywood makes for lightness, which may be important. It is not thick enough to take

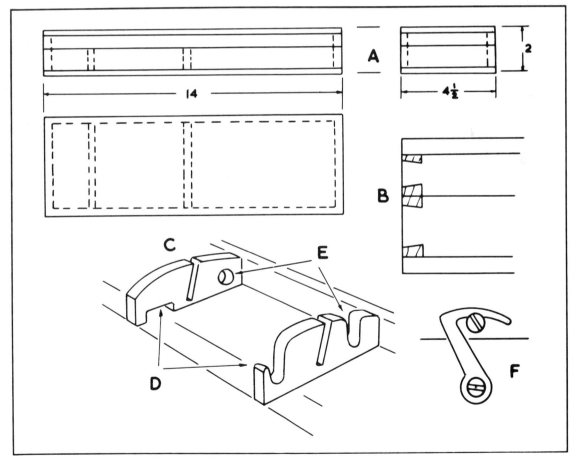

Fig. 6-14. Sizes and details of the carver box.

Fig. 6-15. A portable tool box.

screws for tool holders, but most of them can be screwed from the other side or attached with small bolts. The materials list is for solid wood with plywood back and front; so there will have to be an allowance for other constructions.

The best corner joints are dovetails, as described in the last two projects. The tails should be on the sides so they are in the direction for taking the load when the box is carried. Comb joints could be used. There would also be sufficient strength in one of the joints described earlier for taking nails both ways.

Make up the main part. Mark the shape of the flap (Fig. 6-16B) and make sure the cut will come centrally in a tail or pin of a dovetail, through a finger or comb,

or away from any nails or screws. If you are nailing or screwing, arrange for open of these fasteners at each corner of what will be the opening, so there is no unsupported part of a joint left there.

If you are using 1/2-inch plywood, joints intended for solid wood are unsuitable, and a simple screwed lap may not be strong enough. It is possible to use rather broader fingers than would be employed for solid wood and screw each way through them (Fig. 6-16C). If fitted closely and glued, this method will make very strong corners.

The back and front will probably be satisfactorily nailed or screwed and glued on the edges, but plywood could be let in if you wish. The solid wood edges would then have to be rabbeted and allowance made for that

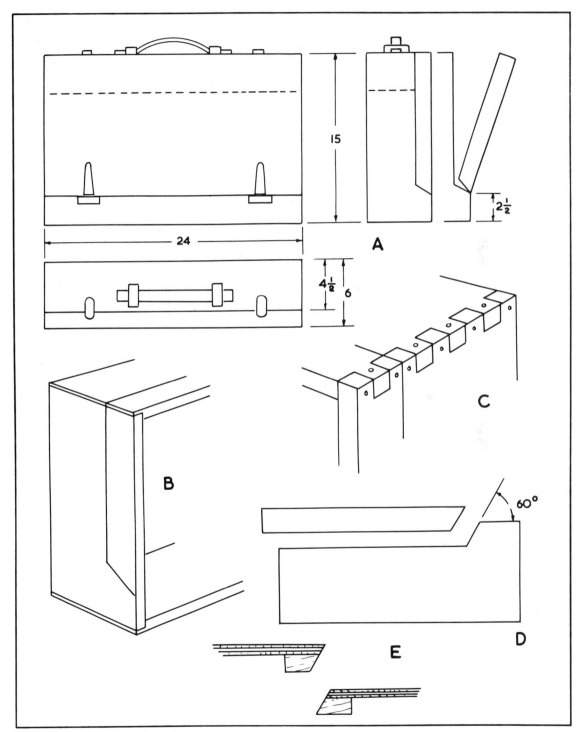

Fig. 6-16. Sizes and details of the portable tool box.

in the corner joints, as previously described. Attach back and front, then true edges and plane or sand the outside, if necessary.

Cutting out the flap is similar to removing the lid in the last two projects, except for the sloping part. The edges have to be cut in line with the angle and that is easier to do with a hand saw, even if other parts are cut with a power tool (Fig. 6-16D). If solid wood or 1/2-inch plywood is used for the front, there will be no need to stiffen the cut edge, but if you use 1/4-inch plywood, put strips inside each edge (Fig. 6-16E).

The inside of the lid is a good place to stow tools that you expect to use regularly. A hand saw can go against the frame so its teeth are protected. It is the longest tool you may want to carry, and it may decide the overall length of the box. Make a shaped block to fit through the saw handle, thick enough to allow a turnbutton to fit on a screw, preferably with a washer under the screw head and another between the turnbutton and the block (Fig. 6-17A). The block does not have to be a precision fit in the handle—let it be easy for the handle to be slipped on. At the other end of the saw, put a block in the corner with a space into which the saw can fit easily (Fig. 6-17B).

A combination square is a good tool to have in a portable kit, even if you use separate tools in the shop, because it can double for many tools when working away from home. It can be held on a shaped block inside the lid, with a wood or metal turnbutton (Fig. 6-17C).

There could be a row of webbing or leather loops for tools to be pushed in. Use screws or nuts and bolts with washers under the heads to prevent the heads pulling through when tools are forced in (Fig. 6-17D). Inside the lid arrange these tools to push down from what will be the top when closed, otherwise they may fall away when the box is transported.

You can make use of spring clips, preferably plastic-coated, so they do not rust and are less likely to mark the tools. Chisels can have their edges protected with a block similar to that for the end of the saw, then their necks gripped by spring clips (Fig. 6-17E). Spring clips are not very successful for heavy tools in a portable box, since they may let them go, but you may use them for screwdrivers and similar light things. Hammers and other heavy things are better in the body of the box.

The tray is long and narrow and resting on supports which allow it to slide out. To prevent it sliding when the box is closed, it should be made as wide as possible. This also gives the maximum capacity, but it means there is no space for a handle. Instead, it can have a hollowed edge to provide a hand grip (Fig. 6-17F). Make the tray of solid

wood with a plywood bottom.

The carrying handle may be of the suitcase type, but the load may be too much for wood screws. Use nuts and bolts through the metal ends. A handle could be a piece from a leather strap. To take the load, fit wood pieces each side, as well as bolts through (Fig. 6-17G).

There could be ordinary hinges between the edges of the flap and the box, but it would be better to use T or strap hinges bolted through (Fig. 6-17H).

Assemble all the tool holders and try everything in place. Make sure you have provided storage for everything you wish to store. When you are satisfied that the tool box is equipped as you want it, finish it with a good, protective coat. This could be several coats of varnish, but it may be better to use paint. If the inside is white or a light color, you can see what there is in it, even when the light is poor. If you paint the outside a bright color, you will have no difficulty in seeing your toolbox, possibly among all the equipment and debris of a building site—red is supposed to be the color easily seen under most circumstances.

Materials List for a Portable Tool Box

2 sides	5 1/2 × 25 × 5/8
2 sides	5 1/2 × 16 × 5/8
2 panels	15 × 25 × 1/4 or 3/8 plywood
2 stiffeners	3/4 × 25 × 1/2
2 tray sides	3 × 25 × 1/2
2 tray ends	3 × 5 × 1/2
1 tray bottom	5 × 25 × 1/4 plywood

PLAIN CHEST

At one time a strong, plain chest was an important part of a family's furniture. In Europe one or more chest were the main depositories of the family possessions. Craftsmen kept a chest to hold their tools and other equipment of their trade. Anyone who traveled carried their belongings in a chest. When the pioneers were moving west, substantial chest contained their most important things. Such a chest is not intended for one-handed carrying. It needs at least two people; so handles are usually provided at the ends. Some larger chests needed sockets for poles to push through so four people could carry them.

Some of the finest chests were those used by woodworking craftsmen for their tools. Externally, they were plain so they could stand up to hard use, particularly when being transported in a wagon, but inside the lid was often

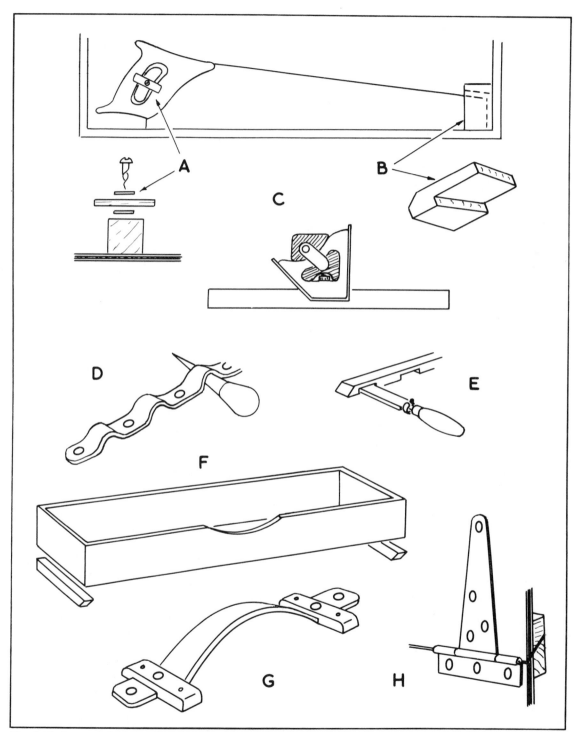

Fig. 6-17. Suggested ways of fitting tools into the portable tool box.

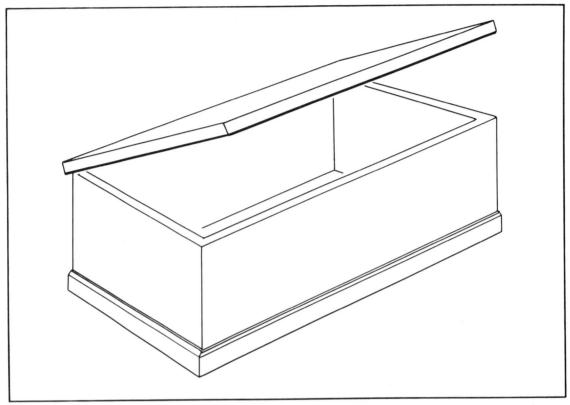

Fig. 6-18. A plain chest with a hinged lid.

decorated with marquetry, possibly used to display to a new employer the skill of the owner. There were also lift-out blocks of trays and shelves for smaller tools and space below and between for the larger ones.

The chest in Fig. 6-18 is without decoration and intended to be made in the traditional way from solid wood. A similar chest might be made from plywood, but that would have to be framed. For the sizes shown (Fig. 6-19A) there must be sufficient wide boards or pieces glued up to make the widths. For old chests, made when there were no waterproof glues, the bottom was often formed of boards across the width, drawn close together when they were screwed on, in the hope that they would not shrink and cause gaps. As they were often over damp earth floors, this was unlikely. For a reproduction chest, this method could be repeated, but the lid should have its grain lengthwise.

You have to decide on the corner joints. The better traditional chests had through dovetails. Less important ones had the edges lapped and screwed or nailed, then the corners bound with metal. Rabbet and comb joints

would be satisfactory, but if you are making a reproduction of a traditional chest, they would not be authentic. Go over machine planing with a hand plane. If some hand plane marks show, they will not matter. It is unlikely that the surfaces of an old chest would have been sanded.

Join the sides and ends, then nail or screw and glue on the bottom to produce the basic box. Check squareness as you assemble, and look across the top to see that there is no twist. Frame underneath the bottom with strips (Fig. 6-19B) to lift the bottom off the ground and make it stand better on an uneven surface than it might directly on a broad base. Make the outer plinth strips go all around the bottom. Bevel their top outer edges and miter the corners (Fig. 6-19C). These parts are best joined with waterproof glue and with nails punched below the surface and covered with stopping.

The single board or glued narrow boards which make the lid should be slightly larger than the box to give clearance at the ends and front. At the back, the lid is not edged, since there must be clearance for it to swing up and back. Make the edging with bevels to match the

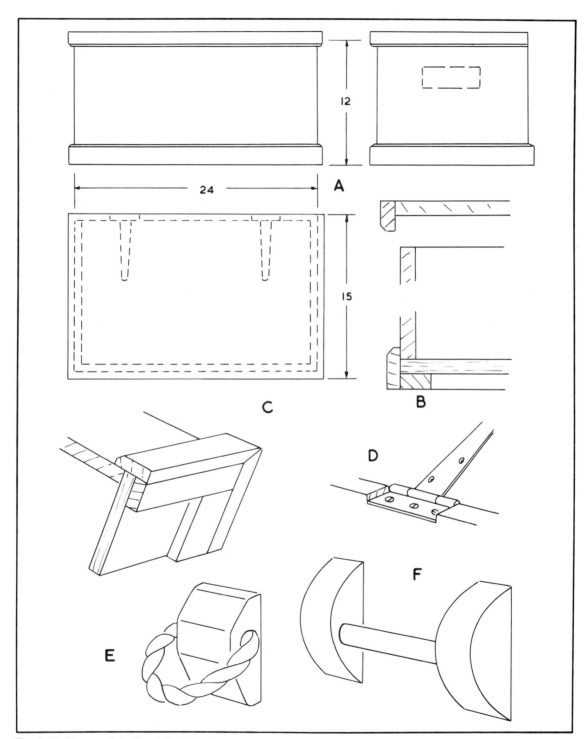

Fig. 6-19. Sizes and details of the plain chest.

plinth and miter the corners. The strips across the ends provide stiffness to prevent the lid warping; so attach them securely. If you think the top needs further stiffening, there can be battens across inside, cut short to fit inside the box.

Some traditional chests have very long blacksmith-made hinges; so the long arm provided additional stiffness across the lid, or a means of holding boards together, when available glues could not be relied on. In this case it will be sufficient to use a T hinge about 6 inches long. Most T hinges are made with a wide clearance between the parts. So the lid shuts fairly closely, put the long arm on the undersurface of the lid, without letting it in, and let the cross part into the box edge fairly deeply (Fig. 6-19D).

Two substantial iron handles could be fitted to the ends—a plain design would be more in keeping with the chest than a more ornate type. Original handles were often of wood or rope. A solid block may take a rope loop (Fig. 6-19E). A seaman's chest often had very elaborate knots and plaits on the handles. Another handle consists of a stout round rod between blocks of wood (Fig. 6-19F), held with glue and screws from inside. Position handles fairly high on the ends, certainly above the halfway line.

That completes the construction of the chest. It could be fitted with a lock. If you have used an attractive wood, the outside might be stained and given a clear finish of varnish or polish; otherwise, it could be painted. If the chest will be taken outdoors, remember to given the bottom as good a paint protection as the sides. Traditional chests usually had a drab paint finish because protection was more important than appearance. Inside there could be paint, but a varnish finish is attractive and suitable if the chest will be used for fabrics. If the box is made of cedar, it could be left untreated for storing fabrics.

You could fit one or more sliding trays, as described for the smaller box. There could be fittings inside the lid for tools or certain sports gear, and you could make compartments for special items. Remember, however, that too much compartmenting restricts total capacity. If you want to pack in as much as possible, it is better to store things loosely.

Materials List for Plain Chest

2 sides	$12 \times 25 \times 5/8$
2 ends	$12 \times 16 \times 5/8$
1 bottom	$15 \times 25 \times 5/8$
4 plinths	$2 \times 27 \times 5/8$
4 plinths	$2 \times 17 \times 5/8$
1 lid	$15 \times 25 \times 5/8$
1 lid edge	$1\ 1/2 \times 27 \times 5/8$
2 lid ends	$1\ 1/2 \times 17 \times 5/8$

TAPERED BOX

If a box is to be made tapered, there are some interesting design points in getting the true shapes and sections, that are not immediately obvious. The problem becomes more acute if the taper is considerable. If a box has only a slight taper both ways, it may be possible to get satisfactory results by trial and error, since the differences between it and a box with parallel sides are slight. If the methods are understood, it is better to use them, even when the taper is slight.

An example is a tapered box, made of plywood with stiffening strips (Fig. 6-20). It could be a trash box in the shop, or it can be used for waste paper in an office. The taper makes it easy to empty. The sides are joined with strips following the corners inside and strips taken around outside at top and bottom. The box bottom is plywood underneath the lower framing strips. It is intended that the box is held together with glue and fine nails and then finished with paint. The size shown is 12 inches square and tapered from a 9-inch-square bottom in a 12-inch height, but the techniques involved are the same for any size box.

Because of the taper both ways, the side view in a general drawing does not show the true shape of a side. In that view the front is sloping towards the viewer, and the vertical height is not the same as the sloping height, although in this case the difference is not much.

To get the true shape of a side, draw the front view fullsize (Fig. 6-21A). Measure the length of an edge (Fig. 6-21B), which is also a side view of the centerline of the adjoining side. Mark this height on the front view centerline (Fig. 6-21C) and draw a new shape on this, keeping the same width at top and bottom. In this case the height of a panel on the slope will be about 1/4 inch more than the vertical height. For practical purposes in a waste bin, this may not matter, but it shows the principle that must be applied when a tapered box of greater precision is needed.

Another thing that may not be immediately obvious is the angle of the wood used in a corner. Although the box is square in plan view, the actual angle between the sides when measured square to a corner is not, and it is the angle there that the corner strips of wood must be, if they are to make a good contact with the plywood. If you joined strips to two opposite sides of plywood, with their cross-sections square, there would be gaps to plane

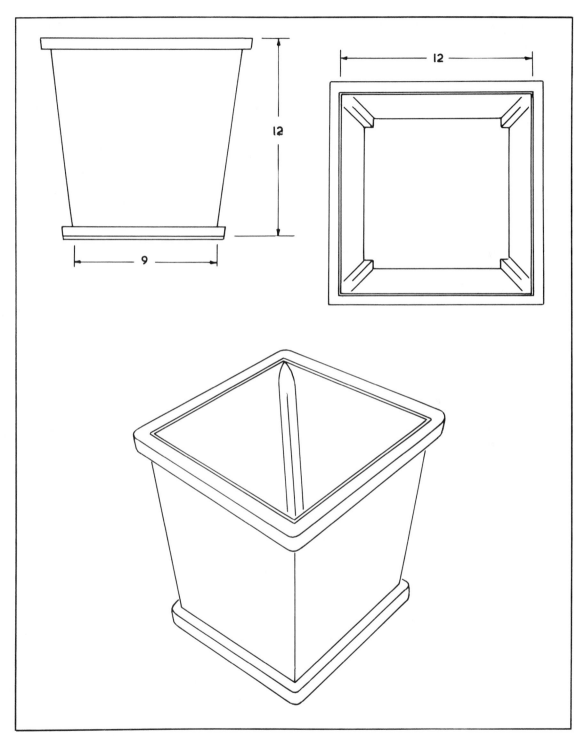

Fig. 6-20. A box tapered both ways.

true when you brought the other sides to them. It might not matter in this case, but for precision working it would be better to prepare the wood to the correct angle before attaching it. Even in this case the difference is enough to make setting out the angle first advisable.

You must get the angle of the corner when viewed squarely to a diagonal of the box, which is 45 degrees to the side. I have the height of the corner edge on the setting out of the side (Fig. 6-21D), and its vertical height is the same as I have drawn in the first side view. Take this corner length and swing it from a vertical line to cut the line showing the true height of the box (Fig. 6-21E). This is the corner line when viewed diagonally. Anywhere on this draw a square horizontally with one corner against the line (Fig. 6-21F). The size of the square does not mat-

ter and will be easier to use if bigger than the 5/8-inch square of the wood. That square is the shape required in plan view, but the wood has to slope with the corner. From its center draw a line square to the corner line (Fig. 6-21G). That will be the actual length of half a diagonal of the square when tilted. Mark that on the square diagonal and join the point to the corners to get the angle the wood must be (shown dotted in Fig. 6-21H). In this case it will be about 95 degrees, which is enough to matter if planing undersize is to be avoided if you start with unprepared square stock. You could plane the inner surfaces to the same angle, if you wish, but for this box it would not matter if they were left square, and the exposed edge rounded.

When the side sizes and the corner angles have been

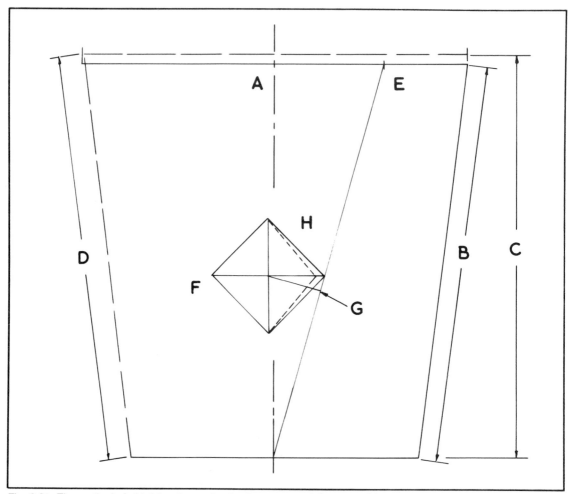

Fig. 6-21. The method of obtaining the angles for the corners of the tapered box.

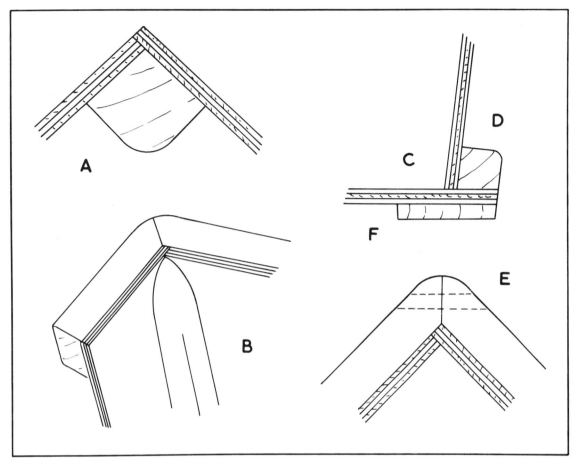

Fig. 6-22. Corner and bottom details of the tapered box.

obtained, construction becomes simple. Cut the plywood for the four sides. Two for opposite sides should be narrower on each edge by the thickness of the plywood at each edge to allow for the overlap. Prepare the strips for the corner joints, with their angles made to those obstained from the development of the corner. Round the inner corners (Fig. 6-22A) and round the upper ends to meet the top edges (Fig. 6-22B). Attach the strips to the narrower plywood sides and plane the plywood edges to match the strips. Plane the bottom edges of the plywood to fit the bottom angle (Fig. 6-22C).

Put strips around the lower edges, planed to fit against the bottom (Fig. 6-22D). Miter the meeting corners of the strips for the best finish, although they could overlap in a simpler construction. The miters may be strengthened by putting dowels through diagonally (Fig. 6-22E). Nail and glue on the bottom. It may be advisable

to raise the bottom off the floor with small blocks at the corners (Fig. 6-22F). If the box is to stand on carpet, the blocks can be faced with cloth or rubber.

Put strips around the top edge. You could plane their top edges to be parallel with the floor, but for most purposes they may be left square and their outer edges rounded. Miter and dowel the corners to leave the upper edges of the plywood exposed. If they are rounded and sanded, that should be satisfactory. If, however, you want to cover the plywood, the top strips may be made wider so they can be rabbeted over the plywood for a neater finish.

A lid for the box would be simple to make. Cut a square of solid wood, plywood, or particleboard to the outside sizes, then put strips underneath to fit inside the box and hold the lid in place. Position a handle or knob on top for lifting. A loop handle placed diagonally looks good and is servicable.

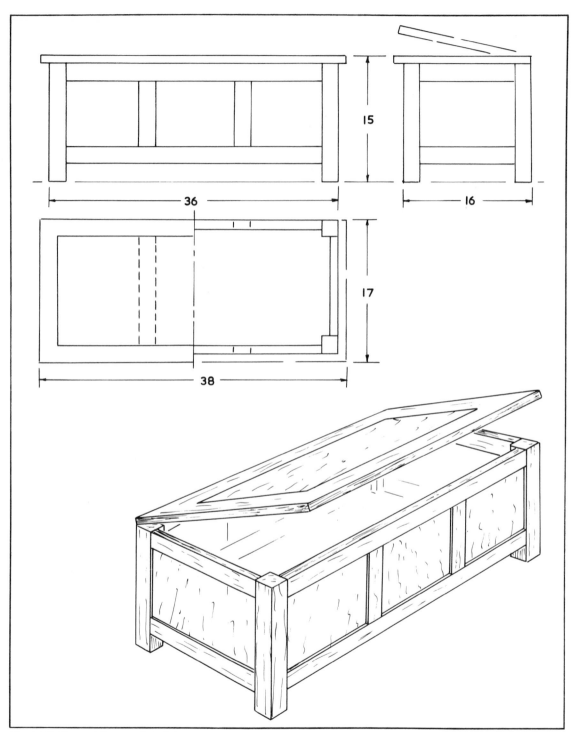

Fig. 6-23. Sizes of the paneled chest.

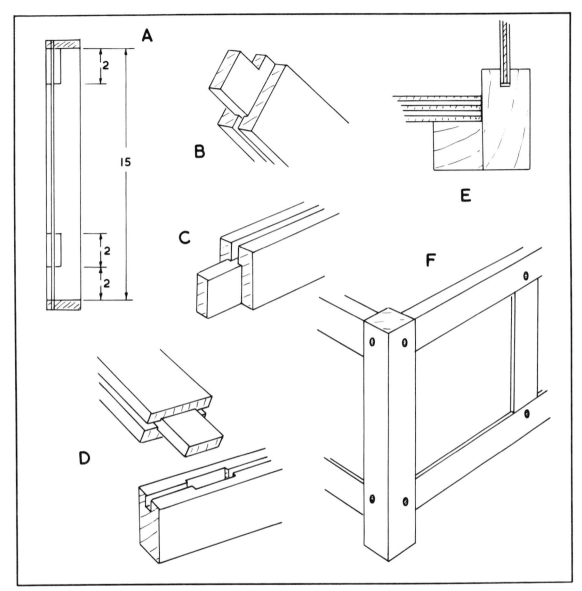

Fig. 6-24. Constructional details of the paneled chest.

Materials List for Tapered Box

4 sides	12 × 13 × 1/4 plywood
1 bottom	11 × 11 × 1/4 plywood
4 corners	5/8 × 14 × 5/8
4 tops	5/8 × 14 × 5/8
4 bottoms	5/8 × 11 × 5/8
4 feet	2 × 2 × 3/8

PANELED CHEST

The chest of Tudor times in England and Europe was often described as the "old oak chest," which gives an idea of its construction. Solid oak chests were very heavy, and where something lighter was needed for use in the living parts of a castle, the chest was made by framing around panels. The panels were limited by the width of wood that could be cut into thin pieces, so the number

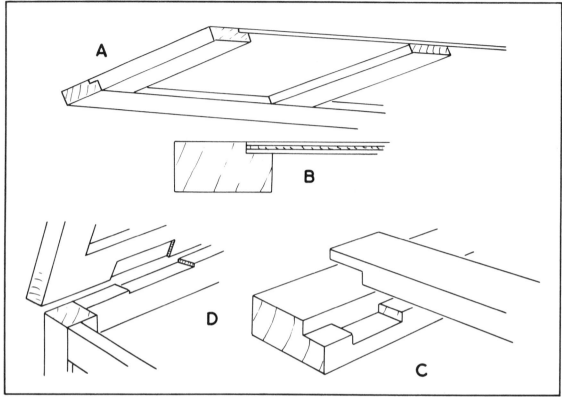

Fig. 6-25. Method of making the chest lid.

of divisions in any part depended on what was available.

With plywood available today, we do not suffer from these limitations, but there is still an advantage in using a panel construction for lightness and an attractive appearance. The chest in Fig. 6-23 does not have to be oak, but the plywood should be veneered to match the surrounding wood, and that may limit the choice of solid wood. The alternative is to stain ordinary plywood to make a near match to the surrounding wood. The chest should be made of hardwood, in any case.

Although the parts could be doweled, this is an assembly where mortise-and-tenon joints are traditional and more suitable. The instructions assume mortise and tenons, but they are easily adapted to suit dowels.

The legs project 2 inches below the bottom of the chest, but this is the stage to change heights if you want to make alterations. As shown, the chest is a convenient height to sit on, particularly if a cushion is made to fit on the lid.

Mark out the legs (Fig. 6-24A) and use them as guides when marking the other parts. The grooves for the panels

may be plowed for the full length. You can then fill them below the bottom rails, if you wish, but they will not be very obvious. Plow similar grooves in the rails. Cut haunched joints at the top (Fig. 6-24B) and plain ones at the bottom rails (Fig. 6-24C). The intermediate pieces are spaced evenly along the rails and held with plain tenons (Fig. 6-24D). In all cases you must cut back to the bottoms of the grooves.

The bottom of the chest can be a piece of plywood resting on strips inside the bottom rails (Fig. 6-24E). Fit the strips to the rails before assembling the chest. Assemble the two long sides first, checking that the second matches the first as you put the parts together. When the glue has set in these joints, add the parts the other way and fit in the bottom to keep the assembly square, even if you do not fasten it down until you have cleaned off surplus glue inside. Make sure the chest stands without wobbling on a level surface.

In a traditional chest, the best glue available was not as strong as we have, and it was usual, for security, to put dowels through the joints. That may be regarded as a decorative touch, and you could add dowels to your joints (Fig. 6-24F). Ideally, they should be made of the same wood as the framing. There is no need to take them right through. Drill far enough to penetrate the tenons, then glue in the dowels and plane them flush.

The lid of a traditional chest was often made with the panels set centrally in the framing, with divisions as necessary, so the top surface was not level. It would, however, be better in a modern version to give the top flush panels. The lid is intended to have plywood in a rabbet and two pieces across underneath to provide stiffness (Fig. 6-25A). Let the plywood overlap about 1/2 inch to give it a strong glue surface (Fig. 6-25B). Join the corners with tenons, but the intermediate strips can be notched in (Fig. 6-25C), level with the rabbets. Cutting too much away from the lid edges with larger joints might weaken them. The lid must be kept level with the back of the chest for hinging, but the other edges overlap 1 inch.

There is no need for the long strap hinges that would have been used in old chests, but this lid could have three 4-inch hinges let equally into the surfaces (Fig. 6-25D), so the lid closes with only minimal clearance over the edge. In this way, it will get support all around when it is sat upon. The weight of the lid will keep it closed, but you could fit a box lock with a keyhole through the front.

Materials List for Paneled Chest

4 legs	2 × 19 × 2
4 rails	2 × 36 × 1
4 rails	2 × 16 × 1
4 rails	2 × 12 × 1
6 panels	9 × 11 × 1/4 plywood
2 panels	9 × 14 × 1/4 plywood
2 bottom supports	1 × 33 × 1
2 bottom supports	1 × 12 × 1
1 bottom	15 × 35 × 1/2 plywood
2 lid sides	2 × 39 × 1
2 lid ends	2 × 18 × 1
2 lid stiffeners	2 × 15 × 3/4
1 lid panel	15 × 36 × 1/4 plywood

Chapter 7

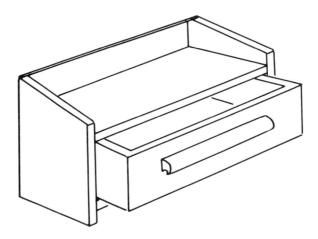

Drawers

If you put a box on a shelf, it is just that, but if you put a box between shelves, it becomes a drawer. Drawers are boxes arranged to slide into containers that protect their contents. They are usually close-fitting, so they need handles or other means of withdrawal. A considerable amount of storage in the home is in drawers. They are convenient, and they keep their contents hidden from view, yet easily accessible and protected from dust and dirt. They will also keep an untidy collection of things hidden from critical eyes, and in some circumstances the contents are protected from prying hands. Drawers can be fitted with locks.

In many ways a drawer is more convenient than a box with a lid. You do not have the problem of moving things off the top before opening. Several drawers may be made to hold the same volume of goods as a large box which are then more easily found, without having to dip vertically into an enclosed pile. A box is usually kept fairly low, if not actually on the floor. Drawers can be at any reasonable height and are then more accessible.

Although a drawer is a box, the loads on it are different from a normal box. It does not have to be lifted, but most strain in use comes when the front is pulled. The contents then tend to press toward the back. Drawer joints are arranged to allow for these loads and are not

necessarily the same on all four corners. Bottoms are usually fixed in a different way from most boxes. There have been developments to allow for modern materials and methods, but most derive from traditional ways.

If a drawer fits between two solid shelves, as it might into a boxlike case (Fig. 7-1A), its sides are guided by the sides of the box; their lower edges run on the bottom part, and the top of the box prevents the drawer from tilting as it is pulled forward. If there are several drawers stacked above each other, there is no need for a solid shelf between each set of two. If the side of the case is paneled, it may not present a smooth surface inside to act as a guide. Traditional drawers slide on their bottom edges and there must be parts to ensure smooth running in and out.

DRAWER GUIDES

What supports the drawer is a runner (Fig. 7-1B) wide enough to take the bearing surface of the drawer side. As the drawer is pulled forward, it will tend to tilt; to prevent this, there is a kicker above the side (Fig. 7-1C). In many constructions, the runner for one drawer forms the kicker for the one below. If the drawer cannot rub along the side of its casing, because of paneling or some other

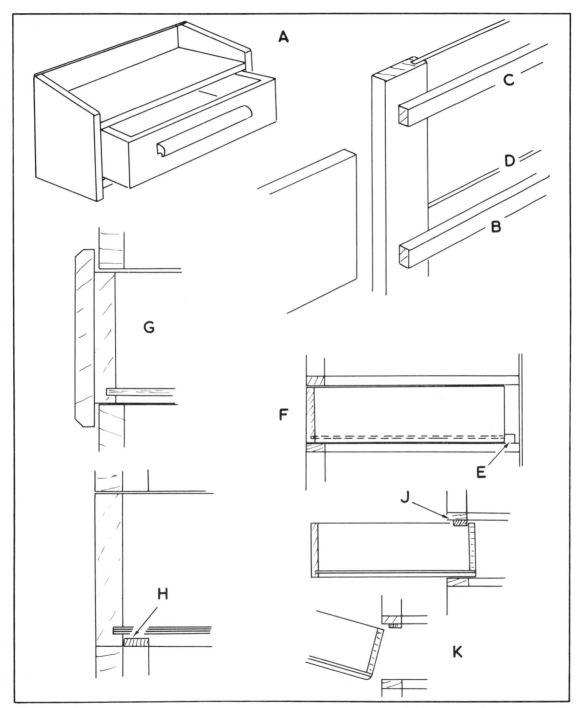

Fig. 7-1. A drawer may fit between shelves (A) or have runners, kickers, and guides (B-D). There may be a stop at the back (E) so the front finishes flush (F), or it could have an overlapping front (G). A stop may come under the bottom (H) or be arranged to stop the back as well (J,K).

reason, there will have to be a guide (Fig. 7-1D). It could be just at the top or bottom, but is better at both positions for a deep drawer.

In some cases the drawer may go to the back of its casing and act as a stop. If the drawer does not reach the back, there may be a stop on each runner of kicker (Fig. 7-1E). The fronts of drawers may fit within the framing (Fig. 7-1F) requiring stops so the front surfaces finish level. If the front overlaps the opening, the edges there may provide sufficient stopping (Fig. 7-1G), but when a heavily loaded drawer is pushed back hard, it exerts considerable thrust. In that case, stops at the back of the drawer are desirable to take at least some of the load from the front edges.

Most drawer bottoms come above the lower edges of the sides. Stops may then be arranged behind the fronts of the drawers (Fig. 7-1H). Two widely spaced stops are better than a single central one. They cannot be very thick, but they are sufficient to ensure the drawer coming level with the surrounding wood when shut.

There may be no need to provide stops to prevent a drawer from pulling right out unintentionally, but if there is, any stops must hold the drawer back in normal conditions. You should be able to remove it without much special action. One way is to put stops at the top (Fig. 7-1J). Their forward edges can act as stops when the drawer is pushed in, instead of putting any below the drawer bottom; then their rear edges come against the back of the drawer as it is pulled, to stop the drawer coming completely out. To get the drawer out, it can be tilted upward to pull the bottom clear (Fig. 7-1K). The normal clearance allowance should be enough to permit this action, but if necessary, the rear bottom corners of the drawer can be rounded.

DRAWER CONSTRUCTION

If you examine an old piece of good-quality furniture with drawers, you will see that the drawers are held together with dovetail joints. The front dovetails are of the stopped type, and the rear dovetails may carry through a little, particularly if the back of the drawer must be stopped by the ends of the sides. This is a place where the old-time cabinetmaker made dovetail joints with the pins very narrow (Fig. 7-2A). There does not seem to be any good reason for this practice, except to show how skilled the craftsman was. Wider pins would be just as acceptable and probably stronger (Fig. 7-2B), even if they were as wide as tails in machine-cut joints. This applies to the back as well as the front of the drawer. To allow

for the stopped dovetails, the front of a drawer is made thicker than the sides and back. It would also be of a wood to match the exposed parts of the furniture, while the inner parts may be a cheaper wood.

In an old piece of furniture, made before the advent of plywood, the bottoms of drawers were more of a problem to be overcome. They had to be made of solid wood, cut as thinly as possible. There is, however, a limit in width to the pieces that can be cut; so many old drawers have the bottoms made in several pieces with the grain running the short way of the drawer, for strength. Even then, many old drawer bottoms will be found to have cracked or shrunk.

The bottom edges of the side of a drawer, fitted in the traditional way, are rubbing surfaces as they run along the bearer, which can be worn away in long use. To have as big a bearing surface as possible, the width of the bottom edge may be increased inside (Fig. 7-2C). You may find that many old solid-wood bottoms are thicker than plywood would be, but the edges are thinned to fit into plowed grooves (Fig. 7-2D). In a modern drawer, particularly if it is supported in a way that does not put the load on the bottom edges of the sides, plywood can be fitted into grooved sides (Fig. 7-2E). Nailing plywood to the sides, as in a box, and the fitting strips underneath is a possible alternative (Fig 7-2F), but not as good as the other methods.

It is usual to have a drawer back fitted above the bottom (Fig. 7-2G). This method avoids the occurrence of an edge across at bottom level, which may catch on other crosswise parts of the framework when the drawer is being pulled out, especially after the sides have worn away a little. For the same reason it is usual to keep the top of the back lower than the sides.

There is a practical advantage when making and fitting the drawer in having the back above the bottom. The bottom may be slid into the assembled drawer and then screwed up into the back (Fig. 7-2H). If this is first done loosely, the drawer can be tried in place, and any adjustment needed can be made to get squareness or the fit of the drawer correct before final screwing.

When making and fitting drawers, care is needed to keep parts square. A drawer that is wider at the back than the front would obviously present difficulties, but so would a framework out of square, or runners and kickers out of parallel, which would have a twisting effect on drawer movement.

Drawer Fronts

Traditionally there was a rail across between drawers

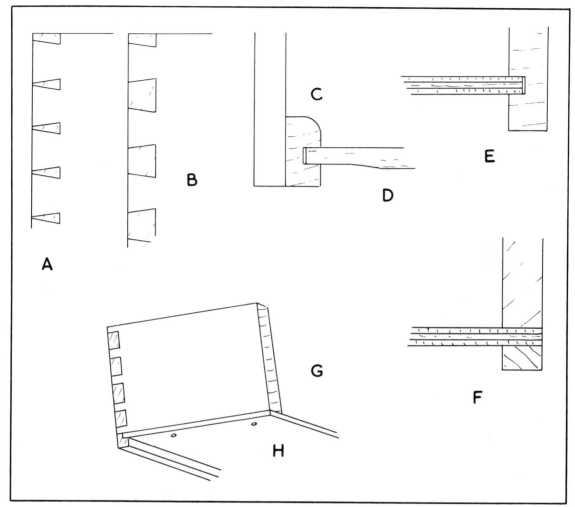

Fig. 7-2. Typical drawers are dovetailed (A,B), and the bottom is supported in a groove (C-E). There could be a false bottom edge (F). The back usually comes above the bottom (G,H).

(Fig. 7-3A) that matched the combined runner and kicker depth and might be repeated across the back; then a thin dustboard fitted into grooves (Fig. 7-3B). You could construct dustboards in modern furniture, but they are uncommon today.

Many modern chests of drawers do not have front rails between drawers and, except for the necessary clearance, the drawers come together. In this arrangement, the drawer fronts extend high enough to cover the front ends of the runners (Fig. 7-3C). Less commonly, they are made to extend downward, or each drawer front may go halfway over the runner ends, up and down.

If a drawer front is to cover the opening when closed, it could be cut from solid wood (Fig. 7-3D). For the production of single pieces of furniture, however, it may be more convenient to have the front in two parts (Fig. 7-3E). If it is an isolated drawer, the front can extend all around. If there are several drawers, they can extend a matching amount at the sides, but only one vertical edge extends toward the next, either upward (Fig. 7-3F) or downward. Overlapping drawer fronts may be shaped in any way at the edges, from simple chamfers or roundings to elaborate moldings.

Making an overlapping front in two parts allows the sides to be joined in with through dovetails, which are easier to cut by hand than are stopped dovetails. The false front can be glued on and strengthened with screws from inside. In many drawers, the screws that hold on the handles will also serve this purpose.

Drawer Bottoms

A drawer bottom should be let into the front, or there may be a grooved strip across to match those at the sides. If it is grooved, the end of it must be hidden by the bottom dovetail. Usually, there is not enough depth to let this be a full tail with a pin below it, and it is more usual to have a half tail there (Fig. 7-3G). This tail also hides a side groove, if there is one.

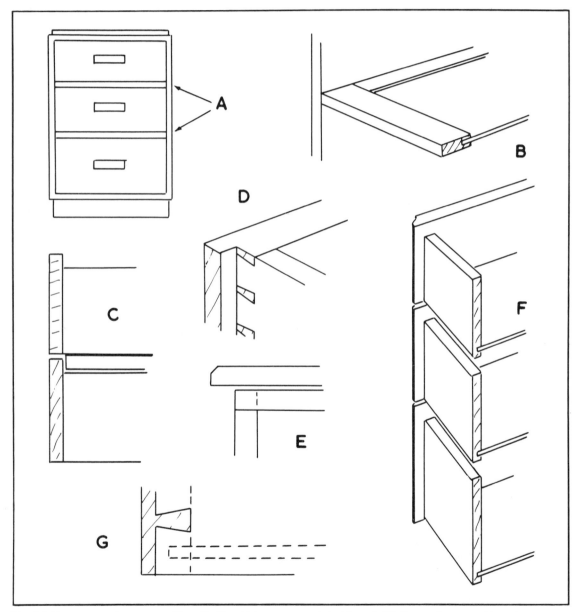

Fig. 7-3. Drawers may be separated by rails (A), which may support dust boards (B). Drawer fronts could overlap runners (C). The drawer fronts may overlap the frame (D-F). The bottom may be hidden behind a dovetail (G).

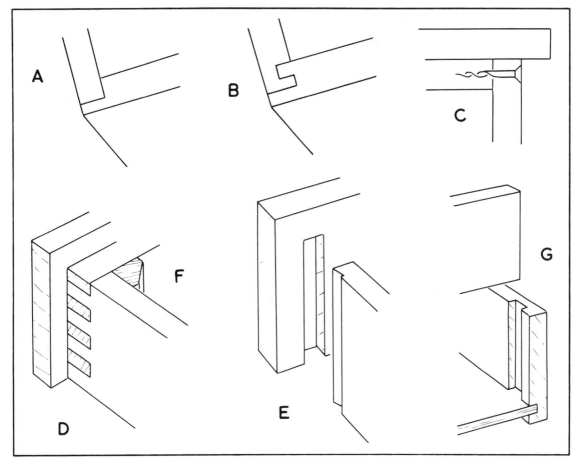

Fig. 7-4. There are several possible alternatives to dovetails in drawers.

If you do not wish to use dovetails, there are other possible corner joints, but in good furniture only dovetails are really appropriate joints. If the front is to finish flush, the sides may go into a rabbet and be nailed or screwed (Fig. 7-4A). A dado, tongue, and rabbet is possible (Fig. 7-4B). If there is a false front to cover the joint, you can merely screw a lap (Fig. 7-4C); with particleboard that may be the most appropriate joint. Behind a false front, wood could have comb or finger joints (Fig. 7-4D). A side could go into a dado in the front, but unless it is given a dovetail form (Fig. 7-4E), there is little resistance to pulling apart. Any of these joints could be strengthened with a glued block inside (Fig. 7-4F).

Drawer Support

At the back of the drawer, the wood may slide into

a dado from the top (Fig. 7-4G). It could be joined to the sides with any of the box corner joints, but even if dovetails are not used, it will still be advisable to keep the back above the bottom plywood. If the rear edges of the sides are to stop the drawer against the carcass back, allow for the sides to extend a little past the drawer back no matter what joints are used.

Drawers can be supported in ways other than on their bottom edges. In some places a drawer may hang from its top edges (Fig. 7-5A). Strips along the tops of the sides are usually supported by L-section pieces, either solid wood (Fig. 7-5B) or built-up (Fig. 7-5C). There could be a combination of methods if the drawer comes against an upright side (Fig. 7-5D). The front appearance may be improved by letting the front overlap the runners (Fig. 7-5E).

Another way of supporting a drawer is to have runners in groves in the drawer sides (Fig. 7-5F). The runners also serve as kickers to prevent the drawer from tilting. The forward ends could serve as stops.

There are several forms of metal drawer mechanisms that can be both. Most of them have to fit between the drawer side and the side of the casing, so there must be some clearance, which can be covered by an overlapping front. These mechanisms use rollers or balls to ease the movement of heavily loaded drawers, and they are arranged to keep a drawer level at any any position and to provide stops.

Some of this equipment is intended for heavy drawers used in industry or for office filing cabinets, and would be rather bulky for domestic drawers. There are other, lighter mechanisms more suitable for drawers in home furniture, and they are either quite thin themselves or capable of reducing the space by letting into one or both surfaces. Some of these items are particularly suitable

for use with particleboard. Many of the projects described in this book could have metal mechanisms, but sufficient clearance would have to be allowed when making and fitting drawers. For most projects, it is assumed that you will make the drawers to run on wood parts, but they are easily adapted to suit metal mechanisms.

Drawer Movement

When designing a piece of furniture which will have one or more drawers, consider the ease of moving the drawers. The easiest drawer to move in and out is deeper back to front than it is wide (Fig. 7-6A). Even if its fit is not very exact, it will still move without difficulty. At the other extreme is one that is very wide in relation to the distance back to front (Fig. 7-6B). As it is moved in or out, any movement other than parallel will cause it to stick (Fig. 7-6C). A carefully fitted wide drawer that does

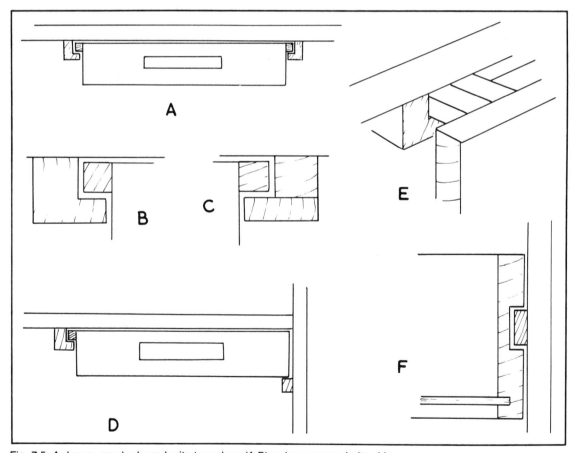

Fig. 7-5. A drawer may be hung by its top edges (A-D) or by a groove in its side.

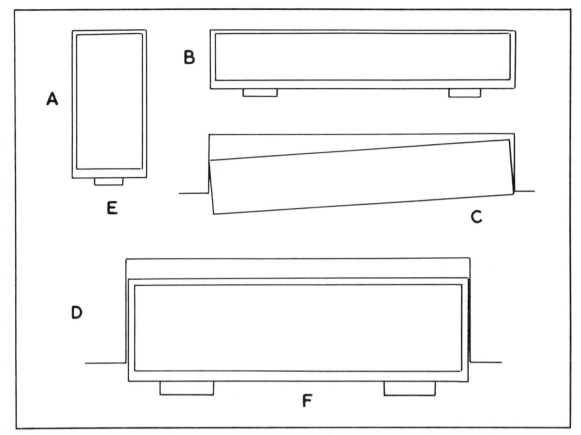

Fig. 7-6. A narrow drawer will run easily (A). A wide one may catch if it pulls at an angle (B,C). Having handles wide apart helps in pulling squarely (D).

not have quite such extreme proportions, will work easily (Fig. 7-6D), but fit and accuracy are more important than with the first drawer described.

Handles can affect drawer movement. The first drawer can have one central handle (Fig. 7-6E), and single-handed operation will be easy. A single central handle on a wide drawer will encourage wobbling and therefore cause jamming. It is better to have two handles, widely spaced, for the right sort of pull to prevent the drawer from jamming (Fig. 7-6F). A large heavy drawer of any proportion will need two handles, in any case.

In a new piece of furniture, drawers may not move smoothly. It is not usual to provide much of a polish finish inside, and drawer sides are often untreated. To ease a drawer, rub wax on the meeting surfaces. You could use any wax polish, although for local sticking, rubbing with a candle is effective. The fronts of drawers will be finished with the surrounding wood. Any stain or polish is usual-

ly taken around the tops and ends of the front only as far as its thickness, although sometimes it is taken an inch or so further on the sides so the lighter wood does not show through the clearance spaces. If the sides and other parts of drawers are to be treated, wax or a coat of thin varnish will seal the wood and reduce its tendency to absorb dirt or moisture.

BASIC CHEST OF DRAWERS

There are many ways to arrange a block of drawers, and this example (Fig. 7-7) makes a block of three that will give a comfortable height to the top, and drawers of graduated depth, with a rather greater capacity in the bottom one for such things as blankets and heavy or bulky items. As shown, the chest is used in front of a wall mirror in a bedroom, but it could stand in a living room or office. The sizes (Fig. 7-8A) give a reasonable proportion

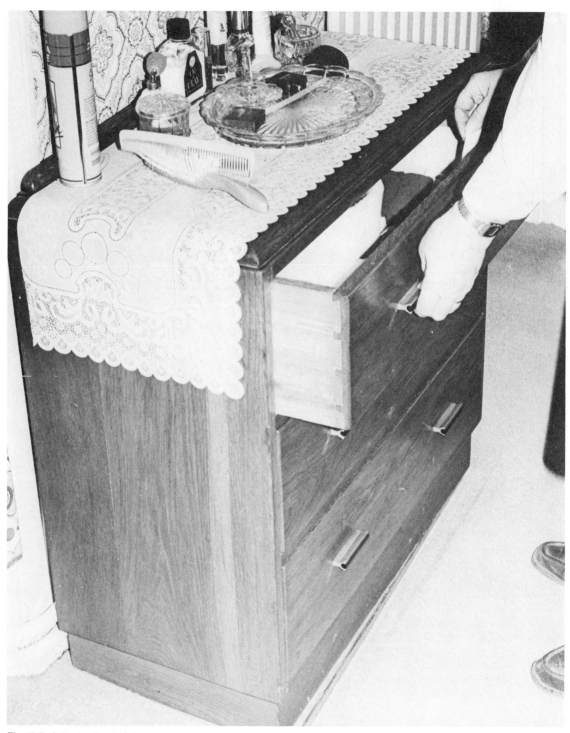

Fig. 7-7. A basic chest of drawers.

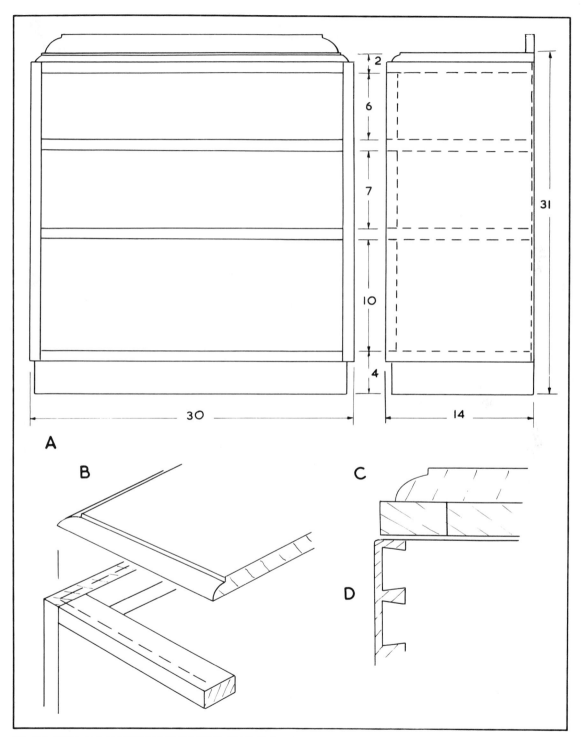

Fig. 7-8. Sizes and construction of the basic chest of drawers.

and capacity, with all of the structural parts 7/8-inch hardwood. The design would not suit particleboard or thick plywood, at least not without alterations to the method of construction.

Frame Assembly

Assembly is based on four identical frames (Fig. 7-9A). They form the top, bottom, and two dividers. Front parts should match the wood being used for the ends and top. The inside, however, may be other wood, although softwood might wear too much, and the drawers eventually work slackly. The frames will be doweled to the ends, but their sides are joined into the back and front with short tenons (Fig. 7-9B). The tenons do not have much strength in themselves, but they will be reinforced when the frames are joined to the sides. Check the squareness of one frame and use it to check that the other three exactly match it.

The sides are solid wood. You may have to glue pieces together to make up the width. Rabbet the rear edges for the plywood back (Fig. 7-9C). Mark where the frames will come and drill the frames and sides for dowels—3/8-inch dowels should do. Arrange two in the end grain, but the others could be more widely spaced (Fig. 7-9D).

The plinth is attached to the bottom frame and ends with dowels, and it would be advisable to prepare the parts there before assembling the frames and sides. If the chest is to go against a wall, there is no need for a back to the plinth. Miter the front corners and reinforce them inside with glued blocks (Fig. 7-9E). Set back the plinth slightly all around. Lay out the dowel holes in the plinth edges and along the front part of the bottom frame, but it will probably be wiser to leave drilling into the ends for the end parts of the plinth until after partial assembly.

Join the frames to the ends and check squareness. Cut the back plywood to size and fit it temporarily with a few screws to hold the other parts in shape, but delay final fitting until after the drawers have been made and fitted. It helps in fitting drawers to be able to get at the open back for adjustment and to see where stops have to come. The plywood back can go in permanently when you are satisfied that the drawers fit and slide properly.

The top is solid wood made to fit over the plywood at the back and to overlap about half the thickness of the ends and the same amount along the front (Fig. 7-8B). Its edges could be left square, but it will look better with molding on front and ends (Fig. 7-8C). It can be attached with glue and screws upward through the top frame. At this stage make a trial assembly with screws, but then remove the top so you can see how the drawers fit and what adjustment may be necessary before gluing and screwing on the top and back.

You could leave the rear edge of the top as it is, particularly if it will come close to a wall, but otherwise it is advisable to put a strip along the edge to prevent things from falling off. The strip may be joined on with dowels. It is shown with its ends shaped to match the section of edge molding (Fig. 7-9F). The drawers could be made by any of the methods described earlier in this chapter, but the following description assumes they will be dovetailed, either cut by hand or machine.

Drawer Assembly

Make the drawer fronts. They will control many of the sizes of other drawer parts; so you have to judge how much clearance to allow. In use, the drawer front will rest on the rail below it; so it should be given the same clearance at the sides and top. If you make a drawer too tight, you can plane something off, but obviously it would be unwise to allow for taking off much wood that way, or you would finish with thin or tapered parts. There must be enough clearance for the drawers to move easily. If you are reasonably certain the carcass is square, 1/16-inch clearance will usually be satisfactory. It is intended that the drawer fronts should project about 1/8 inch and have rounded edges (Fig. 7-8D). It is easier then to get a good appearance than if the drawer fronts are intended to be level with the framing.

Make each pair of drawer sides slightly too long, but plane them to fit their spaces, where the frames are forming runners and kickers. Make the strips that will take the bottom and plow grooves in the fronts at the same level. Square the forward ends of the sides and cut dovetails to the front pieces. At the rear the drawers should be about 1/2 inch forward of the plywood rabbet so you can put stops there (Fig. 7-10A).

Mark the lengths of the sides. Make the back piece and cut the joints to the sides. On all the drawer pieces, use an identification mark at each joint to avoid confusion during assembly. When making the back of a drawer, it can start slightly too long, but the key measurement is inside the joint (Fig. 7-10B). The distance between the insides of the joints should allow for the thickness of the sides, with the total the same length as the drawer front. Any excess on the overall length of the wood can be planned off after assembly. The back of the finished drawer should be the same width as its front. If it is wider,

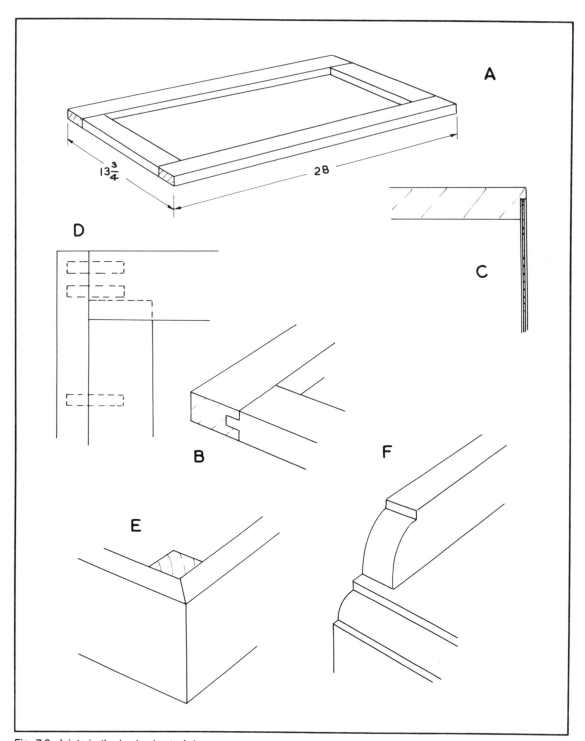

Fig. 7-9. Joints in the basic chest of drawers.

the drawer will not run properly. It could be marginally narrower for ease in withdrawal, but with drawers of this proportion and size, that is unnecessary.

There is no satisfactory way of making a trial assembly of a drawer in its framing. You will have to rely on the accuracy of your measuring and jointing. Glue up the parts of a drawer without its bottom. When the glue has set, plane off any excess wood at the joints, then try the drawer in the frame. While it is in place, make and fit its plywood button. Insert it in its groove from the back. If the drawer must be sprung slightly to get the best sliding fit, do so now, then glue and screw in the plywood to hold the shape. Wait to level the rear ends of the drawer sides and the plywood edge until after this stage.

When all of the drawers have been fitted, round their front edges by the same small amount, then fit stops on the frames to limit movement. All drawers should go in to their stops so their fronts project the same from the framework. When you are satisfied with the fit and ap-

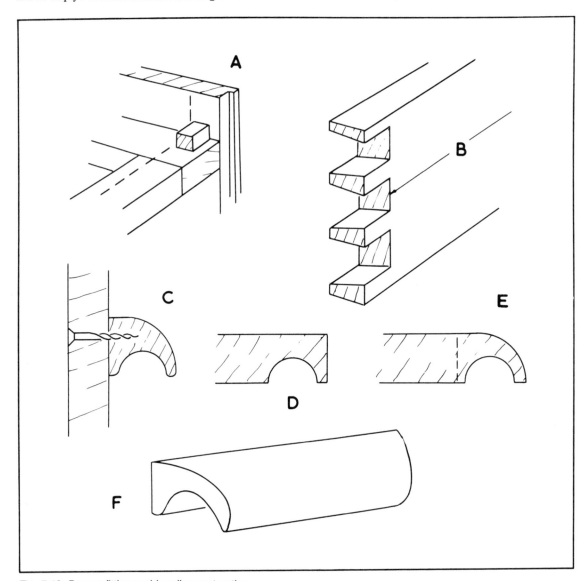

Fig. 7-10. Drawer fitting and handle construction.

pearance of the drawers, you can add stops under the front rails to prevent the drawers from pulling out unintentionally; then the plywood back and solid top may be glued and screwed on.

Handles

Handles on the chest in Fig. 7-7 are metal and plastic, with bolts through them. A large variety of handles are available. Whatever type is chosen, locate the handles widely, so a two-handed pull brings a drawer forward without jamming. If you divide a drawer width into four, the handles should not be further in than 1/4 the width from the ends.

Some wood handles are suggested in Fig.7-10C. The best way to make them is as a long strip, more than enough for them all. It is easier to do the shaping on the edge of a wide board and cut off later, than to start with a strip only just wide enough. Work a hollow first (Fig. 7-10D), then make the outside curve over it (Fig. 7-10E), and round the part where the fingers will hook under. Thoroughly sand before cutting the handle strip from the wide board.

The end of a handle could be cut squarely across, or it might be rounded, but cutting at about 60 degrees gives a good appearance (Fig. 7-10F). Attach the handles with glue and screws from inside the drawers.

Materials List for Basic Chest of Drawers

Frame	
2 sides	$14 \times 28 \times 7/8$
1 top	13 1/2 $\times 30 \times 7/8$
1 top	$2 \times 30 \times 7/8$
8 frames	$2 \times 30 \times 7/8$
8 frames	$2 \times 14 \times 7/8$
1 plinth	$3 \times 30 \times 7/8$
2 plinths	$3 \times 14 \times 7/8$
1 back	$30 \times 30 \times 1/4$ plywood
Top drawer	
1 front	$6 \times 30 \times 7/8$
1 back	5 1/2 $\times 30 \times 5/8$
2 sides	$6 \times 14 \times 5/8$
1 bottom	$14 \times 30 \times 1/4$ plywood
Middle drawer	
1 front	$7 \times 30 \times 7/8$
1 back	6 1/2 $\times 30 \times 5/8$
2 sides	$7 \times 14 \times 5/8$
1 bottom	$14 \times 30 \times 1/4$ plywood
Bottom drawer	
1 front	$10 \times 30 \times 7/8$
1 back	9 1/2 $\times 30 \times 5/8$
2 sides	$10 \times 14 \times 5/8$
1 bottom	$14 \times 30 \times 1/4$ plywood

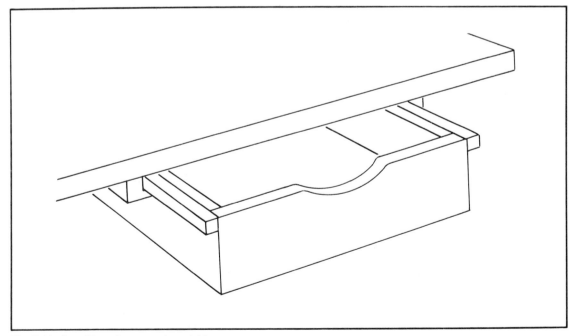

Fig. 7-11. An add-on drawer under a table.

ADD-ON DRAWER #1

A drawer can be added under a table or bench with a flat top. If the table is used as a work bench or desk, it may be convenient to make the drawer as a tray that can be lifted on top of the table so tools or papers are available for use. The drawer in Fig. 7-11 doubles as such a tray; so it is made as a box that can be slid under the table when not required. The sizes suggested (Fig. 7-12A) should suit many needs, but measure the available space and decide on what will hold the intended contents. A drawer could go right across the width of a table, but then it might take up too much space on the work surface when lifted out. It could be made almost any depth, but again you must consider its bulk when brought out. It might be deep enough to have a smaller tray inside, which either slides or can be lifted out separately.

The bottom could be glued and screwed on, in the simplest construction, but it would be neater in a rabbet, and stronger if the plywood fitted into grooves (Fig. 7-12B). Corner joints could be any of those already suggested, but as this is primarily a work tray, through dovetails are shown all around (Fig. 7-12C). If you want

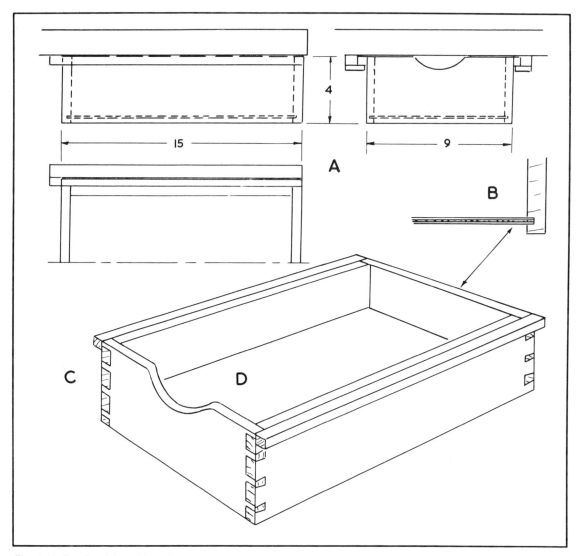

Fig. 7-12. Details of the add-on drawer.

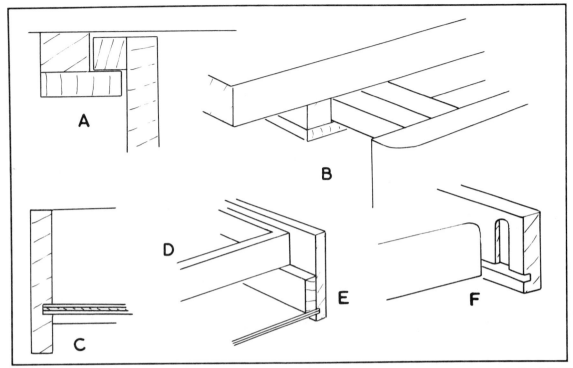

Fig. 7-13. The drawer fits on built-up strips (A,B). Its top may extend below as a handle (C). A tray may be fitted (D,E) and the back let into a groove (F).

to cut the joints by machine, the corners could have stopped dovetails, but in both cases allow for the bottom grooves to be hidden by half a tail.

A metal or plastic handle might be fitted to the front, or you could make a wood one, but a hollow to put a hand in is shown in Fig. 7-12D. A hollow has the advantage of avoiding a projection, which could be a nuisance at a bench front, and is both cheaper and lighter than a handle.

Attach the strips to the sides from inside the tray, using glue and screws. This is better than having screw heads outside against the runners. The supports are shown built-up (Fig. 7-13A), although they could be machined from solid wood. It is easier to get smooth-running surfaces by building up, but make sure no blobs of glue are left inside. Allow for screwing upward into the underside of the tabletop. Make the supports longer than the tray so you can add a stop to each at the back. It should be possible to locate them before screwing to the table, otherwise it would be awkward screwing each little block in position.

The supports could be hidden by putting a false front on the drawer (Fig. 7-13B), wide enough to overlap them.

For shop use you can use a piece of plywood, but for a better appearance you should use solid wood to match the drawer and table.

If it is not important that the drawer should lift out to become a tray resting flat on the tabletop, the front could be extended downward to form a handle (Fig. 7-13C). The extension does not have to be much—less than 1 inch will be enough to put fingers under. It will probably be sufficient to leave the edge with just the sharpness taken off the angles, but you could make a hollow near the center for a more comfortable pull. Even if the tray is to be put on the tabletop, the extension could be allowed to hang over the table front and would then act as a stop to prevent some movement of the tray.

A second tray inside could be full-size, but would have to be able to be lifted out to expose things below it. A sliding tray may be better (Fig. 7-13D). If the whole drawer is not very deep, the inner tray runners may go to the bottom (Fig. 7-13E). An alternative to a sliding tray is a front compartment for small things, like pens and pencils. Round its top and make dado grooves for it so it can be fitted as the drawer is assembled (Fig. 7-13F); otherwise you will have to nail or screw through the sides and bottom.

Materials List for Add-On Drawer 1

2 sides	4 × 16 × 1/2
2 ends	4 × 10 × 1/2
1 bottom	10 × 16 × 1/4 plywood
2 runners	1/2 × 17 × 1/2
2 guides	3/4 × 17 × 5/8
2 guides	1 1/4 × 17 × 3/8

ADD-ON DRAWER #2

Many benches and tables have a deep rail under the front. In some cases it may be possible to put a drawer under that, but usually if you want to add a drawer, it has to go through a rail. This involves a different construction, because you cannot hang the drawer by its top. Instead, it is necessary to make a hole through the rail and build a structure behind it for the drawer to slide into (Fig. 7-14A).

You will have to examine the structure under the tabletop to decide what size drawer is possible. The front

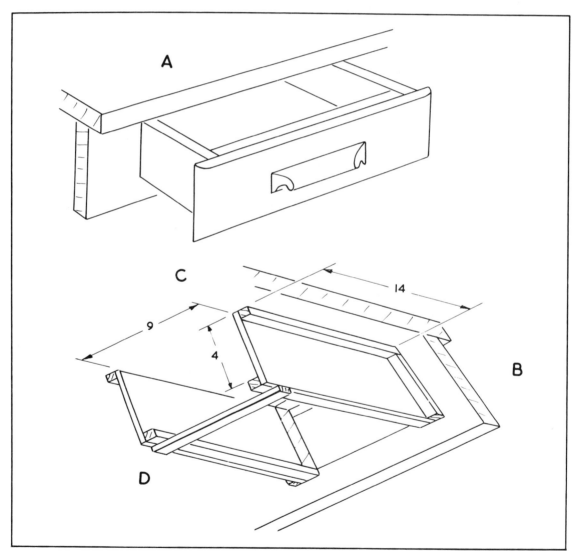

Fig. 7-14. A drawer added to a table top with a deep rail.

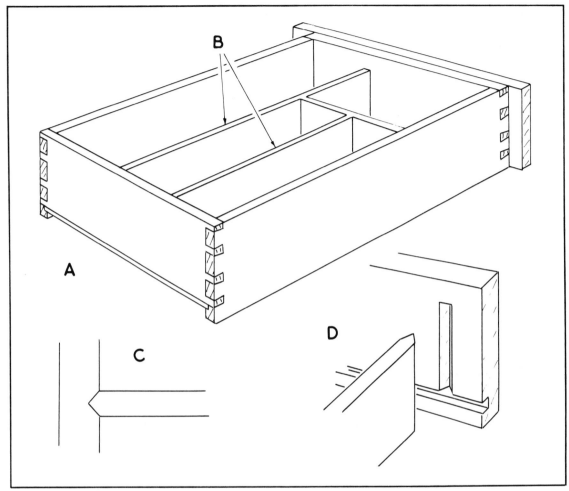

Fig. 7-15. Details of the drawer with partitions.

rail is there for a purpose, so you must not cut it away too much. It stiffens the whole table and provides support for the top. Fortunately, its lower edge contributes most of the stiffness, so if you leave a reasonable amount of wood below the opening, that should be satisfactory. Cut the opening before you make any drawer parts. Square it and get the edges straight. An overlapping drawer front will hide the gap, but do not count on it disguising any but the smallest irregularities. Use the opening as a guide when making other parts.

Behind it must come an assembly of two sides with runners (Fig. 7-14B). If you have cut away the rail fully up to the underside of the tabletop, there will be no need for kickers, but if the top of the opening is lower, include kicker strips along the sides. Sizes are suggested in Fig.

7-14C. Stiff plywood sides, with the other parts glued and screwed to them, should be satisfactory. See that the assembly is square to the front rail. Hold the rear ends at the correct distance apart with a stay underneath (Fig. 7-14D).

The drawer could be made as a tray in the way described in the previous example, but as shown it is a conventional drawer with dovetailed corners and a false front (Fig. 7-15A). Round the edges of the front, except where it comes under the tabletop, and provide a handle, either bought metal or made of wood.

There could be a sliding tray on runners along the drawer sides, or a front compartment, as in the previous drawer. If you want more compartments, they could be made with quite light sections of wood so the divisions

127

themselves do not take up much space. For cutlery there might be divisions arranged over a piece of cloth glued to the bottom before they are fitted (Fig. 7-15B). With straight-grained stiff wood, they need not be much more than 1/8 inch thick.

With wood as thin as that, dado joints are difficult, and there is not enough thickness for screws. One way of dealing with the ends is to cut them pointed to fit in V grooves (Fig. 7-15C), either full depth to put in after the drawer has been made, or stopped, so they have to be positioned before the bottom is slid in from the back (Fig. 7-15D).

Materials List for Add-On Drawer 2

2 sides	4 × 16 × 1/2
1 front	4 × 10 × 1/2
1 front	4 1/2 × 11 × 1/2
1 back	3 1/2 × 10 × 1/2
1 bottom	10 × 16 × 1/4 plywood
2 guides	5 × 16 × 3/8 plywood
4 guides	3/4 × 16 × 1/2
2 fillets	3/4 × 5 × 1/2
1 stay	3/4 × 12 × 1/2

CHEST OF DRAWERS USING POWER TOOL CONSTRUCTION

Many chests of drawers can be made with hand tools or combinations of hand and power tools. Most designs are adaptable to many techniques. If you have the means of cutting dovetails with the aid of a jig and a cutter in a power drill or by other machine methods, drawers can be joined with the usual type of stopped dovetail. If you have a router, it will cut simple dadoes and others with dovetail sections; then with other cutters you can make moldings or do surface decoration.

This chest of drawers (Fig. 7-16) is designed to suit a router and a dovetail cutter. If you do not have these tools, something very similar could be made with hand tools.

The drawer fronts extend below the drawer bottoms; then there is a gap so fingers can be put in to pull any drawer out, without the need for handles on the surfaces. To disguise the plainness of the front, there can be surface decoration, done with the router or by other means. The drawers are supported by strips on the chest sides, which fit into grooves cut with the router.

The chest sides could be solid wood or particleboard veneered to match the solid wood of the drawer fronts. The top could also be veneered particleboard, and it would

be possible to make the drawer fronts of this material, but they might be better made of solid wood. Plywood makes the drawer bottoms and the chest back.

The sizes shown in Fig. 7-17A will make a chest taller than it is wide or deep, but the method of construction could be used for any other size. Lay out one side, so you can see the drawer sizes and the positions of other parts. The drawer fronts overlap the sides (Fig. 7-17B). The top is framed around, with the front framing extending over the top drawer (Fig. 7-18A). There is similar framing at the bottom, but that is set back to give clearance for gripping and pulling the bottom drawer (Fig. 7-18B). All of the framing should be doweled to the sides. The plywood back goes into rabbets in the sides and against the back parts of the top and bottom framing. Prepare the plywood, and it could be positioned temporarily, but it helps to have it out of the way while you are fitting the drawers.

Towards the front, but set back far enough to clear the fingers, are three strips across (Fig. 7-18C). They do not have to support drawers, but they are arranged between drawers as spacers to hold the chest sides at the correct distance, without fear of warping, which would affect the fit of the drawers. Dowel the ends to the sides.

The drawer runners will be glued and screwed to the sides, with their front ends set back 3 inches (Fig. 7-17C). Do not fit them until you have made their drawers; then you can adjust their positions to get the action smooth and level.

Below the bottom frame there is a plinth set back level with the frame front (Fig. 7-18D) and doweled to the frame and to the sides. With all of the crosswise parts made, join them to the chest sides, being careful to make them square across the assembly, otherwise there will be difficulty in getting the drawers to function properly. The top of the chest overlaps half the thickness of the sides and the same amount at the front (Fig. 7-18E). At the back it will cover the plywood against the top frame. Prepare it, but do not fit it finally until after the drawers have been made and tested; then it will be glued and screwed from below.

The drawers are all made the same way, but of different depths. Cut the wood for the front of a drawer to a length that will cover the chest sides. Its width should be enough to come 1 inch below the drawer sides. Cut the wood for the drawer sides, with a little excess length at first. Mark out each pair to match. At the back allow for a dovetail joint above the plywood bottom (Fig. 7-19A), which goes into the usual groove in each side, or it may be better with its own strip (Fig. 7-19B).

At the front use a dovetail dado cutter in the router

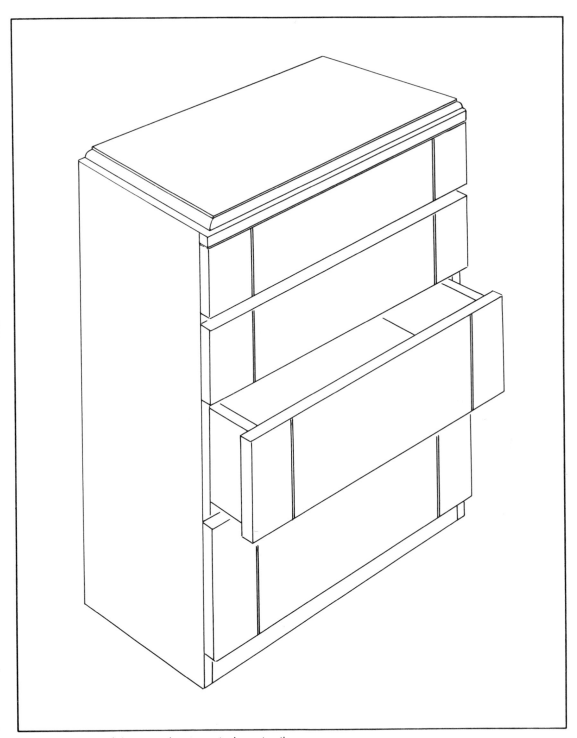

Fig. 7-16. A chest of drawers using power tool construction.

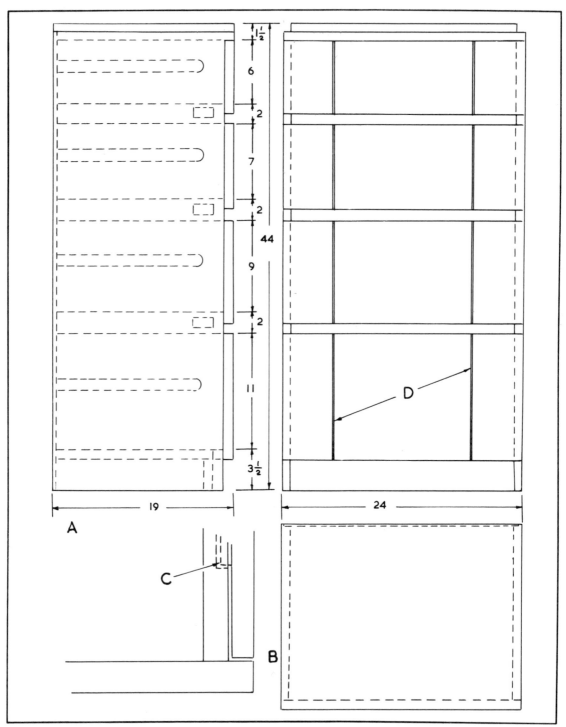

Fig. 7-17. Sizes of the chest of drawers using power tool construction.

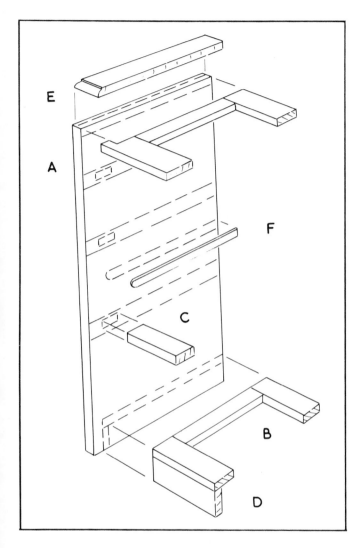

Fig. 7-18. How the main parts of the chest of drawers fit to a side.

to make the joints. With a suitable guide, it can cut both parts (Fig. 7-19C). Arrange the joint so the dado is stopped at the bottom, and the side enters the front from the top. For the front edge of the plywood bottom, the router could be used to make a groove between the dadoes (Fig. 7-19D), or there could be a similar strip to those at the sides.

Make the groove for the runners with one wide dado cutter in the router, or with several passes of a narrower one. The closed end can be left rounded (Fig. 7-19E) or it could be cut square with a chisel. The best position for each groove is just above half the depth of the side.

Have the drawers marked out to give some clearance at the sides; the amount depends on your skill in fitting,

but up to 1/8 inch between the drawer side and the chest side may be acceptable. Some of the slackness can be taken up when you fit the runners by adjusting their thickness, which could be planed to a limited extent after assembly.

Assemble the drawers, remove excess glue, and plane off any excess wood at the joints. Make the runners (Fig. 7-18F), which should all be the same if your drawers are to match in width. In the final assembly, the drawers should slide easily on their runners without excessive wobble or play; so you may wish to make them a little too thick at first and plane them down as you fit each pair and their drawer. Round the front ends of the runners if the grooves are rounded.

Locate the drawers and fit their runners. This procedure is best done in turn starting with the top drawer, but with the assembly inverted. Pack the drawer away from the top frame with paper, to provide clearance, then mark and fit the runners, working from the back. A temporary assembly with a screw near the back and front in each runner will show you if the drawer will push in and out correctly, then you can use glue and more screws in the runners. For the other drawers, you will have to use temporary wood packings against the next drawer, but otherwise the method of fitting runners is the same.

The drawer fronts act as stops; so there is no need to provide stops at the back. When you are satisfied that the drawers work properly, glue and screw or nail the plywood back in place. Keep the assembly standing upright on a flat surface and stand back so you can look

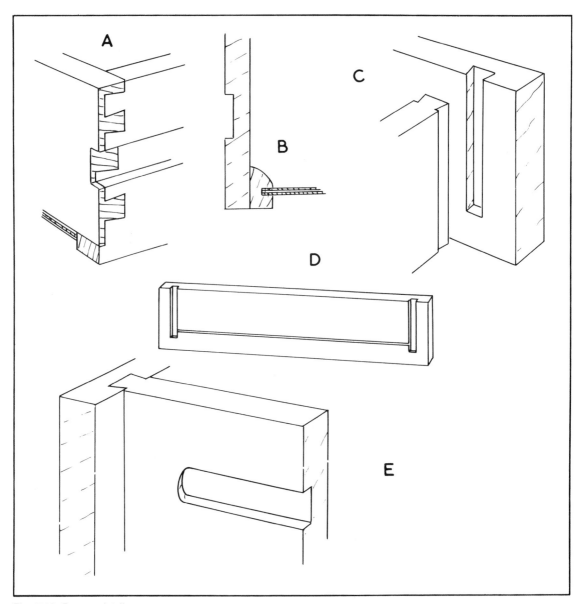

Fig. 7-19. Drawer details.

at it from all directions; then you can check the fit of the drawer fronts and the squareness of the chest. Finally add the top.

If you have used wood with an attractive grain, you may choose to leave the drawer fronts plain, but otherwise it is possible to decorator them with carving or inlays. A simple treatment is a narrow groove near each side, running up and down all the drawers (Fig. 7-17D) and filled with paint of a color to contrast with the surrounding wood. The grooves need not be much more than 1/8 inch and could be made with a router cutter with a semicircular end, either on individual fronts before assembly or across them all after assembly. With a fence running along the chest sides, the latter method would ensure all the lines match. Use polish or varnish on the wood, including in the grooves. When a sufficient amount has been applied, put paint in the grooves and immediately wipe off surplus that has spilled onto the surrounding wood to keep all color restricted to the grooves. If you paint before the wood has been sealed with varnish, the paint will seep along the grain, and you will not get a clear outline to a groove.

Materials List for Chest of Drawers Using Power Tool Construction

Frame

2 sides	$18 \times 44 \times 3/4$
1 top	$19 \times 24 \times 3/4$
4 frames	$3 \times 24 \times 3/4$
4 frames	$2 \times 18 \times 3/4$
3 spacers	$2 \times 24 \times 1$
1 plinth	$2 \ 3/4 \times 24 \times 3/4$
1 back	$24 \times 44 \times 1/4$ plywood

Top drawer

1 front	$7 \times 25 \times 1$
2 sides	$6 \times 19 \times 3/4$
1 back	$5 \ 1/2 \times 25 \times 3/4$
1 bottom	$19 \times 24 \times 1/4$ plywood

Second drawer

1 front	$8 \times 25 \times 1$
2 sides	$7 \times 19 \times 3/4$
1 back	$6 \ 1/2 \times 25 \times 3/4$
1 bottom	$19 \times 24 \times 1/4$ plywood

Third drawer

1 front	$10 \times 25 \times 1$
2 sides	$9 \times 19 \times 3/4$
1 back	$8 \ 1/2 \times 25 \times 3/4$
1 bottom	$19 \times 24 \times 1/4$ plywood

Bottom drawer

1 front	$12 \times 25 \times 1$
2 sides	$11 \times 19 \times 3/4$
1 back	$10 \ 1/2 \times 25 \times 3/4$
1 bottom	$19 \times 24 \times 1/4$ plywood

PULL-THROUGH DRAWER

In some situations it is helpful to have a drawer that can be pulled out from either side. It could be on a bench, used at both sides, where tools in a drawer may be needed at whichever side you are working. It may be a counter or a bench used for serving or eating, where cutlery, kitchen tools, and maybe mugs, will be needed at either side. The drawer may be built into new construction, or it may be added to an existing piece of furniture. In the latter case, many of the installation problems are similar to the earlier examples of add-on drawers that work from one side only.

There are some limitations if a drawer is to be taken right through. It has to be made as a drawer with two fronts, either of which has to follow through when the other side is pulled. This means that you cannot fit overlapping fronts. Each front must be fitted flush or projecting slightly with rounded edges. You cannot support the drawer with runners in side grooves, unless the grooves go right through the two fronts, which would be unsightly, although that may not matter in a workshop situation.

Some bars and counters have the underside sloping back, which may have to be allowed for at one or both sides (Fig. 7-20A). For ease of operation, it is best to have the drawer narrower than its length across the table. If you need width, it may be better to fit two narrower drawers.

There has to be support at each end of the drawer. You may be able to have it against one end of the counter and fit runners and kickers to that. Otherwise, you must fit pieces between the counter sides. Examine the construction under the counter or tabletop. If there are only wide rails under the top at each side, the drawer may fit close under the top and not require separate kickers, but if there is framed plywood, the drawer openings will have to come under the top framing, and kickers must be taken across.

If the distance across the counter is not great, you can make top and bottom guides separately (Fig. 7-20B). Alternatively, use plywood sides with runners and kickers attached (Fig. 7-20C). If the first type of support has to extend very far, there is a risk of warping. Only a slight

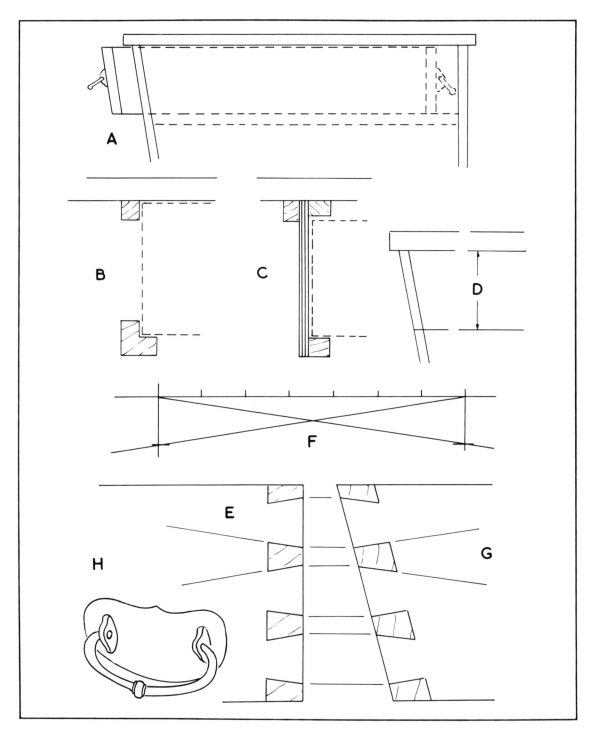

Fig. 7-20. A pull-through drawer under a bar top (A), with its supports (B-D), the layout of dovetails (E-G), and a suitable handle (H).

warp will be enough to affect the movement of the drawer; so the parts should be thick enough to be stiff, or the more rigid second method should be used.

Make sure the openings you cut are squarely opposite each other and their sizes match. If one side slopes, the opening will actually be slightly deeper on the surface than an upright one. The difference is slight, but measure it vertically (Fig. 7-20D). If you are dealing with thin plywood sides, strengthen around the openings with solid strips.

Drawer construction is normal, except you are dealing with two fronts and no backs. The plywood bottom must be fitted during assembly, because it cannot be slid in after the other parts are joined.

If dovetails are used, there is a difference in the way they are cut if the front slopes. For an upright front, their marking out is straightforward (Fig. 7-20E), but for a sloping front it would be wrong to relate the dovetail angles to the front line. If there is much slope, one side of a tail would be almost in line with the length of the wood and the other side would be at an excessive angle; so the load would be taken there by weak short grain. Because of this problem, do not mark tails with a template over the edge, nor use a guide for a power dovetailer, which also relates the cut to the edge.

The angle should be about 1 to 7 in ratio to the long side of the wood (Fig. 7-20F). Mark it both ways and set an adjustable bevel to these angles related to the sloping end of a side (Fig. 7-20G). The angles each way are different in relation to the end, but the same to the side, which is correct.

Fit the handles of your choice, but this is a place where hanging bail handles are suitable (Fig. 7-20H) because they provide a good grip when pulling a loaded drawer.

EXTENDING FLAP

It is useful to have a flap which can be pulled out when you are sitting at a bench or desk so you can have extra surface beside you. It works like a drawer, but obviously has very little depth.

In the simplest situation, there is a rail without inside framing under an overhanging top (Fig. 7-21A). The flap may be a piece of 1/2-inch plywood; so cut a slot to allow this to slide through easily. An extension of about 10 inches square is reasonable; for this you must allow more length to remain under the top when the flap is out, to prevent it from tilting. Ideally, this extra length will be another 10 inches (Fig. 7-21B), but you may have to

settle for less. Do not make it under 5 inches, however.

The guides inside are solid or built-up strips (Fig. 7-21C) similar to those for the first add-on drawer. Fit these pieces squarely under the top, using the piece of plywood for the flap as a guide to spacing. There must be enough clearance for the plywood to move easily, but keep slackness to a minimum so the flap does not sag when pulled out. If there is framing inside, and the slot has to be cut below it, the guides can be grooved strips (Fig. 7-21D).

Thicken the front of the plywood with a piece of solid wood that is the same as, or slightly less than, the amount the top hangs over the front rail. It could take the plywood in a rabbet (Fig. 7-21E); it would be stronger, however, if a tongue on the plywood went into a groove (Fig. 7-21F). To provide a grip, groove under the thickening piece, either the full length (Fig. 7-21G) or with a central hollow made with a router (Fig. 7-21H).

When you are satisfied that the flap slides as you wish, screw a strip of wood across underneath, inside the rail, to act as a stop (Fig. 7-21J). Do not glue it to the flap extension, so if you ever want to remove it to withdraw the flap, you can do so without doing damage.

For a superior flap, you can make it to suit its special purpose. It could be given a rim so it becomes a shallow tray, and small items on it will not roll off. The top could be recessed enough to take a leather or cloth panel, which would be appropriate if you are making or using jewelry. The plywood could be pierced to provide sockets for containers, glasses, or whatever you are using in a particular activity. If you make it a little deeper, it could be a shallow drawer, suitable for such things as drawing instruments or paint brushes and pencils. In that case it could have its bottom lined with cloth or plastic. There will still have to be extensions that remain inside to prevent the flap from tilting, but you may extend the solid sides only to fit in guides (Fig. 7-21K).

BLOCK OF SMALL DRAWERS

In many activities there are a large number of small items that have to be stored separately. In a woodworking or metalworking shop, there are different sizes of screws, bolts, washers, nuts, pins, nails, and other small items that should all have their own places. In many hobbies there are small parts; even in a kitchen there are small packages of food. In an office there are clips, pins, erasers, and similar things. An arrangement of a large number of small drawers will provide storage for these things, and they can be made in sizes to suit the intended contents.

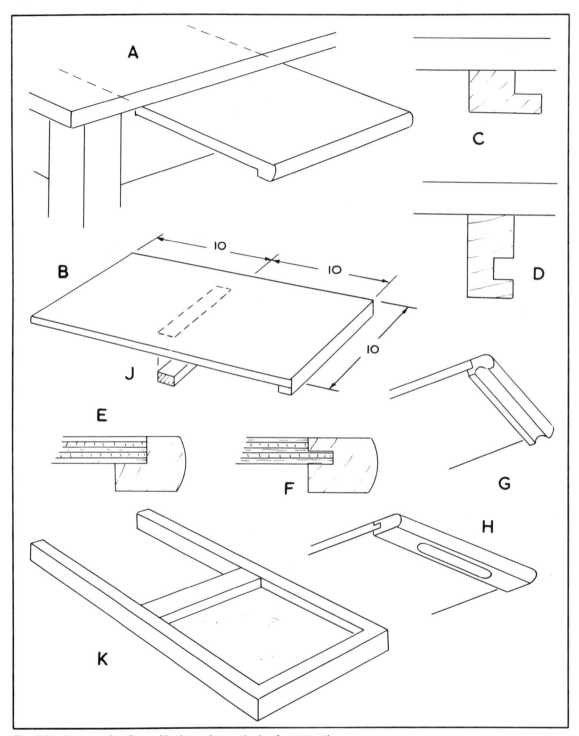

Fig. 7-21. An extending flap, with alternative methods of construction.

The old-time store keeper had a large block of drawers. When the grocer had such things as flour and sugar in bulk to be weighed as needed, a large block of drawers—often mahogany fronted—covered the wall behind his counter. Drug stores and hardware stores had similar arrangements. The block of small drawers described here (Fig. 7-22A) makes a smaller collection of containers of similar type. If you want to continue tradition, they can have wood knobs, but otherwise you can use any type of handle you wish.

Some sizes are suggested in Fig. 7-22B, but you should take into account what you want to store and make the drawer sizes accordingly, then the whole fitment can be designed around the number of drawers you think are necessary. It is usually wise to allow for a few spares as well. The rack shown has two shelves, but there could be more. To prevent the shelves from bending in use, allow for spacers at about three- or four-drawer intervals. To avoid joints that might weaken the shelves if put opposite each other, stagger the positions of spacers.

The drawers could be made with any sort of corner joints. Have the fronts thicker than the sides and backs. As with bigger drawers, dovetails would make the best joints, but simple laps glued and screwed or nailed should be satisfactory, with the front joints hidden in a rabbet (Fig. 7-23A). Bottoms may be thin plywood or hardboard and are best set in grooves (Fig. 7-23B), although they could go into rabbets or be merely nailed on.

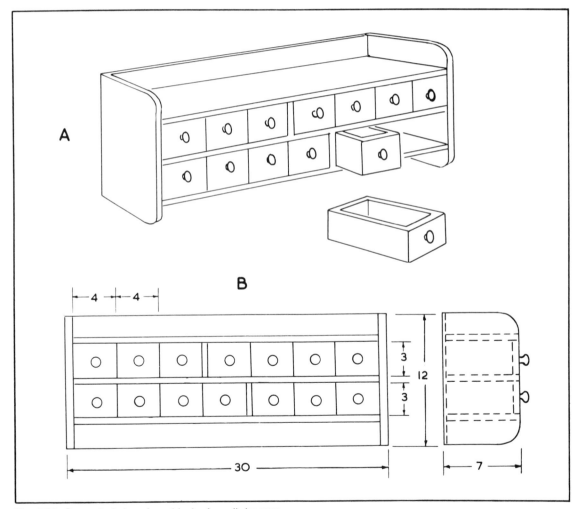

Fig. 7-22. Suggested sizes for a block of small drawers.

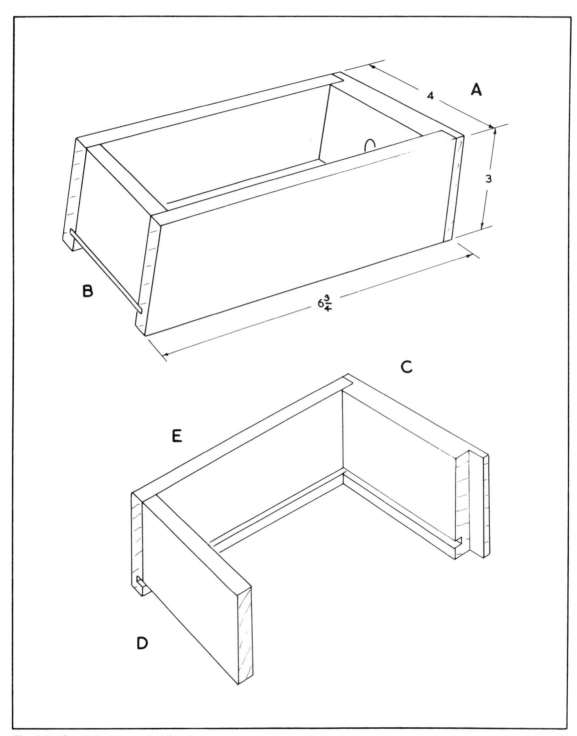

Fig. 7-23. Small drawer construction.

Decide on the drawer sizes and method of construction. Plan to make all the drawers as one batch, preparing enough wood for all parts in long lengths and doing the same jobs to each drawer in step so they will match and all be completed at the same time. They are more likely to make a good set if made that way than if you mark out and make drawers individually. Cut grooves for the bottoms in the long pieces of wood. If you are using a table saw, you can cut parts that have to match to the same length against the fence. Otherwise, you may make up stops on a sawing board for cutting by hand.

Mark out as many identical parts as possible by clamping together and squaring across to get spacing the same. Use the fronts as gauges for the other parts (Fig. 7-23C). Backs will then have to be the same length as the distance between rabbets (Fig. 7-23D) and will be cut above the bottom grooves, in the usual way. The sides fit into rabbets and against the backs (Fig. 7-23E), and the bottom slides in when the other parts have been joined.

Make up all the drawers and measure over them in groups to get the sizes for the rack. This method is easier than starting with the rack and trying to make the drawers fit, although you may have to use the second method if the finished rack has to fit a particular space.

The specimen rack (Fig. 7-24A) is intended to hold 14 drawers in two rows of 7 with spacers between 3 and 4 on each row. Its construction is like a small bookcase

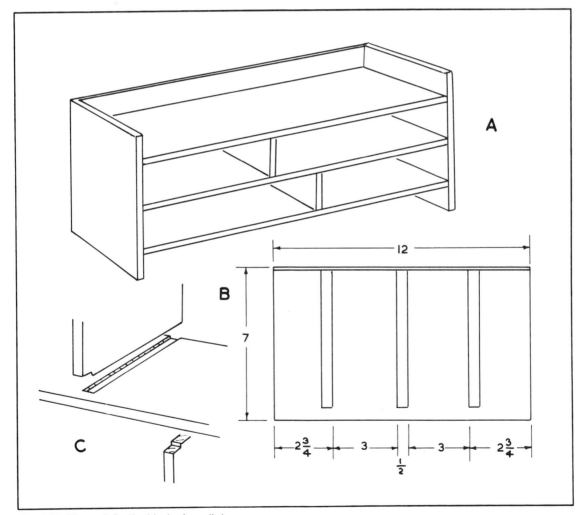

Fig. 7-24. The rack for the block of small drawers.

with a back. Prepare the pair of ends, with rabbets for the back and dado grooves for the shelves (Fig. 7-24B). Along the shelves make dadoes for the spacers, but they can be quite shallow—1/8 inch will be enough (Fig. 7-24C).

The top and bottom edges of the rack are shown cut square to allow the rack to stand on a table or bench. You could put a second rack on top of the first. If the rack is to hang on a wall, you could shape the top and bottom edges of the ends in any way you wish. If you want to make a longer rack, any reasonable length is possible, but put in spacers at intervals. Allow for the drawers to fit easily against each other, but there is no need to make anything between them. The back of the rack will be a stop to bring the fronts of the drawers level.

Materials List for Block of Small Drawers

2 rack ends	7 × 13 × 5/8
3 shelves	6 3/4 × 30 × 1/2
2 spacers	6 3/4 × 5 × 1/2
1 rack back	12 × 30 × 1/4 plywood
14 drawer fronts	3 × 5 × 5/8
14 drawer backs	2 1/2 × 5 × 1/2
28 drawer sides	3 × 7 × 1/2
14 drawer bottoms	3 1/2 × 7 × 1/2 plywood

CURVED DRAWERS

If a drawer is to be fitted to anything with a curved frontage, the size you can make it is often less than you expect. In some circumstances, the capacity possible is so small that the drawer may not be worthwhile. Much depends on the amount of curve and the shape and construction of the other parts where the drawer is to come.

If you want to put a drawer under a square tabletop, the maximum size you can make it is almost as big as the table (Fig. 7-25A) with an allowance for legs and framing. If you want to put a drawer under a round tabletop, its sides must be parallel to allow for sliding in and out; so there can be a narrow drawer across (Fig. 7-25B) or a wider one that does not go as far (Fig. 7-25C). In practice the construction under a round tabletop does not usually permit anything as big as a square top.

If there is to be more than one drawer, the possible sizes are reduced considerably. Drawers opposite each other can meet (Fig. 7-25D). Some Victorian and earlier furniture had four or more drawers fitted into a round top, but the individual sizes are then quite small in relation to the circle (Fig. 7-25E). It would not be impossible to give the drawers pointed backs to fit closer to each other, but the gain in capacity would be slight, and it is

usual to cut the backs square in the normal way. If a round table stands on four legs, they can be positioned between the drawers, without interfering with drawer construction. If the tabletop is supported by a central pedestal, its top will usually have two crossing pieces or a supporting disc, and either of these will limit drawer sizes.

Curves can be avoided if the tabletop is made hexagonal, octagonal, or with even more sides, but although that gives drawers straight fronts, their possible sizes are much the same as with a round top. For instance, a hexagonal top could have drawers on alternate sides (Fig. 7-25F). Elliptical and other curves bring complications, however. It is often difficult to make the drawer front an exact match to the curve around the cutout.

If the part to be fitted with a drawer is only part of a circle, the problems are very similar to a complete circular top. A corner shelf is like 1/4 a round tabletop. A drawer arranged radially under it has similar limitations (Fig. 7-25G) with the probable need to avoid wall supports. A drawer does not have to slide in and out radially, although that is the usual arrangement. You can fit the drawer parallel with one side of the shelf (Fig. 7-25H). That allows a greater length, but if you want to make the drawer very wide, the runner away from the wall becomes shorter with increases in drawer width (Fig. 7-25J). Taking it very far away makes it so short that runner and kicker cease to have much effect on holding the drawer when it is pulled partly out.

CURVED CORNER SHELF AND DRAWER

This is an example of a shelf fitted to the corner of a room, with its front a quarter circle and a drawer set into it (Fig. 7-26) with a matching curve. The sizes in Fig. 7-27A show a shelf that does not project much into a room, but it is large enough for a vase of flowers or a small radio or television set.

Within the 18-inch radius quadrant there is a drawer 9 inches wide (Fig. 7-27B), which allows it to be about 12 inches back to front. A wider drawer would lose quite a lot of that depth. The front is 6 inches high; the drawer 3 inches (Fig 7-27C). It is unwise to use up too much depth for the drawer since the front of the drawer and its surround might distort slightly in relation to each other if there is not much width of wood above and below the drawer.

Match the angle of the top to the corner it is to fit. Not every room is exactly 90 degrees, and it is more important that the shelf matches than that it should be any exact angle in degrees. The top could be 1/2-inch plywood, with half-round edging glued and pinned on (Fig. 7-27D).

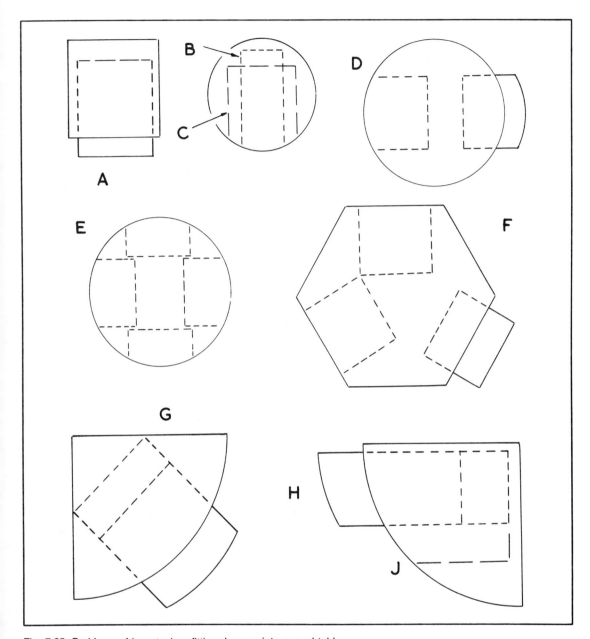

Fig. 7-25. Problems of layout when fitting drawers into curved tables.

Use the underside of the top to mark out the positions and shapes of other parts.

The curved front is too big to cut successfully from one piece of wood. It would be wasteful, and most craftsmen do not have the facilities for cutting curves in wood as thick as that. Instead it is suggested that the front is built up by laminating blocks, which are then faced with veneer bent around (Fig. 7-28A). By using wood 1 1/2 inches thick, the drawer opening can be included as the blocks are built up, thus avoiding special cutting later.

141

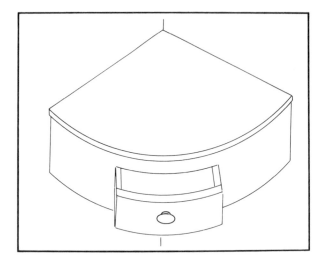

Fig. 7-26. A curved corner shelf with drawer.

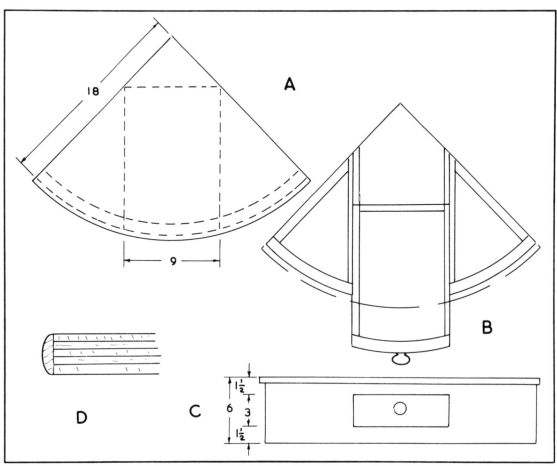

Fig. 7-27. Sizes and parts of the curved corner shelf with drawer.

142

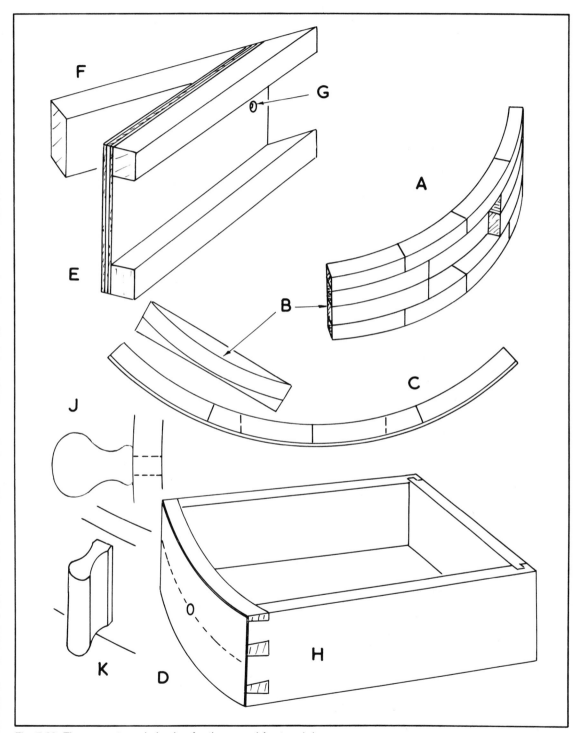

Fig. 7-28. The supports and shaping for the curved front and drawer.

For the center layers, the blocks can be single lengths each side of the opening (Fig. 7-18B). Top and bottom layers are divided so joints are staggered (Fig. 7-28C). In that way, none of the blocks have to be cut wastefully. Make a hardboard or plywood template of the curves, inside and out, longer than any block, and use that to mark the shapes to be sawn. Make the whole assembly too long so it can be treated as one piece of wood when trimming the ends.

The inside of the curved front will not show, and its finish is not important, except that it should be accurate around the drawer opening and where other pieces will meet it. The outside curved surface should be brought to an accurate shape. Look around and across, also testing the second direction with a straightedge. You may like the laminated appearance and decide to leave it uncovered. It would then match any butcher-block furniture nearby. Otherwise, glue veneer around it.

Make the drawer front to match the shelf front. It could be made of two or three glued blocks (Fig. 7-28D), veneered or not, to match. As with the shelf front, make it long at first, then carefully square the ends and match drawer and opening with just a small clearance allowance. Get this part done before you make the inside parts so you can match them to these visible parts to get an overall correct appearance.

Make the drawer guides from plywood with runners and kickers attached (Fig. 7-28E). Put blocks outside the forward ends of the guides to attach them to the sides of the drawer opening in the curved front. Shape the edges of the plywood guides and these blocks to the curve of the front so you get a close fit; the guide joints will show if the drawer is pulled right out. At the back it is best to taper the runners and kickers to the wall if the drawer is to go to the absolute limit. If you settle for a slightly shorter drawer, the ends of these parts may be cut square.

There are strips (Fig. 7-28F) between the ends of the front and the guides for attaching to the wall. The shelf has to be mounted by reaching underneath and driving screws into the walls. To allow for two screws each way, drill for one screw through each guide, underneath its kicker, where it overlaps the side strip (Fig. 7-28G).

The drawer is made up in the usual way, with the front dovetails or other joints cut into the ends of the curved front in the same way as would be done to a straight front (Fig. 7-28H).

Because of the curve, many normal drawer handles cannot be fitted, but a knob with a dowel is suitable (Fig. 7-28J). It can be bought, or you can make your own if you have a lathe. If you prefer a straight handle, one could

be made with a narrow back to fit vertically, with screws from inside (Fig. 7-28K).

Check the action of the drawer and ease it or wax its supports before fitting the top and mounting on the wall. Use a spirit level to get the assembly level, and also check the heights from the floor. Any error will be rather obvious to a viewer across the room.

Materials List for
Curved Corner Shelf and Drawer

1 top	20 × 28 × 1/2 plywood
1 top edge	1/2 × 30 × half round
4 front blocks	2 × 10 × 1 1/2
8 front blocks	2 × 9 × 1 1/2
2 drawer blocks	2 × 10 × 1 1/2
2 wall strips	2 × 12 × 1 1/2
2 drawer guides	6 × 15 × 1/4 plywood
4 drawer guides	3/4 × 15 × 3/4
2 drawer sides	4 1/2 × 15 × 5/8
1 drawer back	4 × 9 × 5/8
1 drawer bottom	9 × 15 × 1/4 plywood

SIDEBOARD

A sideboard may have doors and drawers or drawers only (Fig. 7-29). The assembly is in three main parts. There is a block of drawers, arranged with three in the top row and a pair of slightly deeper ones in a second row. This arrangement could be varied to suit needs. Below that comes a plinth, which is not essential. It does, however, form a base for the block of drawers if they are to be used without a stand, and it makes a visual break between the drawers and stand, if one is used. Without the plinth, the bottom of the block of drawers can go directly on to the stand. The stand is made like the framework for a small table, with square or round legs. As shown in Fig. 7-30, the overall height of the sideboard is slightly more than a dining table, which is convenient for a person standing.

It is best if all the parts are hardwood. Oak was used for the sideboard in Fig. 7-29. Construction is shown with veneered plywood at the ends. Solid wood could be used there. The top is intended to be made of solid wood, but it could be framed plywood or edged particleboard. Suggestions are offered for decorating the fronts of the drawers and their surrounds with flutes and beads. If the wood is to be left plain, the drawer fronts could be thinner.

Start by making the carcass, which consists of two end assemblies, then three frames, which are identical in their overall sizes. Make the front corner strips (Fig.

Fig. 7-29. A sideboard with drawers.

7-31A). Rabbet them for the plywood ends and notch where each frame will come. The notches are primarily for location; so they need not be deeper than 1/8 inch. Strength will come from adjoining parts. At the rear there could be similar strips, but it is simpler to put them inside the plywood so the end plywood will overlap the back plywood (Fig. 7-31B).

Make the parts for the outsides of three frames, using dowels or tenons at the corners (Fig. 7-31C). Notch them to fit into the upright corner strips (Fig. 7-31D). Check that the parts match. Mark them for their positions so there will be no confusion after the next step. Use the middle frame as a guide for the others. Mark on its front rail where the drawer dividers are to come (Fig.

7-31E). Make the dividers and cut barefaced mortise-and-tenon joints for them (Fig. 7-31F). Cut matching joints on the top and bottom front rails. There is no need for dividers in the rear rails, but you must combine runners and kickers across the frames where the drawers come intermediately (Fig. 7-31G). The ends of the frames will also serve this purpose.

Put guides across the runners behind the drawer front dividers (Fig. 7-31H). They could be underneath as well as on top, where appropriate, but having them on the tops only should be sufficient since the drawers cannot move sideways with only bottom guides. Similar guide pieces are needed across the tops of the bottom and middle frames. In all cases, see that the widths of the guides match the widths of the drawer dividers. You should wait to fit the guides until after the frames, dividers, and ends have been assembled; then you can plane each to match its divider, as it is fitted.

Make the back and fit it temporarily to help keep the assembly square. You may, however, want to remove it for access to the backs of the drawers when fitting them.

If the drawer fronts and front framing are to be beaded and fluted, that will have to be done before assembly of the carcass. Because this step is optional, instructions for that work are given later.

The drawers can be made in any of the ways already described, but for good-quality work, dovetails should be chosen. The fronts could be finished flush, but I suggest you let them project about 1/4 inch with their edges rounded (Fig. 7-32A), whether or not there is to be surface decoration. Dovetails should, therefore, be kept far enough back to the hidden when a drawer is closed (Fig. 7-32B). It would be unwise to depend on a drawer hitting the back plywood as a stop. Instead, make the drawers about 1/2 inch short and put stops on the runners (Fig. 7-32C) or use shallow blocks under the fronts.

Turned wood knobs are appropriate on the drawers, particularly if they are decorated. Alternatively, antique-type metal handles would look better than plastic or bright metal ones.

When the drawers are all working correctly, put the back on and make and fit the top. If the top is to be solid wood, you will probably have to glue strips together to make up the width. Arrange the rear edge flush and allow overlaps of about 1 inch at the ends and front. These edges could be left square or rounded, but they will look best if molded. The choice of molding will depend on your equipment. Various patterns can be worked with a router, spindle, or special planes (Fig. 7-32D). A simple one can be made with a rabbet plane followed by sanding (Fig. 7-32E).

Because of the width of the top, it is advisable to allow for any expansion and contraction by slot screwing. Screw upward through the front rail, using plain, round holes so the wood retains the same overlap there. Along the ends, drive screws up through slots (Fig. 7-32F) and make a few similar slots across the back rails. With screws and no glue, the top can then expand and contract as it takes

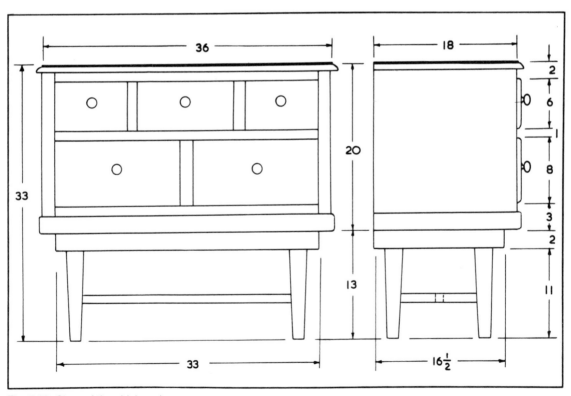

Fig. 7-30. Sizes of the sideboard.

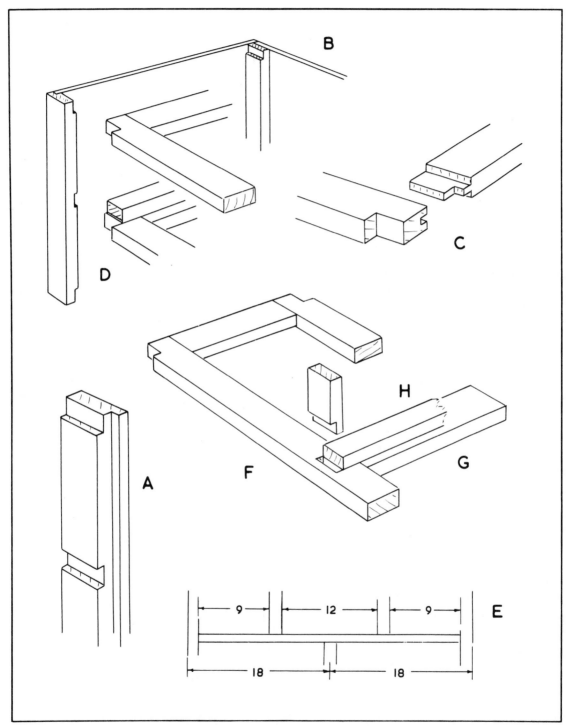

Fig. 7-31. Construction of the main parts of the sideboard.

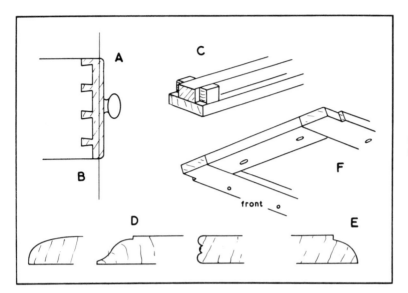

Fig. 7-32. Drawer and top details of the sideboard.

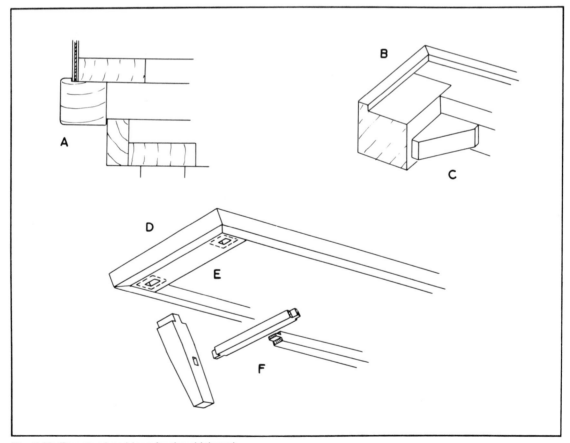

Fig. 7-33. The stand and legs for the sideboard.

up or gives out moisture from the atmosphere, without affecting the appearance at the front.

The plinth fits under the block of drawers, but is not attached permanently to it. It will then fit over the stand, but does not have to be attached firmly to it. The block of drawers should therefore, be completed before making the plinth, then its sizes taken from that. Similarly, the plinth should be completed, then the top of the stand made to fit it.

Prepare the wood for the plinth, by rabbeting so a border 1/4 inch wide is left (Fig. 7-33A). This border fits around the base of the block of drawers; so the important sizes to work to are inside the rabbet, where you allow enough clearance for an easy fit. At the corners, miter the parts that will show. Cut back so the ends butt against each other and can be doweled (Fig. 7-33B) for a stronger assembly than a miter cut right through. Round the outer edges, above and below if the drawers will

mount on a stand, but only around the top edges if it is to be used without a stand.

The stand goes inside the plinth, and its corners come against blocks glued and screwed in (Fig. 7-33C) 1/4 inch above the bottom edges. Make the top frame of the stand with mitered corners (Fig. 7-33D). At each end strips go across to take the tops of the legs (Fig. 7-33E). Tenon the strips into the long parts and glue to the ends. That will also provide strength for the mitered corners. Cut mortises in the crossbars for tenons on the tops of the legs.

The legs are shown tapered square, but they could be left parallel, be decorated with edge carving, or have their lower parts turned. There could be four lower rails, but two end ones and a single lengthwise one are shown in Fig. 7-33F. They provide rigidity to the legs; so make secure joints. There is not much area for dowels, and tenons are advisable.

If some router decoration is to be used on the front,

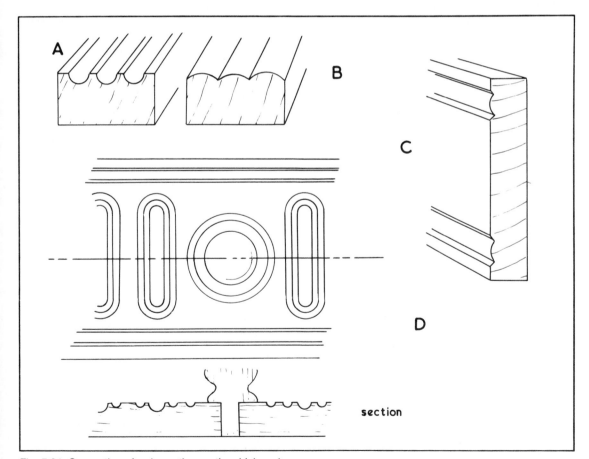

Fig. 7-34. Suggestions for decoration on the sideboard.

it could be on the drawers only, or even one drawer centrally, or it could include some of the framing. Fluting on the upright parts could be just one central strip or two or three grooves (Fig. 7-34A) taken the full length of stopped before the ends, done with a round-ended cutter in a router or spindle. A similar effect could be obtained with a round-bottomed plane.

Instead of making the curves hollows, they could stand out as beads (Fig. 7-34B). With a suitable cutter, there could be one central bead, standing above the background; three would look better on this sideboard. The plainness of the drawer fronts could be broken with beads made across parallel with the top and bottom edges (Fig. 7-34C). This might be done on the top central drawer only, but all the drawers could be done, if the uprights are also decorated.

It is possible to make more elaborate decoration with two sizes of round-ended cutters, but a template or other guide will be needed to keep the patterns regular. The design shown in Fig. 7-34D has a small, circular hollow cut round the knob; then there are larger hollows arranged vertically, with small hollows taken around them.

Materials List for Sideboard

Chest

4 corners	1 1/2 × 20 × 1
6 rails	3 × 36 × 1
6 rails	3 × 17 × 1
6 runners	3 × 18 × 1
10 guides	1 1/2 × 18 × 1
2 dividers	1 1/2 × 9 × 1
1 divider	1 1/2 × 11 × 1
2 ends	18 × 20 × 1/4 plywood
1 back	18 × 36 × 1/4 plywood
1 top	19 × 39 × 1

Drawers

2 drawer fronts	8 × 16 × 1
4 drawer sides	8 × 18 × 5/8
2 drawer backs	7 1/2 × 16 × 5/8
2 drawer bottoms	16 × 18 × 1/4 plywood
1 drawer front	6 × 13 × 1
2 drawer sides	6 × 18 × 5/8
1 drawer back	5 1/2 × 13 × 5/8
1 drawer bottom	13 × 18 × 1/4 plywood
2 drawer fronts	6 × 10 × 1
4 drawer sides	6 × 18 × 5/8
2 drawer backs	5 1/2 × 10 × 5/8
drawer bottoms	10 × 18 × 1/4 plywood

Plinth and stand

2 pieces	2 × 37 × 2
2 pieces	2 × 19 × 2
2 tops	2 × 34 × 1
2 tops	2 × 18 × 1
2 crossbars	3 × 18 × 1
4 legs	2 × 12 × 2
2 rails	1 1/4 × 13 × 1 1/4
1 rail	1 1/4 × 30 × 1 1/4

Chapter 8

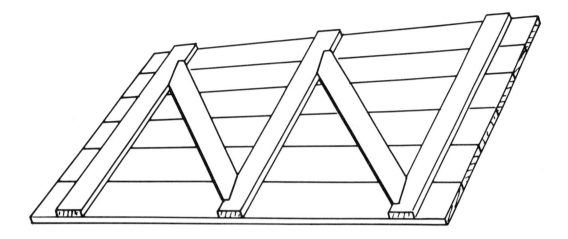

Doors

Since most storage units are fitted with doors, it is important that the craftsman making them should be able to deal with the many forms they can take. In many cupboards, closets, and cabinets, the doors are the most prominent parts so they should have a good appearance. A door is often a design feature; so it should look attractive and blend into the whole piece of furniture. In most furniture, it is the only moving part, and should be made to function properly so it swings on its hinges and opens or closes without either leaving a wide gap or rubbing against its surround. It may have to be fastened with some form of catch, or there may be a lock. The possible forms that a door can take are almost infinite, but many of the usual types are described in this chapter and in examples that follow later in this book.

Doors can be made of solid wood, particleboard, or plywood. The choice may depend on materials used for other parts of the furniture, but it is important that a door keeps its shape, remains flat, and does not expand or contract; otherwise its fit will be affected by its environment. A door that twists or expands with changes in the humidity of the surrounding air will be a nuisance; so it may be necessary to choose a different material for a door from that used for the rest of the item. Fortunately, with modern veneers and other surface treatments, it is possible to get a matching appearance between different base materials.

HINGES

A door is *hinged* when it is provided with a pivot so it can swing open and closed. We usually think of a hinge as being a metal arrangement that is screwed on, but there are other ways of making a pivot. For instance, a door between top and bottom parts which overlap the sides of a cabinet can have screws as pivots (Fig. 8-1A). Top and bottom screws must be carefully lined up, and washers will give clearance. The back of the door edge should be rounded to keep it away from the fixed edge behind it as it swings. For a larger and heavier door, it may be better to use dowel rod pivots (Fig. 8-1B), but the principle is the same. For greater strength there could be metal rods. As an example, a large door for a built-in closet could have a metal rod into a plate in the floor at the bottom (Fig. 8-1C) and the top arranged as described for a dowel, if that would be appropriate, or a metal plate extension used (Fig. 8-1D). Whatever method is used for hinging on screws, dowels, or rods, it is wise to make

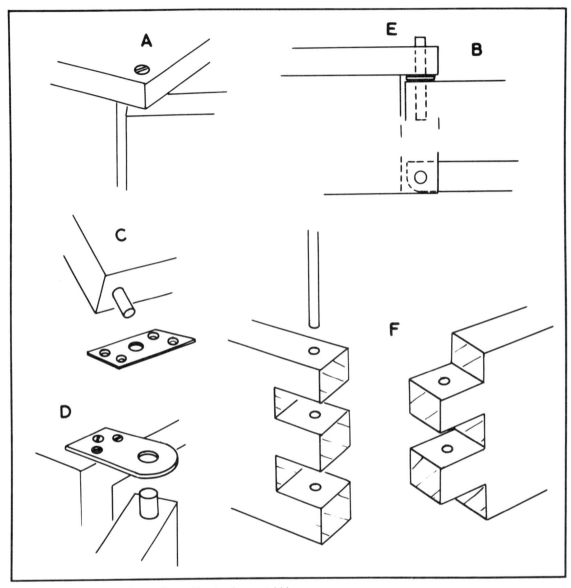

Fig. 8-1. Some ways to pivot a door without using metal hinges.

removal possible so you can take a door away if necessary. Usually the top pivot pin can be arranged to project slightly; then it can be gripped to pull upward (Fig. 8-1E).

A development of this hinging arrangement uses interlocking fingers with a wire or rod through them (Fig. 8-1F). It is found in the brackets under a folding flap on some tables, but it could be used for a small door. For strength, the grain must run across both parts, which is

possible for a small compartment where the door is wide in relation to its height.

Surface Hinges

The simplest way to arrange a metal hinge is to put it on the surface. In old furniture the hinges were made for a particular job by the local blacksmith and were screwed to the front of the door and its support. Some of the hinges were very decorative, and they formed a feature of the whole design. Such large hinges also served to spread the attachments and provide strength to a heavy door. Modern T and strap hinges are used in the same way (Fig. 8-2A), but most of them are plain and would not be regarded as decorative. Besides spreading the load over widely spaced screws, the long, stiff straps help to minimize the risk of warping or splitting wood. Such hinges are mostly on large doors used outside or where appearance is of secondary importance. In some situations, the spread over a great width of door is more important than the less attractive appearance. Where the assembly is painted, the hinge arms are not very obvious, but it is difficult to hide them when the wood is oiled or varnished. Then, it may be preferable to actually emphasize the hinges by painting them a distinctive color.

Black hinges on varnished wood will give a sturdy and tough look, if that is what you want.

There are smaller hinges intended to be mounted on the surface of furniture. They usually have a decorative outline and may be made of brass or given an antique finish (Fig. 8-2B). Several sizes are available, and they are more suitable for reproduction furniture than most modern items. There are plainer versions as well, and they may be used for more utilitarian doors where strap or T hinges are not needed. Plastic versions of these hinges are also made, but they tend to be rather bulky, which may not matter is some situations.

As with any hinges, when you fit surface hinges, make sure they are square to the door edge, and knuckles of a pair are in line (Fig. 8-2C); otherwise the door will not swing smoothly, and screws will be strained. The number of hinges to use, the size to have, and the spac-

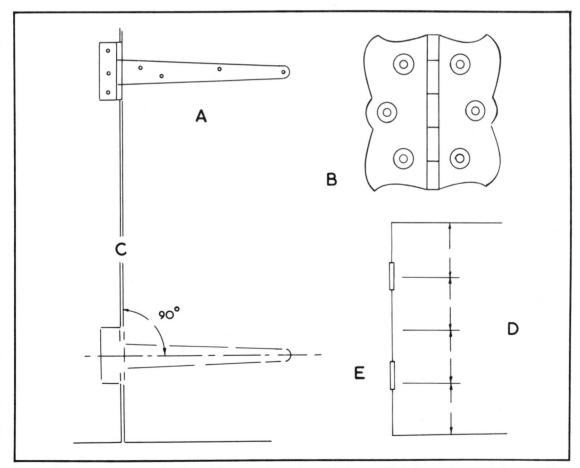

Fig. 8-2. T hinges (A) and decorative hinges (B) screw on the surface. Knuckles must be in line, and spacing is important (C-E).

153

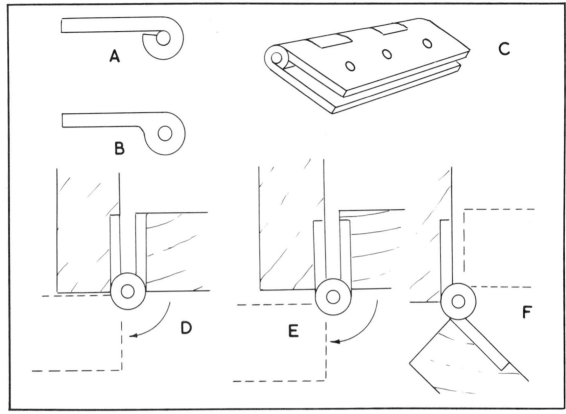

Fig. 8-3. Butt hinges may be wrapped or cast (A-C). The position of the knuckle affects the swing of a door.

ing of them is largely a matter of experience. Look at other similar doors to check the hinges on them. As a rough guide to start planning hinge spacing, divide the door height into four (Fig. 8-2D). Put the top hinge 1/4 the way down, but because of optical illusion, place the bottom hinge a little higher than 1/4 up from the bottom (Fig. 8-2E). Variations from these positions will not matter. Having the hinges too near each other is unsatisfactory, however, and having them very near the ends is only justified if the door is so relatively tall that you put another hinge at the center.

Butt Hinges

Common hinges may be described as *butt hinges* to distinguish them from other hinges. Although they are sometimes screwed to the surface in less important work, they are meant to come between the edge of a door and its post, which form a butt joint, hence the name. Hinges are made in all sizes—from tiny ones for such things as

jewel cases, to very large ones, bigger than would be needed for furniture. Steel is the choice if nothing else is required, but for furniture, brass is often chosen because of its resistance to corrosion. There are other materials available, too. The cheapest hinges have the flaps made of sheet metal wrapped around the pin (Fig. 8-3A), but more expensive brass hinges and large steel ones are cast, so the knuckle around the pin is solid (Fig. 8-3B). Even in brass hinges, the pin is steel for strength, but for a better resistance to corrosion, it could be brass or stainless steel.

If a hinge is closed, the flaps come parallel, but do not touch (Fig. 8-3C) to give clearance to the screw heads if they have not sunk flush in the countersunk holes, which are made to suit a particular gauge size of screw. If you want to use screws of other sizes, you must drill out and countersink to suit, but it is normally advisable to use the gauge the makers have drilled for and get differences in strength by using screws of an appropriate length.

The amount of clearance between the closed flaps

154

of a hinge is the maker's estimate of the clearance you will allow between the door edge and post, but you can vary that by cutting out different amounts. If the hinges are merely screwed on without letting in, the clearance at the door edge will be considerable, which may not matter if what you are making is something unimportant in appearance, such as outside storage for garden tools. For most things you make, however, the hinges should be let in.

The door swings about the center of the pin through the hinge knuckle, so it must be arranged to give enough clearance. If the center of the pin is in line with the edge of the door, it should just swing clear of the flat side (Fig. 8-3D), but it is usually moved a little further out to provide clearance (Fig. 8-3E). Sometimes the door is set in slightly from the surrounding wood. In that case the knuckle must be far enough out to swing clear (Fig. 8-3F). Sometimes it is unnecessary for the door to swing a full 180 degrees and then the knuckle level with the door edge will be satisfactory, but if it is possible to push the door further, even unintentionally, screws could be strained if the wood parts meet.

It is usual to let hinges in equally at each side (Fig. 8-4A). If you are satisfied with the clearance the hinge makers have allowed, let each flap in flush (Fig. 8-4B), but usually you can get a better looking, and still adequate, clearance by letting one or both flaps in a little more (Fig. 8-4C). You do not have to let in parallel. The clearance between screw heads can be improved by sloping the recess for one (Fig. 8-4D) or both flaps. If you let a hinge in too deeply so the clearance at the door edge is insufficient, and you do not want to plane off the door edge, pack out the hinge with a piece of cardboard.

Other Hinges

There have been a number of ingenious hinges developed in recent years, mostly for use in the mass production of furniture from veneered particleboard, but many of them are suitable for use with individual pieces of furniture. There are butt hinges with rounded corners (Fig. 8-5A) that can be used in similar situations to ordinary butt hinges. The recesses can be cut with a suitable cutter in a router, and there is no need to then square the corners by hand work with a chisel.

With particleboard it is difficult to cut clean recesses because of the tendency for wood and resin chips to break out and leave ragged edges. There are some very thin hinges intended for veneered particleboard doors, where one flap fits into the other (Fig 8-5B). The total thickness of metal in these hinges is no more than an acceptable clearance at the door edge; so the hinge does not have to be let in. Fitting then involves screwing on without any preparation other than drilling holes.

Other hinges are intended to throw clear an overlapping door and are particularly used in kitchen cabinets and similar applications. One type screws on (Fig. 8-5C) and will take the door outward as it is opened. This type is suitable for wood as well as particleboard. Other hinges give the same effect, but are more appropriate to particleboard, where they are fitted into holes made with a hole saw or drill bit, which may have to be bought specially to match the hinges. A hinge with a knuckle may be obtained angled to swing a door wider (Fig. 8-5D).

Several hinges are available to give particular actions to doors as they are opened or closed. Some are unsuitable for fitting with hand tools; so they would be unsuitable for anyone tackling a one-off project. Others may require

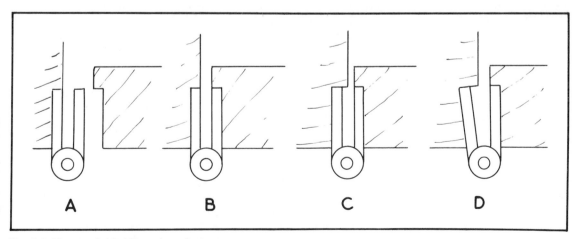

Fig. 8-4. You can let in hinges in various ways.

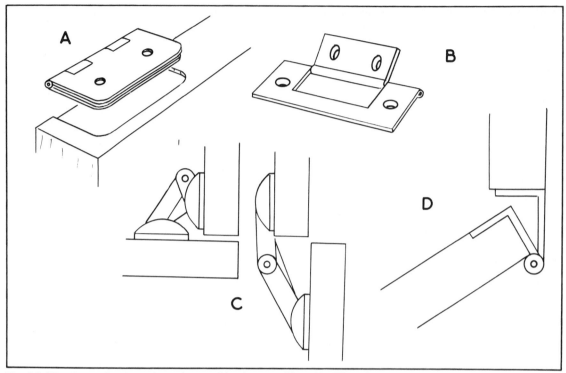

Fig. 8-5. Hinges may be shaped to suit a machined recess (A) or thin (B) so they do not need a recess. Special hinges throw a door clear (C,D).

particular attention in fitting, but if you follow the markers' instructions, you can get good results. For most things you make, however, the simpler hinges are adequate.

HANDLES

There are hundreds of handle designs, and you have a considerable choice in them when you want to match particular furniture. The methods of attachment to the doors, however, are few. In this section we are concerned with the methods of attachment and not with the overall appearance of handles.

The traditional handle is a round, turned knob. The best attachment to the door of a piece of furniture is with a dowel that is turned as part of the handle and glued into a hole, usually right through the door (Fig. 8-6A). If you turn the knob yourself and know the thickness of the door, the inner end of the dowel may be curved slightly above the level of the inside of the door.

Another type of turned knob is cut off at surface level, and there has to be a screw from inside. It is advisable

to put a large washer under the screw head (Fig. 8-6B). Some turned knobs have a short dowel intended to go into a shallow hole, which does not provide much glue area. A screw from the back is advisable. Plastic and metal knobs are made with a screw projecting. They have to be turned to drive the screw into the front of the door or drawer, and strength depends on choosing the right size hole to drill so the screw gets the strongest grip.

Straight wood handles are made in long lengths to cut off, with various forms of molding to provide the grip. They are fixed with screws from the back, with washers under the screw heads or strips of metal drilled for two or more screws, to give an even better spread of pressure (Fig. 8-6C). If you are making these handles, position screws fairly near the ends of the handles and do not drill the holes through the door any bigger than necessary for the screws to slide through. In that way you will reduce the risk of the handle twisting in use.

If a wood handle, whether turned or long, is in a different wood to the door, or you wish to emphasize the handle in any case, a piece of black or colored plexiglass under the handle gives an attractive result (Fig. 8-6D) and in the long term prevents the surrounding surface from becoming soiled.

Bought handles made of plastic or metal often have screwed rods and nuts. Except for careful marking out of the holes for them, there is no difficulty in fitting. For a good fit, tighten the nuts over washers, then cut off the surplus bolt ends and file them level with the nuts (Fig. 8-6E). In furniture, varnish over the end and nut will reduce the risk of rust, if these parts are made of steel.

For use with veneered particleboard doors and drawers, there are many forms of metal moldings for use as handles; most of them attach to the edge of a panel. One type needs a groove along the particleboard, which can usually be made by one or two passes of a table saw; then the handle molding has a projection with ridges to press in (Fig. 8-6F). A little glue can be used in the groove. When you are fitting the door, you need to allow for this handle being the full length of a side, then arrange enough space to get fingers behind.

PLAIN DOORS

Many old doors were made of single pieces of wide boards because they were available, but a piece of wood without anything to strengthen it can have problems. It may warp; its width may alter with expansion and contraction, and it may split. A single piece of wood would only be suitable today for a small door. The best wood would then be with the grain lines at the end across the thickness (Fig. 8-7A), an indication that the wood has been

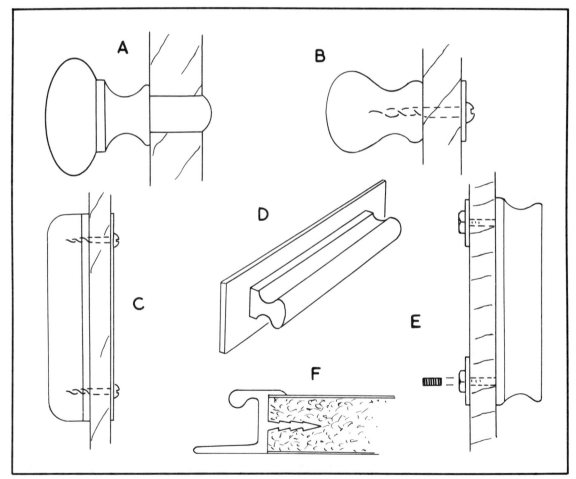

Fig. 8-6. A knob may fit through or be screwed (A,B). Strip handles can screw from the back, have guard plates, or be bolted (C-E). Special strip handles fit on the edge of particleboard (F).

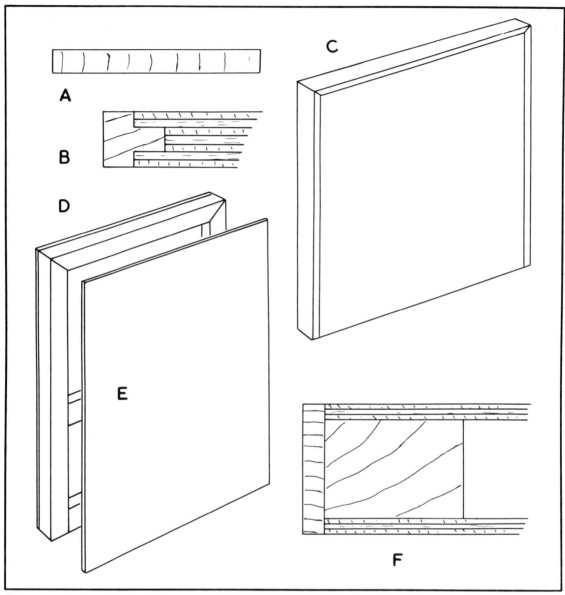

Fig. 8-7. A door may be made from plywood with solid wood edges.

radially cut. It is unlikely to split or warp. If it absorbs or gives up water, it will alter in thickness, but not to any appreciable amount in width, which is the important direction because it affects fit.

It would be better to use a panel of thick plywood or particleboard, which should retain its size in any conditions and may be expected to remain flat. In furniture a particleboard door should have its surfaces and edges veneered, then the appropriate thin hinges (Fig. 8-5B) used, so fitting to an opening is a simple process.

If the door is a single piece of thick plywood, something must be done to hide the edges and provide strength for screws in the hinges. Screws edgewise into plywood only do not have a very good grip. A solid wood lip all around, mitered at the corners and held with a tongue-and-groove joint, is best (Fig. 8-7B), but lips can be attached in other ways, depending on what equipment you have. For some doors you can lip the top and sides, but leave the bottom, which is not normally visible, uncovered (Fig. 8-7C).

One of the lightest ways to make a large, plain door is to use two pieces of thin plywood with framing strips between. In some situations it may be satisfactory to leave the plywood edges exposed; then the framing should be mitered at the top corners (Fig. 8-7D) and at the bottom if they will show there; otherwise the sides may simply overlap the bottom. Other strips can be arranged intermediately (Fig. 8-7E), either for stiffness or where external parts will have to be screwed through. There is no need to cut joints between the frame parts; they can be glued and clamped, although a few fine pins driven, sunk, and stopped in the plywood will supplement the glue and prevent movement of the parts before the glue sets.

It is wiser to assemble the door in two stages. Attach all the framing strips to one piece of plywood and let that glue set, then plane the edges and surfaces, if necessary, before adding the second piece of plywood.

If the plywood edges are to be hidden, they may be covered with thin strips of solid wood (Fig. 8-7F) glued and pinned on. Although the top corners of the framing will be hidden, you should still miter the framing pieces there, since end grain does not take glue as well as side grain, and you will get a stronger attachment of the rim strips over the mitered parts. Usually there is no need to put strips under the bottom of a door.

LEDGED DOORS

A door can be built up from several boards glued together. If the boards cannot be chosen with the end grain lines through the thickness, put them together with any curves going alternate ways on the boards (Fig. 8-8A) to reduce the effect of overall warping. If a number of

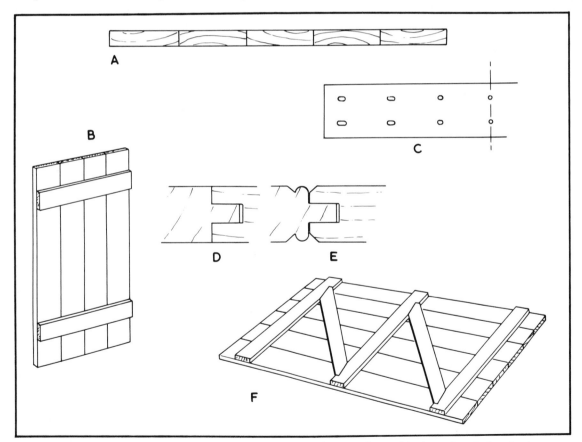

Fig. 8-8. A door made from boards must allow for expansion and contraction and be braced so it stays in shape.

narrow strips are joined in this way, the door would match butcher-block arrangements elsewhere.

A door of more than the smallest size made in this way should be strengthened and held flat with *ledgers* (Fig. 8-8B), which are strips across near top and bottom and possibly intermediately. If the door must fit into a frame, the ends of the ledgers are cut back.

In a large door, you should allow for expansion and contraction of the vertical boards. To do so do not glue the ledgers, but attach them with screws. Near the center of each ledger, put the screws through round holes, but further out use slot holes in the ledger (Fig. 8-8C) so the neck of each screw can slide sideways a limited amount. The amount of allowance depends on the wood and its tendency to expand or shrink, but on a door 24 inches wide made of softwood boards, a possible movement of 3/16 inch could be allowed for at the extremes of the ledgers, with other slots progressively less toward the center.

Large doors can be made of boards tongues and grooved together (Fig. 8-8D). Some of these boards can also be bought with a bead over the joint (Fig. 8-8E). If the boards are made into a door without glue in the joints, the gaps will open and close slightly, but the bead disguises the movement. If such a door is to be painted, you should paint the tongues before the door is assembled; otherwise bare wood may be visible along the joints if the wood shrinks much in use.

If a door is made from tongued-and-grooved boards without glue, the ledgers alone do not provide much resistance against door sagging as it hangs on its hinges. To prevent sagging, there can be braces as well. It is then called a *ledged and braced door* (Fig. 8-8F). To give absolute rigidity to the shape, the braces should be notched into the ledgers as well as be screwed to the boards and sloped up from the hinged side. this is the best construction for a door that will be exposed to the weather, and it might serve for a large closet indoors, but for most indoor situations one of the other door constructions would be more suitable.

PANELED DOORS

Before the days of plywood and other broad, flat, stable panels, any paneled work was limited by the available widths of solid wood. In addition was the need to cut the solid wood thin, which presented practical problems. Some wood allowed the cutting of fairly wide pieces, but in an average construction, 12-inch-wide panels were about the limit. Panels have been used in furniture design for a long time, but if old furniture is examined, you will see that the design was arranged so the framing divided a door or other parts into portions that would accommodate panels of wood of available width. A door we might now fit with a full-size plywood panel was divided into four (Fig. 8-9A). There is a beauty about this arrangement, and some doors and other parts of furniture may still be divided for the sake of appearance.

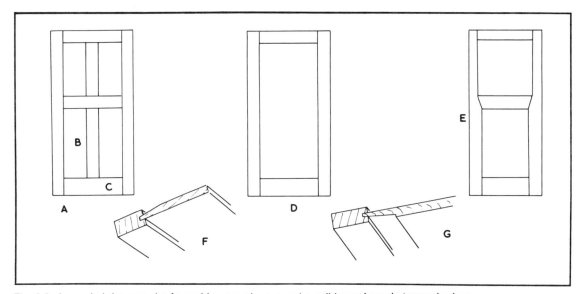

Fig. 8-9. A paneled door may be framed in several ways and a solid panel needs tapered edges.

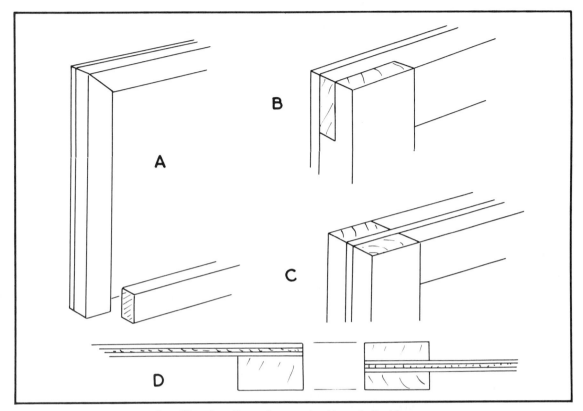

Fig. 8-10. Plywood doors can be stiffened on the surface, preferably on both sides.

When dividing a door into panels, there are optional effects to consider. In most situations the panels will be the same width, but the lower panels are deeper than the upper ones (Fig. 8-9B), and the bottom rail is made deeper than the side and top parts (Fig. 8-9C). This applies when there is only one panel. For the sake of appearance, the bottom rail is wider (Fig. 8-9D), since it would look narrower than the others if it was actually the same width.

Some paneled room doors have the upright parts wider alongside the bottom panel and are said to be gunstock stiled because the upright parts have something of the outline of a gunstock (Fig. 8-9E). It is uncommon, although not unknown, for large furniture doors to be made this way.

If solid wood is used for panels, there is a problem in achieving overall even thinness. A panel would be stronger if thicker, but that would be heavy and cause some constructional problems. We can follow the old-time methods. A panel can be reasonably thick over most of its area, but be tapered all around to fit into grooves (Fig. 8-9F); that is normally done on the back, so only the front shows a level, smooth surface. Another way of using thicker wood cuts a tapered rabbet all around the front (Fig. 8-9G). Thicker wood is less likely to develop cracks. With any solid wood panel, there has to be an allowance for shrinkage; so it is usual to put the edges in grooves that are too deep and to assemble the door with no glue around the panels.

Today, plywood is more common for panels. Hardboard might be used, but obviously would not be as strong, although it may be good enough for some painted furniture. Particleboard is too thick for panels, except in very large construction and, even then, plywood would be better. Glass panels are easy to fit, but you should fit them in a way that allows easy removal without damage to the woodwork, in case they need to be replaced.

Lapped Panel Frames

The easiest way to get a panel effect is to have a piece of plywood the full size of the door and attach framing pieces to its front (Fig. 8-10A), mitered at the corners if you wish, and with intermediate rails to divide up the appearance, if that is part of the design. Corner joints can butt against each other, or the parts could be halved (Fig. 8-10B). The inside surface can be left plain, or you could put strips there as well (Fig. 8-10C). With some plywood treated in this way, solid wood strips on one side only may pull or push the plywood to a curve as the wood loses or takes up moisture from the atmosphere; so it is better to put the plywood between two thinner pieces of wood than to have one thicker piece on one side only (Fig. 8-10D).

Using full-size plywood exposes the edges of the plies and would not be considered good craftsmanship. It's only suitable for the less important type of construction. It is better to hide the plywood edges in rabbets in the framing. How far to take it depends on the joints used in the framing. If the corner joints are to be simple laps, you should take the plywood some way into the wood (Fig. 8-11A) because nailing or screwing it against a board surface provides strength and stiffness.

The simplest way of joining the corners with this type of paneling is with half lap joints. At the front, let the

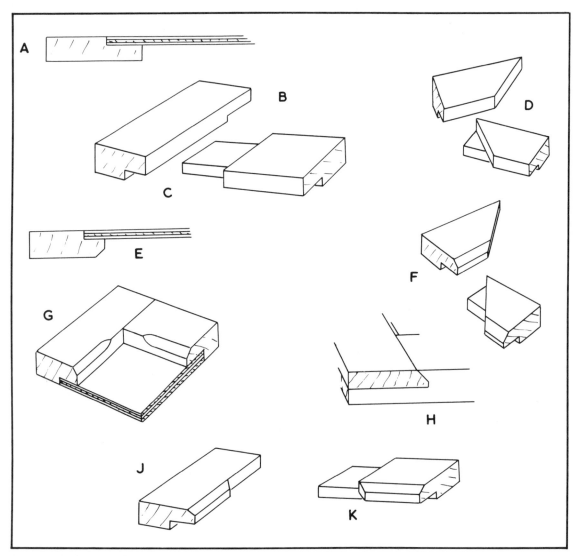

Fig. 8-11. Surface framing with rabbets can be joined at the corners in several ways.

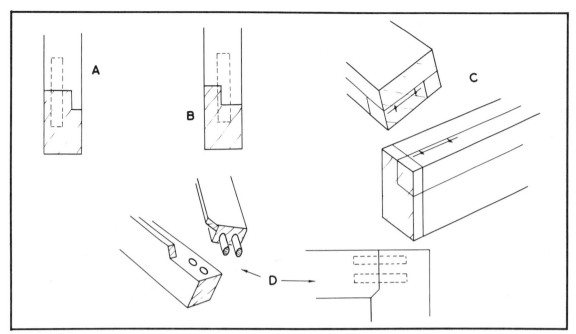

Fig. 8-12. Steps in joining the corner of a frame with dowels.

uprights follow through. A door does not look right if crosswise members go the full width of the door, and there are breaks in the appearance of uprights.

Half is cut out of the thickness of each part in the joint (Fig. 8-11B). The front part of a joint shows the full width of each piece of wood, but at the back they are notched to suit the rabbets (Fig. 8-11C). There is not a very large glue area when the rabbets are wide. If, however, all the parts of the joint and the plywood in the rabbet are glued and some pins or fine screws driven from the back, there is mutual support. A strong door should result.

It is possible to have a miter on the front in this type of joint (Fig. 8-11D). A miter, however, reduces the available glue area in a joint and is usually best avoided, unless the wood outside the rabbet is fairly wide.

There may be a chamfer or bevel on the edges of the framing around the panel (Fig. 8-11E). The edge could be molded. On a door usually only the front angles are molded, and the matching rear angles are left square, but they could be treated in the same way. If a miter is used at the front of the half lap joint, the edge treatment does not affect the making of the joint (Fig. 8-11F), but with the normal joint having the upright part following through there must be a modification. One way of avoiding alterations to the joint is to use a stopped chamfer on each piece

(Fig. 8-11G). You can easily make one with a router, but with hand tools there is difficulty in achieving even angles and ends to the cuts.

If the wood is first prepared with the chamfer or molding going the length of the pieces, there are two ways of dealing with the corner treatment. The joint can be cut in the upright part in the same way as with plain wood, but where the crosspiece meets it, the front must be scribed to fit over the chamfer (Fig. 8-11H). This process is fairly easy if it is a simple chamfer, but there are difficulties in shaping the undercut end grain if you have to match it to a molding, unless you have suitable cutters for a router or spindle.

Another way is to miter just the chamfer or molding width (Fig. 8-11J) by cutting back the edge of the upright part to the width of the chamfer, then the front of the other piece must be that much longer (Fig. 8-11K). In this way, the awkward cutting of the other method is avoided, and the small miter gives an attractive appearance to the front.

Doweled Paneled Frames

Dowels can be used at the corners of framed doors. If the panel is rabbeted in the back, there will usually be enough thickness of wood in front of it for dowels to come wholly in that part (Fig. 8-12A). One piece must be notched into the other, but except for that, marking out and drilling the joint is the same as for other doweled parts.

If there is a deeper rabbet, or the overall thickness is slight, the dowel may have to come over the edge of the rabbet (Fig. 8-12B). In that case holes should be marked and drilled on both pieces before rabbets are cut or the ends notched (Fig. 8-12C); otherwise it would be difficult to keep the drill exactly on its course.

Instead of scribing one rabbeted piece over the other, the wide part, which can be chamfered or molded, can be cut back to a miter so the doweled parts of the joint has flat meeting faces (Fig. 8-12D). In most doweled door frame joints, two dowels should be sufficient, but if the wood is thick, it may be better to use four dowels of smaller diameter.

It is more usual to groove a plywood panel into the frame (Fig. 8-13A). In most assemblies, the groove is not very deep—3/8 inch for a l/4-inch panel is typical. A doweled joint could be made with the pieces cut back to the bottom of the grooves and the remaining wood mitered (Fig. 8-13B). That method allows the two meeting faces to be flat for drilling to take dowels.

Cutting back reduces the area of the joint. In use, doors are subject to a strain which may try to make them sag. The corner joints must provide most resistance to this sagging; so they should be as strong as possible. It would also be better to keep the parts full width.

If you do so with wood of the usual proportions, the dowel diameters will be greater than the thickness of the grooves (Fig. 8-13C). As with the dowels in a rabbet, it is best to drill before making the grooves and shaping the meeting end.

Allow for a stub tenon to fit into the groove. Mark out and drill the parts, then cut the grooves and make the stub tenon to fit its groove. Let the dowel go some way into the end grain to provide strength.

Dowels could be used instead of a butt or lap when strips are put on a full-size plywood panel (Fig. 8-10A). In that construction, however, strength is provided by the plywood, and in most cases dowels would not be necessary.

TENONED-AND-GROOVED FRAMES

Most doors are held together with Mortise-and-tenon joints, and they should be the choice if the door is to have a craftsmanlike appearance. The tenons may go right through to give the strongest joints. They should be used if the appearance of the tenon ends outside does not matter; otherwise, there can be stub or stopped tenons finishing inside the wood. The method of cutting and forcing together a mortise-and-tenon joint puts a thrust on the end grain outside the mortise. At a door corner that grain may be rather thin, and therefore easily broken out; so it is usual to leave some extra length on a door side until after the door is assembled. If the door will not be immediately used, the ends can be left to protect the door corners from knocks and cut and leveled just before the

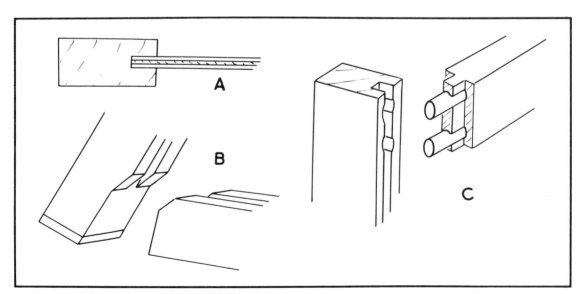

Fig. 8-13. If the panel fit in grooves, the corners of a frame can be doweled.

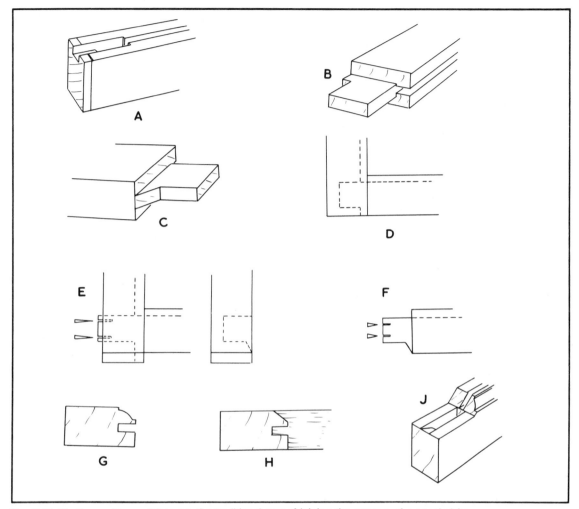

Fig. 8-14. Mortise-and-tenon joints are the traditional way of joining the corners of a paneled frame.

door is fitted.

Mortise-and-tenon joints can be used with rabbets or grooves, but for most doors plywood is likely to be let into grooves rather than rabbets. Rabbets are only used for glass (see next section). In light framing, it is possible the tenon can be the same thickness as the width of the grooves, but usually the tenon and its mortise must be wider than the grooves. The tenon of a door corner should be about 1/3 the thickness of the wood.

At the corner of a grooved frame, cut back the end that will have the tenon to the bottom of the groove and mark out the other piece with some extra at the end (Fig. 8-14A). Cut back a haunch outside the tenon, either square (Fig. 8-14B), or tapered (Fig. 8-14C) if you do not wish

the haunch to show. Cut the joint in the usual way (Fig. 8-14D). If the tenon is to go right through, make it a little too long at first and mark out the mortise at both sides so you can cut both ways and avoid breaking out the grain. If you are using stub tenons, make the mortises slightly too deep so the shoulders will pull tight as they are clamped.

If the tenon goes through, make one or two saw cuts across its end so you can drive in wedges during assembly (Fig. 8-14E). Do not cut off the wedges and the tenon end until after the glue has set. With stub tenons, you can tighten with foxtail wedges. Make one or two saw cuts and put wedges into them as you drive the joint together (Fig. 8-14F).

165

With this type of construction, arrange the grooves to be slightly deeper than the plywood panel is expected to reach so there is no risk of the plywood tightening before the corner joints are closed. A little glue in the bottom of the grooves will lock in the panel and so strengthen the construction, but be careful of using so much glue that it oozes out around the panel, where it is difficult to clean off without a trace.

If one or both edges around the panel are chamfered or molded to the corner, they will have to be treated in a similar way to that described for rabbets. If stopped decoration is used, the corner joints are not affected. For convenience in production, it is usual to make the chamfer or molding the same width as the depth of the groove (Fig. 8-14G). The upright parts of the door frame should be carried through and the crosswise parts fitted into them. You can scribe the shoulders of the tenon to the other piece (Fig. 8-14H), but unless you have a suitable router or spindle cutter, this is difficult with anything except a simple chamfer. The alternative is to cut back to the bottom of the groove in the mortised part, then the molded edge can be mitered (Fig. 8-14J), and the tenon joint becomes simple.

Where rails meet intermediately, the joints are similar, but two-sided because there are panels on each side of the part coming into the other. You can cut back to the bottoms of the grooves on both sides of the tenon where the parts are square-ended (Fig. 8-15A). If you have to consider a chamfered or molded edge, you can scribe over (Fig. 8-15B) or cut back and miter (Fig. 8-15C). These joints can be wedged like the corner joints, but the strain on them is not usually as great so it is not often necessary.

In some doors that is a wider central rail. Cutting the mortises and tenons the full width of the rail might weaken the mortised part, so it is better to use multiple tenons with stubs between taken to the same depth as the groove. This occurs with a gunstock stile with a sloping joint, but it is made in the same way, with sloping shoulders (Fig. 8-15D).

TENONED-AND-RABBETED FRAMES

If glass is to be fitted into a frame, it is usually held in a rabbet by a fillet (Fig. 8-16A). If another part of the same door framing has a plywood panel, it is best to cut the rabbet to the same distance from the surface as the groove (Fig. 8-16B). The fillet can be made to finish level

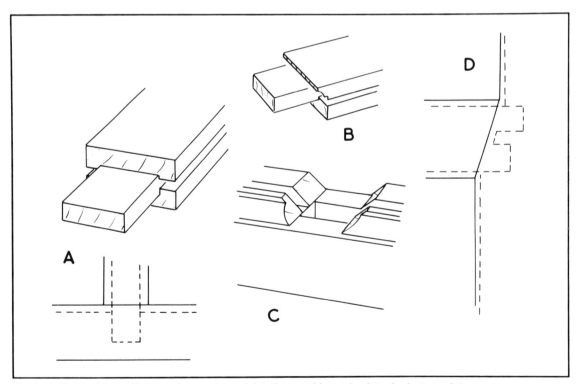

Fig. 8-15. For an intermediate mortise-and-tenon joint, the wood is cut back to the bottom of the groove.

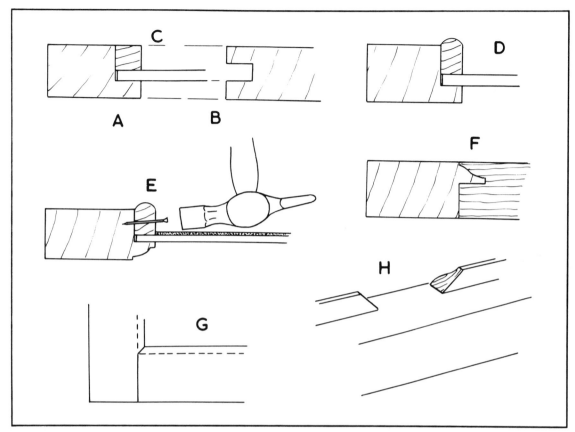

Fig. 8-16. A glass or plywood panel in a rabbet is held with a fillet. Joints can be scribed (F) or mitered (G,H).

with the adjoining wood (Fig. 8-16C) or it can project slightly with a rounded edge (Fig. 8-16D). Where the fillets meet in the corners, they should be mitered. Fix them with a few pins or fine nails only; then it is possible to lever them out if you have to replace the glass. It helps in driving the pins safely to have a piece of card on the glass on which the hammer can slide (Fig. 8-16E).

At the corner of a rabbeted frame, the shoulders of the tenoned part are stepped over the other piece. In most constructions it is possible to have the mortise and tenon wholly in the rabbet. It is not impossible to have them partly in the two levels, but cutting the joint is easier if they are not.

Cut the joints in a similar way to that for grooved parts, with square or tapered haunches outside the main tenons. Leave some excess length on the mortised parts for cutting off after assembly.

For a molded or chamfered edge, scribe the shoulder of the tenoned part over it (Fig. 8-16F) or cut down to the rabbet level and milter the parts (Fig. 8-16G). Similarly, intermediate joints can be scribed over or mitered both ways (Fig. 8-16H). If the intermediate rail comes between glass and plywood panels, it is important that the grooves and rabbets are to the same level, if you are to avoid complications in the joint. With multiple tenons on a wide rail, take the haunches below the level of the rabbet.

DOOR ASSEMBLY

The door is usually the most obvious thing when anyone looks at a piece of furniture; so it should be without flaws. It must be square and flat. What surrounds it should be square, but if there is a slight error that cannot be rectified, it is better to start with a paneled door square and then fit it by planing the outside no more than absolutely necessary.

If the panel is made square at each corner the assembly will not move far out of true. Because the plywood does not normally touch the bottoms of all grooves, however, there can be some movement. Measure diagonally inside the corners of the assembled door (Fig. 8-17A).

Sometimes joints are cut slightly out of true. If this lack of true goes the same way at each corner, the door will assemble with a twist, which must be removed. Sight across the door (Fig. 8-17B) to see if there is a twist. If the door is not very big, you can test it on a flat surface. Before the glue starts to set, force the door slightly too far the other way by holding it diagonally over the edge of a bench (Fig. 8-17C). This procedure should cure the twist, but recheck squareness in case you altered it while pushing. Leave the door on a flat surface with strips of wood across and weights on top until the glue has thoroughly set.

DOOR FITTINGS

We have already discussed hinges, but a door needs something to stop it from closing too far, something to pull it open, and usually something to hold it closed. A craftsman may call these things *door furniture*, but that name could be confusing.

If a door shuts against the outside edge of the opening (Fig. 8-18A), that opening acts as all the stop that is necessary. If the door closes inside its frame; the fastener, lock, or catch you use may also act as a stop, but in many assemblies it is advisable to provide one or more stops as well. If they come at top and bottom, and there is some sort of fastener near in the middle, they combine to hold the door in place without fear of it twisting.

There could be a stop the whole length of the clos-

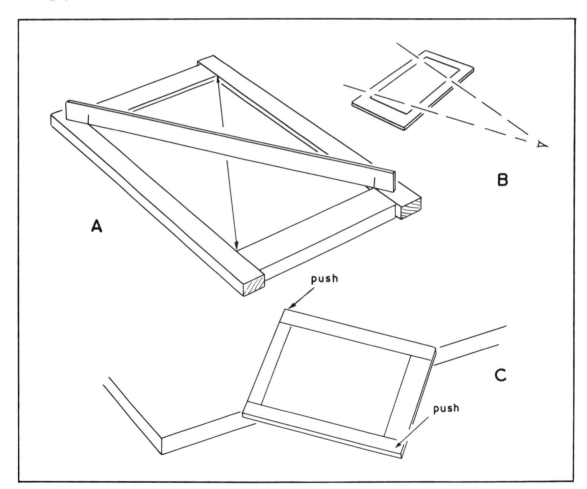

Fig. 8-17. An assembled frame should be checked square and free from twist.

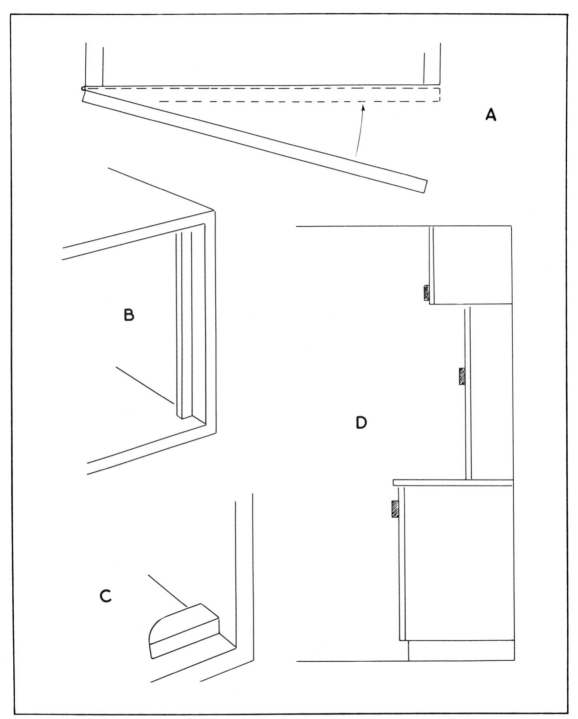

Fig. 8-18. A door on the surface will be stopped by its frame (A). Otherwise stops should be provided (B,C). Handles should be positioned where they can be reached (D).

ing side of the door (Fig. 8-18B) which could also provide draught-and dust-proofing. If either of these things are important, similar strips may go all around the opening.

It is more usual to fit small blocks as stops (Fig. 8-18C), large enough to serve the purpose, but kept small enough to be neat and with most edges rounded. They can go at the top and/or bottom of the door. In some situations it may be better to have one stop near the center of the door side.

Handles have been mentioned in connection with drawers. Their appearance and position influence the visual effect of the furniture. For a single handle to get the best pull on a door, it should be near the middle of the side and not far from the edge. In practice, the handle is placed just above the center of the side, for visual effect, if there are no other requirements. If the door is low, as it might be under a working surface, the handle could be quite close to the top. Similarly, if the door is high, it is more accessible near the bottom of the door (Fig. 8-18D).

At one time, most furniture doors were held closed by a catch which required a turn or other movement of a handle or knob on the front of the door. Catches are still available, and the handle that works the catch may be all you need to pull the door open. Many furniture doors, however, are held closed by spring or magnetic catches, and a sharp pull on the handle is all that is needed to release them. In that case the catch should be near the middle of the door edge and preferably in line with or not far from the handle used for pulling to keep any load on the door even.

If a lock is used, it will mount between the back of the door and the side of the cabinet, with a keyhole through the door. As with a catch, it should be near the center of the door edge.

Unless the door is very tall in relation to its size, it is wisest to rely on single catches, since it is often difficult to locate and operate two or more catches as you move the door, and there is a risk of distorting it. This is particularly so if you arrange catches at the extreme top and bottom of the door and have a handle near the middle.

A very large variety of door fittings is available. Handles, in particular, are very obvious in the finished furniture, and care in needed in their selection. If there are drawers as well as doors, the handles should match, even if they are not the same. Catches and fasteners must be related to the size of the door. Fortunately, most of them come with detailed fitting instructions. If you have

any doubts, look at other comparable furniture and see how the doors have been equipped.

SLIDING DOORS

If sliding doors are to be fitted, the method used depends on the size and weight of the doors. There are usually two that overlap slightly at the center when they are drawn across; so the interior is fully hidden. Both doors should be able to slide across completely so either half of the space exposed can be used for access. Unless the doors are removable, no more than half can be open at one time. The method of sliding has to be duplicated; so guides and tracks must be arranged parallel at no greater spacing than is required to let the doors clear each other. Therefore, flush handles or grips need to be used, because there is insufficient space between for projecting handles to pass.

The smallest and lightest doors can slide in grooves, but heavier doors need rollers and tracks to overcome friction and allow the doors to move easily. Examples are seen on sliding doors to rooms, and there are lighter versions for cabinets and closets. Where the door is glass or plywood up to 3/8 inch thick and of sizes such as are used in kitchen and bathroom cabinets, it is possible to arrange for sliding within the woodwork without special parts.

For small glass or plywood doors, the weight is taken by the bottom edges running in grooves (Fig. 8-19A). The grooves could be plowed in the bottom part of the cabinet, or there could be another strip added (Fig. 8-19B). The added strip would mean anything inside would have to be lifted over it to get it out. If you want to be able to slide things on the bottom of the cabinet, cut grooves into it or let in the extra strips.

The top can be grooved in a similar way or be an added strip, but have these grooves twice as deep as the bottom ones (Fig. 8-19C) so doors to be lifted out. Gravity keeps them in the bottom grooves, but the clearance left above allows you to lift a door high enough into the top groove for its bottom to clear, allowing removal.

A plain plywood door should have its bottom edge sanded particularly smooth; then it and the groove should be waxed for easy sliding. Glass may need rubbing on abrasive paper to remove any roughness. Top edges are not as important, but they should be reasonably smooth and the grooves waxed.

There are plastic strips available for this type of door (Fig. 8-19D), with deepened grooves at the top. They could be let into the wood or screwed to the surfaces (Fig.

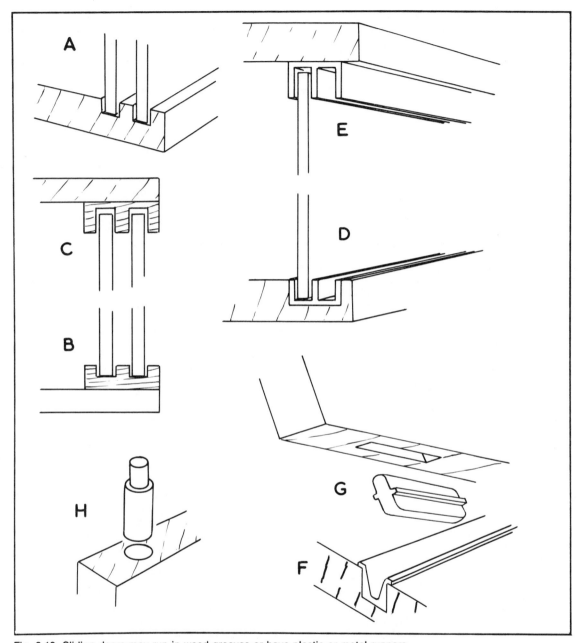

Fig. 8-19. Sliding doors may run in wood grooves or have plastic or metal runners.

8-19E). For rather heavier doors which are too thick to slide in grooves, such as those made from particleboard, it is possible to use plastic lower parts, while the top edges are controlled by grooves in the wood. In one system a plastic trough lets into a groove in the bottom woodwork (Fig. 8-19F). Two glides are fitted into the ends of the bottom of a door. They are designed to be pressed and glued into slots; then their extensions fit into the trough (Fig. 8-19G). At the top, a groove to take a particleboard door would be very wide. Instead, two pegs are fitted into the door so their projections will run in an inverted track or just in a groove plowed in the wood (Fig. 8-19H).

For heavier doors where the friction of sliding would make the difficult to move, fittings are available that include rollers. There is a choice of two methods: The rollers could be in the bottom of a door so the weight is taken by them running in a bottom track, or the rollers could be above the top of the door and run in a track there, which takes the weight of the door. A track at the bottom merely provides guidance. Top rollers and track take up space above the door, nearly 3 inches with heavy equipment, and woodwork must be arranged to hide it. Where the furniture design would not permit covering that much, bottom rollers cause less of a problem since they need not require much more clearance than in a sliding system.

In one hanging system, the top track is metal with its edges turned in (Fig. 8-20A), and two sets of rollers (Fig. 8-20B) must be bracketed to the top of each door. At the bottom there may be guides at intervals instead of a continuous track. This type of sliding door mechanism is appropriate to room doors and large closets or storage units with doors comparable in size to room doors. It is unnecessary for smaller doors.

For doors too large to slide in simple tracks, yet not large enough to justify the heavier hanging equipment, rollers let into the bottom of a door are appropriate. There are plastic tracks for top and bottom, to be let into the woodwork. In one type, the roller assembly fits in from the back surface of the door, with only enough of the roller projecting to fit into the track (Fig. 8-20C). At the top,

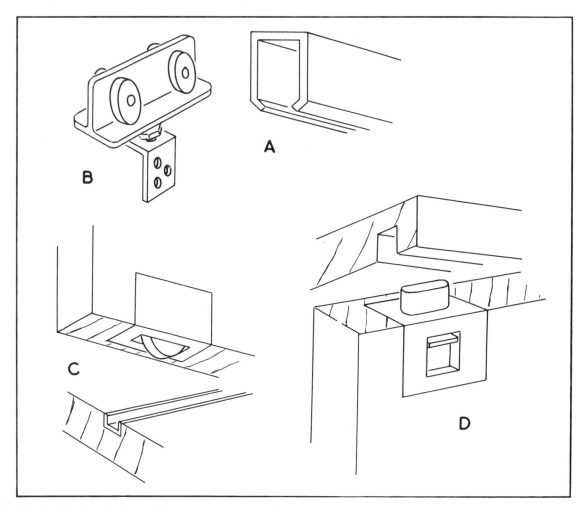

Fig. 8-20. For heavier doors, there are rollers at top or bottom.

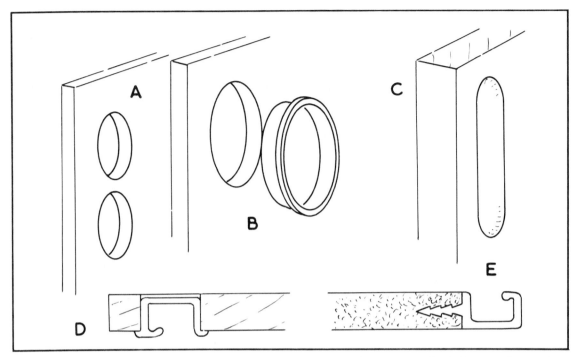

Fig. 8-21. Sliding doors cannot have projecting handles, but there may be finger holes, handles let in, or handles on edges.

a fitting needing a similar cutout in the wood has a projecting pin for guiding along the track. A pair of fittings go on each door. The upper pins may be made to retract into their inserted bodies, so the top of a door may be freed to allow it to be tilted forward and removed (Fig. 8-20D).

The choice of handles for sliding doors is limited by the clearance between the doors, at least for the handle on the inner doors. It is usual, however, to have the same type of handle on the outer edges of both doors for the sake of appearance, although you could have one with more projection in the outer door, if you wish. The simplest way to provide grip is to make a hole for a finger or a pair for two fingers near the edge of a light door (Fig. 8-21A). Such open holes may not be acceptable in some situations. There are circular plastic inserts that can be glued in or held with pins (Fig. 8-21B). They have a minimal projection back and front.

For thicker solid-wood doors, a hollow cut with a router will provide a grip (Fig. 8-21C). For doors not thick enough for a cut, and for particleboard, a hole can be made right through and a metal handle let in (Fig. 8-21D). There are plastic handles that fit in a similar way, but they require more clearance between the passing doors. Some

aluminum edge strips, similar to those intended for drawers, are arranged with sufficient hook shape to allow pulling a sliding door (Fig. 8-21E). Such handles are made the full depth of a door so they can be gripped at any point to push or pull. They take up some of the space of the doorway, so the door itself is narrower.

LIFT-OUT DOORS

Some sliding doors can be lifted out with varying degrees of ease. Sliding doors are always in pairs, however, and you may want to enclose a space with a single lift-out door. It would be illogical to provide sliding door equipment, then, for the sake of lifting out and not for sliding. A lift-out door completely clears access, and you can use the removed door as a drawing board; it may have tool racks on it, or it may fit in another position as a tabletop.

A light plywood door may drop into a groove at the bottom (Fig. 8-22A). At the top it goes against a stop or rabbet (Fig. 8-22B), where it may be held by a turnbutton, either from above, if the framework does not project, or with a block projecting through a notch in the door edge (Fig. 8-22C).

If the door is made of thicker wood, it can be rabbeted at the bottom to form a lip to engage with a notch (Fig. 8-22D). Alternatively, use two dowels in the bottom edge of the door to engage with holes. Taper the ends of the dowels for ease in locating (Fig. 8-22E). If the wood is not thick enough for wood dowels, you can use wood screws, driven in and the heads cut off (Fig. 8-22F).

The top edge of a thicker door can have a ball, spring, or magnetic catch to keep it in and a handle for pulling it open. There could be a lock engaging with the framing and a keyhole arranged through the door.

If the plywood door is to fit into plywood framing of similar thickness and not into a solid wood surround, it may have a lip added inside the bottom edge (Fig. 8-22G),

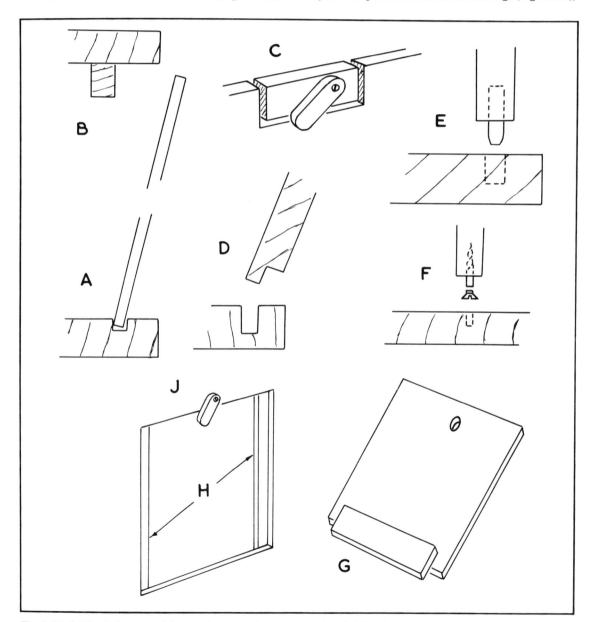

Fig. 8-22. A lift-out door may fit into a slot or peg into holes and be held at the top by a turnbutton.

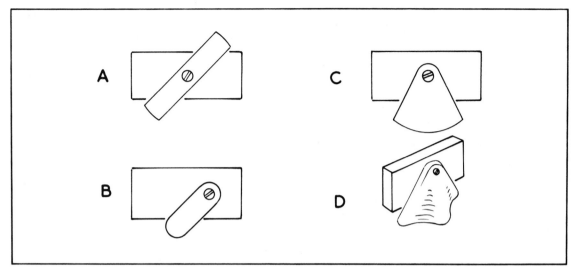

Fig. 8-23. Turnbuttons may be plain or weighted to close by gravity.

then strips inside the framing at the sides prevent it being pushed through (Fig. 8-22H). A turnbutton at the top will keep the door closed (Fig. 8-22J). There may be holes for pulling the door open, or a handle if its projection does not matter.

A turnbutton may be made of wood in the usual balanced way (Fig. 8-23A), but only half a button is needed to hold a vertical door (Fig. 8-23B). It can be tapered for neatness, but if you make its end heavy, gravity helps make it stay down. A piece of thick wood can be cut as a quandrant (Fig. 8-23C) to give it a heavy end, or solid woods can be both wider and thicker at its end (Fig. 8-23D). In any case, let the turnbutton turn easily on its screw and put a washer back and front for easy swinging.

Chapter 9

Simple Cupboards and Cabinets

There are many pieces of furniture fitted with doors, with varying degrees of complexity. Many are simple, however, and some examples are given in this chapter. If you have little or no experience, you should make a simple item first, before moving on to more advance furniture with doors. A single door does not involve much skill in getting a satisfactory result. A pair of doors are more difficult to fit to get the appearance and action correct.

When a door is included in a piece of furniture, it is often the most prominent part; so you should consider it a major part of the design. Whether you make it plain or framed, let it include glass, or have prominent hinges or handle can affect the appearance as well as its action and purpose. You must decide if it is to be hinged on the right or left, and if it is to swing wide open or to a more limited amount. You must decide if the door will come within the framework, be wholly in front of it, or in front of the sides and within the top and bottom.

Squareness is important in any furniture, but it is more so if there is a door. It is possible to make an open-fronted assembly where opposite uprights are slightly twisted in relation to each other, and it will not be ob-

vious. If however, a door comes between them, it will be hinged parallel to one side, but at the other side the twist will show by an uneven fit. Lack of squareness in front view becomes more obvious if a door has to be planed out of square to fit. When assembling furniture to take a door, pay extra attention to getting the door frame square and without twist, even if there must be a slight error elsewhere.

In nearly all furniture, the door is made last. You may prepare its parts, but you should usually wait until the other parts are made, with joints cut and ready to assemble, before using them as a guide to marking out the door parts. Even then it is often better to wait until the carcass is completed before making and fitting the door. I do not mean you should not do any work on the door and its frame. It will be easier to cut recesses for hinges in a door stile before building it into an assembly, when you can put the wood flat on the bench or in a vise, without other things attached to it. Similarly, you can make provision for stops and other things associated with the door that involve work on the wood, before assembly. Prefabrication while dealing with single pieces of wood is always easier than waiting until you have made the whole or part of an assembly.

MEDICINE CABINET

This is a simple box-on-edge type of assembly with a hinged door (Fig. 9-1A). The suggested sizes allow for storing bottles and boxes and other things needed for first aid or medication in the home (Fig. 9-1B). Top and bottom overlap the door, making the assembly reasonably dustproof.

Prepare the wood for top, bottom and sides. Rabbet the rear edges for the back. In a bathroom or other damp atmosphere, the back should be plywood bonded with waterproof glue, or you could use the type of hardboard that is oil-impregnated to give it a water resistance.

Top and bottom overlap the sides at the ends as well as at the front. Joints could be merely butted and held with nails or screws in the simplest construction. If the cabinet is to be finished with paint, this construction would be disguised; so it may be more acceptable than you expected. There could be dowels between the parts, but construction is shown with dado joints (Fig. 9-2A). Dadoes and back rabbets should be taken to the same depth. Dovetailed dadoes would be stronger, but plain glued dadoes with a few pins driven diagonally from inside should be strong enough (Fig. 9-2B).

The shelf fits into the sides with dado joints (Fig. 9-2C), or you could use glass or wood to lift out from strips on the sides (Fig. 9-2D). Round the front edges of the cabinet top and bottom, then assemble these parts.

The door is framed with a panel in a rabbet to allow you to choose between a plywood panel, a mirror, or a piece of glass with a clear or decorated finish. Corner joints can be any of those described for rabbeted frames in Chapter 8, but that shown is halved (Fig. 9-2E). Make the sides to the full height of the door, with a little extra to trim off after assembly. Allow for a little clearance at top and bottom. Get the actual distances from the assembled cabinet (Fig. 9-2F); this is always a wiser course than measuring with a rule, whenever it is possible. Prepare the pieces the other way. In this case it is the distance between the shoulders which is important. Deduct the widths of the sides of the door from the width of the cabinet and mark the shoulders, then extend outward a little more than will finally be needed (Fig. 9-2G).

Cut the halving joints and assemble the door with glue and screws from the back, checking squareness both with a try square and by putting the door over where it is to go on the cabinet. Fit the chosen type of panel with fillets at the back (Fig. 9-2H), but if it is glass, remove it after

a trial assembly until you have painted or otherwise finished the woodwork.

Use a pair of butt hinges, preferably brass for a damp situation. Let the flaps into both surfaces, although for simplicity you could let in deeper in one edge and leave the flap on the surface of the other part. This choice moves the pivot point of the knuckle slightly. If you let in deeper in the door, it will throw slightly wider from the front of the cabinet, but letting equally looks better.

This is the stage where you adjust the fit of the door. Hinge it in place, possibly with only a single screw each way in each hinge, and note the fit. The edge further from the hinges should finish level with the cabinet side. Top and bottom should have slight clearances and be parallel. Put a piece of card under the door while you are driving the temporary hinge screws to provide clearance. If the first assembly with hinges is not quite right, take out a screw and drive another in a different hole until you are satisfied. Note which are the correct screws for reference when you make the final assembly with a full set of screws.

Fit a handle. It could be one of the many bought types; it could be a straight wood strip, and a turned knob is also appropriate to this cabinet (Fig. 9-1C). Put it just above the center of the side. Behind it arrange a fastener or catch of the type where a spring or magnet has its main part inside the side of the case, and there is a plate or other thin part on the inside of the door.

Finish the wood in any way you wish. If the panel is a mirror or plain glass, you may get a reflection of the inside of the rabbet that spoils appearance. That reflection can be minimized by painting the inside of the rabbet with a matte black paint. If it is clear glass, you may also wish to paint the inside surface of the fillet black.

Materials List for Medicine Cabinet

2 sides	4 1/4 × 15 × 5/8
1 top	5 1/2 × 12 × 5/8
1 bottom	5 1/2 × 12 × 5/8
1 shelf	3 1/2 × 10 × 1/2
1 back	10 × 15 × 1/4 plywood
2 door sides	1 1/2 × 15 × 3/4
1 door top	1 1/2 × 10 × 3/4
1 door bottom	2 × 10 × 3/4
1 door panel	9 × 13 × 1/4 plywood or glass

HANGING CABINET

Books are usually arranged on shelves which are open

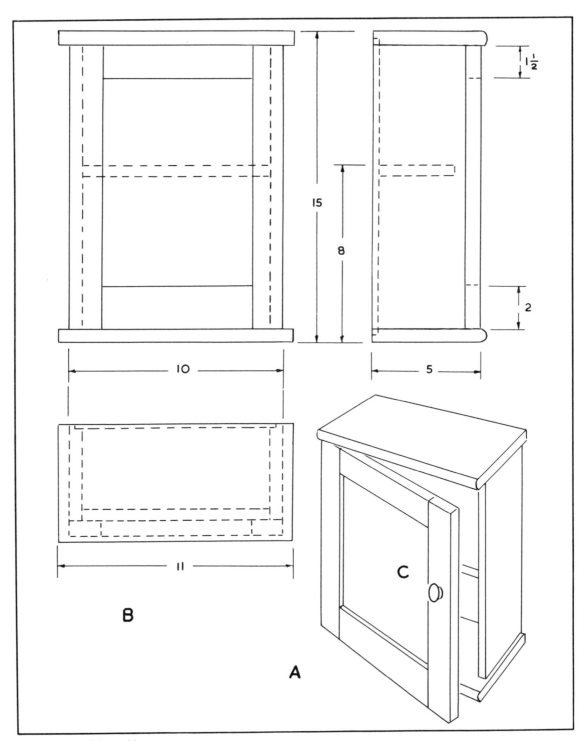

Fig. 9-1. A medicine cabinet.

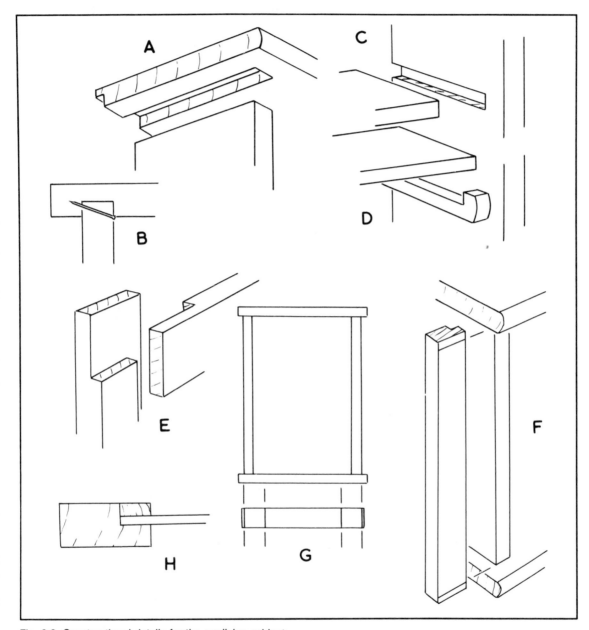

Fig. 9-2. Constructional details for the medicine cabinet.

to the front, but if you want to arrange a similar hanging cabinet to enclose a variety of things, it is better, for the sake of tidiness and to keep the contents in place, to provide a door. The example in Fig. 9-3A is similar in outline to many bookcases and might be made to match one. It can be hung by screws through its plywood back and

could be made in any shape or size. Typical sizes are given in Fig. 9-3B as a guide to proportions. The door is shown inside its framing and made with a plywood panel and mortise-and-tenon joints at its corners. If a glass panel would be preferred, the frame should be rabbeted and the door made as described for the previous example.

179

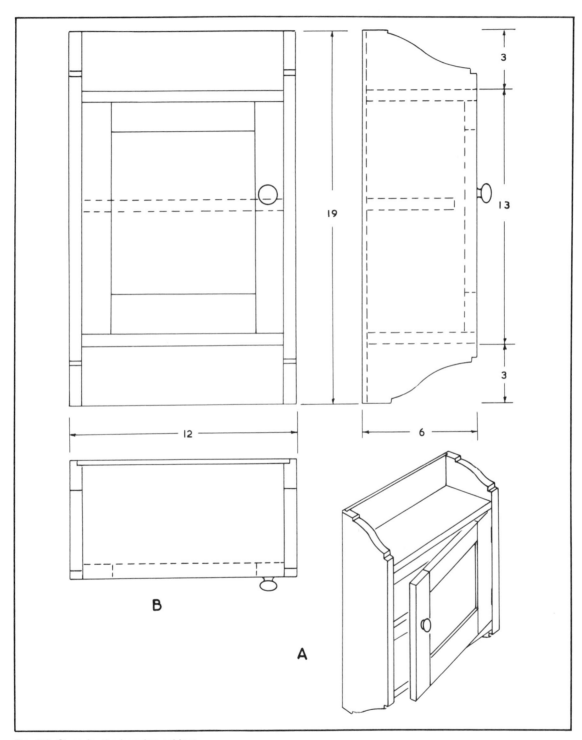

Fig. 9-3. Sizes for the hanging cabinet.

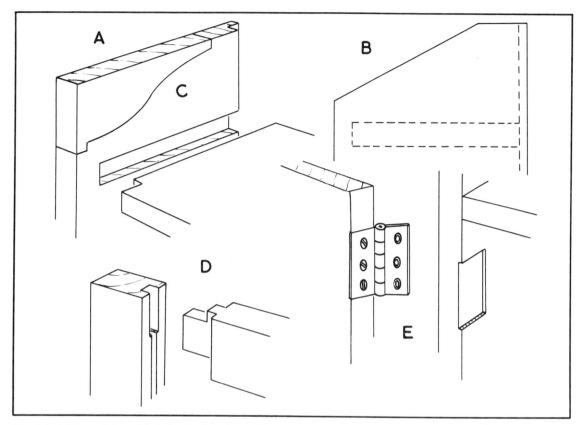

Fig. 9-4. Joints and door details for the hanging cabinet.

Prepare the wood for the sides and rabbet the rear edges for the plywood back. The back is shown going the full depth, for simplicity. If solid wood is wanted at top and bottom, the plywood could finish at the shelf levels, and solid wood be let into deeper rabbets above and below, as described for some of the earlier blocks of shelves. Make the two shelves and cut joints for them to fit into stopped dadoes in the sides (Fig. 9-4A). Decorate the extensions of the sides with simple bevels (Fig. 9-4B) or with curves (Fig. 9-4C). If you want to put books on top, it may be better to leave the tops cut square. If you want one or more shelves, set them into stopped dadoes or rest them on supports, as described for the medicine cabinet.

Assemble the parts. Check squareness as you bring the joints together; then the plywood back should hold the shape. So there is no twist, leave the assembly with its back on a flat surface while the glue hardens.

As you mark out the door parts, check lengths against the actual opening, allowing only slight clearance all around. Plow grooves for the plywood panel, or cut rabbets if you are to use glass.

At the corners, the tenons are on the horizontal rails and the mortises in the upright parts. If the panel is 1/4-inch plywood, the joints can be the same width, but otherwise make the mortises 1/3 the thickness of the wood with haunches at the ends to the groove depth (Fig. 9-4D).

After assembling the door, plane its edges so you get an easy fit in the opening. Use pieces of card as packing to check that spaces are the same all around. When this first trial seems satisfactory, mark and fit the hinges into both parts (Fig. 9-4E). You will have to adjust the depths of the recesses to get the clearance you planned at that edge. Arrange the knuckles of the hinges with their centers just outside the line of the wood so the door swings clear to 180 degrees. If you want to make sure it will swing further than that without straining the hinges, set the knuckles further out. Too much projection, however, becomes ugly. Try the door action with single screws in each hinge flap; then when you have experimented and found the best position and have adjusted clearance, if necessary, mark the position for one or more door stops. If you will be using a spring ball catch in the edge of the door, the stop can be a short block of wood behind the center of the door. If you will be using a catch that has its body on the inside of the cabinet side, it may be sufficient to act as a stop as well; if not, there could be a stop block at top and bottom. When you are satisfied with the working of the door, remove the hinges until after you finish the woodwork.

Buy or make a handle. For a cabinet of the size shown, a simple knob or small metal handle will suit, but if you make a deeper cabinet, a strip wood handle may be better. Finish with stain and polish or varnish. If a painted finish is used, the inside could be white or cream to make the contents easier to see.

Materials List for Hanging Cabinet

2 sides	6 × 20 × 5/8
1 top	5 3/4 × 12 × 5/8
1 bottom	5 3/4 × 12 × 5/8
1 shelf	4 1/2 × 12 × 1/2
1 back	12 × 20 × 1/4 plywood
2 door sides	1 1/2 × 13 × 3/4
1 door top	1 1/2 × 12 × 3/4
1 door bottom	2 × 12 × 3/4

BEDSIDE CABINET

Particleboard, bought already veneered with plastic or wood on two surfaces and two edges, is particularly suitable for a bedside cabinet type of project, since it

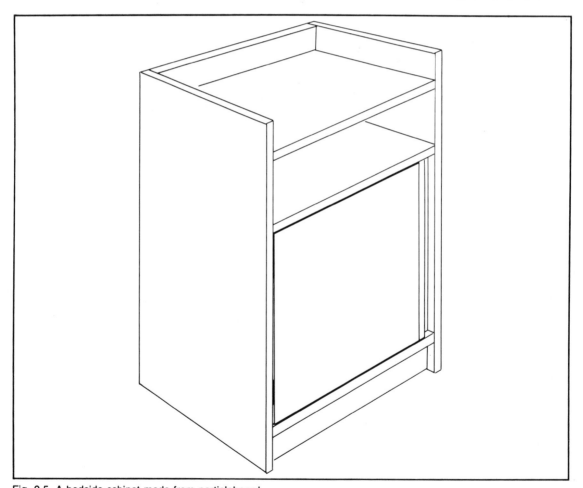

Fig. 9-5. A bedside cabinet made from particleboard.

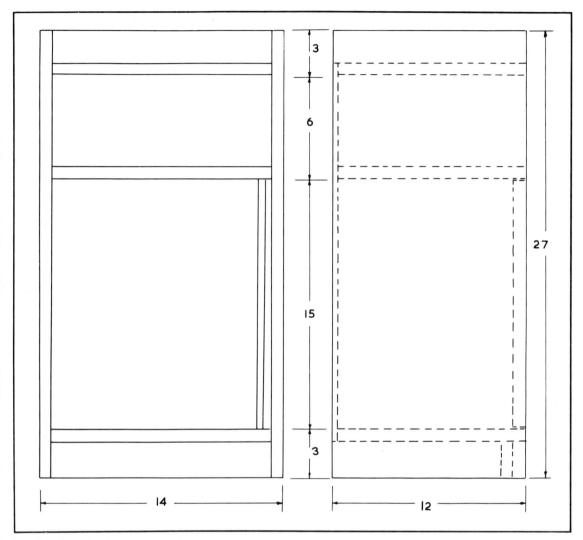

Fig. 9-6. Sizes for the bedside cabinet.

keeps its shape and can be used with a minimum of preparation. The cabinet shown in Fig. 9-5 is intended to be made with stock width panels. See Fig. 9-6. Most of the parts are 12 inches wide. The door has a full-length metal handle at one side. If you wish to make the door without cutting it to width, check the total width it will occupy with the handle attached and make this the measurement between the sides of the cabinet, with a small allowance for clearance. As drawn, the door will have to be reduced a little from the 12-inch width, with a handle of standard section.

Preparation of the parts consists of cutting the par-

ticleboard panels squarely to matching lengths. All ends can be left as cut and planed, except the tops of the sides, which should be veneered to match the surfaces. If the strip at the back of the top is cut from the edge of a panel, it will already have a veneered edge; otherwise it should be treated with a strip of veneer. The plinth does not need veneering on either edge; so it can be an offcut from other parts. Be careful of damaging surface veneers when cutting, but get the ends square in both directions; otherwise discrepancies will show in the butt joints.

All of the parts could be doweled—1/4-inch dowels at 3-inch intervals should be satisfactory across the main joints. Alternatively, most of the joints could be joined with screwed fillets. Unless you have special equipment for rabbeting particleboard, the plywood back must be fitted in with fillets (Fig. 9-7A) cut above and below the shelf. The ends of the top back piece are best doweled (Fig. 9-7B), but its lower edge could be screwed upward through the shelf (Fig. 9-7C). The plinth could be doweled in both directions (Fig. 9-7D). When making and fitting the plinth, make sure it does not finish with its lower edge below the side pieces, or the cabinet may stand

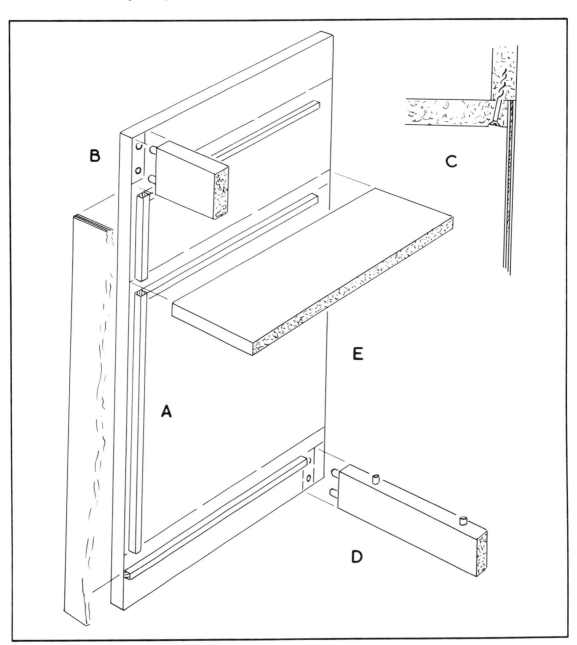

Fig. 9-7. How the parts fit to one side of the bedside cabinet.

184

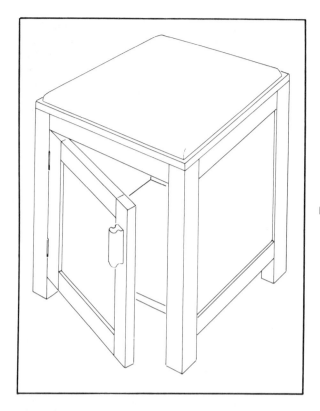

Fig. 9-8. A bathroom stool with door.

unsteadily. Making it up to 1/8 inch narrower is unlikely to show, particularly if the cabinet stands on carpet.

Prepare the pair of sides, with dowel holes drilled and fillets attached (Fig. 9-7E). Stop the fillets under the shelf to allow for the thickness of the door. They can then act as door stops. It is easier to assemble the crosswise parts with the assembly inverted. Attach the top pieces, then the shelf, and then the bottom, with the plinth attached. Check squareness and put in the plywood back temporarily to hold the parts in shape while they are resting face down on a flat surface for the glue to set. Leave the permanent fitting of the back until all the other parts are made and fitted, because you may need to see and work on them from the back.

Make and fit the door. The hinges should be the thin type with one flap closing into the other. The closed thickness determines the clearance at that side. Use that as a guide to the clearance at the other edges. Make a groove for the handle at the opening edge, if that is the type of handle to be fitted; otherwise make the door full width and add a handle to the surface.

Remove any blobs of glue that have squeezed out of joints. With particleboard you need to use adequate glue

in joints, but estimate it so there will not be too much, since with some veneered surfaces it is difficult to remove an excess without damaging the plastic or wood veneer. If it is a plastic surface, wipe off the inside parts with a damp cloth to remove grease and dirt before finally attaching the plywood back. If it is wood veneer, finish the surface in the same way as you would for solid wood.

Materials List for Bedside Cabinet

2 sides	$12 \times 28 \times 3/4$
3 shelves	$12 \times 13 \times 3/4$
1 back	$3 \times 13 \times 3/4$
1 plinth	$2\ 1/4 \times 13 \times 3/4$
1 door	$12 \times 16 \times 3/4$
1 back	$13 \times 23 \times 1/4$ plywood
9 fillets	$1/2 \times 12 \times 1/2$

BATHROOM STOOL

A stool with storage space below it is always useful. The one shown in Fig. 9-8 is intended for use in a bathroom, but it is adaptable to other purposes. It is of framed and paneled construction, with four legs and a top that might be covered with cork for use in a bathroom. The sizes (Fig. 9-9A) combine a comfortable height with a roomy storage space. Construction could be with softwood and ordinary plywood and given a painted finish, or hardwood could be used with plywood having a matching surface veneer and given a clear finish.

Legs are joined with rails in the same way on three sides. On the fourth side there is a top rail, but instead of a lower rail, the inside bottom piece braces the stool, and its edge is covered by the door, which is also framed.

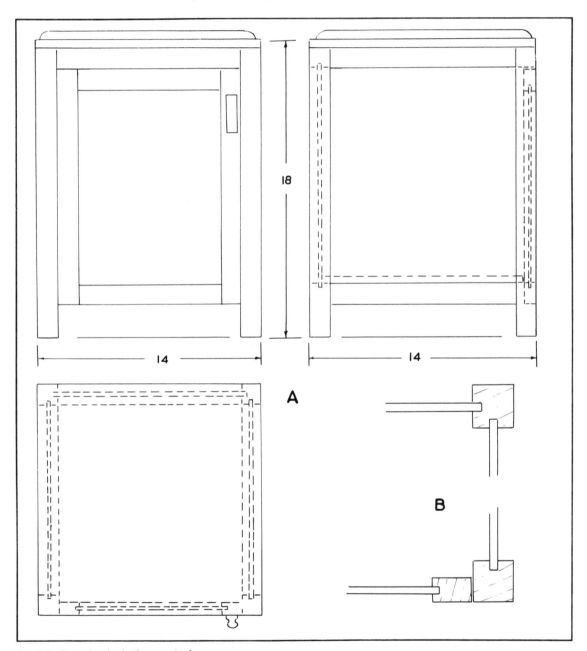

Fig. 9-9. Sizes for the bathroom stool.

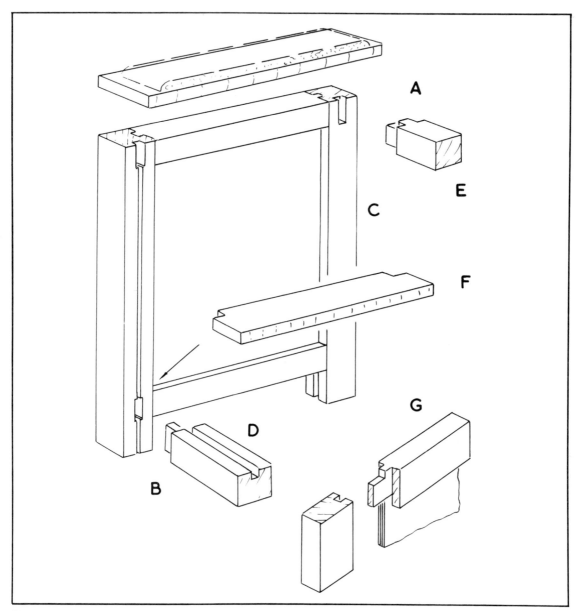

Fig. 9-10. Joints for the bathroom stool.

Groove the wood for the legs, to suit the plywood. There is no need to go deeper than 1/4 inch. The two back legs are grooved on two faces, but the front pair are not grooved on the sides toward the door (Fig. 9-9B). Although the panels will not go the full depth of each leg, it is easier to plow the grooves for the full length. The unused grooves below the bottom rails will not be very obvious. If you wish to hide them, they can be plugged with glued strips after the parts have been assembled. Groove all the rails similarly, except the one above the door.

Prepare mortise-and-tenon joints for the rails, using haunches at the top (Fig. 9-10A) and cutting back the tenons to the bottoms of the rail grooves (Fig. 9-10B).

Make up a pair of opposite frames complete with panels (Fig. 9-10C). Join them with rails (Fig. 9-10D) as well as their panel at the back and the ungrooved rail at the front (Fig. 9-10E). At the same time, fit the bottom (Fig. 9-10F). Cut it with its grain across the front and notch it around the legs. Give it clearance for the door, which must close in front of it.

Before fitting the top, reach inside to clean off any excess glue. The top and bottom are best made of solid wood, but they could be plywood, especially if the stool is to be painted, when the exposed veneers of the top plywood can be protected and hidden by paint. Glue the top to the framing. If it is to be covered with cork or unholstery, nails or screws can supplement the glue. If you have the top slightly oversize, you can plane the edges level after it has been glued on.

The door is made with strips grooved for the plywood and haunched mortise-and-tenon joints at the corners (Fig. 9-10G). For neatness the tenons should not go right through. The bottom edge of the door should come level with the bottom edge of the lower rails in the sides of the cabinet.

Let in brass hinges and provide a catch at the other side—a ball catch in the edge of the door is suitable. The bottom of the cabinet may provide sufficient stop behind the door, but if anything else seems necessary, put a stop block on the leg behind the top of the door. Anyone reaching down to open the door needs a grip close to the top, so provide a handle or knob there.

Materials List for Bathroom Stool

4 legs	1 1/4 × 19 × 1 1/4
7 rails	1 1/4 × 14 × 1 1/4
3 panels	13 × 15 × 1/4 plywood
1 top	14 × 15 × 1/2
1 bottom	13 × 13 × 1/2
2 door sides	1 1/4 × 16 × 3/4
2 door rails	1 1/4 × 12 × 3/4
1 door panel	11 × 15 × 1/4 plywood

CORNER TABLE WITH DOOR

When the space below a table is to be enclosed and fitted with a door, the door must be fairly rigid. A light door that flexes when opened and closed would be a nuisance and probably would not be strong enough to last very long. If the door is paneled, the framing should be wide so the corner joints are of adequate size to hold the door in shape. The corner table in Fig. 9-11 is at the usual

height and designed so two walls border part of the enclosed space below, with the narrower direction closed with a panel and a door in the wider side. There is only one leg; screws to the walls provide the other supports.

Sizes are suggested in Fig. 9-12A. The top hangs over and is probably best surfaced with faced particleboard, although solid wood pieces could be glued to make up the width, or thick plywood could be used. The edge of the top is thickened and covered with molding; so the edges of the top material will be hidden. You should make up the underframing and fit it to the walls before you cut the top to size and edge it. This method is easier than starting with the top and trying to fit the framing to it, particularly if the corner of the room is slightly out of square.

Start with the end assembly (Fig. 9-13A). The key member is the leg (Fig. 9-13B), which settles the height of the table. Prepare it and the rear post with grooves to suit the plywood. Groove the top and bottom rails to match. Joints in this assembly could be doweled, but they are better made with mortise and tenons, having haunches to the depths of the grooves. Grooves 3/8 or 1/2 inch deep should be satisfactory.

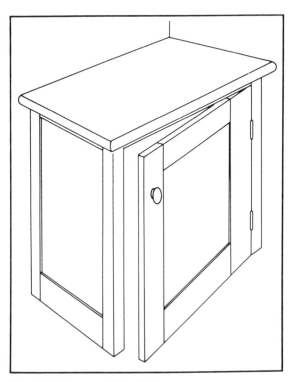

Fig. 9-11. A corner table with door.

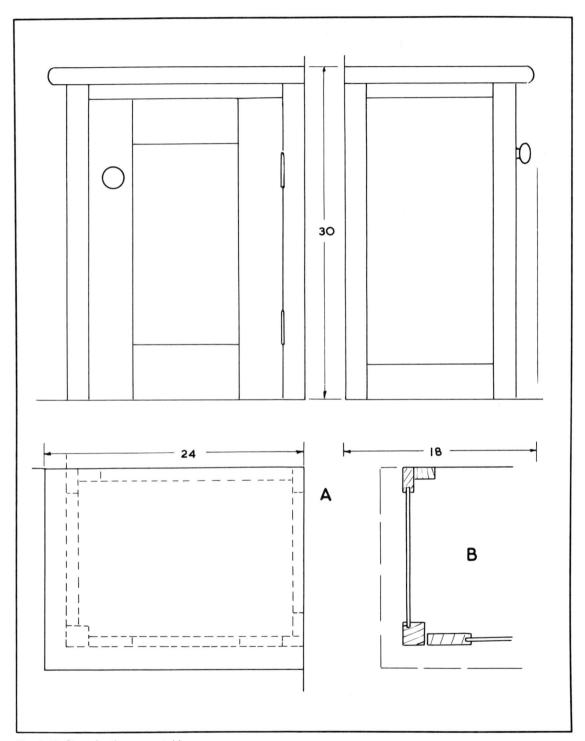

Fig. 9-12. Sizes for the corner table.

Lengthwise rails should also be joined with mortises and tenons (Fig. 9-13C). At the rear post, join in another vertical strip (Figs. 9-12B and 9-13D) for taking screws to the wall. It is shown to the full depth, but it need not reach the floor, providing there is space for two or three screws to the wall. If there is a baseboard on the wall, the post should be notched to suit and the other strip cut short.

At the side of the front against the wall, another post should match the leg in front view (Fig. 9-13E). At the wall corner another post may go to the floor, or it could be cut short (Fig. 9-13F). Its purpose is to provide a link between the rails and a place for screwing into the wall. A strip behind the front post also takes screws into the wall (Fig. 9-13G). Join the rails with dowels or mortise-and-tenon joints.

There are no lower rails inside the assembly. Care is needed to get the parts attached to the wall so the end panel is vertical, and the opening for the door is both parallel and untwisted. With the rear post screwed to the

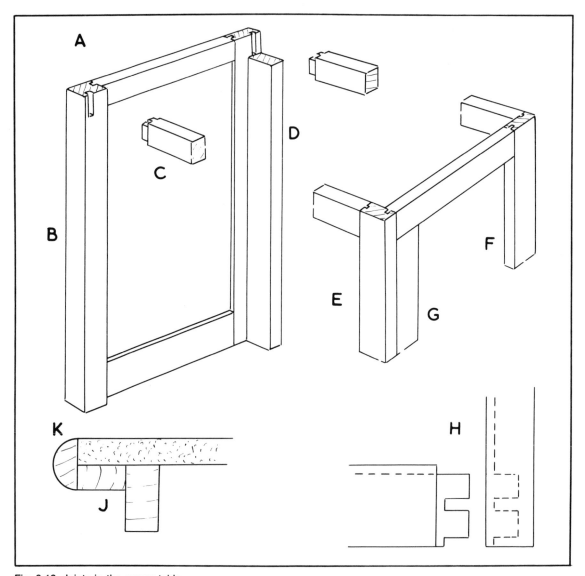

Fig. 9-13. Joints in the corner table.

wall, it should be sufficient to dowel the leg to the floor. If it is impractical to do so, put a strip inside the bottom rail of the end framing and screw downward through it.

It will probably be simplest to start fixing the table from the corner of the room; so mark heights on the wall to match the height of the leg and its end assembly. Attach the corner post to the wall, then add the rails both ways, with the rear post of the end framing screwed next and the frame checked square to the wall. When you fix the front post to the wall, check that it is vertical, but also sight across the front of the leg to check that there is no twist obvious between the leg and the post on which the door will swing. Check also that the door opening will have parallel sides.

The doorway is without a bottom rail so heavy items can be moved in and out without having to be lifted. The door, therefore, is full depth, but do not make it too close to the floor. A tight fit is not usually necessary; so you can leave as much as 1 inch if there is a carpet to be cleared when the door swings. It could be hung at either side, but in most situations it is better for the door to swing open against the wall, unless it would then interfere with a room door.

Prepare the door parts by grooving them to suit the plywood panel. Because the pieces are wide, it would be unwise to have single tenons. Instead, cut back to the bottoms of the grooves, arrange haunches outside, and divide the remainder into two with a narrow haunch between (Fig. 9-13H). Take stub tenons about 3 inches deep to give stiffness. Assemble and fit the door in the usual way. For the sizes shown, 3-inch hinges would be suitable. At the leg, put stops on it, either full length ones or just short pieces at the top and bottom of the door. Fit a knob or other handle at a convenient height for a person to grip while standing.

Fit the top edge pieces (Fig. 9-13J) to the top rails with glue and screws from inside the rails. Now you have the size for the tabletop. Plane the edges that will touch the wall, allowing for any irregularity or lack of squareness, then mark the other two sides for the edge pieces. Fit the top with glue and screws from below through the edge pieces and a few pocket screws upward through the rails along the walls.

The table edge is shown half-round (Fig. 9-13K), but it could be any molding you choose. Miter the corner and attach the pieces with glue and pins punched below the surface and covered with stopping.

Materials List for Corner Table with Door

1 leg	$2 \times 30 \times 2$
5 posts	$2 \times 30 \times 1$
2 top rails	$2 \times 22 \times 1$
2 top rails	$2 \times 16 \times 1$
1 bottom rail	$3 \times 16 \times 1$
1 end panel	$15 \times 27 \times 1/4$ plywood
2 door sides	$4 \times 28 \times 1$
1 door rail	$4 \times 20 \times 1$
1 door rail	$5 \times 20 \times 1$
1 door panel	$12 \times 20 \times 1/4$ plywood
1 top	$17 \times 23 \times 3/4$
1 top frame	$1 \ 1/2 \times 24 \times 3/4$
1 top frame	$1 \ 1/2 \times 18 \times 3/4$
1 top edge	$1 \ 1/2 \times 24 \times 3/4$ half-round
1 top edge	$1 \ 1/2 \times 18 \times 3/4$ half-round

ENCLOSED BENCH

Many shop benches are open underneath. If they are enclosed, however, there is valuable storage space and the bench is stiffened. The bench in Fig. 9-14 has a substantial top to withstand hammering and other heavy work without bending. The structure below is equally strong and is made without cutting into it for the paneling which encloses the lower part. The design shows closed panels at the ends and back, with two doors at the front. If the bench is to be used from both sides, there could be doors at the back as well, without affecting the strength of the assembly.

If the entire bench is made of a close-grained hardwood, it would be suitable for good-quality woodworking. For metalworking or general purposes, it would be cheaper and lighter to make the entire bench of softwood. A compromise would have a hardwood top to withstand wear, and a softwood structure underneath. The suggested sizes in Fig. 9-15A would make a general-purpose bench, but check width of doorways and passages, even if you make it in the place where you will use it—you may want to move it out later.

All of the underframing is made of wood 3 inches square. Top joints should be haunched mortise and tenons (Fig. 9-16A). The lower rails and the posts to the long rails do not require haunches (Fig. 9-16B). Make the tenons 1 inch thick and take them at least 1 1/2 inches into the other parts. Besides glue, there could be dowels across the tenons.

Assembly of the structure is straightforward, but be carefully to get the parts square and opposite assemblies matching. It will probably be best to assemble the back first, put it on a flat surface, and assemble the front over it in the correct relative position. See that both assemblies

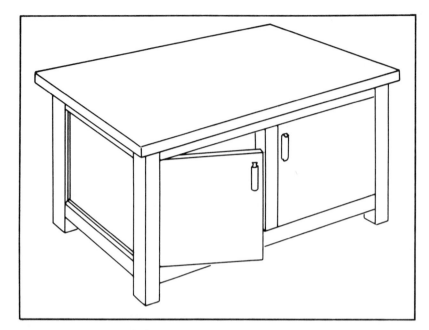

Fig. 9-14. An enclosed bench.

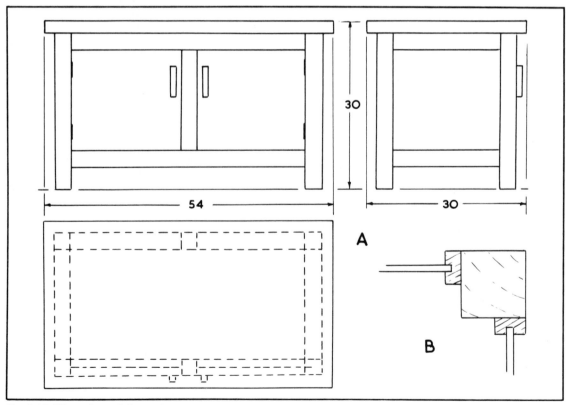

A

B

Fig. 9-15. Dimensions of the enclosed bench.

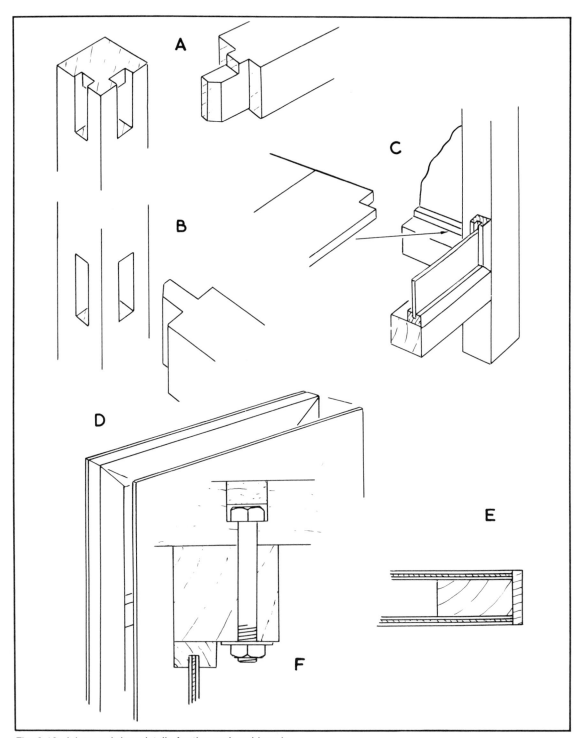

Fig. 9-16. Joints and door details for the enclosed bench.

are flat, then let the glue harden before joining them with the shorter rails across. Check squareness in all directions by measuring diagonals.

The panels must be framed within the spaces between the 3-inch-square parts. For this framing, prepare enough 3/4- × -1 1/2-inch strips with grooves for the plywood (Fig. 9-15B). Cut them with miters or laps at the corners, then fit the plywood, and glue and nail the strips to the legs and rails, with their outer edges flush with the outsides of the structure. Do so at the back and ends, but leave the front untreated.

The bottom is made up of a number of boards laid lengthwise and fitted inside the panel strips on the lower rails. Notch around the legs, but at the front set back enough to clear the doors (Fig. 9-16C). Final fitting of the front board should be left until you are certain what space the doors will require; then its edge can be planed to suit.

The doors are made with flush plywood panels inside and out. In the simplest construction, the plywood is taken to the door edges (Fig. 9-16D). For a better finish, there can be strips around the edges (Fig. 9-16E). In both cases, miter the top corners of the wood forming the framing, but at the bottom the side pieces may overlap the bottom ones.

The amount of intermediate framing you put in a door depends on what you want to do with it. If there are to be tool racks on the inside, you may want stiffeners where they come, or you may screw the racks from the inner plywood before putting on the outer panel. If the doors are to be left plain, one stiffener across the center of each is advisable.

The best way to make the doors accurately is to cut an inside piece of plywood to a suitable fit with clearance, then add the framing to it. When that glue has set, put on a slightly oversize outer panel and plane it to fit when the glue has set. Hinge the doors in the usual way and add handles within reach from above. The bottom boards will act as stops for the doors. Catches are best fitted near the top so the handles pull or push near them.

Make up the width of the top with several boards. If they vary in width, put the wider boards at the outsides. For strength it is best to bolt the top on, with the bolt heads sunk beneath the surface (Fig. 9-16F). Alternatively, use long, thick wood screws sunk in the same way. Use washers under the nuts and position the holes so the bolt ends come inside the panel strips. Plug the holes over the bolt heads with wood.

The type of treatment you give the bench top depends on its intended use, and for most purposes it is better left plain. The appearance of the bench can be improved, however, if all that comes below the top is stained and varnished. If the inside is painted a light color, its contents will be more easily seen.

Materials List for Enclosed Bench

4 legs	3 × 30 × 3
4 rails	3 × 50 × 3
4 rails	3 × 25 × 3
2 posts	3 × 22 × 3
1 top	30 × 55 × 2
16 panel strips	1 1/2 × 21 × 1 1/2
4 panels	20 × 22 × 1/4 plywood
4 door panels	19 × 21 × 1/4 plywood
10 door frames	2 × 21 × 1
1 bottom	24 × 50 × 1

SHALLOW CABINET

Doors with hinges at the sides hang best when they are taller than they are wide. If they are much wider, there is a tendency to sag. A small amount of slackness in screws or wear in the hinges will cause the door to fall under its own weight. A gap that was parallel across the top of the closed door shows that it has fallen, and its free side may begin to rub at the bottom. Where wide doors are needed, sliding becomes preferable to hinging.

The shallow cabinet in Fig. 9-17 is a simple container with a pair of sliding doors. It is a type of fill-in furniture. It could go above another item in the angle between wall and ceiling. It could form the base of a bookcase or some other item you wish to raise above table level, while also offering increased storage space. It could stand at the back of a desk or table to accommodate the many things needed during work, but which are better hidden away afterward.

As shown, the width is about three times the height (Fig. 9-18A) which allows long doors with good bearing surfaces; so they should slide easily. If you want to be able to get at the whole interior, the doors lift out.

Suggested construction is of solid wood, which allows plowing for the grooves at the bottom. If particleboard or thick plywood is used, the bottom grooves should be in a separate strip of solid wood, similar to the top strip, but not as deep. The bottom board is shown thicker than the rest of the construction, for stiffness even when grooved.

Rabbet the backs of the pieces for plywood. Corner joints may be whatever you choose and depending on how important appearance is. The upright parts could be nailed or screwed to the horizontal pieces for the simplest

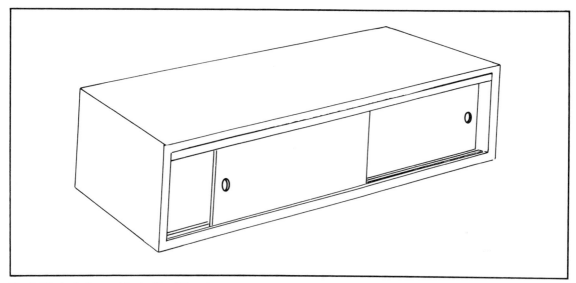

Fig. 9-17. A shallow cabinet with sliding doors.

construction. Dowels could be used; for the sake of appearance, the top should then overlap the ends, but the ends must overlap the bottom to hide the ends of the grooves (Fig. 9-18B).

Another way of hiding the ends of the grooves and making a neat joint at top and bottom is to use a rabbet across the ends (Fig. 9-18C). Besides glue you can then drive fine nails both ways to make secure joints. The best corner joints are dovetails. If you use the machine-cut stopped type, the tails should be on the horizontal parts; then the stopped part will cover the ends of the grooves. For through dovetails, the tails may come in the upright parts, but you must allow for the end of the groove section by cutting away for it (Fig. 9-18D) and the end cut back to fit (Fig. 9-18E).

Make the grooves an easy fit on the plywood. If the plywood is 1/4 inch, the grooves could be 5/16 inch and about the same depth at the bottom, but twice that in the top strip so the doors can be lifted out. Make the top strip first (Fig. 9-18F) and use it as a guide for plowing the grooves in the bottom (Fig. 9-18G).

Wrap sandpaper around a piece of plywood and rub it along the grooves to smooth them. Follow with cloth over the plywood to rub in wax polish. Do this step before assembly, whatever finish is to be used on the completed cabinet, so the doors slide easily. Glue the strip to the top piece, with a few fine nails driven and punched at the bottoms of the grooves if you think they are necessary.

Check squareness and fit the plywood back. Make the two doors long enough for about 2 inches overlap at the center. Heights should be sufficient to lift to the top of an upper groove and just clear the surface of the bottom piece. The door can be dropped into the bottom groove ready for sliding, but will come clear if you lift it. Finger holes are shown for moving the doors, but you could fit plastic inserts, providing they project less than the clearance between the doors. Treat the door edges the same way as the grooves, by sanding and waxing.

Materials List for Shallow Cabinet

1 top	12 × 31 × 3/4
1 bottom	12 × 31 × 1
2 ends	12 × 11 × 3/4
1 back	10 × 30 × 1/4 plywood
2 doors	10 × 16 × 1/4 plywood
1 door guide	1 1/2 × 30 × 1

BENCH WITH LIFT-OUT DOOR

A bench which can be disguised as another piece of furniture is useful if a hobby is pursued in what is normally a living room. It is useful then to enclose the lower part so all the things needed for the hobby can be hidden away when out of use. A refinement on this theme is to have a door to this lower part, which can be fitted with tool racks and lifted out to stand at the back of the bench with your equipment all there within reach. When the

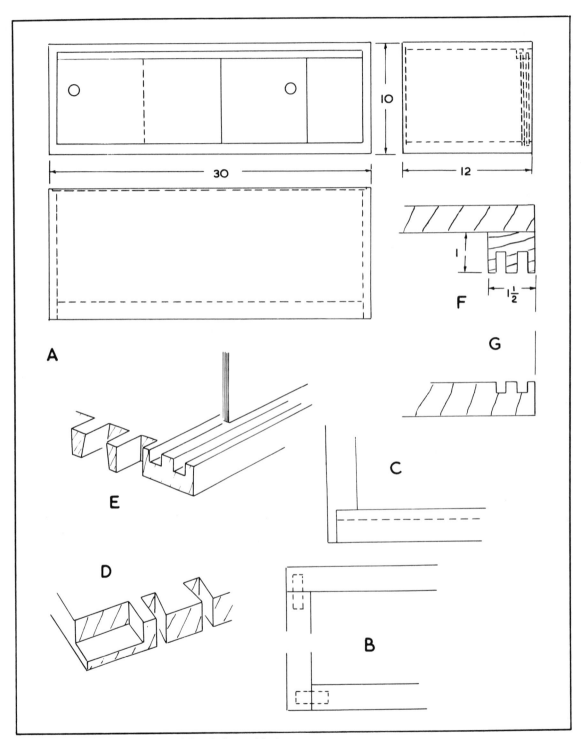

Fig. 9-18. Sizes and construction of the shallow cabinet.

bench is not used for your hobby, it will look like a piece of furniture, especially if its top is covered with a cloth, and a vase of flowers stands on it.

This bench (Fig. 9-19) is a size to suit such hobbies as model making, fabric craft and macrame, but it could be made in other sizes if you need more space for work on larger pieces.

The construction uses four legs and flush panels at back and sides (Fig. 9-20A), with a door that closes flush. If the bench will always be against the wall, there is no need for a good finish on it, but if the bench must be moved about, it should have a good appearance in any direction. If you will need to move it to and from a work position, put casters under the legs and allow for the depth they occupy when you make the legs.

The four legs are identical, with joints for the horizontal rails at two levels, except the rails are set back to suit the plywood panels on three sides, enough to clear the top of the door at the front, and to the full width of the leg at the door bottom. The plywood goes over the side and back rails at top and bottom (Fig. 9-20B). Between the rails are 1/4-inch square strips on the legs (Fig. 9-20C)

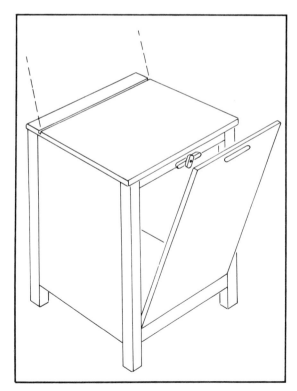

Fig. 9-19. A bench with a lift-out door.

to support the plywood flush with the outsides of the legs.

Join the rails to the legs with dowels or mortise-and-tenon joints. Assemble the two sides first so they match as a pair, then join them with the rails the other way, fitting in the plywood panels at the same time to keep the structure square. The bottom front rail must be grooved to hold the bottom of the door; so check the thickness of the plywood for the door and its extension at the bottom (Fig. 9-21A). Make the groove to suit so the door will close flush with the outsides of the legs. At the top make the rail behind the door a suitable thickness for the door to close flush there.

Check diagonals across the top corners of the legs. The bottom can be a single sheet of plywood, or it could be made up from several boards laid across (Fig. 9-21B). At the front make it level with the groove in the front rail (Fig. 9-20D). Fit it closely inside the panels and fasten it down to the bottom rails so it keeps the assembly square.

The simplest door is a piece of 3/4-inch plywood, which is stout enough to be unlikely to warp and thick enough to take screws from tool clips and whatever fittings you put in the inside to hold equipment. Many tools can be arranged to drop into holes in narrow shelves, or you can screw on loops of leather belting. Obviously, open racks would be inadvisable since tools might drop out when the door is moved. Make the door to fit neatly between the legs while resting on the bottom rail. Allow ample clearance under the top.

At the center of the top of the door, make a hole large enough to put your hand through (Fig. 9-21C). Round its edges so it becomes a handle to lift out the door. Arrange the lower edge of the hole to come about level with the lower edge of the top rail behind it. Put a block on the rail to easily pass through the handle hole and make a small turnbutton to turn on a screw, and washers at its center (Fig. 9-21D) to hold the door shut.

The extension strip on the bottom of the door should drop easily into the groove. Rounding its edge will help in location, particularly if you are positioning a door heavily loaded with tools.

The top is shown as solid wood 1 inch thick, which will have to be made from several pieces glued together. You can either use whatever wide boards are available or a pattern of narrow pieces to give a butcher-block effect. Make the top flush with the back, but let it hang over on the other sides. Arrange the grain parallel with the back.

When the door is lifted out, it can be turned over and stood against the wall at the back of the bench so the tools

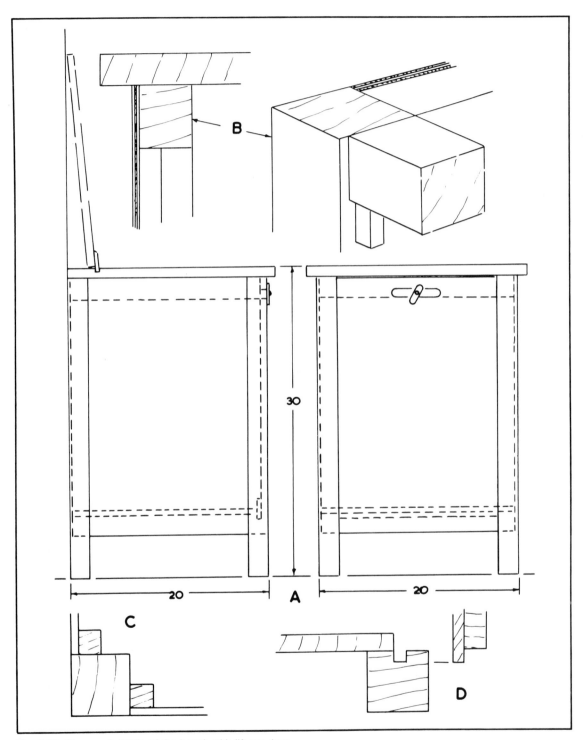

Fig. 9-20. Sizes and details of the bench with lift-out door.

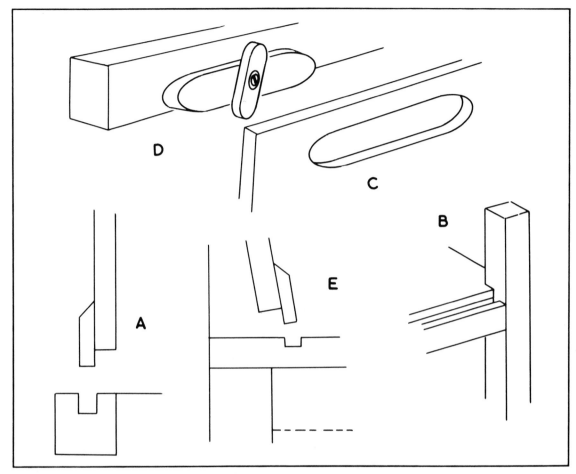

Fig. 9-21. The door fits into a groove and has a turnbutton at the top through a hand hole.

are in their racks facing forward. Make a groove in the top about 3 inches from the wall to take the extension on the door (Fig. 9-21E). The door may then be firm enough when sloping against the wall, but if there are heavy tools projecting some way from it to make it unsteady, put a hook on the wall so you can drop the handle over it as you lower the door into the slot in the bench top.

Materials List for Bench with Lift-Out Door

4 legs	2 × 30 × 2
6 rails	2 × 20 × 1 3/4
1 rail	2 × 20 × 2
1 rail	2 × 20 × 1 1/4
6 panel strips	3/4 × 24 × 3/4
3 panels	16 × 27 × 1/4 plywood

1 door	16 × 25 × 3/4 plywood
1 door extension	2 × 16 × 1/2
1 bottom	19 × 20 × 1/2
1 top	21 × 23 × 1
1 handle block	1 × 5 × 3/4

TILT-BIN TABLE

A lift-out door may have a bin attached so the bin as well as the door may be lifted out and used independently or taken away to empty. This small table or bench (Fig. 9-22) is at working height, where it could be of use in a kitchen or laundry, or it might serve as a stand for a machine in a shop. It is strong enough to be

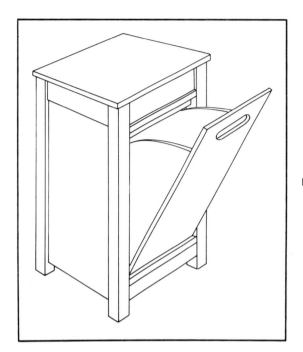

Fig. 9-22. A tilt-bin table.

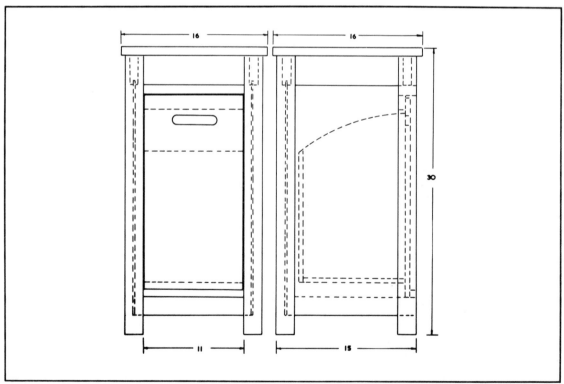

Fig. 9-23. Sizes for the tilt-bin table.

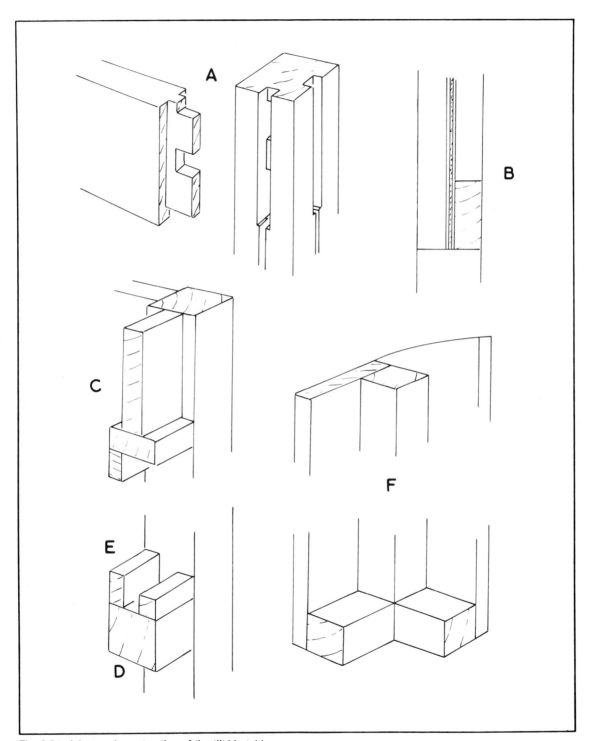

Fig. 9-24. Joints and construction of the tilt-bin table.

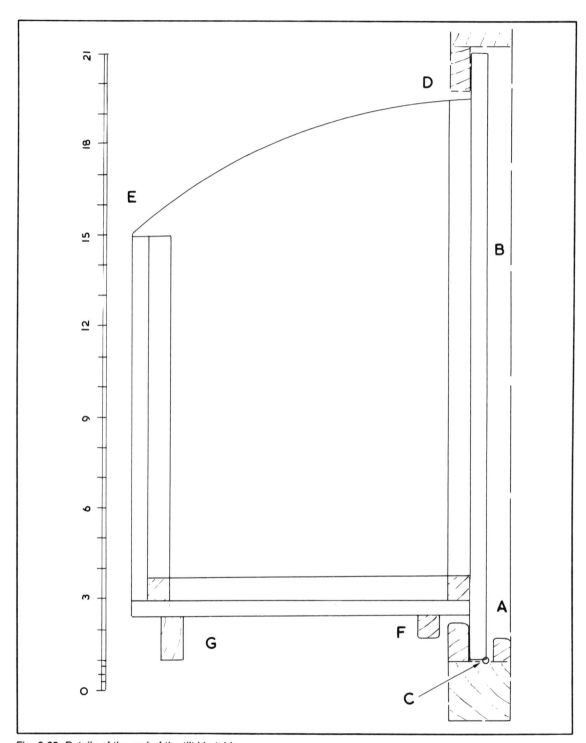

Fig. 9-25. Details of the end of the tilt-bin table.

a small bench for holding metalworking stakes, a bench grinder, or a small band saw. The sizes suggested in Fig. 9-23 provide a bit with an inside capacity about 11 inches square and 15 inches deep, mounted in a table with a top 16 inches square and 30 inches from the floor. The bin tilts forward on its front, either to put things in, or to come clear of the table and be lifted out. It will stand upright if put on the floor after removal.

Mark out the legs first. Plow grooves for the plywood centrally in two faces of each of the back legs and one face of each of the front legs. The top rails can be joined into the legs with dowels or mortise-and-tenon joints (Fig. 9-24A). Groove the rails for the panels on three sides. Bottom rails could be made similarly with grooves, but they are shown with the plywood overlapping (Fig. 9-24B), which is simpler and avoids ledges that would catch dust.

Below the top rail at the front comes a strip across, with a stop for the bin front attached (Fig. 9-24C). Glue it to the rail and dowel or tenon it to the legs. The bottom rail at the front is a square piece which provides the support for the bin front (Fig. 9-24D). Attach two guides to it. They do not have to make a close fit on the bin front; they are there to guide it into place when replaced and allow it to tilt easily (Fig. 9-24E and 25A). Round the top edges of the guides and allow at least 1/8 inch clearance on the plywood that will drop between them. There is no need for a rear support for the bin.

With all the parts prepared, assemble the pair of sides first, then add the back panel and rails and the front rails. Squareness in all directions is important; otherwise it will be difficult to make the bin move in and out without rubbing where it should not.

For the bin itself, it will help to make a full-size drawing of a side view (Fig. 9-25). Check the measurements inside your table and draw the bin's main outlines to suit. The front rests against the upper and lower guides (Fig. 9-25B). It will pivot on its bottom front edge, which is the point for the center of your compasses to draw the curved top of a side (Fig. 9-25C). Give the side a little clearance under the top guide (Fig. 9-25D). Make the height of the back to fit into the end of the curve (Fig. 9-25E).

Plywood will not make strong joints with nails or screws into its edges. Instead, use 3/4-inch square fillets in all joints (Fig. 9-24F), with glue and pins or fine nails.

Lap the front over the sides so the edge grain does not show in the front. For the other edges it does not matter which pieces go over.

The bottom edge of the front will take the weight of the bin and serve as a pivot. Sand it smooth and round its edges. A retaining strip under the bin (Fig. 9-25F) is not essential, but it may help in locating the front when dropping it into place. Toward the back put another strip across as a foot (Fig. 9-25G), at the same level as the front edge so the bin will stand level when lifted on to the floor.

Before assembling the bin parts, cut a hand hole through the front. Locate it below the guide strip so the front touches when closed. A hole 5 inches long and 1 inch wide gives sufficient space. Round its edges, since the weight of a loaded bin must be lifted by it. There is no need for a catch or fastener of any sort; the bin will be kept closed by its own weight.

Put a top on the table when you have tested the action of the bin. It is shown as solid wood which may be glued up from strips to give a strong work top, but plywood or particleboard could be fitted. Blocks inside may be screwed into the rails and upward into the top, or dowels could be used between the top and the edges of the rails.

Materials List for Tilt-Bin Table

Table
4 legs	$2 \times 30 \times 2$
4 top rails	$3 \times 14 \times 1$
1 bottom rail	$2 \times 14 \times 2$
3 bottom rails	$2 \times 14 \times 3/4$
2 front rails	$2 \times 14 \times 1$
3 panels	$14 \times 25 \times 1/4$ plywood
2 bin guides	$1\ 1/4 \times 14 \times 3/4$
2 bin guides	$3/4 \times 14 \times 5/8$

Bin
1 front	$11 \times 21 \times 1/2$ plywood
2 sides	$11\ 1/2 \times 18 \times 1/2$ plywood
1 back	$11 \times 13 \times 1/2$ plywood
1 bottom	$11 \times 13 \times 1/2$ plywood
4 frames	$3/4 \times 11 \times 3/4$
4 frames	$3/4 \times 17 \times 3/4$
1 foot	$1\ 1/2 \times 11 \times 3/4$

Chapter 10

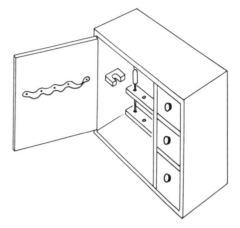

Simple Furniture
with Drawers and Doors

In furniture doors and drawers will often complement each other. Each has its uses. If you want to open a container and reach in horizontally, it can be closed with a door. If it would be better to have the particular items in a box, a drawer serves as such a sliding container. Large items, particularly if they should stand upright, are better in a cupboard or closet, with one or a pair of doors. Small items that would have to be piled high in a cupboard would be better in a drawer.

Another consideration is access. In most furniture or storage units, drawers should usually be below eye level so you can see into them when they are pulled out. If they are higher, you must stand on something to look into them, and that is a nuisance that may have to be accepted in some circumstances. If a large block of drawers, as may be needed in industry, must occupy a whole wall, some high ones have to be accepted.

Probably more important with drawers is the physical effort needed in moving them in and out. You may put a drawer just below eye level, but having to reach to that height makes moving a heavily loaded drawer difficult. Large drawers should not usually come above waist level if they are to be moved without difficulty when you are standing on the floor.

Doors are easier to move at any level. You may have

to reach down to a low one, but if the handle is near its top, that is not difficult. It is not so easy to see into a low cupboard as it is into a withdrawn drawer. High doors are certainly easier to use than drawers above eye level, and you can see most of what they enclose. At middle levels, there is not much difference between drawers and doors with regard to ease of working and visibility of contents.

Many pieces of furniture intended for use as storage units can be made with combinations of doors, drawers, and shelves. Besides offering a range of storage facilities to suit the usual variety of storage items, the mixed arrangement allows designs that are often more attractive in appearance than items which have only one method of storage. A particular piece of furniture standing on the floor can have one or more doors, with one or more drawers above, or the arrangement can be reversed. A hanging unit can combine bookshelves with a display cabinet, possibly with a small drawer underneath. Of the very large number of possible combinations, some are suggested in this and the following chapters.

BEDSIDE CABINET WITH DRAWER AND FLAP

This cabinet has one deep drawer and a compartment

above with a door hinged along its bottom edge so it lowers as a flap to extend the bottom of the compartment (Fig. 10-1). The top has a low border to stop things from falling off, and the flap reaches the same height when closed. Both the flap and drawer front overlap the sides of the cabinet and have handles for the full width, making it easy to pull in the dark or when still sleepy. The sizes shown in Fig. 10-2A are for a small cabinet, but they could be increased to suit your needs. Instructions are for building from veneered particleboard for all parts, except the back, the plinth, and the inner drawer parts, which could be solid wood or plywood.

Prepare the two sides. Put veneer on the top edges, but there will be no need to cover the particleboard surface at the bottom or rear edges. There could be rabbets in the rear edges for the back plywood. If, however, you do not have the equipment to rabbet particleboard, the plywood may go flat on the edges, if you do not mind the edges of the plies being exposed. You can put fillets inside—3/8 inch square is suitable—for the plywood to come inside the sides and shelves.

Mark out the sides where the top and shelf will come. The top and the shelves are all the same size, and they are doweled to the sides—1/4-inch dowels at about 3-inch

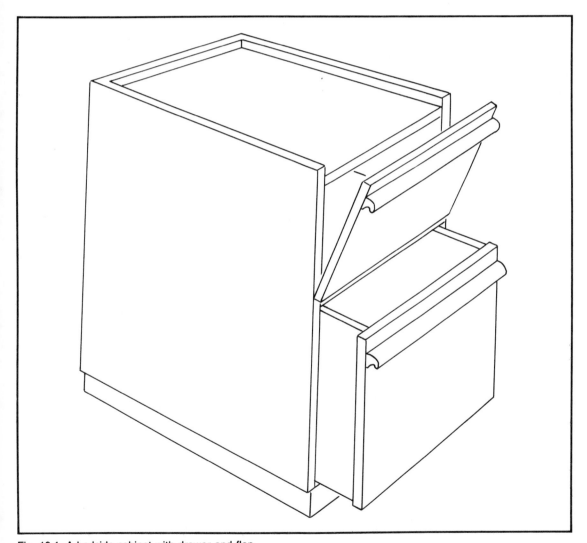

Fig. 10-1. A bedside cabinet with drawer and flap.

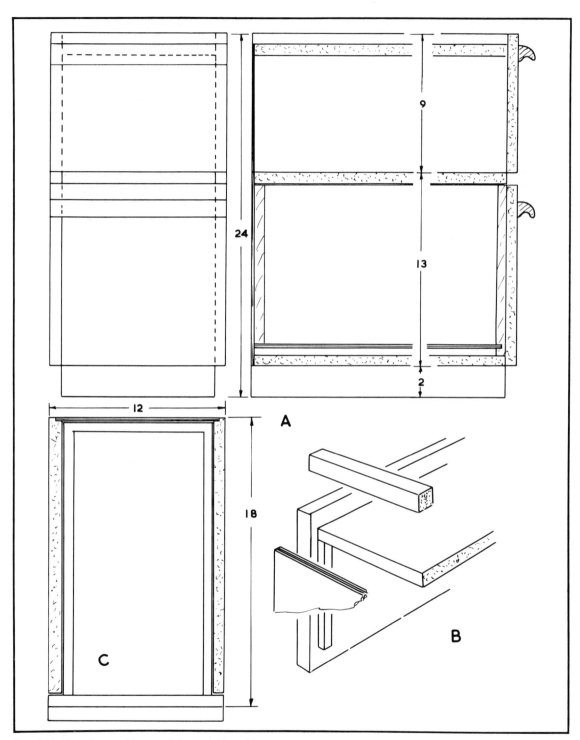

Fig. 10-2. The sizes and layout of the bedside cabinet.

intervals should be satisfactory. At the rear allow for the plywood back, which will overlap all three pieces (Fig. 10-2B).

The plinth is set in on three edges. There is no need for a part across the back. The plinth parts could be particleboard. The cabinet can be given an attractive appearance by using white plastic-covered particleboard for the main parts, with the plinth and the handles in solid wood stained and given a dark finish. If wood is used, miter the front corners and strengthen them with blocks inside (Fig. 10-3A). Attach the plinth parts with dowels into the bottom shelf.

Assemble the main parts of the cabinet. Have the back piece of plywood ready to fit in so it can be used to hold the parts square while the glue sets, but do not fix it in yet.

For the flap to drop level with the shelf, its hinges must be set into the surfaces (Fig. 10-3B). There could be two ordinary hinges, but this is a place where a piano hinge could go right across the joint. This hinge is obtainable in a long piece which you can cut and drill to suit your needs. When you assemble the flap to the cabinet, include a folding strut to hold the flap level when it is down (Fig. 10-3C). Make the flap so it comes from the level of the sides to the top of the shelf. There must be a gap between it and the drawer edge to allow it to swing into its lowered position. At the rear of the top, put a strip of wood or particleboard between the sides to come above the plywood back (Fig. 10-3D).

Make the drawer front to overlap the cabinet sides and the bottom shelf (Figs. 10-2C and 10-3E). Make the drawer sides so they fit easily between the shelves. Cut the inner front piece to the same depth, but its length must allow for the joints. Groove the sides and inner front piece for the plywood bottom. Make the drawer back to fit above the bottom grooves. The overlapping front will act as a drawer stop, so there is no need to allow space for stops at the rear. Make the drawer with any of the corner joints described in Chapter 7, but dovetails are best (Fig. 10-3F). Slide the plywood into its grooves and secure it by screwing under the back piece. When you are satisfied that the drawer will slide properly into place, drill for screws at the front. It will be easier to attach the handle before you screw the drawer front parts together.

You may be able to get plastic handle-section material in long pieces, but wood handles are suggested (Fig. 10-3G). The materials list gives the overall sizes, but it is easier to make handles if you can start with a wider board and not cut the handle off until it has been fully shaped. Attach the handle to the drawer with screws from

inside. Their heads will be covered when you screw the inner front on. The flap handle could be attached with short dowels, or you could screw from the back, with the heads counterbored and covered with plastic plugs. The folding flap stay may have enough friction in it to hold the flap closed, but if not, put a spring or magnetic catch at one side to hold the flap up. If the cabinet is going beside a bed, arrange the stay and catch on the side further from the bed so they do not interfere with access.

Materials List
for Bedside Cabinet with Drawer and Flap

2 sides	18 × 25 × 3/4
1 top	10 1/2 × 18 × 3/4
2 shelves	10 1/2 × 18 × 3/4
1 back	12 × 23 × 1/4 plywood
1 flap	9 × 13 × 3/4
1 drawer front	12 1/4 × 13 × 3/4
1 drawer front	12 × 12 × 5/8
2 drawer sides	10 1/2 × 18 × 5/8
1 drawer back	10 × 12 × 5/8
1 drawer bottom	10 1/2 × 18 × 1/4 plywood
handles	1 1/4 × 26 × 1 1/4
1 plinth	2 × 12 × 3/4
1 plinth	2 × 18 × 3/4

STOOL WITH DRAWER

A stool with enclosed storage below it is useful in a bathroom or elsewhere, and if it has a drawer as well, many things can be stored conveniently. The stool shown in Fig. 10-4 has a framed construction, and there are handles at the sides for easy moving. The size (Fig. 10-5) gives a useful capacity and is a convenient height for sitting. Construction is based on four legs with plywood panels.

Start by making a pair of opposite sides (Fig. 10-6A). Groove the legs for their full lengths to take the plywood—on two edges for the back legs and one edge on each of the front legs. Top and bottom back and side rails (Fig. 10-6B) are also grooved for plywood. A suitable spacing is 1/4 inch in from the outer edges. At the front there are similar rails for the top and below the drawer, but they are not grooved.

The lower rails and the rail below the drawer are joined to the legs with plain mortise-and-tenon joints. The four top rails are not deep enough for haunched mortise-and-tenon joints; so they must be made open (Fig. 10-6C). This type of joint is not very strong in itself, but there

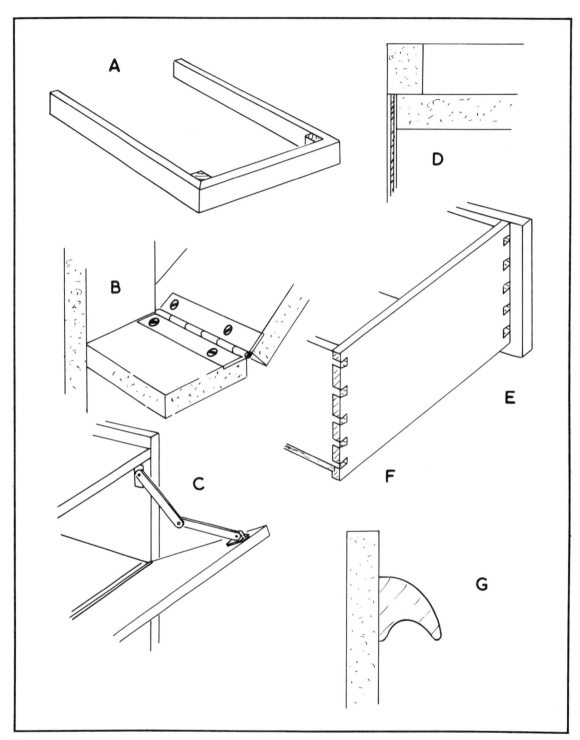

Fig. 10-3. Constructional details of the bedside cabinet with drawer and flap.

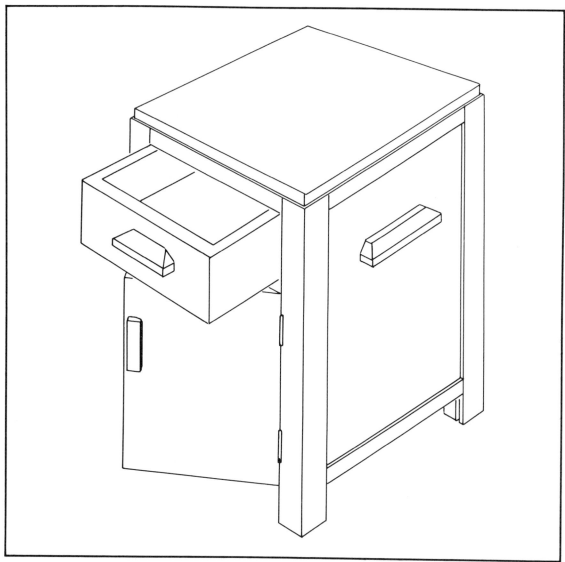

Fig. 10-4. A stool with a drawer and door.

can be screws downward through the tenons, and the top, when it is put on, will provide more strength.

Assemble the pair of sides and have the parts ready to fit the other way, but first make the drawer guides and runners (Fig. 10-6D). The thickness of the guide inside the plywood should come exactly level with the insides of the legs, and the runner top edge must be level with the top of the drawer rail across the front.

Join in the strips and the back panel to make the stool square. For the bottom make a panel to rest on the bot-

tom rails and fit close to the back and side panels. At the front, set back the plywood enough to allow for the thickness of the door (Fig. 10-6E).

There is nothing to close the gap between the drawer and the space below. This will probably not matter, but if you will be storing things below which should be kept clear of the drawer, you can groove the drawer rail and the two runners to take a plywood panel.

Make the drawer before you fit the door and the top. You can choose any of the methods described earlier for drawers, preferably using dovetail joints. Make the drawer so its front finishes level or very slightly forward of the legs and rails.

You could put knobs or bought handles on the drawer, door, and sides, but an angular wood type is shown, with three the same for the drawer and lifting, and a matching one on the door. Each handle starts with a square section; then a strip for all three can be beveled (Fig. 10-7A) and marked out for the outside cuts (Fig. 10-7B). Before

cutting there, however, mark and cut inside (Fig. 10-7C). The door handle has tapers at both sides (Fig. 10-7D) and the ends. All are fixed with glue and screws from inside. The lifting handles will be easier to fit before the stool sides are joined with the crosswise rails.

The top of the stool is set back a little from the edges, although it could be made level if you wish. A few screws upward through the top rails will supplement glue. The wood top could be upholstered before it is screwed down.

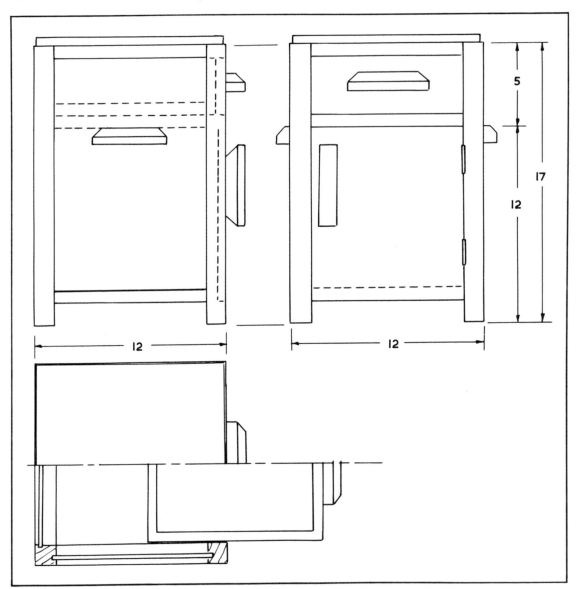

Fig. 10-5. Dimensions of the stool with drawer and door.

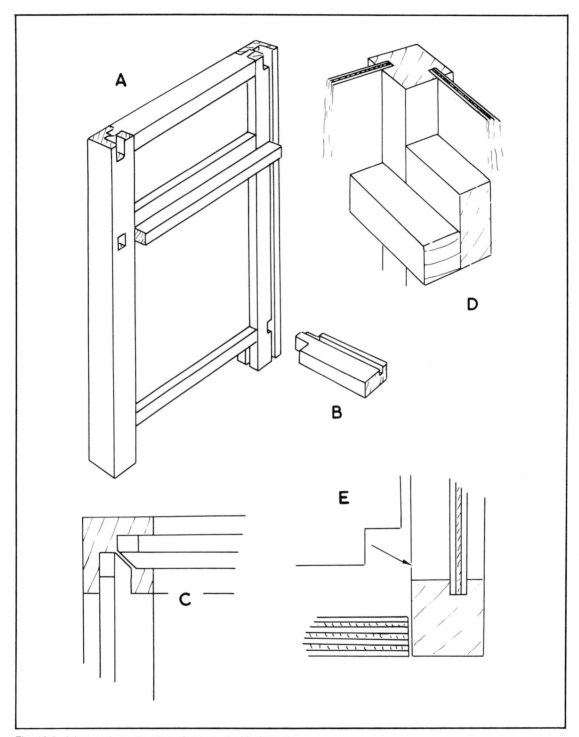

Fig. 10-6. Joints and construction of the stool with drawer.

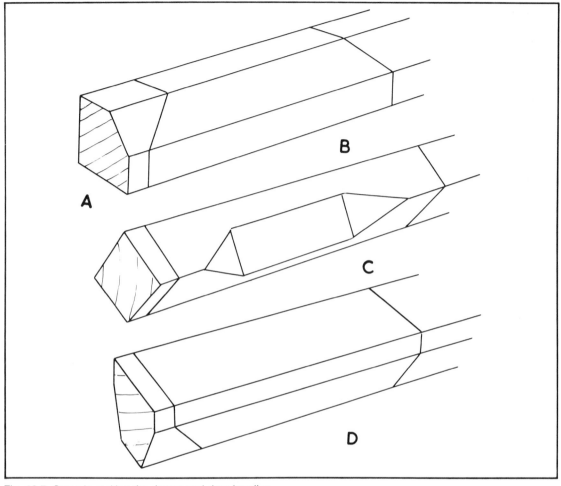

Fig. 10-7. Steps in making the drawer and door handles.

In that case, do not use glue so you can take off the top easily if you ever need to replace the upholstery. Alternatively, you could glue a piece of cork on the top for use in a bathroom.

Materials List for Stool with Drawer

4 legs	1 1/4 × 18 × 1 1/4
7 rails	1 1/4 × 12 × 3/4
2 drawer guides	1 1/4 × 11 × 3/4
2 drawer runners	3/4 × 12 × 3/4
1 top	12 × 12 × 1/2
1 bottom	11 × 12 × 1/2
3 panels	11 × 15 × 1/4 plywood
1 drawer front	3 1/2 × 10 × 5/8
2 drawer sides	3 1/2 × 10 × 1/2
1 drawer back	3 × 10 × 1/2
1 drawer bottom	10 × 10 × 1/4 plywood
1 door	9 1/2 × 10 × 1/2 plywood
4 handles	1 1/4 × 6 × 1 1/4

HOBBY TOOL CABINET

For many of the lighter and smaller crafts, there are just a few tools and many small items, such as buttons and fasteners for sewing, dollmaking, and similar fabricwork. There may be studs, fasteners, and eyelets for leatherwork. Some sort of storage unit is worth having, but it does not need to be as large or extensive as would be needed for woodworking or metalworking.

Two versions of small cabinets are suggested in Fig. 10-8. Each has a cabinet space enclosed with a door, where racks can be arranged for tools around the sides and inside the door; then there are drawers for small items. The sizes (Fig. 10-9) make units that could be attached to a wall or stood on a table or bench. They are also small enough to be portable so they can be put away and brought out only when needed, or they can be carried with you if you are occupied with demonstrating or teaching your craft.

Both cabinets are made in the same way; only the layouts are different. Check the sizes of tools and equipment you want to store. Sizes may need to be adapted to suit long tools, or a drawer may need to be made deeper to suit particular things. The following instructions are for the cabinet with three drawers alongside the door. Some notes are provided if you wish to make the cabinet with two bottom drawers.

Three-Drawer Cabinet

Prepare the parts for the outside of the cabinet, with rabbets at the back to take the plywood. Cut the wood for the divisions to the width inside the cabinet. The corner joints could be dovetails; rabbets with fine nails each way would also be satisfactory (Fig. 10-10A). Plain

nailed or screwed laps would do for less important construction. The wood is too thin for satisfactory dowel joints.

There will not be much load on the division joints when the whole cabinet has been assembled. Shallow stopped dado joints (Fig. 10-10B) will ensure exact locations, which are important for door and drawer fitting, since lack of squareness there will spoil the action and appearance.

Assemble the cabinet, including fitting the plywood back to hold the other parts square. If there are wood racks that must be fitted against the sides and back, they could be given their own dadoes and be fitted during main assembly. If you think you may want to alter rack arrangements later, it may be better to merely screw the racks in, without cutting joints, so they can be removed with a minimum of trouble.

The door is a plain piece of 1/2-inch plywood. You could frame thinner plywood instead to give a recess inside, which may be of value in storing thin books or paper patterns (Fig. 10-10C). In either case, allow for letting in a pair of hinges, providing a catch at the opening side,

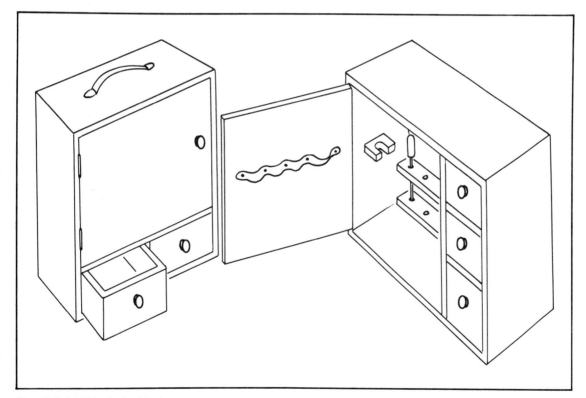

Fig. 10-8. A hobby tool cabinet.

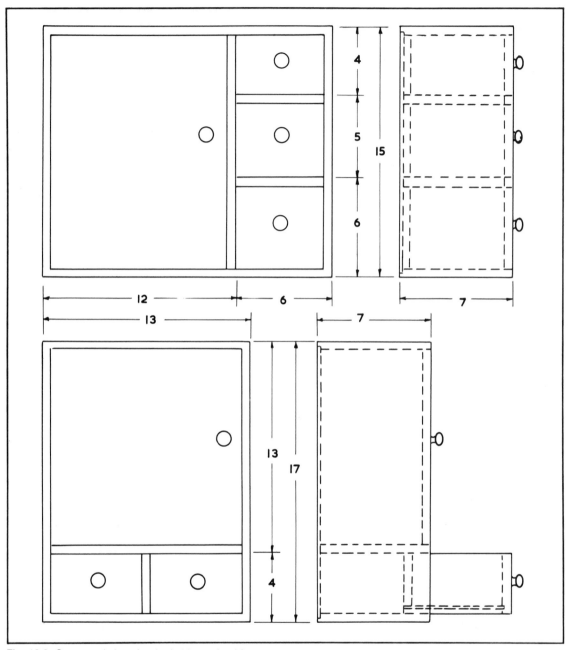

Fig. 10-9. Suggested sizes for the hobby tool cabinet.

and adding a handle. For neatness the handle can come level with the handle of the middle drawer.

Make the drawer fronts, cutting them to fit fairly closely in their spaces. Use them as guides when mak-

ing the other drawer parts. For the best work, use dovetails. These small drawers would, however, still be satisfactory with the sides glued and pinned into front rabbets and with the backs in dadoes above the bottoms

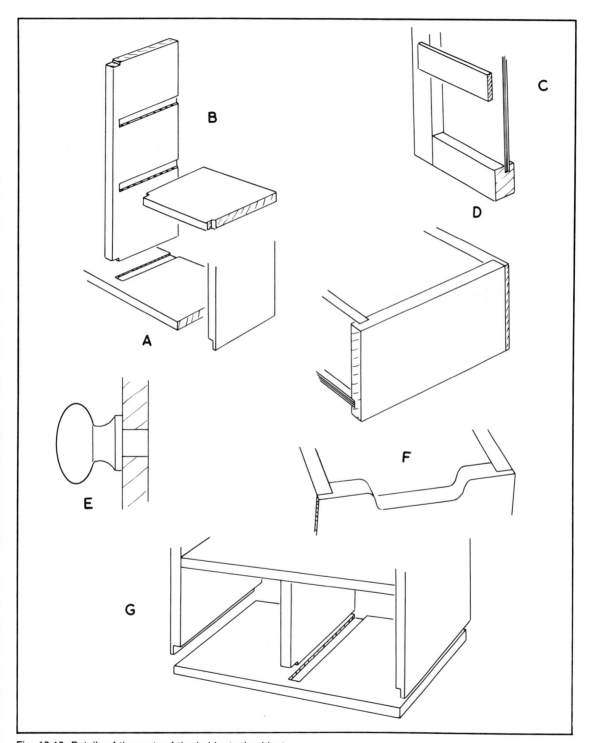

Fig. 10-10. Details of the parts of the hobby tool cabinet.

in the usual grooves (Fig. 10-10D). Hardboard could be used instead of plywood for the bottoms, but for hard or sharp contents, it is more liable to damage.

Round knobs are shown as handles (Fig. 10-10E), preferably placed just above the drawer center and with dowels through the fronts. If you want to avoid projections because you need to frequently transport the cabinet, handles with drop nails might be used, or you could let in handles almost flush. Even simpler would be notching the edge of each drawer and the door, just enough to get two fingers in (Fig. 10-10F). Fit a carrying handle, if needed. A piece of leather strap may be all that is required, or you could choose a leather or metal handle with bolts through. You can stop the drawers from sliding out during transport by fitting spring ball catches in their edges.

Materials List for
Three-Drawer Hobby Tool Cabinet

2 sides	7 × 16 × 1/2
1 top	7 × 19 × 1/2
1 bottom	7 × 19 × 1/2
1 division	6 3/4 × 16 × 1/2
2 divisions	6 3/4 × 6 × 1/2
1 back	15 × 19 × 1/4 plywood
1 door	11 × 15 × 1/2 plywood
1 drawer front	3 1/2 × 6 × 1/2
2 drawer sides	3 1/2 × 7 × 1/2
1 drawer back	3 × 6 × 1/2
1 drawer front	4 1/2 × 6 × 1/2
2 drawer sides	4 1/2 × 6 × 1/2
1 drawer back	4 × 6 × 1/2
1 drawer front	5 × 6 × 1/2
2 drawer sides	5 × 7 × 1/2
1 drawer back	4 1/2 × 6 × 1/2
3 drawer bottoms	5 1/2 × 7 × 1/4 plywood

Two-Drawer Cabinet

Details of construction of the other cabinet are the same. Use shallow dadoes for the division between the drawers (Fig. 10-10G). The door can be hinged at either side. In the first cabinet, it would be inconvenient if it was hinged on the drawer side. The layout of the second design assumes there are no weight problems. If your hobby involves heavy tools and light materials in the drawers, it would be better to make the cabinet with the drawers above the door; that is, turning the whole assembly upside down, but with no other differences to the main construction. You will probably want to pull the drawers right out for use on the table, but otherwise there could be stops inside to hold a drawer back an inch or so inside its casing.

Materials List for
Two-Drawer Hobby Tool Cabinet

2 sides	7 × 18 × 1/2
1 top	7 × 14 × 1/2
1 bottom	7 × 14 × 1/2
1 division	6 3/4 × 14 × 1/2
1 division	6 3/4 × 4 × 1/2
1 back	13 × 17 × 1/4 plywood
1 door	12 × 13 × 1/2 plywood
2 drawer fronts	3 1/2 × 6 × 1/2
2 drawer sides	3 1/2 × 7 × 1/2
2 drawer backs	3 × 6 × 1/2
2 drawer bottoms	6 × 7 × 1/4 plywood

WALL CABINET WITH DRAWERS

A cabinet mounted on the wall has uses in many parts of the home, including bedroom, bathroom and kitchen. It would also have a use in a utility room or shop. It could be equipped to suit your needs, but the example in Fig. 10-11 is shown as it might be equipped for use in a kitchen or laundry room, with two lower rails to take towels and pegs at the sides for hanging other things. There are double doors and two small drawers.

Top and bottom are shown with decorative curves. The cabinet could be made with straight cuts, but if the top is kept fairly high it will hold a row of books upright. Construction of the main parts is very similar to a hanging bookcase. The sizes shown in Fig. 10-12A will produce a cabinet of average size, but they could be altered. If you redesign it, however, keep each door higher than it is wide and do not make the drawers much wider than their depth back-to-front, or they may not slide in and out easily.

If you intend to curve the edges, make card or hardboard templates of the shapes. The ends of the sides are all the same (Fig. 10-12B), and a half template of the back curves can be turned over to get them symmetrical (Fig. 10-12C).

Mark out the pair of sides and cut the dado joints before shaping the ends (Fig. 10-13A). Make a rabbet along the back for the plywood, then widen above and below the outer shelves for the thicker back pieces (Fig. 10-13B). Either use dovetailed dado joints or drive thin screws or nails diagonally upward near the fronts of the top and bottom shelves. The plywood back will secure the rear ends of the dado joints. Fit the plywood to the backs of all three shelves, as well as into the rabbets. Stop it at the outer edges of the top and bottom shelves so the

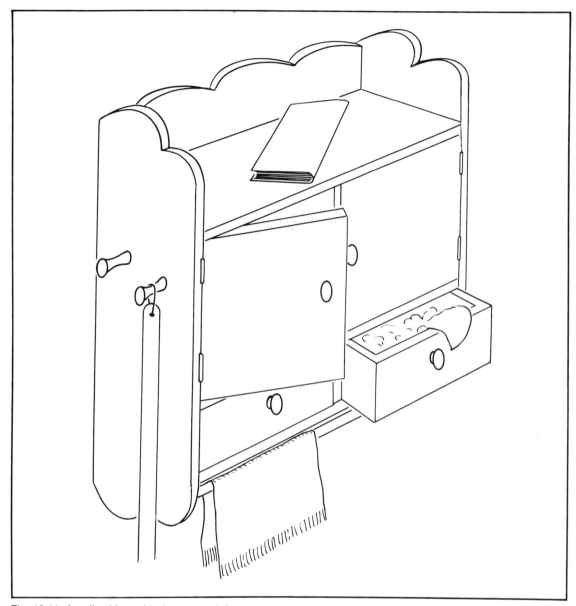

Fig. 10-11. A wall cabinet with drawers and doors.

thicker pieces can be put into the rabbets and be glued to the shelves.

Do all of the edge shaping before you assemble the parts. Be careful that the curves match and remove all signs of saw and other tool marks. Sharp angles can be rounded off slightly, but the effect is better with clean cuts square across than with the sections rounded. Drill

for the pegs and the towel rails before assembly so both sides will match. The rails could go right through or be put into stopped holes (Fig. 10-13C). You can buy turned "Shaker" pegs, but your own turned shorter ones may be better (Fig. 10-13D).

The doors are plain pieces of 1/2-inch plywood. The edges can be left untreated, or you can glue on thin strips,

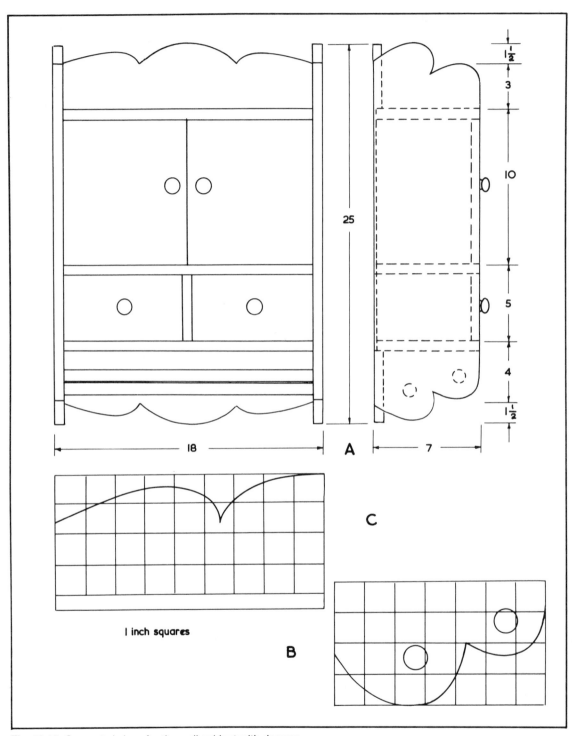

Fig. 10-12. Suggested sizes for the wall cabinet with drawers.

either all around or just along the meeting edges (Fig. 10-13E). Hinge the doors in the usual way and put small stops at top and bottom for them to close against (Fig. 10-13F). Spring or ball catches will keep the doors closed. Round knobs are shown, but any type of handle could be used, with the door and drawer handles in matching designs.

Make the drawer fronts to fit the openings with a little clearance; then make the drawers in the way suggested for the previous project (Fig. 10-10D). They should be stopped by the plywood back when the fronts are either level or projecting about 1/8 inch. Fit handles or knobs (Fig. 10-10E).

There could be a shelf inside or racks for tools and

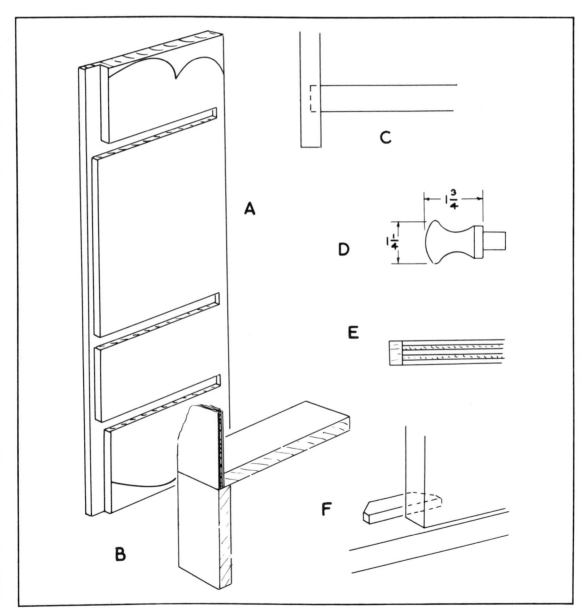

Fig. 10-13. The parts of the wall cabinet with drawers.

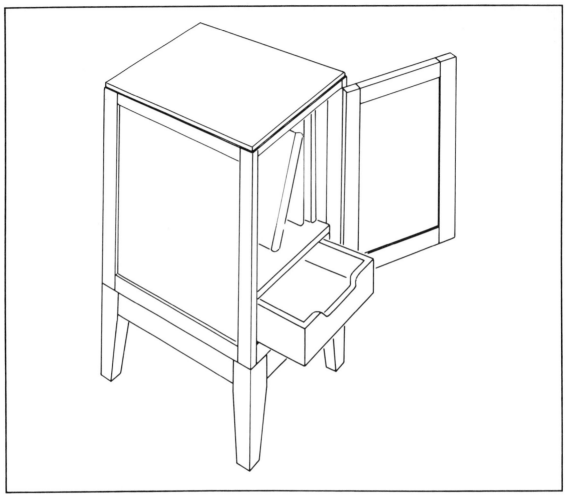

Fig. 10-14. A vertical filing cabinet.

equipment, but for varied use it is better to leave the interior plain so as much as possible can be put in. Hang the cabinet with two widely-spaced screws high in the plywood back. Two should be enough, unless the rip in the wall is not very secure.

Materials List for Wall Cabinet with Drawers

2 sides	7 × 26 × 5/8
3 shelves	6 3/4 × 18 × 5/8
1 back	4 1/2 × 18 × 5/8
1 back	5 1/2 × 18 × 5/8
2 doors	8 1/2 × 10 × 1/2 plywood
1 back	16 × 18 × 1/4 plywood
1 divider	5 × 7 × 1/2
2 drawer fronts	4 3/8 × 9 × 1/2
2 drawer sides	4 3/8 × 7 × 1/2
2 drawer backs	4 × 9 × 1/2
2 drawer bottoms	7 × 9 × 1/4 plywood
2 rails	3/4 × 18 round

VERTICAL FILING CABINET

This cabinet has an optional stand, intended primarily for storing filed papers, account books, documents, and important small items in an office or study, but it could be used in the home for general storage. The cabinet is of framed plywood construction (Fig. 10-14), arranged inside for upright storage with a drawer underneath. The door encloses the drawer; so if it is provided with a lock,

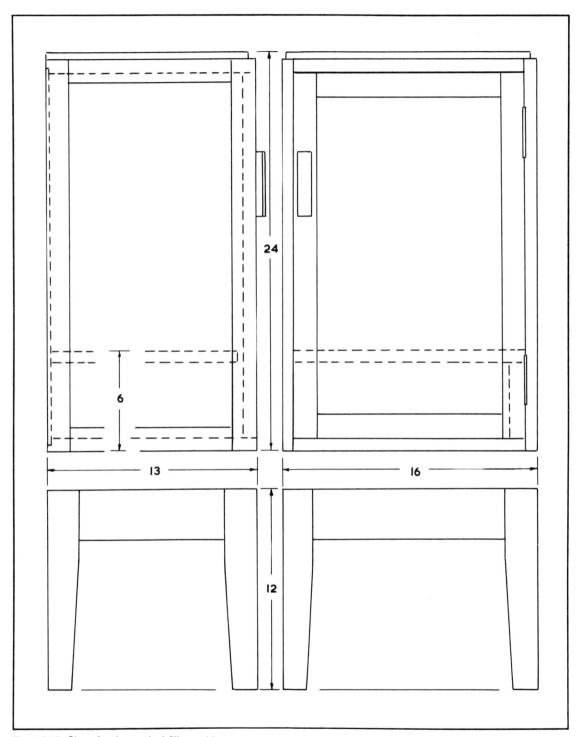

Fig. 10-15. Sizes for the vertical filing cabinet.

everything inside is secure. The cabinet is 24 inches high and might stand on a table, but if it is to be independent, there is a stand to go under it and raise the top to 36 inches. The two parts are separate pieces, so they can be moved independently. If arrangements are changed, and the cabinet is to be put on a table, the stand can have a top added to make it into a stool or small table.

The sizes (Fig. 10-15) allow more than enough vertical space for the usual paper files, and larger account books can also be stood with them. Check what you want to store and adjust the sizes to suit, but allow some extra space so the contents can be handled easily.

The cabinet is made with a pair of frame sides joined with top and bottom frames and a shelf above the drawer. The plywood back goes into rabbets in the sides. The door, which is framed, fits within the other parts.

Make the pair of sides (Fig. 10-16A). Rabbet the rear edges to take the back. Groove the inner edges centrally to take the plywood panels. Corners can be mortise and tenon jointed, or there could be dowels. Where the shelf is to come, notch the uprights to take it. At the rear, notch the full width to the depth of the panel groove (Fig. 10-16B). At the front make a similar notch, but stop it about 1/8 inch back from where the door will come (Fig. 10-16C).

For the bottom of the cabinet make a frame with rabbets to take a piece of plywood (Fig. 10-16D). Make sure the plywood and its frame finish flush, since the drawer slides on this surface. At the top make another frame of exactly the same size, but without the plywood (Fig. 10-16E). Both frames fit against the inside edges of the rabbet, and the plywood back will be taken over them. They are doweled to the sides—3/8-inch dowels at about 3-inch intervals should be satisfactory.

Make the shelf from 1/2-inch plywood. For the best finish, lip its front edge with solid wood. When you assemble the cabinet, it must fit closely to the side plywood panels. For the best fit, wait until the top and bottom have been doweled in place, then cut the shelf so it will slide in tightly from the rear before you fit the plywood back there. If the door is swung wide open, it clears the front of the cabinet so a full-width drawer will slide out, but if it is opened little more than 90 degrees it will obstruct the movement of the drawer. So that you do not always need to swing the door wide, put a strip under the shelf on the hinge side to make the drawer a little narrower and to clear the partly open door (Fig. 10-16F).

Above the top frame there is a piece held with glue and screws from below. It looks best if it is level at the back, but set in about 1/8 inch on the other three sides.

In that way it covers the back plywood edges and looks neater elsewhere than a flush treatment. There are several ways of making the top. It could be a simple piece of plywood with its edges exposed. It would be better lipped, and even better with the lip widened so the edges might be molded on all sides except the back (Fig. 10-16G).

The drawer may be made in any of the usual ways. It could be kept far enough back for a handle to project without touching the door. If you want the drawer to be as deep as possible, back to front, make it to the front of the shelf, then a finger notch (Fig. 10-14) will serve instead of a handle.

The door is made like the sides, with a plywood panel in central grooves in the solid wood frame, which can have mortise-and-tenon or dowel joints at the corners. Keep the knuckles of the hinges far enough out for the door to swing 180 degrees when required. A strip wood or plastic handle is shown, but a turned knob could be used. The shelf may act as a door stop, but if it is set too far back, put a small strip of wood as a stop on the side near its center. If a lock is needed, arrange it below the handle and make a keyhole through the door side.

If the cabinet is mounted on a stand, make it the same size as the cabinet bottom or set it back about 1/4 inch all around. If set back in this way, slight errors in the fit

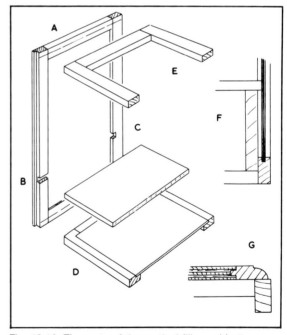

Fig. 10-16. The parts of the vertical filing cabinet.

222

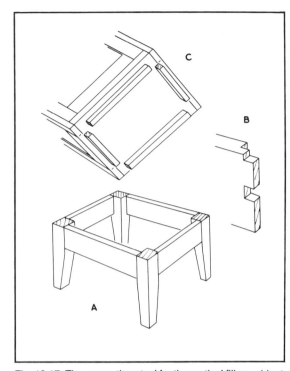

Fig. 10-17. The supporting stool for the vertical filing cabinet.

2 top frames	1 1/2 × 16 × 3/4
2 top frames	1 1/2 × 13 × 3/4
2 bottoms	1 1/2 × 16 × 3/4
2 bottoms	1 1/2 × 13 × 3/4
1 bottom	12 × 15 × 1/4 plywood
1 shelf	12 × 16 × 1/2 plywood
2 side panels	11 × 22 × 1/4 plywood
1 back	16 × 25 × 1/4 plywood
1 top	13 × 16 × 1/2 plywood
2 door frames	1 1/2 × 24 × 3/4
2 door frames	1 1/2 × 15 × 3/4
1 door panel	13 × 21 × 1/4 plywood
4 drawer parts	4 3/4 × 15 × 3/4
1 drawer back	4 1/4 × 15 × 1/2
1 drawer bottom	13 × 15 × 1/4 plywood

Stand
4 legs	2 × 13 × 2
4 rails	3 × 14 × 3/4
4 guide strips	3/4 × 13 × 3/4

DESK WITH SIDE STORAGE

There are many uses for a table with a flat top and some storage at one side so it is possible to sit with ample knee room, yet have many of the things needed stored within reach. The obvious example is a desk, but the same thing would be valuable for any craft where the worker sits more than he stands. The table shown in Fig. 10-18 has a top 24 inches wide and 48 inches long, standing on strong legs and with a drawer and cabinet extending downward under one side, but not to the floor. The sizes suggested in Fig. 10-19 give a good working area and no restrictions on knees when sitting. The drawer is large enough to take the common sizes of paper, with plenty of space, as well, for pens and other office accessories or for small tools. The space below is very roomy and can be divided to suit whatever you want to store.

The design is basically a table, made in the standard way, with deep rails to support the top and lower rails around three sides. It is modified to take in the cabinet. Two methods of construction are possible. The traditional way uses mortise-and-tenon joints in most positions; dowels can also be used, however. The materials list allows enough length for cutting tenons. The drawings show ends cut off level, as they would be when being prepared for dowels. Either method would be satisfactory.

The key parts are the two end assemblies. The table is shown with the storage at the left, but it could be either way. Where instructions refer to directions, they assume

of the meeting parts are not obvious. Make the stand like the framework of a table (Fig. 10-17A). The legs are shown tapered on the inner surfaces only. They could be tapered all around; they could be given feet, or they could be turned below the rail level if the whole assembly must match other nearby furniture.

Join the rails into the legs with dowels or mortise-and-tenon joints (Fig. 10-17B). The rails are shown with their outer surfaces level with the leg surfaces, but they could be set back, without altering the method of mounting the cabinet. Assemble the square the stand. Check its size and shape against the cabinet bottom. At this stage it may be possible to alter the stand, but the cabinet bottom is now unalterable.

To locate the cabinet on its stand, put strips under to fit into the stand (Fig. 10-17C). Unless you want to make the whole assembly into one unit, these strips are attached to the cabinet, but they are a sliding fit into the stand so the cabinet will lift off.

Materials List for Vertical Filing Cabinet

Cabinet
| 4 side frames | 1 1/2 × 25 × 3/4 |
| 4 side frames | 1 1/2 × 13 × 3/4 |

223

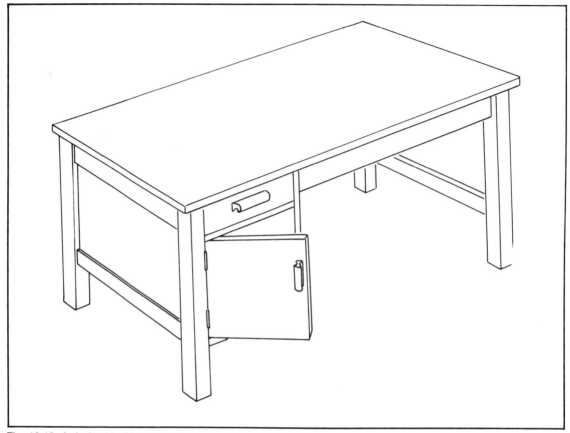

Fig. 10-18. A desk with side storage.

storage is on the left. Mark out the legs together to get important parts level, particularly the main rails, which are the same at both ends. Continue with the assembly at the right (Fig. 10-19A) which is the same as for a simple table. Cut the joints or drill the dowel holes for the rails that come back to front. Prepare also for the lengthwise rails; there is no lengthwise lower rail at the front.

Assemble that end, making sure it is square and flat. Use it as a pattern for the other end assembly (Fig. 10-19B) which has rails in the same place, but they and the legs should be grooved for a plywood panel (Fig. 10-20A). Allow for letting in a full-depth panel at the back (Fig. 10-20B). Beside the rails and panel across between the legs, there must be pieces to control the drawer.

At the front there is a piece on edge at the bottom of the cabinet (Fig. 10-20C) and another piece between the door and the drawer (Fig. 10-20D). Prepare the legs to take these parts. At the top of the end there is a piece

the same thickness as the front rail to serve as a kicker (Fig. 10-20E and F). At the drawer bottom, another piece makes a runner with the strip above it brought out to the thickness of the legs as a guide (Fig. 10-20G and H). Join these pieces as you assemble the end, checking that the assembly makes a pair with the opposite end.

At the other side of the cabinet is another piece of framed plywood (Fig. 10-20J), At its back notch it around the top and bottom rear rails and use dowels to attach them, even if you are using tenons for most other joints. Also at the back include a grooved piece to take the edge of the back plywood panel (Fig. 10-20K). Put kicker, runner, and drawer guide across (Fig. 10-20L) at levels to match those on the end assembly and prepare the front edge of the frame for the rails to the leg.

The bottom of the cabinet is a piece of plywood fitted inside the bottom rails and resting on bearers glued and nailed to them (Fig. 10-20M and N). Fit the bearers before assembling the main parts of the table.

Have the two end assemblies made up, with as many parts attached as possible. Let the glue set and clean off any surplus. Sand parts that may be difficult to get at after assembly. Have the interframe made up as far as possible. With all the other loose parts ready, assemble the table on a flat surface. Check diagonals frequently to get all parts square to each other. Put in the rails that go full-length first, then add the interframe with its shorter rails. Make sure the front rail (Fig. 10-20P) joins the cabinet so the top edges are in a straight line between the legs.

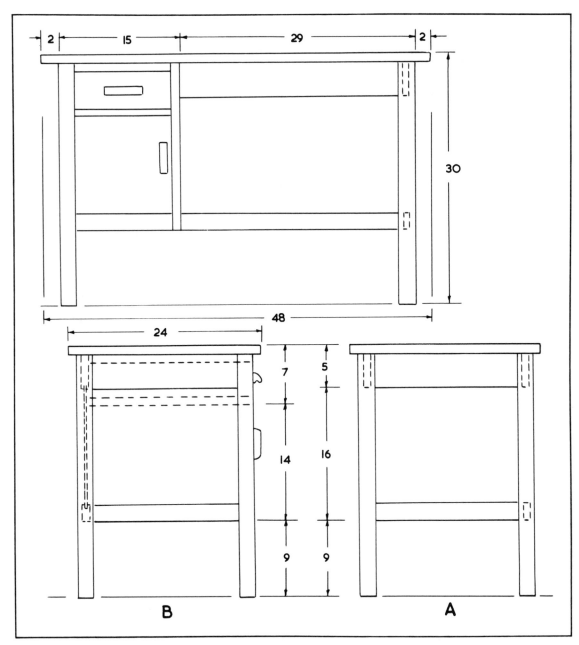

Fig. 10-19. Suggested sizes for the desk with side storage.

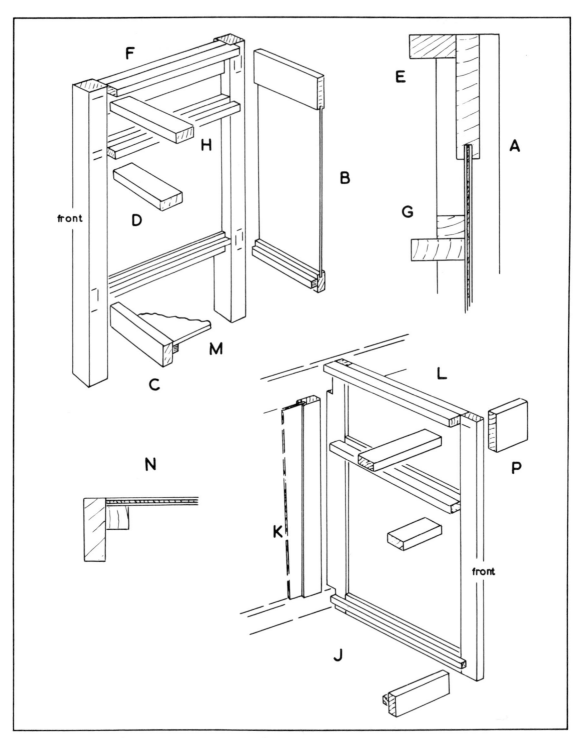

Fig. 10-20. Assembly of the parts of the desk with side storage.

Put the bottom in the cabinet when you are satisfied that all the other parts are correct.

Make the door with a single piece of plywood, preferably lipped. Hinge it to the leg so the door opens to swing away from the user. If you make the drawer to go right across the width of the table, it is a considerable length. You may want to shorten it. In that case, put stops on the runners to suit the drawer. It is shown as having a flush front, but it could be made to overlap, if you wish. Make the drawer in any of the usual ways. Fit matching handles to the door and drawer.

The top could be made in several ways. Whatever type is chosen, it can be fitted with dowels to the rails, with buttons engaging with slots in the rails (if the top is liable to expand and contract), with screws driven upward through pockets in the rails, or with screws through metal plates let into the tops of the rails.

The choice of top will depend on the intended use. Plastic veneered particleboard would suit kitchen, floral, or greenhouse use. Thick plywood makes a tough work surface for many activities. It should have solid wood lips all around. Thin plywood could be framed. A fairly substantial frame, possibly 1 × 4 inches, could take a piece of 3/8-inch or 1/2-inch plywood in rabbets. If the framing is hardwood, and the plywood is faced with an attractive veneer, you can finish it with clear polish. Plywood could be used in a similar way, but sunk below its surround just enough to allow for a piece of leather or simulated leather to be glued in to give a traditional desk-top finish.

A solid wood top would have to be made with boards glued to make up the width. This choice would be best if fairly heavy and rough work is contemplated on the top. The table then becomes a metalworking or woodworking bench, but it is not stout enough for the heaviest work.

Its large, flat surface makes it very suitable in a shop for assembly work, after heavy hitting and cutting has been done on another bench. The top could be made of narrow, solid wood strips to give a butcher block effect, either for the sake of its strength and rigidity for working on or in order to match other furniture treated in that way.

The top is shown overlapping 2 inches at the ends and 1 inch at front and back, enough for clamp-on lamps and tools at the ends. Excessive overhang can be a nuisance; so do not make the top much more than that shown over its lower parts.

Materials List for Desk with Side Storage

Table structure

4 legs	2 × 30 × 2
1 top rail	4 × 44 × 3/4
3 top rails	4 × 29 × 3/4
2 lower rails	2 × 22 × 3/4
1 lower rail	2 × 44 × 3/4
2 end panels	18 × 19 × 1/4 plywood
1 top	24 × 48 × 1

Cabinet

3 uprights	2 × 20 × 3/4
4 rails	2 × 22 × 3/4
4 bottom bearers	3/4 × 19 × 3/4
1 bottom	14 × 20 × 1/4 plywood
2 drawer runners	2 × 20 × 3/4
2 drawer kickers	1 1/2 × 20 × 3/4
2 drawer guides	3/4 × 20 × 3/4
1 door	13 × 13 × 1/2 plywood
1 drawer front	4 1/2 × 13 × 3/4
2 drawer sides	4 1/2 × 22 × 5/8
1 drawer back	4 × 13 × 5/8
1 drawer bottom	13 × 22 × 1/4 plywood

Chapter 11

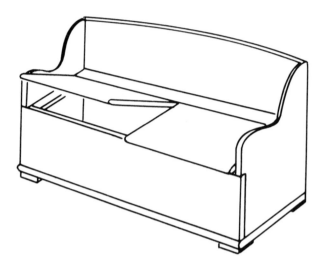

Reproductions

Just about everything in the world is in a state of development, including furniture. Besides developments due to new materials and equipment, there are changes in design. In both cases the changes are not always for the good, although many of them are. We are in the fortunate position of being able to learn from the past, adopt what we like from it, and discard the earlier mistakes or anything that does not appeal to us.

Obviously, none of us want to go so far back into history as to fell a tree, split it into boards, and fashion it crudely into something of use. Neither do we want to convert logs to boards by using a pit saw. We do not want to do any of the laborious tasks that were usual when there were no power tools, but what we do now could still have similar results, if we use power for routine jobs and hand tools for finishing.

Not so long ago, only solid wood was available, and glues were not as reliable as they are today. Construction reflected this situation. Panels were limited by available wood widths; backs were filled with several strips. Now we have plywood, particleboard, and hardboard, as well as other solid wood substitutes, in widths that are unlimited in relation to most furniture. Coupled with that development we have less good-quality solid

wood available, and what there is may be expensive. These conditions have brought about something of a revolution in furniture design. Not all of this revolution has been successful, however. Too many of the new benefits have been directed towards mass-production of furniture. In the future, those who look back will certainly find faults.

In the comparatively recent past, from the 17th century onward, some very fine furniture has been designed and made, and much of it survives. There is much we can learn from the actual furniture and pictures of it. One thing we can learn is to be selective. For instance, in Victorian days over-elaborate things were made. It seemed that plain wood had to be covered by carving or other means, and the complexities of finish on what was basically a simple object would not be acceptable today.

We can marvel at what was done by hand work, much of it really heavy physical labor. Now you can substitute machines, however, either by buying wood already sawn and planed to the sizes you want, or by using our own power saw and planer. You can also substitute man-made panels for some of the solid wood parts in the originals. You can certainly use better glues.

The experience of those who came after will indicate

if an old design was successful and worth considering for reproduction. Did it serve its purpose adequately? Did it look right? Appearance and use are not necessarily different requirements. There is something about fitness for purpose. In most instances something that does its job well also looks good. For instance, a chair designed to be comfortable has a beauty in its shape, without added decoration.

If we want to follow an old design for something to be used today, we must decide if we want a reproduction as exact as possible, or if a piece of furniture with basically similar appearance will do. If the first method is chosen, the glue should be traditional, and all wood should be solid. If the second method is chosen, you can use any modern glue and put plywood in where appropriate according to modern usage. The decision is yours. Obviously, you do not want plywood or particleboard in something that is intended to be a close copy of what the first settlers made or was made by one of the great early cabinetmakers, but plywood backs or drawer bottoms could be sensible choices, and there might even be plywood door panels, provided they are veneered or made to look less obviously like plywood. The choice of hinges, handles, and other hardware will affect authentic appearance. Some modern manufacturers specialize in reproduction hardware, but you may decide that modern hinges would not be very obvious, and wood handles would blend into the design. Obviously, there was no plastic or bright-plated metal when the original furniture was made.

A design from the past may just be used to give you ideas for overall design, shape, capacity, size, or whatever your requirements are. In that case you make something with modern materials and methods. The product is then modern, with no pretentions at a reproduction. At the other end of the scale, you may want to produce something just like mother used to have. Then your efforts must be directed toward making a reasonably close reproduction using similar materials and finishes. It depends on what you want. The furniture described in this chapter is intended to be a fairly close copy of its original design, but you can easily adapt the instructions if your requirements are for something less closely related, and suited to needs rather than history.

There are two broad divisions in the choice of reproductions. There are the examples made by Chippendale and other great craftsmen designers. For reproduction of their products, you need skills that most people do not possess. You may also need woods that are not readily obtainable. Not very many of their products were

storage units, and their various forms of seating are not appropriate to this book. If you are selective you may find some of their plainer pieces that are within your scope. Alternatively, you can copy some of the simpler items made by the first settlers and those who came after as the pioneers moved west. Those who could afford it imported fine furniture, but most people depended on what the local carpenter could make from wood he found locally. It is some of those simpler pieces that are worth reproducing by those with limited skill and equipment. They have their uses in a modern home, and they provide decoration as well as nostalgia.

Coupled with the latter selection are examples dating from before the settling of America and taken from the home woodworking of people in Europe, particularly the furniture used in ordinary homes, much of which influenced immigrants in their designs. You can also go further back into history to find European designs worth copying.

SHAKER SHELVES

People wanted to get things off the floor, which was probably dirty and uneven in early Colonial dwellings; so much use was made of shelves of many sorts. Many were blocks of shelves between end supports, similar to several designs already described, but another way of holding the shelves was to have the supporting boards at the back instead of the ends. This method can be seen in a set of Shaker shelves, designed to hang from hooks or nails so they can be taken down for moving or cleaning (Fig. 11-1A). By arranging the hanging points high on the supports, the load ensures that gravity keeps the assembly reasonably steady on the wall.

The back boards are parallel strips with rounded tops (Fig. 11-1B). The bottoms could be rounded in the same way, but in some Shaker originals the bottoms are narrower (Fig. 11-1C), presumably to act as handles if the shelves are to be moved.

The shelves could be notched around plain back boards and nailed from the back, but it is neater and stronger to cut shallow dadoes across the back boards to positively locate the shelves (Fig. 11-1D).

The shelves could be made with square ends, or their front corners could be rounded, but they are shown with a molded outline (Fig. 11-1E) as in an original. The brackets are important. Besides supporting the shelves, the brackets should be taken right across them to reduce the risk of warping. For greatest strength, cut the brackets with the grain running diagonally (Fig. 11-1F). The curves of the brackets complement those at the ends of the shelves. In the originals, the joints would have been glued and nailed, but it would be stronger to use screws, which could be disguised by sinking the heads and covering them with stopping or plugs.

The exposed edges can be left square in section or with just the sharpness taken off. Molding them would not be appropriate, but they could be given a moderate rounding (Fig. 11-1G).

Materials List for Shaker Shelves

2 back boards	$5 \times 32 \times 1$
2 shelves	$7 \times 40 \times 1$
4 brackets	$5 \times 5 \times 1$

DISPLAY AND HUTCH SHELVES

Some shelves were used in early American homes to display the best plates and other crockery or to hold the more everyday things. The shelves, therefore, served as a hanging hutch, when a complete floor-standing piece of furniture was not practicable. Construction is straightforward and similar to many other blocks of shelves, but decoration peculiar to the period was often provided at the ends, where alternating inward and outward curves often appeared in New England racks and shelves.

Some racks were made with open backs. The simplest versions were light and had shaped ends with plain shelves (Fig. 11-2A and B) let into dado grooves but allowed to project a short distance forward with rounded corners (Fig. 11-2C).

The sides could have holes near their tops for hanging with cord. In a modern version, however, a more rigid attachment to the wall would be preferable, and could be provided by letting in a projecting cross brace under the top shelf (Fig. 11-2D). It serves more than one purpose: its ends can be drilled for screws, and it provides stiffness for the block or shelves.

If the shelves are to display plates, they must be arranged to prevent the plates from slipping. A light strip with a rounded top makes a good stop (Fig. 11-2E). A plowed groove may be sufficient (Fig. 11-2F), but you can avoid the necessity of making it very wide by beveling its inner edge (Fig. 11-2G). If the rack is held tightly to the wall, the plates can lean against it, but if the rack is merely hanging, there must be something behind the top edges of the plates. The brace can be positioned to serve this purpose as well, with another in the lower space, not necessarily projecting, unless you need further means of screwing to the wall.

There are problems with open shelves. A closed back would improve them and protect and hide the wall. Dust from above would have been a problem in many early homes, and some protection from above would also be welcomed. This protection could be just a wider shelf above the rack, but it developed into a more substantial molded top. Something very like the original open rack then became closed at the back and with a prominent top (Fig. 11-3A). If its purpose was utilitarian, and cups, saucers, and plates were stored on it for everyday purposes, arrangements would be added to hold cutlery and some of the things needed in food preparation.

The example shown in Fig. 11-3B has the same sort of decoration at the ends as the first rack, but the tops of the ends are cut square. The shelves also fit into dado grooves, but there must be an allowance at their rear edges for the back.

A plywood back could be let into rabbets in the sides, but it would not be authentic. In an original rack there would have been thin boards arranged vertically—3/8 inch is a probable thickness, and they would be in random widths, possibly with chamfers to show Vs at their meeting edges (Fig. 11-3C). They can butt against the sides without being let into rabbets. Ideally, the boards would have had tongue-and groove joints, but it is unlikely that method would have been used. More likely, if the wood was unseasoned and liable to shrink, the vertical joints would be covered with strips, attached to only one piece so the other was free to slide under it (Fig. 11-3D) and so reduce the risk of shrinkage cracks showing.

The back strips could finish at the bottom shelf or be taken to the depth of the sides. If they project below, it is possible to arrange pegs into them for hanging kitchen tools or towels. At the top there is a covering board, which could be plain with a small overhang at the front and sides. For a molded appearance, it can project further, and separate molding strips can be added to build up the section (Fig. 11-3E), either stopping at the sides or carried around them, with mitered corners (Fig. 11-3F).

Use strips along the fronts of shelves or plowed grooves for plates arranged to slope, unless the crockery is to be stacked level. If cutlery is to be included, it could be through slots at the front of one or more shelves. A full-length slot would be inadvisable because the narrow strip would bend, but there could be slots divided by solid parts (Fig. 11-3G). Drill holes and cut between them. Router grooves would not be authentic.

Another way of making a cutlery rack is to put a separate batten along the front of a shelf, held off by small blocks at intervals (Fig. 11-3H).

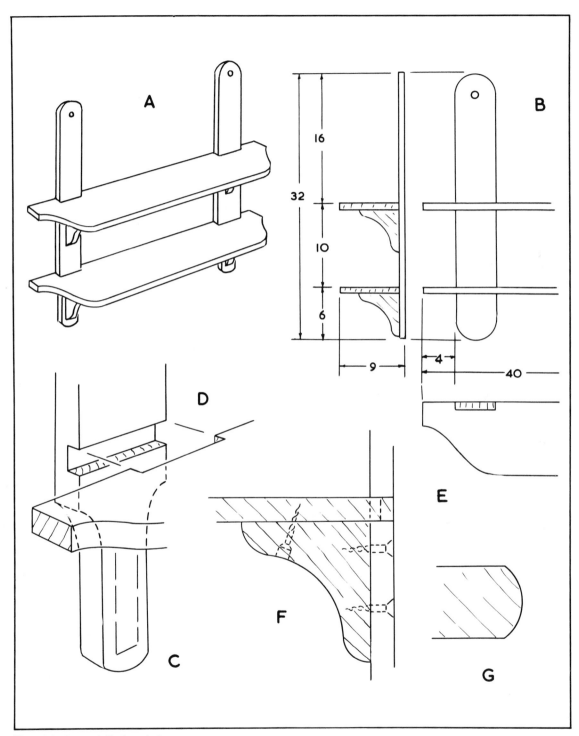

Fig. 11-1. A set of Shaker shelves.

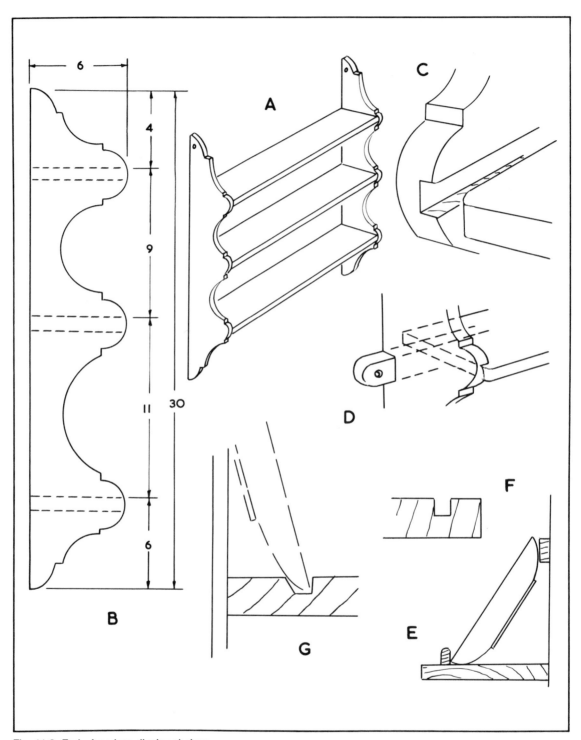

Fig. 11-2. Early American display shelves.

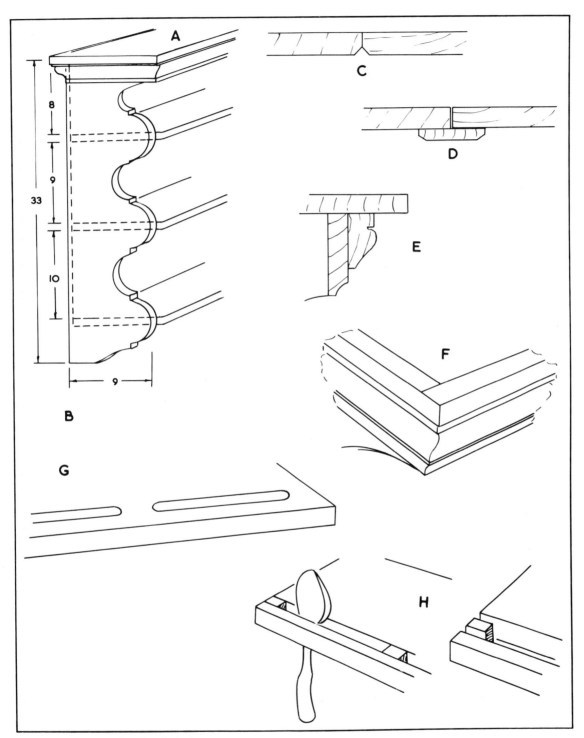

Fig. 11-3. Early American hutch shelves.

Materials List for Display Shelves

2 sides	6 × 30 × 1
2 shelves	6 1/2 × 36 × 1
1 brace	1 1/2 × 40 × 1

Materials List for Hutch Shelves

2 sides	9 × 33 × 1
3 shelves	9 × 30 × 1
1 top	12 × 33 × 1
1 molding from	2 × 46 × 1 1/2
1 top rail	3 × 33 × 1
1 back, built up to	30 × 30

KITCHEN BOX

Boxes with handles had many uses among early settlers, particularly the women. There were chests with handles at the ends for two people to lift, but many other boxes were small enough for one person to lift with two hands or to share with a helper if the load was heavy. The example in Fig. 11-4 is such a box of moderate size. Originally, it might have contained flour, grain, sugar, or other loose food. It could have been used for carrying firewood, or it might have served as a soiled linen container. Boxes for use with food were made of light-colored woods without resin or smell that would affect the contents. Boxes for firewood would have been made of any wood available.

The sizes and choice of wood for a reproduction will depend on the intended use, but the dimensions will produce a box comparable with many originals and suitable for many modern uses. The originals were mostly left as untreated natural wood, but if you want to use the box indoors, it could be stained and varnished without detracting from its appearance as a replica. Ideally, the wood should be solid and chosen from a type available locally. Obviously, plywood would not be appropriate, unless you are only concerned with making a box to use and not bothering about making it as a reproduction of something made earlier.

The key pieces are the pair of sides (Fig. 11-5A) since all the main parts fit between them. Work from a centerline to get the shape symmetrical. The exact angles of the ends are not vital, providing they are the same.

The extended ends have the grain the long way, so the part above the hand holes has short grain, which could be weak if that part is too narrow. As shown in Fig. 11-5B there is about 1 3/4 inches of width there above a

1 1/2-inch slot, which should be strong enough with most woods. Drill holes at the ends of the hand slots and cut away the waste between them. Round the edges of the slots to make comfortable hand grips. Round the outer corners of the tops and take the sharpness off the edges of all parts that will project upward. Bevel the bottoms of the pieces to match the angles of the sides.

Cut the bottom to fit between the sides and the ends. Assemble the box parts with nails. Screws might be better, but the original boxes would not have had them. Use glue as well and punch the nail heads below the surface so they can be covered with stopping.

The box is shown with strips across the top inside the ends. These strips are optional. If the box is to be used with contents that need to be poured or tipped out, it is better not to have them so there is no hindrance to complete emptying. For other contents, the strips stiffen the ends of the box and provide a base for the lid. Fit the strips between the sides and bevel to make a close fit against the ends.

If there are no strips, the lid must be taken close to the box ends and beveled to fit. Otherwise, it overlaps the end strips a short amount. In either case it overlaps the sides and could be made with a slight overhang, having rounded corners and edges, if you wish. Put stiffeners across under the lid to fit inside the box opening.

It is possible to remove the lid without a handle, but a wood handle was usual. A metal handle would be inappropriate. The handle could be placed straight, but it was more often diagonal, possibly to provide some help in resisting warping of the lid, although it also looks more attractive that way.

The handle shown in Fig. 11-5C can be sawn from a block of wood; then all edges, except those that come against the lid, can be thoroughly rounded so the actual grip is given an elliptical section, without any remnants of the original flat surfaces. Attach it with glue and nails from below.

Materials List for Kitchen Box

2 sides	11 × 22 × 5/8
2 ends	10 × 19 × 5/8
1 bottom	10 × 17 × 5/8
2 strips	1 1/2 × 11 × 5/8
1 lid	12 × 19 × 5/8
2 stiffeners	1 1/2 × 11 × 5/8
1 handle	2 1/2 × 13 × 1 1/4

SEAT CHEST

Many early chests had to serve as seats as well as

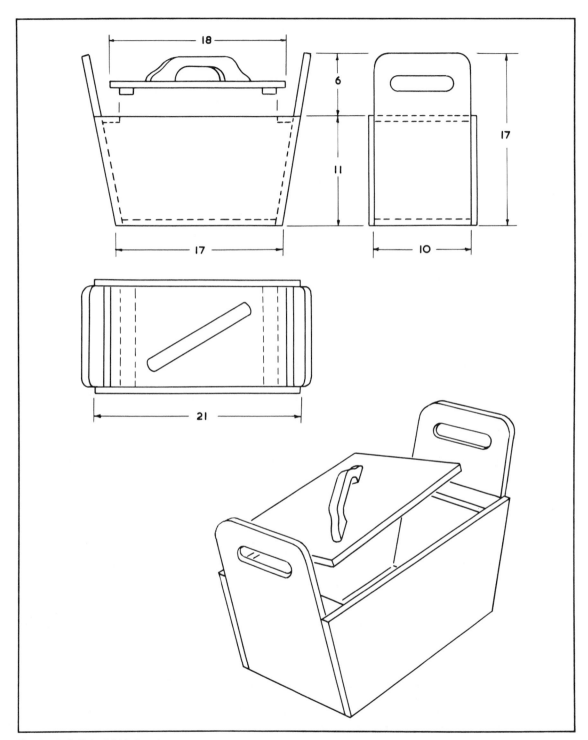

Fig. 11-4. A Colonial kitchen box.

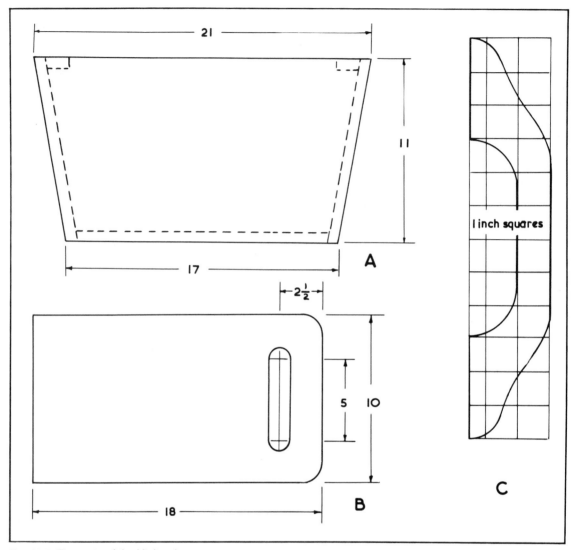

Fig. 11-5. The parts of the kitchen box.

storage places. A plain chest may be reasonably comfortable if it is near a wall you can lean against, but elsewhere the lack of back suppoort makes it uncomfortable after a short period. Some chests developed into seats with backs and ends. In some cases the development was such that the piece of furniture became a chair or settle with some storage space under the seat. Less ambitious seating was still primarily a storage chest that could also offer reasonable comfort as a seat. This type of seat chest was common in European homes as well as in the early days of the settlement of America.

The example in Fig. 11-6A is a roomy chest that has been extended upward to give a low back and some shape to the arms. It could have a single lifting lid, but it is shown with a lid in two parts. There could be a division in the chest for different storage, or the body of the chest could be clear and only the lid divided. In either case there is the advantage of being able to open half of the chest without disturbing anyone or anything on the other half. Fitted cushions would make the chest into a very comfortable seat.

Although it would be possible to make the ends with

their grain across, as it would be in a simple chest, it is stronger to have the grain upright. The lengthwise parts, therefore, cannot be dovetailed into the ends, as this method of jointing is only suitable when end-grained parts are meeting. Much early furniture was merely nailed together. Alternatively, you could use dowels at the corners, with the dowel ends exposed. Early dowels would not have been machine-made, but as they were driven through a dowel plate they would have shown round ends. The chest ends should notch over the front (Fig. 11-7A) for nails or dowels. For greater strength the front could extend enough to allow for a dado joint to the end (Fig. 11-7B).

The ends will overlap the back. Mark out the pair

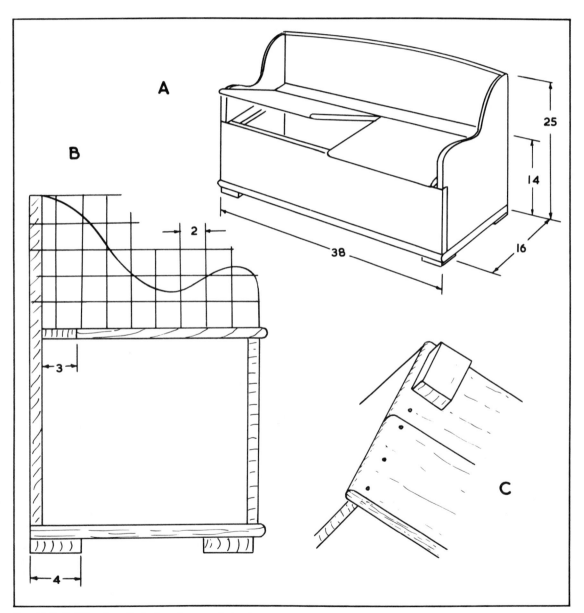

Fig. 11-6. Details of an Early American seat chest.

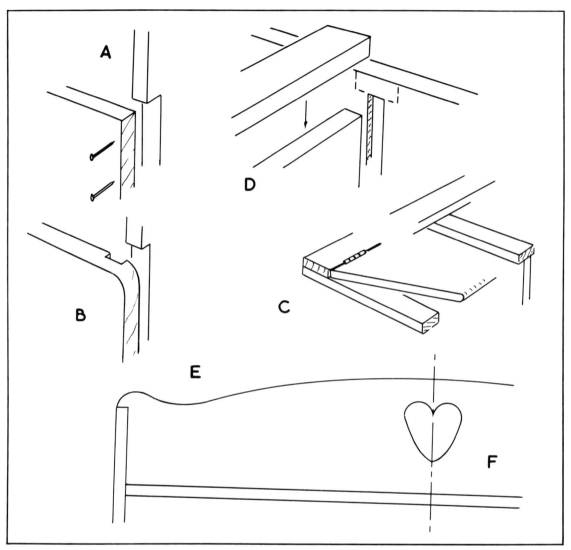

Fig. 11-7. Joints for the Early American seat chest.

of ends (Fig. 11-6B). Do not shape the tops until you have prepared the constructional parts. In addition to cutting to their outline, well round the shaped arm parts.

All the main parts will probably need to be made up to width by gluing boards together. Keep the joints between boards away from joints to other parts. In particular, do not have a joint between boards in the back near seat level.

The lids rest on the front of the chest and on strips across—at the ends only if it is a single lid, or over a central strip as well, if the lid is divided. At the back is a

strip to which the lids are hinged (Fig. 11-7C). If there is a division in the chest, it may go into dado joints at back and front (Fig. 11-7D), and the central lid support goes on top of it. Otherwise, the support should be notched into the back and front of the chest.

The bottom would have been made up with boards across (Fig. 11-6C), brought close together and nailed from below. In a modern chest seat, the bottom could be framed around with solid wood, and the main area closed with plywood let into rabbets. Blocks under the corners will keep clear of the floor. Originally that was advisable on a dirt floor, but today it keeps the bottom off a carpet.

The seats are solid wood, cut to overlap the front enough for rounding there. They are hinged to the strip at the rear and have their grain lengthwise. To reduce the risk of warping you could put battens across under the tops, cut to fit inside the openings.

The back of the seat could be cut straight across or given a moderate curve (Fig. 11-6A). Further shaping could be done to complement the curves of the ends (Fig. 11-7E). A cutout pattern, such as a heart (Fig. 11-7F), was often provided at the center.

There should be no need for handles or fasteners, but a box lock could be put under a lid, with a keyhole through the front. The finish could be anything you wish. You could leave the wood untreated, use stain and varnish, or paint it plain or with decorative patterns. Any of these treatments would have been used by some early owners.

Materials List for Seat Chest

1 front	14 × 39 × 1
1 back	25 × 39 × 1
2 ends	16 × 26 × 1
1 bottom	16 × 39 × I
2 seats	16 × 19 × 1
1 seat rail	3 × 39 × 1
1 division	14 × 16 × 1
3 seat supports	2 × 16 × 1

DRY SINK

Few people today would have a use for a dry sink in its original purpose of providing a working area to accommodate and use water that had to be brought in from a pump or well. The pans and pitchers of water were stood in the enclosed top, which may have been lined with metal, but was more likely merely planked. The lower part of the dry sink provided storage space in drawers and behind doors. In a modern home a dry sink can still provide useful storage, while its top serves as a side table or a place for potted plants and floral decorations.

Dry sinks were made in a large variety of patterns and sizes. Some had the border around the top at the same level on all sides, but the cutdown front version would be more suitable for today's alternative uses. The lower part still has very commodious storage space, and drawers as well as doors should be provided if the available space will permit the dry sink to be big enough. The specimen in Fig. 11-8A is typical of many from that early era.

A dry sink was functional. It was not intended to be decorative, but fitness for purpose gives it a certain attraction. Most sinks were made of softwood and left plain so they could be scrubbed occasionally. A modern version would have its grain sealed to keep the wood clean, but stain or a high glass finish would not be appropriate. Nailed joints were usual. In a reproduction a modern strong glue will supplement nailing, with the nails punched below the surface and covered with stopping. Many of the parts are wide boards, and it is unlikely that they will be available as single pieces; so glue up sufficient strips before starting construction.

The key pieces are the ends (Fig. 11-8B); so make them and mark them out first. With the top and bottom they form the main parts of the unit. Use shallow dado joints for these parts (Fig. 11-8C), with a few screws or nails driven diagonally upward from below to strengthen them.

Before you fit the top and bottom, you must decide how you will make the back. In original construction there may have been tongued-and-grooved boards or thin wide boards with covers over their joints (Fig. 11-8D). If exact authenticity does not matter, you could have a plywood back. In normal use it will not show. Rabbet the rear edges of the ends to suit the back, and allow for solid wood above the top board (Fig. 11-9A). At the front there will be a frame covering the edges of the ends; so do not rabbet any part of the front edge. Make the top and bottom to allow for the amount cut away by the rear rabbets.

The division between the drawers and the other part is another wide board. To provide mutual assistance in resisting warping, it should have dado joints at top and bottom (Fig. 11-9B). The division must remain flat to allow the drawers to slide properly.

The front assembly (Fig. 11-9C) should be made as a unit. Cut away its top edge and round it well. The corners and the parts between doors and drawers can be tenoned (Fig. 11-9D). When the frame has been attached to the other parts there will not be much strain on these joints. Arrange the lower edge of the top piece to come level with the underside of the board forming the base of the top recess and the upper edge of the lower piece level with the inside of the bottom. Cut away the lower edge to match the ends.

The drawer runners and guides are glued and nailed in place (Fig. 11-9E). Strips go across between the drawers at the front (Fig. 11-9F). As with any drawer assembly, see that all the parts related to drawers are parallel and square.

The doors could be ledged and braced matched

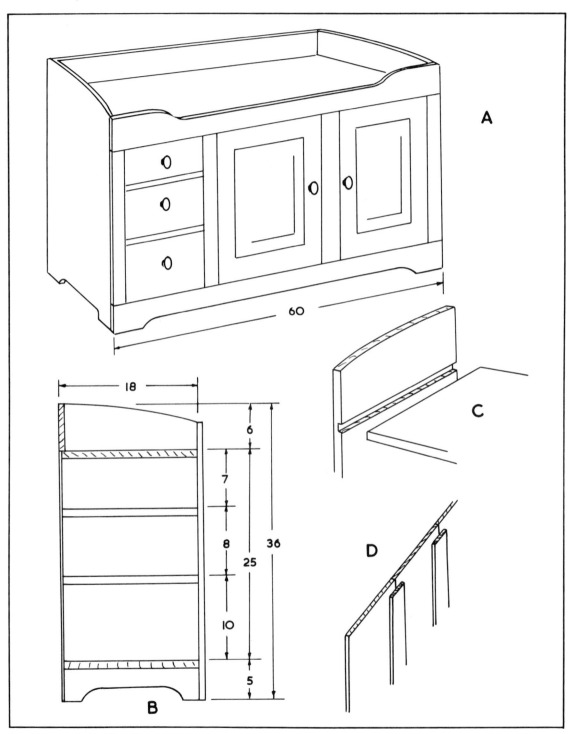

Fig. 11-8. A Colonial dry sink.

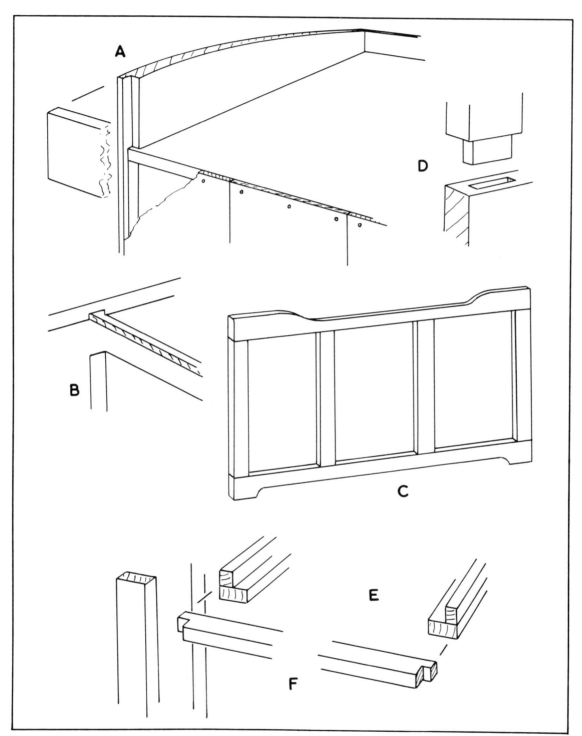

Fig. 11-9. Methods of assembling the parts of the dry sink.

boarding, or they could be framed and paneled. In some dry sinks the panels were perforated zinc to provide flyproof ventilation in the days before refrigerators. Plywood panels would not look right; so solid wood would have to be used. Door corners should be tenoned in the usual way and the frame grooved. The wood could be thinned to leave a level surface on the outside, or careful tapering all around will make a decorative front (Fig. 11-10A).

The drawers can be made in the traditional way, using dovetails at the front (Fig. 11-10B). Original drawers were made with their fronts closing flush with the frame. It is only in modern design that there are overlapping drawer fronts. If you want to produce an exact reproduction, the drawer bottoms must be solid wood strips laid across and thinned below if necessary (Fig. 11-10C).

Turned wood knobs are appropriate for the drawers and doors. Put stops at top and bottom of the door divider (Fig. 11-10D). If you can find or make them, use fasteners of the type where a handle on the front has a turnbutton inside to go behind the door divider. Otherwise, use spring or other catches.

Materials List for Dry Sink

2 ends	$18 \times 37 \times 1$
2 shelves	$18 \times 60 \times 1$
1 divider	$18 \times 25 \times 1$
1 back	$6 \times 60 \times 1$
1 back	$17 \times 60 \times 3/8$ in strips
1 front frame top	$7 \times 60 \times 1$
1 front frame bottom	$5 \times 60 \times 1$
4 frame uprights	$2 \times 33 \times 1$
4 drawer runners	$1\ 1/2 \times 18 \times 1$
4 drawer guides	$1 \times 18 \times 3/4$
1 drawer front	$6 \times 18 \times 1$
2 drawer sides	$6 \times 18 \times 5/8$
1 drawer back	$5 \times 18 \times 5/8$
1 drawer front	$7 \times 18 \times 1$
2 drawer sides	$7 \times 18 \times 5/8$
1 drawer back	$6 \times 18 \times 5/8$
1 drawer front	$9 \times 18 \times 1$
2 drawer sides	$9 \times 18 \times 5/8$
1 drawer back	$8 \times 18 \times 5/8$
4 drawer bottoms	$18 \times 18 \times 3/8$ in strips
4 door sides	$3 \times 25 \times 1$
4 door ends	$3 \times 18 \times 1$
2 door panels	$14 \times 20 \times 1/2$

WELSH DRESSER

A cupboard with shelves above might form the main focal point in a living room, with the best plates displayed

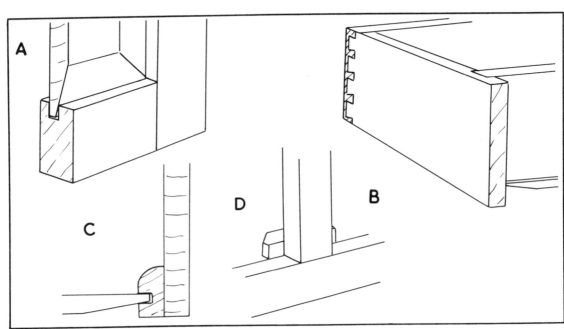

Fig. 11-10. Drawer and door details of the dry sink.

simplified. Softwoods may have been used and finished with paint, except for working surfaces, which would have been left untreated so they could be scrubbed occasionally.

The sizes suggested in Fig. 11-12A show a height of 72 inches, a width of about 36 inches, and a projection from the wall of about 24 inches. These are reasonable proportions, and they give a considerable storage capacity. Sizes could, however, be adapted to suit available space or needs. The following instructions are for a dresser with ends going through to the full height in one piece. The upper shelved section could be made as a separate assembly to lift off, which is advisable if there is difficulty in access to the room where the dresser is to be used. If the ends are to be full height, they are made from two or more boards glued together (Fig. 11-12B). The tabletop will also have to be made from several boards glued together. It is laid in a dado groove at each side and extends over the ends (Fig. 11-12C). At the back, boards closing the lower part overlap it, and a strip above takes the ends of the boards behind the shelves (Fig. 11-12D).

The front edge of the tabletop is expected to get the most wear; so it can be covered with a piece of harder wood, that is preferably tongued and grooved. This framing is carried around the ends with other pieces mitered at the front corners (Fig. 11-12E), having tongues into the top and a plain overlap on the sides (Fig. 11-12F).

At the bottom of the dresser, the sides are cut square across, and there is a plinth set back. If it would suit the situation better, there could be cuts into the bearing surfaces so only the corners take the weight. This choice would be better for an uneven floor, but otherwise it is wiser to leave the lower edges straight so the weight is spread over as large an area as possible. The bottom is made of boards glued up to width, and it is fastened to battens below (Fig. 11-13A). If the battens are taken to the floor, they increase the bearing area.

There are two similar frames above and below the drawer (Fig. 11-13B). The upper frame goes immediately below the tabletop and will be fixed to it and to the sides when the dresser is assembled. It need not be let into the sides, but the lower one is better made long enough to notch into shallow stopped dadoes (Fig. 11-13C). Tenon the parts of the frames together. Because they will control the movement of the drawer, they must be square, without twist, and with level surfaces.

There is one shelf in the cupboard. It could fit permanently into dadoes, but it may be better to let it rest on battens (Fig. 11-13D) so it is loose and can be removed.

Fig. 11-11. A Welsh dresser.

on the open shelves and the things in everyday use, including cutlery and tablecloths, stored in the drawer and cupboards. A similar, but plainer, version might be used in the kitchen. It was the forerunner of the cabinets in a fitted kitchen today. This furniture was popular in all parts of Britain, but the design was particular to Wales; so it was generally known as a *Welsh dresser,* although the name *dresser* today may be more often applied to a table used in a bedroom, also possibly called a *dressing table.*

Welsh dressers had the same basic layout, but there were varying degrees of decoration, and one version had a curved top. The example in Fig. 11-11 is a typical square-topped version, such as would have been made by the local carpenter. For use in a living room, such a dresser would have been made of good hardwoods, with correct cabinetmaking joints and an appropriate finish. For use in a kitchen, some of the decoration would have been omitted, and construction would have been

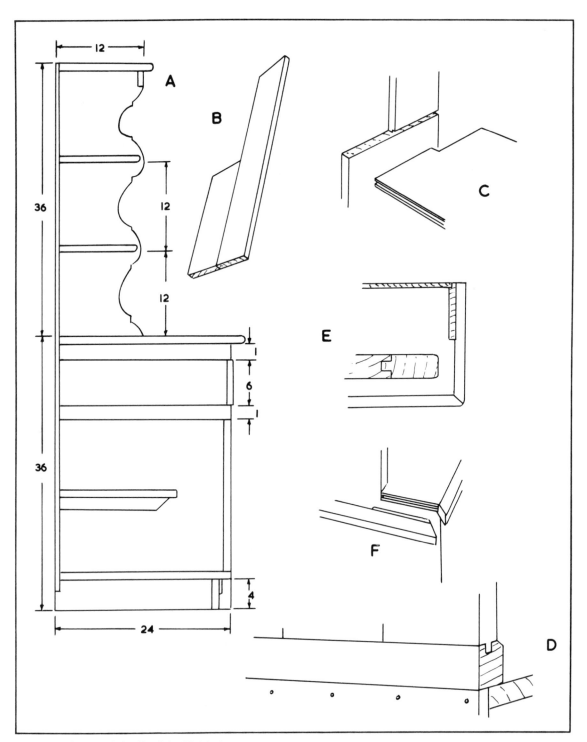

Fig. 11-12. Sizes and details of the Welsh dresser.

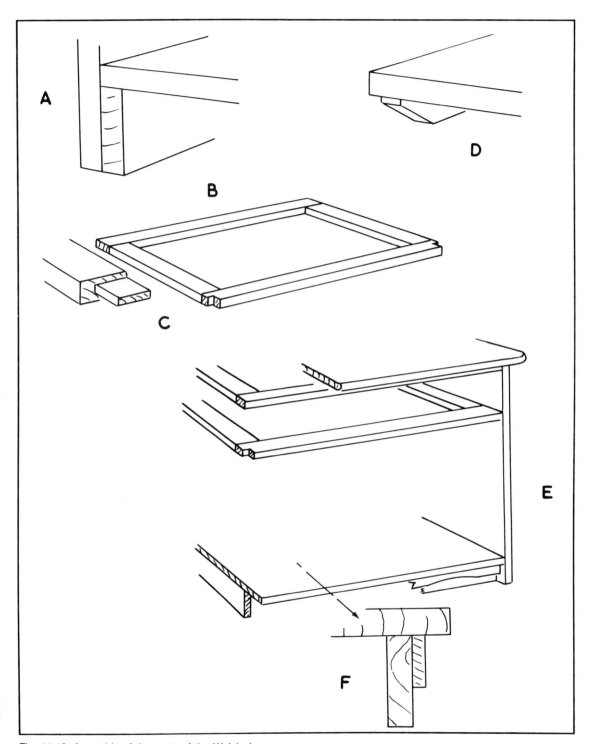

Fig. 11-13. Assembly of the parts of the Welsh dresser.

Arrange the front edges of the frames to come level with the sides (Fig. 11-13E). The plinth is set back a short distance under the bottom (Fig. 11-13F) so it fits against the ends of the battens supporting the bottom. It may be attached to them or let into its own dado grooves in the ends. An overlay will be added to the plinth after assembly; it can be given an undulating pattern to match the rail under the top.

The decoration of the front edges of the sides between the shelves is similar to that of the hutch shelves described earlier. If the two pieces of furniture are used in the same room, they could be made to match, but there is a design consideration if the dresser does not have to be related to anything else. Many early dressers had the decoration drawn with compasses (Fig. 11-14A), sometimes without the step between reversed curves, but that break improves appearance. A curve other than part of a circle is generally considered more attractive, either part of an ellipse or an assymetrical one that tends to emphasize height (Fig. 11-14B). All the curves must be comparable and may be drawn freehand, although where they should be the same, as over the ends of shelves, a template will ensure uniformity.

Make the shelves with rounded front edges to fit into stopped dadoes (Fig. 11-14C). Cut grooves to hold plates. Make a rail to go across the top at the front, with tongues into grooves at the ends (Fig. 11-14D). Shape its lower edge by scalloping, which could be regular undulations or a pattern taken to points (Fig. 11-14E). Use this rail as a pattern for marking a similar edge on the overlay at the plinth.

The top is a plain board with overlapping rounded edges. It can be nailed or screwed from above, since this will be above the normal line of vision. It is better attached with multiple tenons (Fig. 11-14F).

The back, which shows between the shelves, should be made of several vertical boards. Do not use plywood if you want a true reproduction. Many older dressers had thin boards halved over each other with rabbets and a bead to disguise the joint (Fig. 11-14G). This method is not as good as a full tongue and groove because there is a risk of one board warping in relation to its neighbor and leaving a gap, which could not happen with a tongue and groove. At the sides the boards are best let into rabbets. At the top the boards can be nailed to the back of the cover board. At the bottom they may go behind a strip on the tabletop, or preferably be tongued into the strip there (Fig. 11-12D).

At this point, you are finished making all the parts for the body of the dresser. Some prefabrication may have been done already, but do not join the main parts until all are ready. Do all the preparation possible while you can handle separate pieces. It is easier to cut grooves and prepare parts of joints before anything is joined together. Do all of the main assembly in one session so the dresser can be squared before glue begins to harden. Then it can be left standing on a level surface to set.

The doors can be made in several ways. All of the usual door constructions will have been used somewhere on a Welsh dresser. Ledged and braced doors may be appropriate to a kitchen or other working situation, but for display purposes, it is better to make doors with panels. Frames should be mortised and tenoned. The panels could be made in any of the ways described for the dry sink, but good-quality Welsh dressers often had *fielded and raised* panels. This choice is a step further than merely beveling edges to fit into grooves. Instead there is a step between the bevel and the raised flat central part of the panel (Fig. 11-15A). The step can be quite shallow, but the shadow it produces gives an attractive appearance and a sense of quality to the panel.

This work could be done with suitable tools in a power spindle or router, but the original craftsmen would have done it with hand tools. Cut a panel to size and pencil on the shape of the raised part and the thickness to taper to at the edges. Cut in the outline of the flat part, either with a cutting gauge or with a knife along a straightedge. This step is particularly important across the grain, where there is a risk of a plane tearing out the end grain. If posssible, cut the full depth you intend to do the fielding. If not, cut as far as you can, then cut more after some of the wood has been planed away. The amount raised need not be much—1/16 inch is probably enough on these panels.

Some of the waste can be cut away with a paring chisel outside the knife lines (Fig. 11-15B). Cut the fielding to the depth you want, but without the bevel (Fig. 11-15C). You can do so with a fillister plane, using its stops and fences to control the depth and width, but you will probably have to deal with the width in two stages. A low-angle rabbet plane is the best tool for working across the grain. When you have cut to the depth, tilt the plane to make the angle (Fig. 11-15D). The finish from the plane may not be good enough, particularly across the grain; so sand the tapered fielding, but use the abrasive paper wrapped on a flat block. Be careful not to round the edges of the raised part. Try to keep a definite miter line between the flats you are sanding.

You can hang the doors with plain butt hinges, but some original dressers had ornamental hinges on the sur-

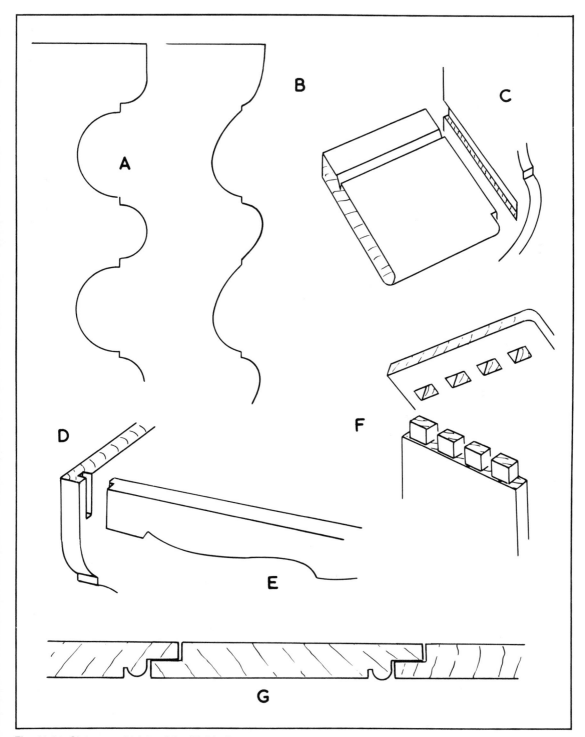

Fig. 11-14. Shapes and joints of the Welsh dresser.

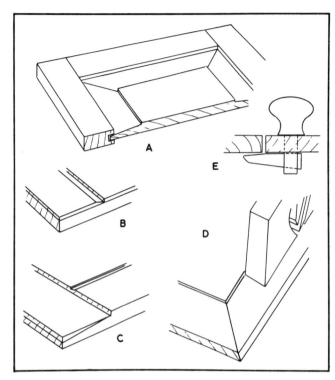

Fig. 11-15. Door panels for the Welsh dresser.

face. In that case, the door handles should match the hinges. Antiqued metal is the obvious finish. Drop handles are appropriate. Put stops inside. One door could have a bolt to the bottom, then the other door be given a turnbutton catch operated by a knob or handle. Metal drop handles can be bought for this purpose.

If butt hinges are sunk into the door joints, it would be more appropriate to use wood knobs on the doors and drawers, preferably doweled through the fronts. A knob with a turnbutton could be made in the way some early ones were, by cutting a slot through an extended knob dowel so a peg through it can be turned by the knob to hold the door to its neighbor (Fig. 11-15E).

The drawer is straightforward and made in the manner described for earlier projects. To be a good reproduction, however, the joints should be hand dovetails at back and front, and the bottom should be made with pieces of thin wood—in this case from back to front, since it is a wide drawer. The front of the drawer may finish flush with its frame or be made to project up to 1/4 inch with rounded edges. The handles could be knobs to match those on the doors. They could also be swinging bail types, set fairly wide apart, since a strong pull will be needed with two hands when the drawer is heavily loaded.

Materials List for Welsh Dresser

2 sides	$12 \times 72 \times 1$
2 sides	$12 \times 36 \times 1$
1 tabletop	$26 \times 36 \times 1$
1 tabletop	$2 \times 40 \times 1$
2 tabletops	$2 \times 16 \times 1$
1 cupboard shelf	$18 \times 36 \times 1$
2 shelves	$11 \times 36 \times 1$
1 top	$14 \times 38 \times 1$
1 top rail	$2 \times 36 \times 1$
4 drawer dividers	$1\ 1/2 \times 36 \times 1$
4 drawer dividers	$1\ 1/2 \times 24 \times 1$
2 door panels	$16 \times 21 \times 1/2$
1 upper back rail	$2 \times 36 \times 1$
1 upper back	$36 \times 36 \times 5/8$ in strips
1 lower back	$34 \times 36 \times 5/8$ in strips
1 plinth	$4 \times 36 \times 1$
1 plinth	$2 \times 36 \times 1/2$
1 drawer front	$6 \times 36 \times 1$
2 drawer sides	$6 \times 24 \times 3/4$
1 drawer back	$5 \times 36 \times 3/4$
4 door sides	$4 \times 23 \times 1$
4 door rails	$4 \times 18 \times 1$

Chapter 12

Combination Storage Units

Separate boxes, cupboards, shelves, bookcases, and other storage items are attractive and useful in themselves, but if there are many of them in a room the total space they occupy may be more than you wish. Besides the actual sizes of the furniture, there is the need for further space around it. The problem can be reduced by combining at least some of the units into one piece of furniture. If that unit can then be built in to the wall, it reduces the occupied area to a minimum, while giving maximum storage space.

Thought should be given to what you expect from a combination storage unit and its final size. The bigger a piece of furniture and the more varied its purpose, the more difficult it is to change your mind if it does not serve the intended needs. While you may be able to move around a small item or adapt it or even scrap it in favor of something else, you may have put so much wood and effort into a big, involved piece of furniture that you may have to live with your mistakes.

Unit construction is one way of allowing changes. Although what you make assembles as an overall large piece of furniture with a combination of uses, it is actually made of several units that merely stand together or are bolted and can be taken apart and rearranged. This method of assembly has an advantage for transport. A large wall unit may be built in position, but because of its size it has to stay there since it is too big to pass through a door or window. If it can be disassembled into smaller units, you can build it elsewhere and bring it in; it could removed to another room or rearranged in the same room, or you could take it with you if you move.

There are plastic connecting blocks available, particularly with veneered particleboard. They will link parts, either with bolts from one plastic block to another or by screws into the particleboard, so it is possible to separate units if necessary, yet they are firmly connected in normal use. A similar arrangement can be made with square strips of wood along a joint where two parts meet, so you can drive screws both ways, instead of using glue and dowels or other more permanent connections.

Veneered particleboard is particularly suitable for many combination storage units since it is obtainable in many widths, and the panels remain stiff and flat. In most situations dowels are the best way to form joints, although take-down connectors or screwed strips can be used where appropriate. Counterbored screws with plastic plugs over them may be used in place of dowels, but the screws should be long enough to go well into the particleboard so there is plenty of grip in the resin/wood chip material, which may not provide as good a hold as wood.

If solid wood is used for making combination storage units, most of the joints can be those usual with other constructions. Many of the parts, however, are simply and satisfactorily made with dowels, particularly where wide boards meet, and dadoes or other conventional joints might be difficult to make over a great width.

Many combination units are built-in or stand so they appear built-in. If there are errors in the squareness of corners or the verticality of walls, it is never wise to follow the errors in the furniture. Instead, parts should be made square and true. Doors and drawers need to be square and with parallel sides. If you must adapt to faults in the walls, floor, or ceiling, make the unit small enough to fit closely where a meeting edge comes out of true and use a filler piece or cover strip that blends the new edge to the wall while not spoiling its trueness. You may be able to make a front piece with one edge vertical for the furniture and the other edge matched to an inaccurate wall.

BASIC ROOM DIVIDER

There is often a need to divide a room into areas of different uses without erecting a partition that makes it into two smaller rooms. That divider may be large and designed to obscure much of one side from the other. In other places a divider may be welcomed, but it does not have to hide as much as define two areas. An example is a bedroom used by two children who would welcome some degree of privacy, yet are happy to communicate with each other much of the time. The simple divider shown in Fig. 12-1 is intended for that type of situation. It does not reach the ceiling, and it only projects from the wall about the length of a bed. The lower part is arranged as cupboards, with two accessible from each side. There is a working top at table height and part of it, toward the wall, is arranged as a bookcase, not only to hold books, but to increase privacy at that end. Two open shelves come above. When things are stored on them,

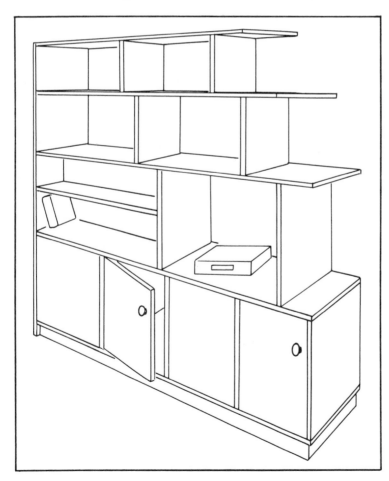

Fig. 12-1. A basic room divider.

there will not be much of a see-through element left.

Lighting must be considered. Artificial light may have to be rearranged, but you cannot do much about natural lighting via windows. With the fairly open construction and the fact that the divider does not reach the ceiling nor project far into the room, there should be plenty of natural lighting getting through to both sides, but you may want to temporarily erect something to check light flow. You may find it better to move or omit the bookcase part so light can get through.

With the cupboard in use and not too many heavy items on upper shelves, the divider would probably be safe standing free, but in most situations it would be better screwed to the wall—two screws fairly high on the back would probably be enough.

As shown in Fig. 12-2A the divider is intended to be made of particleboard veneered with wood or plastic. All of the joints are doweled. With the usual thickness of particleboard, 5/16- or 3/8-inch dowels would be suitable. Along most joints a 4-inch spacing should be adequate.

Cut all parts squarely, both across a sheet and in the thickness, if close joints are to be obtained. Veneer any exposed cut edges. Do not make the doors until after the other parts are assembled, but cut and prepare the other parts for dowels before you assemble anything.

The board against the wall is the key one for settling most sizes (Fig. 12-3A). Mark it out with the positions of shelves, plinth, and bookcase parts. In other directions it is the working surface shelf that gives key measurements (Fig. 12-3B). Figure 12-2B shows the arrangement of doors. They could also be made in other ways to suit needs. The backs of the cupboards are pieces very similar to the doors fixed between the shelves and uprights.

Arrange the plinth strips to be set back a short distance from the edges of the bottom shelf (Fig. 12-4A). Then cut pieces to fit between the shelves to make the backs of the cupboards (Fig. 12-4B).

The bottom shelf, the work top, and the shelf above it are all the same length, but the others are set back in 6-inch steps (Fig. 12-4C). Supports for the shelves are set back 6 inches from their ends. The supports could be narrower than the shelves, if you wish, but they are shown the same width. Intermediate supports should be placed midway between the end supports and the board at the wall to give the effect of staggering the support positions, which looks attractive and avoids the need to drill dowel holes in the same section of the shelf.

Locate the bookcase shelf above the midway point in the space between the main shelves. The upright pieces

that divide the bookcase could be in line, without weakening since there are dowel holes, but they are shown staggered in Fig. 12-4C. If it is not important to obstruct the view through, you could put strips along to stand only about 3 inches high, which would be enough for books to push against, but there would also be a gap above them. Similar strips could be put along the centers of other shelves, if you want the use of opposite sides without the risk of things being pushed right through.

The doors are shown with knobs. They could have aluminum edge strip handles if you want to avoid any projections. Use the thin hinges intended for particleboard so you do not have to cut recesses to let them in. Hang the doors to suit requirements, but if there is no reason for having them otherwise, it is usually better for them to be hinged toward the wall, as shown. Fit stops and suitable catches. There could be a pair of doors to the bookcase compartment if it is to be used for other loose things. In that case, set the bookcase shelf back enough to give clearance to the doors.

Materials List for Basic Room Divider

All veneered particleboard between 5/8 and 1 inch thick

1 wall board	15 × 72
3 shelves	15 × 72
1 shelf	15 × 66
1 shelf	15 × 60
2 plinths	4 × 72
1 plinth	4 × 14
4 cupboard divisions	15 × 25
4 cupboard backs	18 × 25
4 cupboard doors	18 × 25
2 uprights	15 × 11
2 uprights	15 × 14
2 uprights	15 × 17
1 bookcase shelf	15 × 39
1 bookcase back	9 × 39
1 bookcase back	8 × 39

BASIC WALL UNIT

Storage units attached to walls can be made in a great variety of patterns, for capacity to suit whatever is required. They can be adapted to suit the equipment for a hobby, the requirements of an office, or general home needs. If you are uncertain of total requirements, or they are likely to change, it is unwise to make a wall unit with

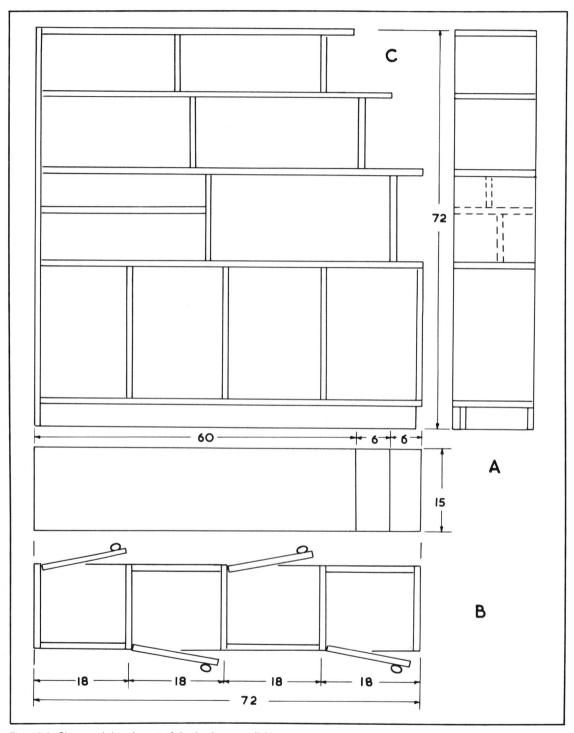

Fig. 12-2. Sizes and door layout of the basic room divider.

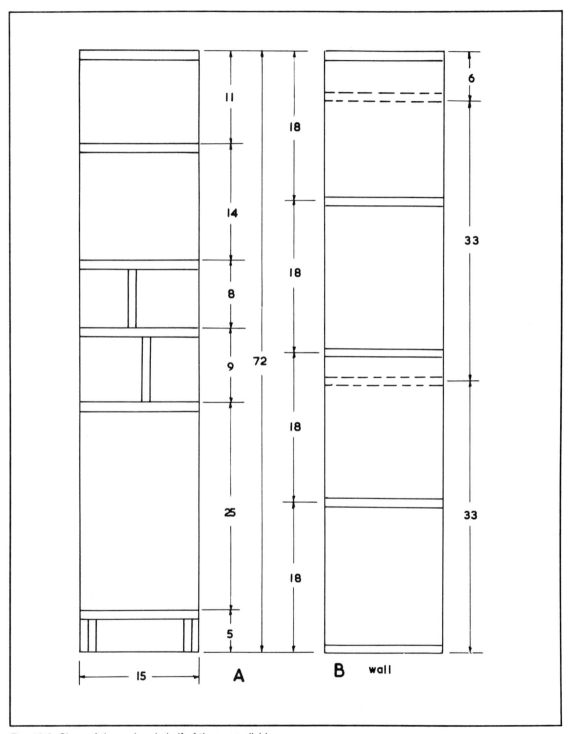

Fig. 12-3. Sizes of the end and shelf of the room divider.

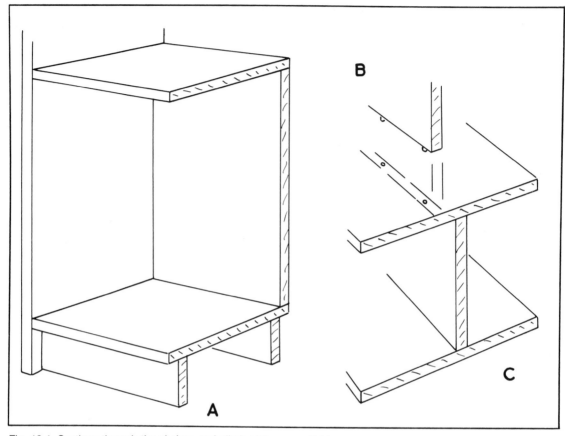

Fig. 12-4. Sections through the shelves and plinth of the room divider.

its capacity restricted to certain things, or to make compartments fitted to the record player of the moment or some other item that might be changed or replaced.

Another problem with special compartmenting is the way divisions and special shelves take up space which might be better used. There is no need to put divisions between things that will stand quite well and not interfere with each other if stored as close neighbors.

Wall fitments are examples of furniture that may be better made in unit. An advantage of units is that you can start with small ones and build on until a whole wall is covered. The example in Fig. 12-5 is a basic design that would suit many purposes, but it is particularly appropriate to a family room. There are two identical units (Fig. 12-6A) and a shelf unit (Fig. 12-6B) that can be fitted between them. A space below this middle unit allows some other piece of furniture to be pushed back out of the way. The two main units do not have to be identical in all respects, as long as the overall heights are the same.

There could be different arrangements of shelves, or one unit could be a different width than the other.

The parts could be solid wood or 3/4-inch plywood with lipped front edges, but particleboard faced with wood or plastic veneer is satisfactory and easiest to work with. All joints could be doweled, using 5/16-inch or 3/8-inch dowels at about 4-inch spacing in most joints. What is done at the back depends on location. If the edges will not show when the unit is attached to the wall, thin plywood or hardboard could be glued and nailed directly on (Fig. 12-7A). If the edges will show, plywood could be let into rabbets in solid wood or most plywoods, but rabbeting particleboard is not usually very satisfactory, and the plywood may have to come inside against strips of wood if the edges are to be hidden (Fig. 12-7B). Since the wood strips would show between the shelves, it may be better to accept the plywood showing outside and avoid using strips. Construction that way is easier.

Mark out the four main sides with the positions of

other parts (Fig. 12-7C). The sides rest on the floor, and the plinth is a strip set back at the front (Fig. 12-6C). Mark out the pair of sides for the central shelf unit (Fig. 12-7D). All of the shelves are the same widths as their sides, except the bottom main ones, which are cut back by the thickness of the doors. Be careful, however, to get each set exactly the same length and with the ends cut square.

Mark out and drill dowel holes in all parts of a unit before you assemble any part of it. Have a back already cut squarely to put on as you assemble a unit so it can be used to keep the assembly square. In any case, check squareness by measuring diagonals. It is important for appearance and the fit of the doors that corners be 90 degrees. Check the second main unit against the first and make the shelf unit to fit between.

The doors go under the shelf at table level and overlap the bottom shelf. Use special thin hinges to avoid cutting away the particleboard. Fit handles and spring or magnetic catches. The bottom shelves will act as door stops.

Attach the units to the wall with a few screws. The main requirement is to prevent the units from falling forward; two screws through each back near the top should be sufficient. One or two screws lower down will keep

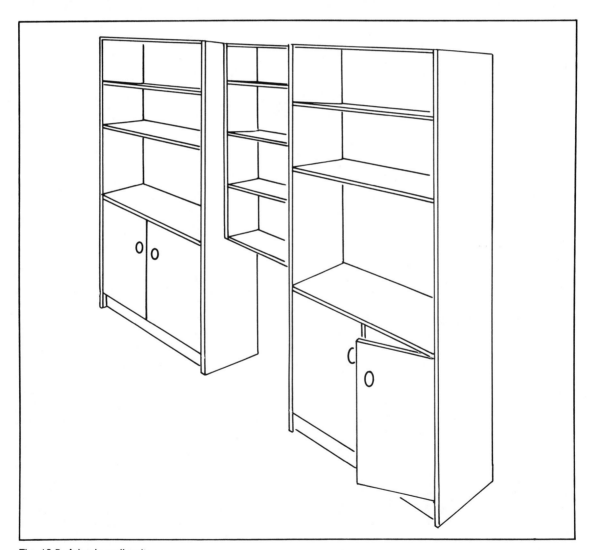

Fig. 12-5. A basic wall unit.

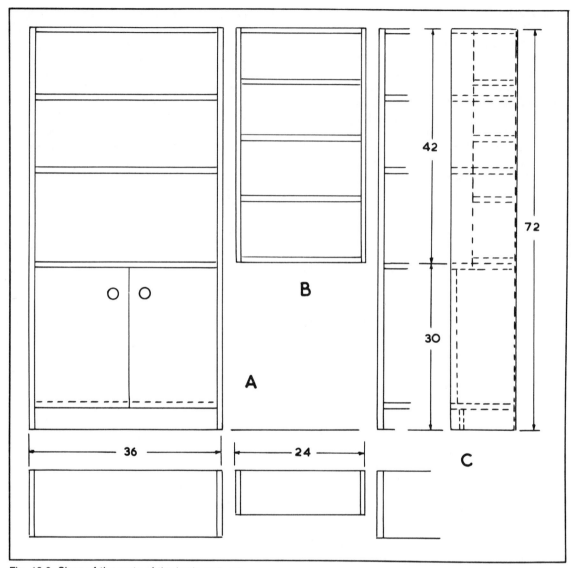

Fig. 12-6. Sizes of the parts of the basic wall unit.

the backs close to the wall. Washers under the screw heads are advisable. A flathead screw pulling into plywood might eventually go right through; a roundhead screw through a washer is stronger.

The shelf unit must be joined to the main units, but there will not be much load on these attachments unless the shelf unit is to be mounted without screws to the wall. A screw or bolt near the top and bottom of the shelf unit should be enough. There could be screws through washers (Fig. 12-7E), but choose lengths that will almost

go through, to get maximum grip. Small bolts may be better. Carriage bolts have inconspicuous heads. The nuts should bear against washers (Fig. 12-7F).

Materials List for Basic Wall Unit

All veneered particleboard between 5/8 and 1 inch thick

4 sides	12 × 72
10 shelves	12 × 36
2 plinths	4 × 36

2 sides	8 × 42
5 shelves	8 × 24
4 doors	18 × 27
2 backs	36 × 70 plywood
1 back	24 × 42 plywood

CORNER CABINET AND SHELVES

The corner of a room is often left unfilled, or a piece of furniture is put diagonally across it. Space is wasted in both cases. A fitted table or cabinet can be made to fill the corner, or there can be a shelf with storage underneath it. If furniture intended to go flat against a wall is brought together at a corner, there are complications where the pieces meet. Shelves meeting in a corner have a space there which is difficult to use. For instance, books cannot be stacked on the shelves right into the corner because those going one way will block the others.

One way of dealing with the problem is to cut the shelves short at a cabinet made to fit the corner (Fig. 12-8). Sizes and arrangements can be varied, but as shown the cabinet top is at low table level, and the shelves are a suitable width for books and most other things. The

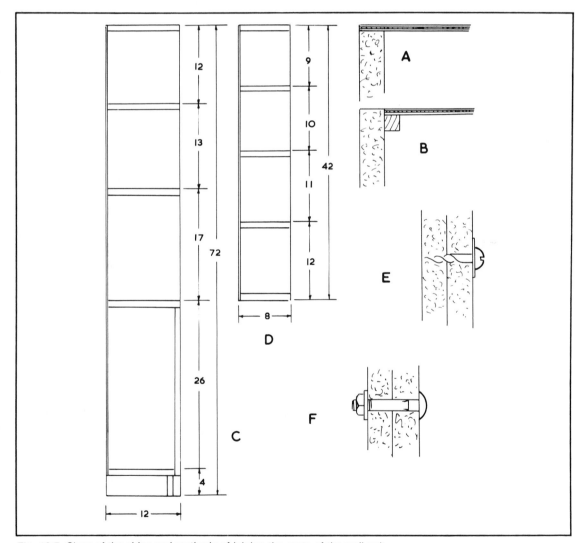

Fig. 12-7. Sizes of the sides and methods of joining the parts of the wall unit.

widths of the shelves affect the proportions of the corner cabinet. If the overall size of the cabinet is kept the same but shelves are made wider, the door must be narrower. To avoid this situation, the cabinet would have to be made to extend further from the corner. The shelves can be whatever length you need, and they need only project one way if that suits the particular situation. If they are more than 48 inches long, however, some intermediate uprights are advisable. The shelves could be open-backed or closed with plywood.

The main parts are assumed to be solid wood in the instructions, but it is possible to use veneered particleboard, either alone or with solid wood. The only very wide boards would be the top and bottom of the cabinet, and a way of building them up with framed plywood is suggested as an alternative. Since the unit is made around the cabinet, make all the parts for the cabinet first. Joints for the shelves can be prepared, then the cabinet assembled. Draw a full-size plan of the cabinet (Fig. 12-9A). The top can be given a slight overhang, but the bottom will come flush with the side and front. For a solid wood top and bottom, have the grain diagonal (Fig. 12-10A). For a framed plywood construction, rabbet pieces for the front edges and cut the other pieces to go under the plywood against the wall (Fig. 12-10B). Glue these parts together. Handle carefully until they get their final strength by being attached to the other parts. If the top is to overhang, round its outer edges.

The main parts of the cabinet backs are made up with plywood on strips (Fig. 12-10C). The sides should be rabbeted for the plywood (Fig. 12-10D), although if the shelves are also to be backed with plywood, the cabinet plywood could be taken halfway over the sides of the shelf plywood made to meet it later.

In order for the door hinge screws to have more wood to bite into than if the doorway was formed only by the sides cut to an acute angle, put stile strips on each side of the door opening (Fig. 12-10E), mitered to the sides. All of these parts should be doweled to the top and bottom, although there could be screws from inside through fillets attached to the plywood.

Before assembling the cabinet, you must prepare the sides for the shelves and decide what you want to do inside the cabinet. You cannot fit or remove shelves after assembly. For storing tall things, the inside could be left clear, but there is space for one or more shelves. You will get the most shelf capacity if you bring the shelf edges close to the door (Fig. 12-10F), but that may make it difficult to see very far into the corner. It may be better to stop any shelves at the diagonal (Fig. 12-10G).

The 9-inch door could be a piece of solid wood or veneered particleboard, or you could put lips around thick plywood. A paneled door may look better (Fig. 12-10H); make it the usual way with grooved parts joined with mortise-and-tenon joints (Fig. 12-10J). You could use decorative surface hinges and a matching handle. If you let in butt hinges, a turned knob or a strip wood handle would be appropriate (Fig. 12-10K).

If you want to put plywood at the back of the long shelves, rabbet the top shelf to suit. You could also rabbet the bottom shelf (Fig. 12-11A), but as it does not show, it is not as important. The simplest way of attaching the shelves to the cabinet is with dowels (Fig. 12-11B). There could be tenons right through (Fig. 12-11C), but if you want to use the traditional craftsman's method, cut shallow stopped dadoes and combine them with mortise-and-tenon joints (Fig. 12-11D). In some circumstances there could be considerable strain on these joints, so make them secure.

Spacers are shown at different positions toward the ends of the shelves (Fig. 12-9B and 11E). They can be doweled to the shelves. Dowels downward may be taken right through, but for the sake of appearance, take them upward as far as possible without going through. You could use dovetailed dadoes or mortise-and-tenon joints if you prefer, but dowel joints are easier to make cleanly and accurately.

In use, things put on the cabinet or top shelves may mark the wall if nothing is done to protect it. Strips are shown in Fig. 12-9C along all rear edges. If the unit is not attached to the wall, the strips will also prevent small things from falling over the back. These strips are parallel for most of their length, but at the ends they could slope or taper. They are shown curved (Fig. 12-11F). If the strips on the shelves go to the ends, they would cover a plywood back, even if it was not rabbeted into the shelf. Attach these strips with dowels into the shelves—3/8-inch dowels at about 6-inch spacing should be sufficient.

The whole assembly is best raised on a 3-inch plinth. Set it back a short distance (Fig. 12-11G) and miter the meeting ends. If the unit is to be attached to the wall, there is no need for the plinth strips along the rear edges. You may want to put a few pieces at intervals, however, to maintain the correct height (Fig. 12-11H). Join on the plinth with glue and a few dowels.

If the assembly is to be free-standing, carefully square by measuring diagonals, particularly if the shelves are without plywood backs. If the assembly is to be built-in, try it in its position as you assemble it. You may want to do final gluing of the shelves to the cabinet while the

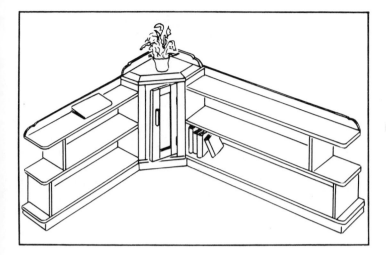

Fig. 12-8. A corner cabinet with shelves.

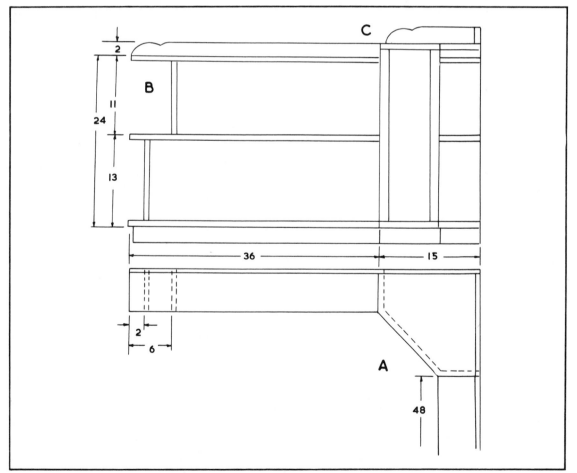

Fig. 12-9. Suggested sizes for the corner cabinet with shelves.

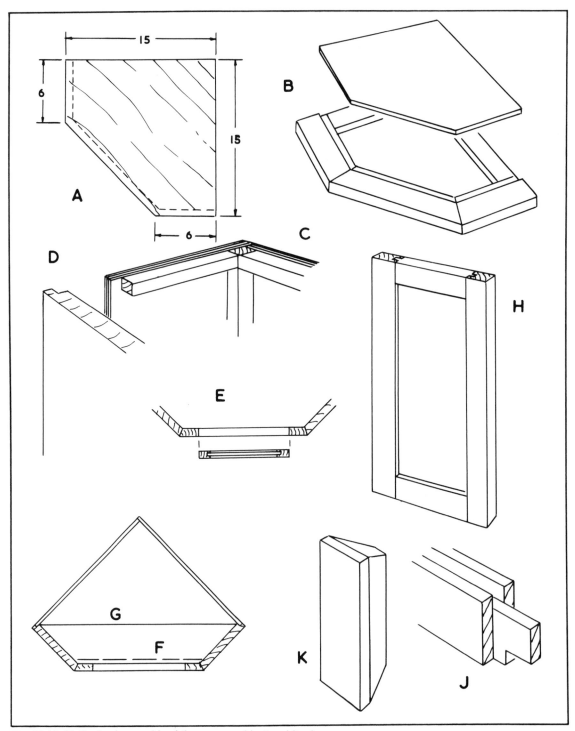

Fig. 12-10. Methods of assembly of the corner cabinet and its door.

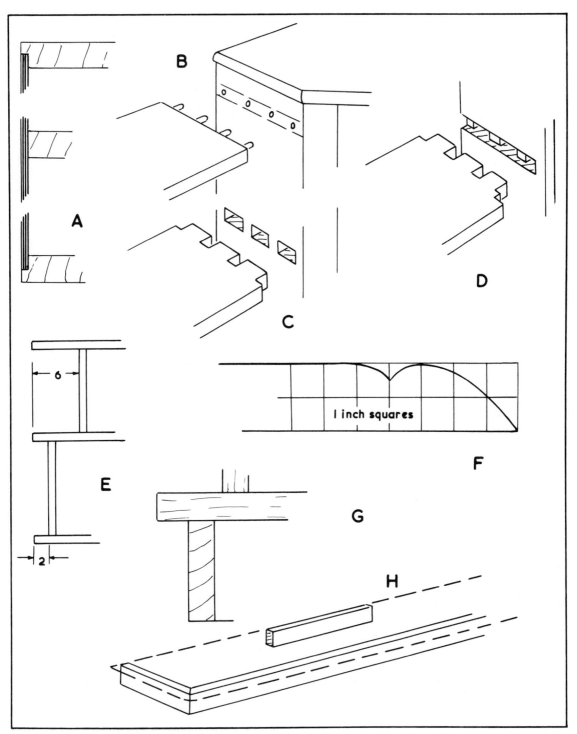

Fig. 12-11. Construction of the shelves and their attachment to the cabinet.

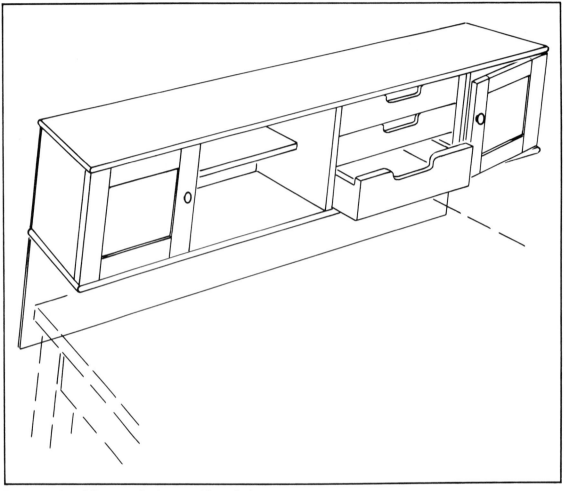

Fig. 12-12. A wall fitment to fit above a table or desk.

assembly is in place to get the closest fit to the walls. If there are plywood backs, you can screw through them to the walls. With open shelves there could be a few metal plates with screw holes under the shelves or blocks of wood screwed upward to them and then to the walls.

When finishing, the plinth may look best darker than the other parts. If the unit is to be attached to the walls, it may be better for finishing if you have the top rear strips ready with dowels attached, but do not join them to the shelves and cabinet top until all parts have been varnished or otherwise finished.

Materials List for Corner Cabinet and Shelves

1 cabinet top	$15 \times 22 \times 3/4$
1 cabinet bottom	$15 \times 22 \times 3/4$
or from 2	$3 \times 24 \times 3/4$
and 4	$2 \times 15 \times 1/2$
and 4	$14 \times 22 \times 1/4$ plywood
2 cabinet sides	$6 \times 28 \times 3/4$
2 door stiles	$2 \times 28 \times 3/4$
2 door stiles	$2 \times 28 \times 3/4$
2 backs	$15 \times 28 \times 1/4$ plywood
back fillets from 1	$1/2 \times 150 \times 1/2$
1 door	$9 \times 28 \times 3/4$
or 2	$2 \times 28 \times 3/4$
and 2	$8 \times 27 \times 1/4$ plywood
and 1	$2 \times 9 \times 3/4$
3 shelves	$6 \times 36 \times 3/4$

3 shelves	6 × 48 × 3/4
2 shelf spacers	6 × 11 × 3/4
2 shelf spacers	6 × 13 × 3/4
1 back (if required)	24 × 36 × 1/4 plywood
1 back (if required)	24 × 48 × 1/4 plywood
2 top cover strips	2 × 16 × 3/4
1 top cover strip	2 × 36 × 3/4
1 top cover strip	2 × 48 × 3/4

WALL FITMENT

If you use a table against a wall as a desk, it is useful to have something on the wall that will accommodate all your books, papers, pens, and other items so the desk top is kept clear. If you work at a hobby that entails standing or sitting at a table to use paper, glue, model parts, jewelry, artist's equipment, or any large quantity of small items, a fitment on the wall behind the table can hold most of your hobby things and keep the working area clear. If a child uses a table for school work, playing with toys, drawing, or any other activity, he needs somewhere to put things if the table is to be kept tidy. A similar fitment may have uses behind a bed to hold a variety of things that you want within reach while you are in or near the bed.

The wall fitment shown in Fig. 12-12 has two cupboards at its ends. They are shown with paneled doors, which could be glass if you want to display anything, or plywood to hid the interior. Between them comes a block of drawers, which can be lifted out and put as trays on the table, and a space with a shelf that will take books and papers. Below these parts the back extends downward to protect the wall when the table is pushed back; but it could also have other uses. There may be racks or clips on it to hold tools needed for a hobby. It could be painted matte black so a child could chalk on it. It could be faced with softboard or cork so it becomes a bulletin board. If this extension does not suit your needs, it can be omitted without affecting the rest of the construction.

As shown in Fig. 12-13A, the sizes should suit many needs, but now is the time to make modifications, if you wish. All the main parts should be solid wood, but they could be veneered particleboard or thick plywood with solid wood lips on the exposed edges. Making the main joints with dowels would be satisfactory, but the uprights could go into dado grooves, and the ends could be dovetailed, if you wish. Top and bottom are shown overlapping the ends enough for rounding. If dovetails

are used, they should be cut square and level with the ends.

In section, the cupboard doors are set between the top and bottom, so the cupboard sides are set back to suit (Fig. 12-13B). There could be shelves or other arrangements inside to suit your needs. The open section is shown with one shelf (Fig. 12-13C), with enough space below it for books of average size. The three drawers (Fig. 12-13D) have hand slots at their fronts, but they could have knobs. They slide on runners, which are hidden by the fronts.

Mark out the top and bottom boards as a pair (Fig. 12-14A). The central division is full-width, but the other uprights are set back by a little more than the thickness of the doors (Fig. 12-14B). It will probably be satisfactory to put the back flat on the other parts, but if you want to let it in, rabbet the top and ends and reduce the widths of other parts.

The shelf may fit into grooves in the adjoining uprights, if you want to make it permanent. If you think you may want to alter the position of the shelf later, it would be better to support it on short strips attached to the uprights.

The upright between the drawers and cupboard will need special treatment. If the drawers slide against it, they come very close to the edge of the door, and there could be interference. To prevent this situation, put a strip down the front edge to limit the widths of the drawers (Fig. 12-14D). Put strips across to act as guides (Fig. 12-14E) and make up the width for combined runners and guides (Fig. 12-14F). The limiting strip must overlap the side of the cupboard to allow for the door being set back, and the runners must be kept back by the thickness of the drawer fronts (Fig. 12-14G).

At the other sides of the drawers, the combined runners and kickers are simple strips on the central divider. Assemble all the main parts at this stage, but leave off the back until after you have fitted the drawers and doors.

The doors should be framed in the usual way. If there are plywood panels, groove the framing (Fig. 12-15A). If you want to fit glass to one or both doors, cut rabbets and hold the glass in with fillets (Fig. 12-15B). Let hinges in between the doors and the ends so they can swing wide open, giving clear full-width access to the interiors. Knobs are shown, but you can use the handles of your choice. The uprights act as door stops, but you will need spring or magnetic catches inside.

The drawers can be made in any of the ways previously described, but you must allow for the fronts of the bottom two drawers extending over the ends of the runners

263

(Fig. 12-15C) to hide them. The drawers could reach the plywood back, but it would be better to let the fronts against the runners act as stops for the two lower drawers and put stops at the backs of the runners for the top drawers. You could make divisions or sliding trays in the drawers to suit your needs, and plan these layouts before assembling the drawers so divisions and guides can be fitted in.

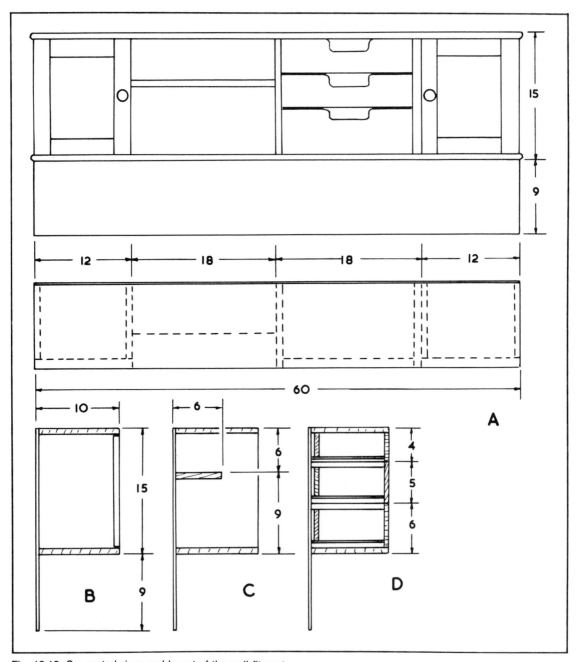

Fig. 12-13. Suggested sizes and layout of the wall fitment.

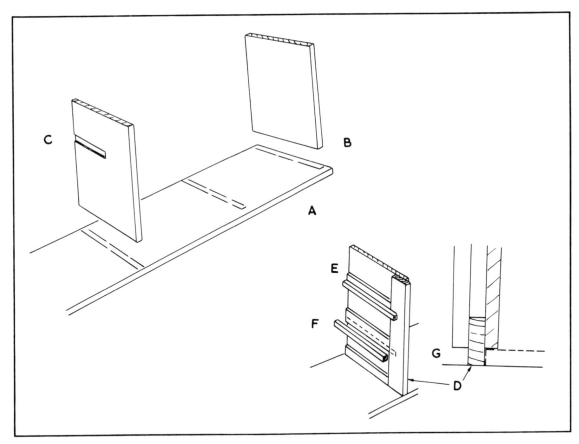

Fig. 12-14. Construction of the wall fitment parts.

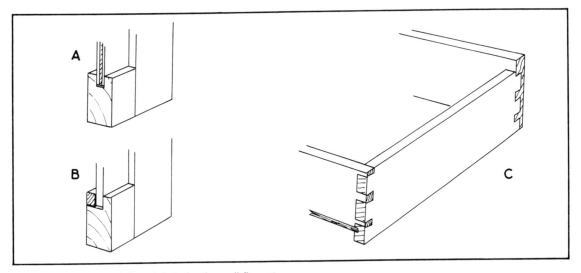

Fig. 12-15. Drawer and door details for the wall fitment.

Add the back to complete the assembly. It will probably be sufficient to screw through the back to attach the assembly to the wall, but if extra strength is needed, put strips under the top at the backs of the cupboards and screw through them. In any case, the screws near the top of the back will take the most load.

Materials List for Wall Fitment

1 top	10 × 62 × 5/8
1 bottom	10 × 62 × 5/8
1 divider	10 × 15 × 5/8
4 uprights	9 × 15 × 5/8
1 shelf	6 × 18 × 5/8
1 back	24 × 62 × 1/4 plywood
4 door frames	2 × 15 × 3/4
4 door frames	2 × 12 × 3/4
2 door panels	10 × 13 × 1/4 plywood
1 drawer limiter	3 × 15 × 3/4
3 drawer guides	1 1/2 × 10 × 3/4
4 drawer runners	1/2 × 10 × 1/2
1 drawer front	6 × 18 × 3/4
2 drawer sides	5 1/2 × 10 × 1/2
1 drawer back	5 × 18 × 1/2
1 drawer front	5 × 18 × 3/4
2 drawer sides	4 1/2 × 10 × 1/2
1 drawer back	4 × 18 × 1/2
1 drawer front	3 1/2 × 18 × 3/4
2 drawer sides	3 × 10 × 1/2
1 drawer back	2 1/2 × 18 × 1/2
3 drawer bottoms	10 × 18 × 1/4 plywood

HALL LOCKER

This is a piece of furniture to put inside the front door (Fig. 12-16) to hold hats, gloves, and other small outdoor things at the top and all kinds of footwear below, with umbrellas, walking canes, fishing poles, and anything long and thin in the end rack. Without the umbrella stand, the locker might have uses elsewhere, such as for toy storage in a playroom, or food in a kitchen. It could also be used as storage in a shop, possibly with a light machine mounted on top of it. The instructions, however, are based on the assumption that it is to serve as a hall locker.

The main parts should be made of solid wood, although you can use veneered particleboard for some parts. Check sizes in relation to the position the locker will occupy. Make sure it will not interfere with the movement of a door. Will anyone be likely to knock against it? It may have to be used with a mirror on the wall or

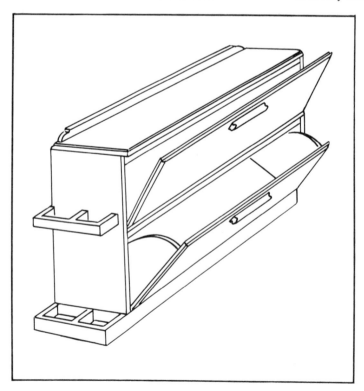

Fig. 12-16. A hall locker with a door, a bin, and an umbrella stand.

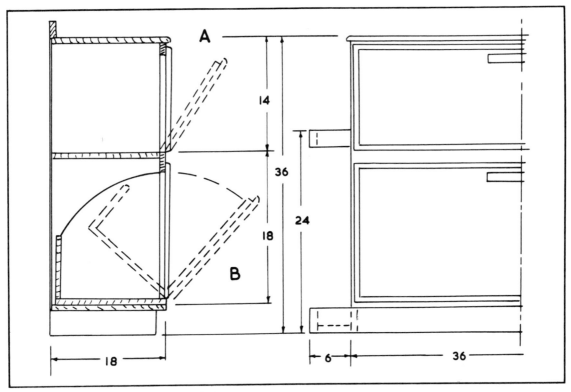

Fig. 12-17. Suggested sizes for the hall locker.

near a coat rack. Make sure it fits in with other things and alter sizes if necessary. Length can be altered without affecting constructional details.

Most of the important dimensions are on the end section (Fig. 12-17A). Glue up wood to width for the ends and mark out the pair. Also on one of the ends mark out the tilting bin so its size and action are clear (Fig. 12-17B). It pivots on the center of the hinge knuckle (Fig. 12-18A); so when you draw the curve of the bin end, the compass point goes on that corner (Fig. 12-18B).

Mark out the locker ends with the positions of the lengthwise parts, which will be doweled to them (Fig. 12-18C). Rabbet the rear edges for the plywood back. The center shelf goes behind its front rail (Fig. 12-18D), and these parts will be glued and doweled to each other as well as to the ends.

Instead of solid wood, you could make the center shelf with strips of solid wood framed around plywood rabbeted into their top surfaces. The bottom could be made in the same way. Use 2- or 3-inch strips if there is ample solid wood to take the screws into the plinth. At the top there are lengthwise strips at back and front, to which the top

board will be attached after other parts have been assembled.

Assemble the lengthwise parts to the ends and square the frame you have made. Fit the plywood back to hold the other parts square, but check diagonals and see that there is no twist in the assembly.

The top door is made in a double thickness (Fig. 12-18E). Make the inner part to be an easy fit in its opening. Allow for letting in two or three 3-inch hinges in its lower edge to connect to the middle shelf. Make a trial assembly. When it works satisfactorily, add the false front, which will overlap at ends and top. It is shown with molded edges in Fig. 12-18F, but it could be left square with rounded front edges or shaped with other moldings, depending on whether router or spindle cutters are available.

The bottom locker front should match the top door. Draw the bin end shape (Fig. 12-18B), checking it with the marking out you did on one locker end. At the front, where much of the tilting load will come, dowel or screw into the end of the inner part of the front (Fig. 12-18G). Assemble the other parts of the bin in the same way.

267

Round the top edges of the bin ends and back. Fit the hinges to the bottom edge of the bin front in a similar way to the top door. Tilt the bin fully forward to get at the screws in the front edge of the bottom. Make a trial assembly, with one screw in each hinge, then remove the bin until after you have fitted the plinth.

In use, you can let the bin swing out as far as possible, but usually you will tilt it a short way to drop something in or take something out. Without restraint the top door would drop too far, but it should be stopped when horizontal. You can put a folding strut at each end, or it may be sufficient to use cords between screw eyes (Fig. 12-18H).

The top of the locker should be glued up to width from attractive wood, since it is the most prominent part of the piece of furniture. It comes level at the back, but overlaps at front and ends. Treat the visible edges in the same way as the drawer fronts, with matching moldings (Fig. 12-19A and B). Screw upward through the rails, counterboring where necessary. At the rear of the top add a strip with dowels to protect the wall and prevent things from falling off (Fig. 12-19C).

The plinth is a box shape that fits under the bottom, with its edges set back at the front and the end away from the umbrella stand. At the umbrella stand end, there is an extension of the plinth and a piece across level with the side of the locker (Fig. 12-19D). At the other end, the corners can be mitered with strengthening blocks inside (Fig. 12-19E). For the stand, dovetail or dowel the corners and include a bottom piece inside (Fig. 12-19F). Attach the plinth to the bottom of the locker with screws (Fig. 12-19G) or with dowels and glue. There could be

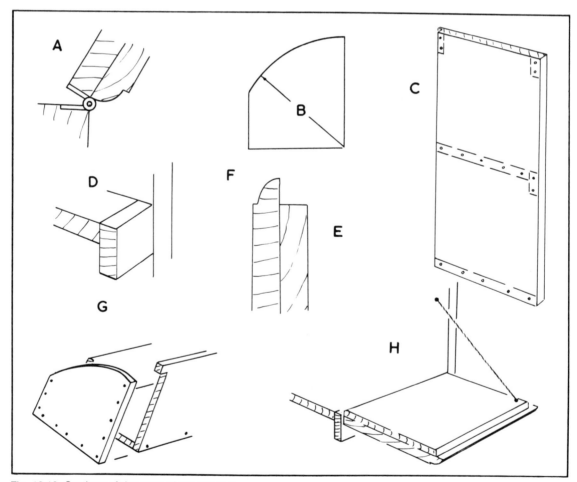

Fig. 12-18. Sections of the parts of the hall locker.

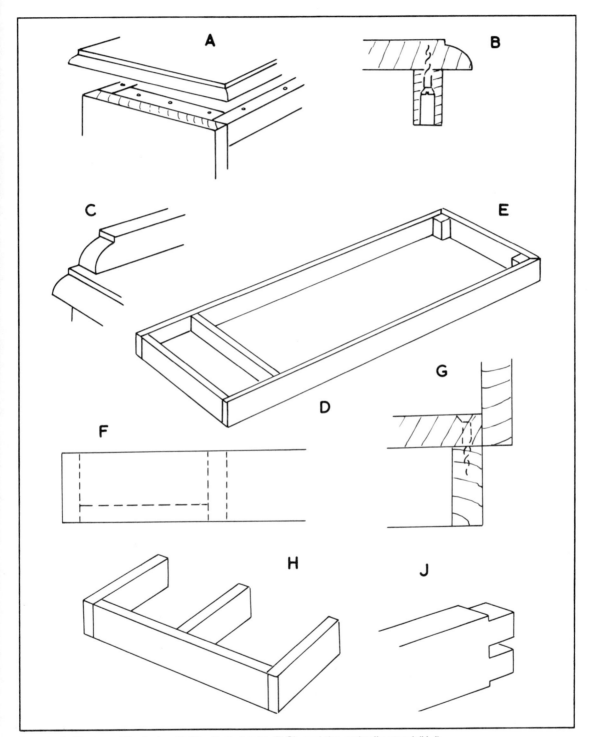

Fig. 12-19. The top of the locker (A-C), plinth details (D-G), and the umbrella stand (H,J).

a central division across the box which is formed, but it may be sufficient to leave it full-width and have a division in the top part only.

At the top repeat the outline of the plinth extension, with a central division to prevent umbrellas or canes from tilting too much (Fig. 12-19H). Dowel or tenon these parts to the locker end (Fig. 12-19J).

The two doors should have similar handles, and they could be quite long wood ones so you can reach to pull a door open at almost any position. The bin should stay shut under its own weight, but you could give the top door a spring or magnetic catch.

Have the top door and the bin removed until you have completed the finishing treatment, then screw through the hinges to complete the assembly. If the heavily loaded bin slams noisily against its frame, it could be edged with strips of cloth or self-adhesive foam plastic of the type put around door recesses.

Materials List for Hall Locker

2 ends	18 × 33 × 3/4
1 top	19 × 39 × 3/4
1 shelf	18 × 36 × 3/4
1 bottom	18 × 36 × 3/4
3 rails	2 × 36 × 3/4
1 front	12 × 36 × 3/4
1 false front	13 × 36 × 3/4
1 front	16 × 36 × 3/4
1 false front	17 × 36 × 3/4
2 bin ends	16 × 16 × 1/2
1 bin back	7 × 36 × 1/2
1 bin bottom	15 × 36 × 1/2
1 locker back	33 × 36 × 1/4 plywood
2 plinths	4 × 43 × 3/4
3 plinths	4 × 18 × 3/4
1 plinth bottom	6 × 18 × 3/4
1 umbrella stand	3 × 18 × 3/4
3 umbrella stands	3 × 6 × 3/4
2 handles	1 1/4 × 8 × 1 1/4
1 back ledge	3 × 39 × 3/4

CLOTHES CLOSET

If you want to store a reasonable amount of clothing on hangers, a closet must be quite large. You usually have to weigh the need for capacity against the space available for positioning the clothes closet. The large piece of furniture might be quite an elaborate construction and rather daunting to the woodworker conscious of the limits of his

ability. This clothes closet (Fig. 12-20) is intended to finish with an attractive appearance, yet the construction is little more than "hammer and nail" carpentry. It could be given a painted finish; so wood surfaces do not need to match. The sizes in Fig. 12-21A are full-size clothes closet that will take adult suits and dresses. With a bright painted finish and possibly some decals, however, the closet could be used in a child's room, and would still be big enough for his clothing when he has grown.

It would not be difficult to adapt the design to being built into a corner of a room, using the meeting walls as the back and one side. You would, however, need a few strips against the wall for screwing through. Alternatively, the closet could be completed free-standing, then the back screwed to the wall, if you want to prevent the closet from being moved.

The main parts are 1-4-inch plywood panels on strips 1- × -2 inch. The strips could be softwood. A few knots on the parts against plywood will not matter, but keep clearer and more straight-grained pieces for the doors and framing away from panels. Joints should be made with strong glue and some fine nails, which can be punched and stopped where they come on outside surfaces. Assemble the panels so each side overlaps a strip, and its edge is hidden by the front (Fig. 12-22A). At its rear edge it extends over the strip enough to cover the back plywood

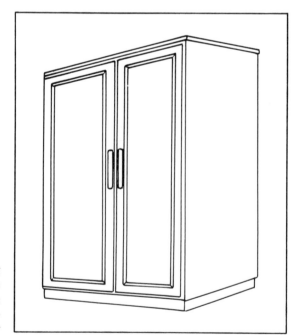

Fig. 12-20. A two-door clothes closet.

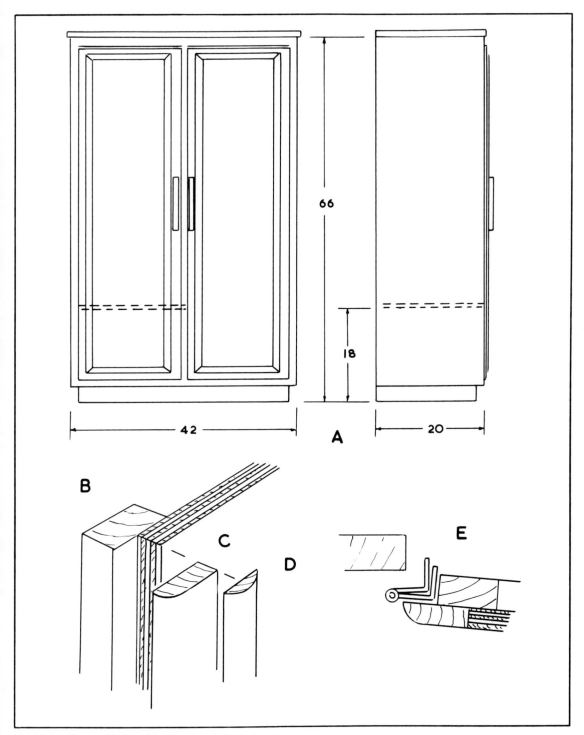

Fig. 12-21. Sizes and door details of the clothes closet.

(Fig. 12-22B). The bottom plywood has a frame under it so it fits inside the other parts (Fig. 12-22C). The top has a frame which overlaps the other parts, and its plywood could be set back on the surface, since it is above the normal line of sight (Fig. 12-22D). It could be let into rabbets, if you wish.

Start by making the pair of sides (Fig. 12-23A). At the corners there is no need to cut joints between the strips because the glued plywood will secure them, but you could miter or halve them if you wish. The design shows drawers at one side. Above them hangs shorter clothing, while there is ample length at the other side for longer dresses. On both sides put extra strips for the ends of the top rail, and on the side you want the drawers, put two more strips. Of course, if the closet is only for men's clothing, which do not require deep hanging, there could be drawers at both sides. The plywood comes flush with the frame, except at the back where it projects enough to overlap the back.

Make the bottom (Fig. 12-23B) with the framing level with the plywood all around. Across the ends make it the same as the width of the side frames. Make its length to suit the width you want the closet to be (39 1/2 inches for 42 inches outside width). Use the bottom as a guide for making the top (Fig. 12-23C), which has the plywood and frame level at the rear so the back plywood can go over it. At the other edges the frame projects (Fig. 12-22D), and the plywood is set back. The central strip is to take a rail block. These parts give you key measurements for the back and front.

The front is a frame (Fig. 12-23D). At the sides its outer edges must come level with the plywood (Fig. 12-22A), and at the top it is covered by the overlapping strip (Fig. 12-22D). At the bottom its upper edge should come level with the inside surface of the bottom (Fig. 12-22E). Its height is the same as the sides, and the bottom must be positioned at this level when the closet is assembled.

It will be best to dowel the corners and central part of the front frame (Fig. 12-23E), although mortise-and-tenon joints are also suitable. Strength will come in the final assembly to other parts.

Before you assemble the main parts, prepare the drawer framing. At the side build out the central rail to the thickness of the front overlap (Fig. 12-22F), then add a runner inside the rail (Fig. 12-22G). Put a similar thickener on the upper rail, but no runner. When you assemble the closet, put another thickener on the bottom so the drawers will be guided through the front and will not catch on it as they are pulled out.

To support the other sides of the drawers, make a frame with a runner to match the opposite side and at a height to support a top frame (Fig. 12-22H). Arrange the frame so the side support can be positioned with its edge level with the center division of the front; then there will be no need for packing to let the drawers clear the front opening.

There are several ways of assembling the main parts. Where screw heads would not show, there could be simple screwing from outside surfaces. Elsewhere they could be sunk and plugged. In several places it is possible to screw from inside, through counterbored holes (Fig. 12-22J). Dowels could be used in many of the joints. Have the back already cut square so it can be fitted to hold the assembly in shape while the glue sets. Fasten everywhere that parts meet so there is mutual support.

To lift the closet a short distance off the floor, fit a plinth (Fig. 12-22K) inside the overhanging front and sides, with screws through the bottom and outward into the front and sides.

Inside the top there must be a rail across, but with a full load of clothing it would sag if unsupported near the center. It could be a piece of dowel rod, but a metal tube would also be suitable. You could drill for the rod and position it during assembly, with a central block screwed through the closet top, but to add the rod after assembly, and make it possible to remove it again if ever necessary, put blocks at the sides and screw them in position (Fig. 12-22L).

The doors are pieces of 1/2-inch plywood stiffened inside and edged with solid wood. The joints covered with halfround molding (Fig. 12-22M).

Cut the plywood for each door 1 inch smaller all around than its opening. Edge the plywood with 1- x -2 inch strips that will make an easy fit in the opening (Fig. 12-21B). For neatness the top corner could be mitered, but the side pieces can overlap the bottom strips. If necessary, plane the edges to size, but there is no need for a close fit in the front, since the other strips will hide any gaps. The front pieces are shown with rounded edges (Fig. 12-21C). They could be molded or left square, with just the sharpness taken off. Glue and pin these strips close to the plywood. Miter the corners. Pins near the joint will be covered by the half-round molding. Glue on the molding, using a few pins as well (Fig. 12-21D).

There are decorative hinges cranked to fit on the surface and overlap the front of the doors. If they are used, there should be matching handles; if not, you can use cranked hinges to fit between the surface (Fig. 12-21E). Handles can be any type you wish, but there is not much

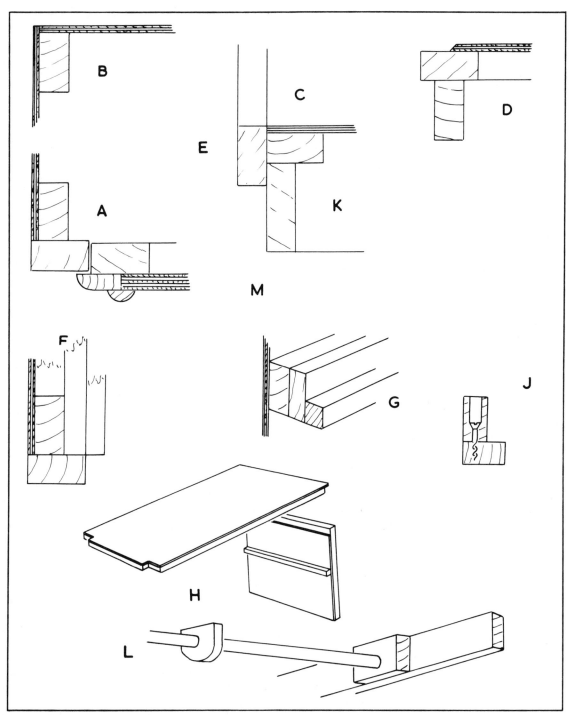

Fig. 12-22. Details of the framed plywood parts (A-F), the drawer compartments (G,H), the screwed assembly (J), and the hanging rail (L).

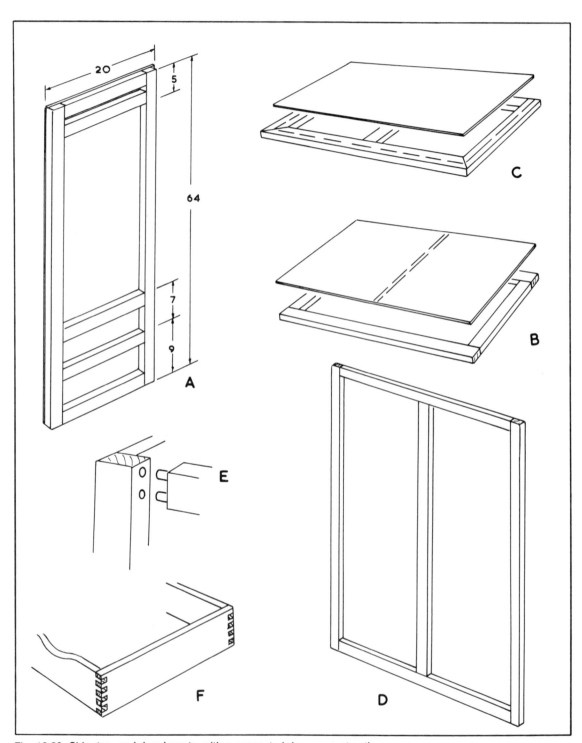

Fig. 12-23. Side, top, and door layouts, with a suggested drawer construction.

width for fitting them, and tall narrow types will look best. Fit catches where the doors close on the central post.

The drawers can be simple trays with hand notches at the front. Comb joints might be used at the corners (Fig. 12-23F) and the plywood or hardboard bottom let into grooves in line with a comb. The top edge of the front of the bottom tray should be carried above the sides enough to hide the ends of the runners.

Materials List for Clothes Closet

2 sides	20 × 65 × 1/4 plywood
4 sides	2 × 65 × 1
10 sides	2 × 17 × 1
1 bottom	20 × 42 × 1/4 plywood
2 bottoms	2 × 42 × 1
2 bottoms	2 × 20 × 1
1 top	20 × 42 × 1/4 plywood
2 tops	2 × 44 × 1
3 tops	2 × 21 × 1
3 fronts	2 × 65 × 1
2 fronts	2 × 42 × 1
2 doors	19 × 61 × 1/2 plywood
4 doors	2 × 63 × 1
4 doors	2 × 20 × 1
4 doors	1 1/2 × 63 × 1/2
4 doors	1 1/2 × 21 × 1/2
4 doors	1 × 63 × halfround
4 doors	1 × 21 × halfround
2 plinths	3 × 42 × 1
2 plinths	3 × 20 × 1
1 drawer cover	20 × 21 × 1/4 plywood
4 drawer covers	2 × 21 × 1
1 drawer upright	16 × 20 × 1/4 plywood
4 drawer uprights	2 × 20 × 1
8 drawer parts	8 × 21 × 1/2
2 drawer bottoms	20 × 21 × 1/4 plywood
1 rail	3/4 × 42 × round

Glossary

The making of shelves and storage items is only a small part of the whole range of woodworking. A complete glossary of all the words that might be encountered would be too large for this book. The words that follow are those likely to be met, including a few that are obsolete or have had their meanings altered.

annular rings—The concentric rings in the cross-section of a tree that form the grain pattern; one ring is added each year.

apron—A piece of wood in the form of a rail, usually below a drawer.

backboard—The wood forming the back of a cabinet or block of shelves.

bail—A swinging loop handle.

batten—Any narrow strip of wood. It may be across other boards to join them, cover a gap, or prevent warping. It may support a shelf.

blind—Not right through, such as a stopped hole or mortise.

bracket—An angular piece used to support a shelf or flap.

cabinet—Any case or boxlike structure, usually with shelves, drawers, and doors.

cabinetmaking, cabinetry—The craft of making all kinds of furniture; not just cabinets.

cast—Twisting of a surface that should be flat.

chamfer—An angle or bevel planed on an edge.

clamp—A device for drawing things, especially joints, together. The tool may be called a cramp. Wood used as a clamp may be called a cleat.

closet—A cupboard for storing clothes and other things. A small room.

core—Base wood on which veneer is laid.

counterbore—To drill a large hole over a small one so the screw head in it is drawn below the surface and can be covered by a plug.

countersink—To bevel the top of a hole so a flat-headed screw can be driven level with the surface.

cupboard—A closet or cabinet particularly intended for storing cups, saucers, plates, and food.

dado—A groove cut across the grain, usually to support the end of a shelf.

dovetail—The fan-shaped piece that projects between pins in the other part of a dovetail joint.

dowel—A cylindrical piece of wood used as a peg when making joints.

escutcheon—A keyhole or the plate covering and surrounding it. A shield bearing a coat-of-arms.

fall front—A flap that lets down to be supported in a horizontal position.

fastenings (fasteners)—Collective name for anything used for joining, such as nails and screws.

featheredge—A wide, smooth bevel, taking the edge of a board to a very thin line.

fillet—A strip of wood used between parts to join or support them.

fillister—A rabbet plane with fences to control the depth and width of cut.

framed construction—Furniture or other woodwork where the main parts are formed of wood strips around panels.

gauge—A marking tool or a means of testing.

half-lap joint—Two crossing pieces notched into each other, usually to bring their surfaces level.

handed—Made as a pair.

hanging stile—The upright at the side of a door to which the hinges are attached.

haunch—A short cutback part of a tenon that joins another piece near its end.

housing joint—Another name for a dado joint, particularly where a shelf is supported in a groove in another piece of wood.

jointing—The making of any joint, but particularly planing edges straight to make close glued joints, edge-to-edge.

kerf—The slot formed by the cut of a saw.

laminate—To construct in layers with several pieces of wood glued together, particularly in the making of curved parts. Plywood is made by laminating veneers.

lap joint—The general name for joints where one piece of wood is cut to overlap and fit into another.

lineal—Length only. The term is sometimes used when pricing wood.

locking stile—The upright against which a door shuts.

matched boarding—Joining boards edge to edge with matching tongues and grooves, or less commonly with the edges rabbeted to lap over each other.

miter—A joint where the meeting angle of the surfaces is divided or bisected, as in the corner of a picture frame or plinth.

mortise-and-tenon joint—A method of joining the end of one piece of wood into the side of another, with the tenon projecting like a tongue on the end of one piece to fit into the matching mortise cut in the other piece.

nosing—A semicircular molding.

pedestal—A supporting post.

pegging—Putting dowels or wooden pegs through joints.

piercing—A decoration made by cutting through the wood.

pigeon hole—A storage compartment built into a writing desk.

pilot hole—A small hole drilled as a guide for the drill point before making a larger hole.

planted—Applied instead of cut in the solid. Molding attached to a surface is planted. If it is cut in the solid wood, it is stuck.

plinth—The base part around the bottom of a piece of furniture.

plowed (ploughed)—Grooved along the grain, usually to take a panel.

plywood—A board made with veneers glued in laminations with the grain of each layer square to the next.

rabbet—An angular cutout section at an edge, as in the back of a picture frame.

rail—A member in framing, usually horizontal.

rake—Inclined to the horizontal.

rod—A strip of wood with distances of construction details marked on it, to use for comparing parts, instead of measuring with a rule.

router—A power or hand tool for leveling the bottom of a groove or recessed surface. With special cutters it can cut moldings and other shapes.

rule—A measuring rod.

run—In a long length. Lumber quantity can be quoted as so many feet run.

setting out—Laying out details, usually full-size, of a piece of furniture or other construction.

shelf—A flat board fixed horizontally on which to store things.

slat—A narrow, thin wood.

splay—Spread out.

spline—A narrow strip of wood fitting into grooves, usually to strengthen two meeting surfaces that are to be glued.

stile—A vertical member in door framing.

strap hinge—A hinge with long, narrow arms.

stretcher—A lengthwise rail between the lower parts of a table or similar assembly.

stub tenon (stopped tenon)—One that does not go through the other piece of wood. It fits into a blind mortise.

template—A shaped pattern to draw around when marking out parts, usually when several must match.

trunnel (treenail)—A peg or dowel driven through a joint.

veneer—A very thin piece of wood intended to be glued to a backing, which could be wood or particleboard.

veneer pin—A very fine nail with a small head.

waney edge—The edge of a board that still has bark on it or is still showing the pattern of the outside of the tree.

winding—A board or assembly that is not flat and whose twist can be seen when sighting for one end.

Index

Edited by Suzanne L. Cheatle

OTHER POPULAR TAB BOOKS OF INTEREST

TAB · TAB BOOKS Inc.

Blue Ridge Summit, Pa. 17214

Send for FREE TAB Catalog describing over 750 current titles in print.